Studies in the Wisdom Tradition

by
David Reigle
and
Nancy Reigle

Eastern School Press

Cotopaxi, Colorado 81223, U.S.A.
mail@easterntradition.org
ISBN 978-0-912181-11-0
ISBN 0-912181-11-7

published June 2015
corrected reprint, October 2015

Contents

Introduction

> To be *true*, religion and philosophy must offer the solution of every problem. That the world is in such a bad condition morally is a conclusive evidence that none of its religions and philosophies, those of the *civilised* races less than any other, have ever possessed the *truth*. The right and logical explanations on the subject of the problems of the great dual principles—right and wrong, good and evil, liberty and despotism, pain and pleasure, egotism and altruism—are as impossible to them now as they were 1881 years ago. They are as far from the solution as they ever were, but—
>
> To these there *must* be somewhere a consistent solution, and if our doctrines will show their competence to offer it, then the world will be the first one to confess, *that must* be the true philosophy, the true religion, the true light, which gives *truth* and nothing but the *truth*.
>
> —the Mahā-Chohan, 1881

There is alleged to be a once universal but now hidden Wisdom Tradition, the original source of the known religions and philosophies of the world. Its existence was made known in the late 1800s when some of its teachings were brought out under the name Theosophy. It has its own distinct doctrines, providing solutions to the great problems of life. The great problems of God, of self (*ātman*), of spirit and matter, of unity and diversity, etc., are explained in opposite ways in the known religions and philosophies of the world. We may thus wonder how there could be a single Wisdom Tradition behind them. How were its distinct doctrines both elaborated and obscured in the religions and philosophies of its homeland, ancient India? Based on the portions of its teachings that were brought out, the studies assembled here attempt to trace this tradition in the extant sources, and thereby to ascertain more fully and exactly the doctrines of the Wisdom Tradition.

While the Wisdom Tradition is supposed to be the original source of all the known religions and philosophies of the world, those of ancient India have preserved its teachings in more complete and less altered form. These are three: Hinduism, Jainism, and Buddhism. Because these are more direct sources, our studies have focused on these.

On the great problem of the existence of God, the position of the Wisdom Tradition was stated clearly and unmistakably in Mahatma letter no. 10: "Neither our philosophy nor ourselves believe in a God, . . ." This letter goes on to say, "the idea of God is not an innate but an acquired notion." If it is true that there is a once universal but now hidden Wisdom Tradition, that it is the original source of the known religions and philosophies of the world, that it is preserved most fully in the three religions of ancient India, from which it went out to the rest of the world, and that the notion of God was never part of it, but was acquired as its teachings were altered over time and as they spread out from their homeland in ancient India, history should show this. Of the three religions of ancient India, Jainism and Buddhism have never accepted such a being, while the third, Hinduism, has. However, there is considerable evidence that Hinduism did not originally accept God, and thus that all of ancient India was once non-theistic, in full accord with the Wisdom Tradition. To show this, chapter 5 attempts to trace "God's Arrival in India."

On the great problem of the existence of an impersonal universal principle, Advaita Vedānta accepts such a principle as the absolute *brahman*, equated with the *ātman*, a universal self. The Buddhist teaching of *anātman*, "no-self," denies the *ātman*. However, the teaching of a permanent personal *ātman* by other Hindu schools was once widespread. A compelling case was made by Kamaleswar Bhattacharya to show that what Buddhism originally denied was only the personal *ātman*, not the universal *ātman*. His book forms the basis of chapter 8, "*Ātman/Anātman* in Buddhism and Its Implication for the Wisdom Tradition."

The Wisdom Tradition posits an "omnipresent, eternal, boundless, and immutable principle," discussed in chapter 3, "The First Fundamental Proposition of the Secret Doctrine." This is much like the non-dual *brahman*, which is equated with the universal *ātman*, in Advaita Vedānta. The great problem that is associated with this doctrine is how the cosmos can arise from an immutable or unchangeable principle. To describe this indescribable process, the model used here by H. P. Blavatsky is that of radiation. An immutable principle can radiate or shine and still remain immutable. Such a model was also used in one school of Advaita Vedānta.

Śaṅkarācārya is the great promulgator of Advaita Vedānta. It appears, however, from the evidence provided in chapter 4, that "The Original Śaṅkarācārya" is not the same as the author of the major texts that define Advaita Vedānta's teachings today and have for the past twelve hundred years. The latter author has made some important changes to the original teachings. He has brought in God, alongside the non-dual *brahman/ ātman*, thus complicating the issue on these two great questions. That aside, the Advaita school of Vedānta has always been known for its non-dualistic teaching of *brahman* as "one without a second." It therefore holds that the appearance of diversity, the manifold cosmos, can only be illusory (*māyā*), a false projection on the one real *brahman*, like that of a snake on a coiled rope.

Tsongkhapa taught just the opposite. As understood in the Gelugpa order that he founded, the Prāsaṅgika Madhyamaka school of Buddhism teaches that there is no such thing as the one real *brahman* or *ātman*. For them, the only ultimate reality is the ultimate emptiness of everything. The manifold cosmos is conventional reality, but this does not mean that it is illusory. Without an ultimate reality other than emptiness, which is a mere absence, conventional reality is the only reality we have. Both Śaṅkarācārya and Tsongkhapa are claimed to be teachers of the Wisdom Tradition; yet two more opposing worldviews would be hard to find. Śaṅkarācārya's is similar in kind to that of the Jonangpas, which was strongly refuted by the Gelugpas. Near the end of chapter 6, "Tsongkhapa and the Teachings of the Wisdom Tradition," the Ri-mé writer Mipham reconciles the Gelug and Jonang views as only being different approaches to the same goal. In note no. 28, Mipham repeatedly says that Tsongkhapa taught a provisional understanding of emptiness that his Gelugpa followers mistook for definitive and final.

"Great Madhyamaka" is the name used by Jonangpas and some other Tibetan Buddhists for the teachings that they take as ultimate, in contradistinction to the Prāsaṅgika Madhyamaka teachings that Gelugpas and most other Tibetan Buddhists take as ultimate. Until recently, the Great Madhyamaka teachings remained little known. In chapter 7, "The Doctrinal Position of the Wisdom Tradition: Great Madhyamaka," the agreement of these teachings with those of the Wisdom Tradition as we now have them is pointed out. This is not only in terms of doctrine, i.e., the first fundamental proposition of the Secret Doctrine, but also in technical terms shared with the "Book of Dzyan," and in the sources claimed, the books of Maitreya. This specific agreement is with the formulation of the Wisdom Tradition we now have, and is not intended to imply that there are not other important formulations of the Wisdom Tradition.

When portions of the Wisdom Tradition were brought out in the late 1800s, a new name was coined for them: Theosophy. H. P. Blavatsky said in 1875 that this tradition may be described as pre-Vedic Buddhism, but since no one now admits there was any Buddhism before the Vedas, it may best be thought of as Esoteric Buddhism. So for a while Theosophy was presented as Esoteric Buddhism, until the public began limiting Theosophy to only one religion among others instead of seeing all religions as expressing more or less of it. To counter this, Blavatsky then distanced Theosophy from Buddhism, saying it should have been spelled Budhism. Chapter 1, "Theosophy and Buddhism," shows that Blavatsky's teachers did in fact consider themselves Buddhists. The indication is that Buddhism is the most direct descendant of the Wisdom Tradition, and that the many texts of Northern Buddhism now becoming available preserve more of its teachings than are found elsewhere. Yet these texts must be understood esoterically. Other than in little-known teachings such as Great Madhyamaka, we do not find taught in Buddhism even the first fundamental proposition of the Secret Doctrine.

The one omnipresent, eternal, boundless, and immutable principle taught in the Wisdom Tradition is conceived under two aspects. These correspond, in the manifested cosmos, to spirit and matter. Ultimate reality is usually thought of as spirit and not matter. But since the two are ultimately one, it follows that ultimate reality can be described as matter or substance. Indeed, as put in the striking words of Mahatma letter no. 10, "we believe in matter alone." This is the one substance-principle of *The Secret Doctrine* (vol. 1, p. 273). Among the systems of old India, such a teaching is found only in Sāṃkhya, regarded as the oldest philosophical system in Hinduism. Sāṃkhya teaches two main principles, spirit (*puruṣa*) and matter (*prakṛti*). The cosmos evolves from matter while spirit passively looks on. It is thus usually considered to be an ultimate dualism. However, the Sāṃkhya of the old Purāṇas depicts *puruṣa* and *prakṛti* as aspects of a single *brahman*. These two principles are clearly regarded as one in the Wisdom Tradition, as we read in Mahatma letter no. 22: "it is one of the elementary and fundamental doctrines of Occultism that the two are one." As with Buddhism, Sāṃkhya must be understood esoterically, or in its ancient sense. Matter as primary substance (*pradhāna*, a synonym of *prakṛti*) is a way to refer to the ultimate principle. This unique teaching on the great problem of spirit and matter is the subject of chapter 2, "Sāṃkhya and the Wisdom-Religion."

An appendix provides a compilation made from the early Theosophical writings on the first fundamental proposition of the Secret Doctrine: an omnipresent, eternal, boundless, and immutable principle, the one reality of the Wisdom Tradition. The doctrines of the Wisdom Tradition are scattered through the Theosophical writings to such an extent that some of them have remained obscure even to lifelong students of Theosophy. When gathered together in one place, as in this compilation, a clear picture of them emerges as distinct doctrines that may be compared and contrasted with doctrines found elsewhere.

Most of the studies assembled here have been published previously. They are here reproduced with a few slight changes. This book is a sequel to our 1999 book, *Blavatsky's Secret Books: Twenty Years' Research*. Since the publication of that 1999 book, and also since the first publication of the studies that comprise this book, some important long-standing questions have been answered. In 2009, Daniel Caldwell found a reference showing that the final "t" on the word *svabhāvāt*, as found throughout the Theosophical writings, is an error resulting from mistakenly copying from an 1867 book by Max Müller (*Chips from a German Workshop*, vol. I: *Essays on the Science of Religion*, p. 281). Müller had used the word *svabhāva* as declined in the ablative case, *svabhāvāt*, "due to its inherent nature" or "by itself," as follows:

> There is the school of the Svâbhâvikas, which still exists in Nepal. The Svâbhâvikas maintain that nothing exists but nature, or rather substance, and that this substance exists by itself (svabhâvât), without a Creator or a Ruler. It exists, however, under two forms: in the state of Pravritti, as active, or in the state of Nirvritti, as passive. Human beings, who, like everything else, exist svabhâvât, 'by themselves,' are supposed to be capable of arriving at Nirvritti, or passiveness, which is nearly synonymous with Nirvâna.

Blavatsky in her early book *Isis Unveiled* (1877, vol. 2, p. 264, later copied in *The Secret Doctrine*, vol. 1, p. 3), wrote:

> The Svâbhâvikas, or philosophers of the oldest school of Buddhism (which still exists in Nepaul), speculate but upon the active condition of this "Essence," which they call Svabhâvât, and deem it foolish to theorize upon the abstract and "unknowable" power in its passive condition.

In another article, she wrote (*Collected Writings*, vol. 13, p. 309):

> . . . of the Svābhāvikas. "Nothing exists in the Universe but Substance—or Nature," say the latter. "This Substance exists by, and through itself (Svabhavat) having never been either created or had a Creator."

As may be seen, Blavatsky copied this material and the spelling *svabhāvāt* from Müller, not realizing that he was using *svabhāva* as declined in the ablative case, and she continued to use this spelling throughout her writings. Thus, it is a simple error for *svabhāva*. My suggestion in our 1999 book (pp. 99-100, 106) that she may have intended *svabhāvatā* is now seen to be needless, as is G. de Purucker's that it is the present participle *svabhavat*. Her spelling with the final "t" has been retained in the present book in quotations, but the correct word is *svabhāva*.

Then in 2010 the long-standing question of what specific Sanskrit term is behind the fundamental but somewhat generic English term "space" of the "Occult Catechism" became clear. Many occurrences of this basic term in the early Theosophical writings can be seen in the appendix on the first fundamental proposition of the Secret Doctrine. This Sanskrit term, it seems, is not *ākāśa*, nor even *śūnyatā*, but is *dhātu*. As shown by its two Tibetan translations, *khams* and *dbyings*, this word is understood in two senses: "element" (as in "the one element") and "space" (or "expanse" or "realm" or "sphere"). The *dhātu* is the central theme of the book attributed by Tibetan tradition to Maitreya titled *Ratna-gotra-vibhāga*. Blavatsky in a private letter had linked the Book of Dzyan to "the Secret Book of 'Maytreya Buddha'." This provided a strong clue, but whether *dhātu* was behind only "the one element" of the Theosophical writings, or also behind "space" remained uncertain. What determined the case was the evidence provided by a catechism-like statement that is found repeated throughout the Buddhist scriptures. As an example:

> "Whether there is an arising of Tathāgatas or no arising of Tathāgathas, that element [*dhātu*] still persists, the stableness of the Dhamma, the fixed course of the Dhamma, specific conditionality." (*Saṃyutta-nikāya* 2.20, *The Connected Discourses of the Buddha*, translated by Bhikkhu Bodhi, vol. 1, 2000, p. 551)

This example is translated from Pali, in which the word *dhātu* is the same as in Sanskrit. Many more examples of this statement are found in Sanskrit Buddhist texts. Compare the statement from the esoteric Senzar Catechism given by Blavatsky:

> "What is that which was, is, and will be, whether there is a Universe or not; whether there be gods or none?" asks the esoteric Senzar Catechism. And the answer made is—SPACE. (*The Secret Doctrine*, vol. 1, p. 9; see also p. 11)

This is further explained by Blavatsky as follows:

> Hence, the Arahat secret doctrine on cosmogony admits but of one absolute, indestructible, eternal, and uncreated UNCONSCIOUSNESS (so to translate), of an element (the word being used

> for want of a better term) absolutely independent of everything else in the universe; a something ever present or ubiquitous, a Presence which ever was, is, and will be, whether there is a God, gods or none; whether there is a universe or no universe; existing during the eternal cycles of Maha Yugas, during the *Pralayas* as during the periods of *Manvantara*: and this is SPACE, . . . (*Collected Writings*, vol. 3, p. 423)

The parallel between the statement that is often repeated in the Buddhist scriptures, with small variants, and the statement from the esoteric Senzar Catechism is clear. This parallel allows us to conclude that the central Theosophical technical term "space" is the Sanskrit term *dhātu*. Knowing this, we are in a position to trace this teaching in known texts, and thereby to ascertain more fully its significance.

References to "space" in relation to *ākāśa* and *śūnyatā* may be found in our 1999 book (pp. 102 and 119-120, respectively), and to *śūnyatā* in the present book, where a note about the *dhātu* has been added (p. 164). Some more examples of the statement from the Buddhist scriptures can be found in the 2013 article by David Reigle, "The Book of Dzyan: The Current State of the Evidence" (*Brahmavidyā: The Adyar Library Bulletin*, Supplement, 2013, pp. 87-120). This article along with others, including the ones in this book, can be found on our website: www.easterntradition.org. Much of our continuing research is being posted at the "Book of Dzyan" blog: prajnaquest.fr/blog, or dzyan.net.

The present book brings together a series of studies that pertain specifically to the doctrines of the Wisdom Tradition, insofar as we can now ascertain them.

David and Nancy Reigle
May 8, 2015

Theosophy and Buddhism

Theosophy is the modern name given by H. P. Blavatsky to what is described by her as the once universal but now hidden Wisdom-Religion, the parent source of all known religions. This original Wisdom-Religion had been preserved intact out of the reach of the many conflicting sects, who each thought that their piece of it was the only truth. Blavatsky was now entrusted by its custodians with the task of making publicly known its existence and bringing out some of its teachings. She presented it to the modern world as Theosophy. In her early writings she referred to this Wisdom-Religion as pre-Vedic Buddhism.

> We can assert, with entire plausibility, that there is not one of all these sects—Kabalism, Judaism, and our present Christianity included—but sprang from the two main branches of that one mother-trunk, the once universal religion, which antedated the Vedic ages—we speak of that prehistoric Buddhism which merged later into Brahmanism.[1]

> We repeat again, *Buddhism is but the primitive source of Brahmanism.*[2]

> Pre-Vedic Brahmanism and Buddhism are the double source from which all religions sprang; . . .[3]

When the Theosophical Society was founded by Blavatsky and others in 1875, she was asked about this Wisdom-Religion by William Q. Judge, one of the co-founders. He in his question referred to the custodians of the Wisdom-Religion as Masters, as did Blavatsky, since they were her teachers. Her reply indicates that while pre-Vedic Buddhism is a correct designation for the Wisdom-Religion, she considered that it might best be thought of as esoteric Buddhism. As reported by Judge:

> . . . on my asking her [Blavatsky] in 1875 what could the Masters' belief be called she told me they might be designated "pre-Vedic Buddhists," but that no one would now admit there was any Buddhism before the Vedas, so I had best think of them as Esoteric Buddhists.[4]

The title chosen for the first book to attempt an outline of the tenets of Theosophy or the Wisdom-Religion was *Esoteric Buddhism*. Its author, A. P. Sinnett, obviously also felt that this was an accurate designation. This book was written on the basis of correspondence with two of the custodians of the Wisdom-Religion living in Tibet. These, Blavatsky's Masters or teachers, also came to be called by the name used in India (where Sinnett and Blavatsky were then living), Mahatmas. Their letters, later published and now preserved in the British Library, became known as the Mahatma letters. However, as made clear in them, the term Mahatma is not used in Tibet. Instead, the Tibetan term *byang chub* is used, whose Sanskrit equivalent is Bodhisattva rather than Mahatma. Sinnett's book based on these Mahatma letters was responsible for establishing the idea among the Western public that Theosophy is esoteric Buddhism. But the public did not correctly apprehend what was meant by esoteric Buddhism, as the Mahatma K.H. commented several months after the book of that name was published:

> . . . that public having never heard of the Tibetan, and entertaining very perverted notions of the Esoteric Buddhist System. . . . the Tibetan School will ever be regarded by those who know little, if anything of it, as coloured more or less with sectarianism.[5]

Thus arose the misconception that Theosophy is derived from one religion among others, namely that known in the world as Buddhism, rather than from the Wisdom-Religion which was the source of all religions.

In order to counter this misconception, and to stress the universality of Theosophy, Blavatsky opened her greatest work, *The Secret Doctrine*, with a refutation of the idea that Theosophy is esoteric Buddhism. She said that Sinnett's book should have been titled, *Esoteric Budhism*, spelled with one "d," to distinguish the Wisdom-Religion, or Budhism, from the exoteric religion known as Buddhism. She repeated this in Section I of *The Key to Theosophy*. We can certainly understand the need to correct the misconception that had arisen in people's minds; but was the problem really with the book title, or was it with people being too ready to jump to unwarranted conclusions? We may recall that at the time the book was being written, the Mahatma K.H. thought *Esoteric Buddhism* was "an excellent title."[6] One must wonder if this distancing of Theosophy from esoteric Buddhism has not produced its own misconceptions; e.g., the idea that the Mahatmas lived in Tibet among Buddhists, but were not themselves Buddhists as such. The literary evidence from Blavatsky's Mahatma teachers indicates that they were in fact Buddhists.

Starting with the first known Mahatma letter, written to Blavatsky's aunt in 1870 in the Mahatma K.H. handwriting, we find the following (translated from the original French):

> She [Blavatsky] has been very ill, but is so no longer; for under the protection of the Lord Sang-gyas she has found devoted friends who guard her physically and spiritually.[7]

The word "Sang-gyas" (*sangs rgyas*) is the Tibetan translation of the Sanskrit word "Buddha."

Then in letters from the Mahatma K.H. to A. P. Sinnett and A. O. Hume, written in the early 1880s, we find a number of references to Sang-gyas or Buddha as "our Lord:"

> They *cannot* place—however much they would—the birth of our Lord Sangyas Buddha A.D. as they have contrived to place that of Chrishna.[8]

> . . . the ecclesiastical system built upon the basic ideas of our Lord Gautama Buddha's philosophy, . . .[9]

> . . . for the information gathered as to what takes place beyond we are indebted to the Planetary Spirits, to our blessed Lord Buddha.[10]

> . . . and necessity of the practical application of these sublime words of our Lord and Master:—"O ye Bhikkhus and Arhats— . . ."[11]

> Our Lord Buddha—a sixth r. man—[12]

> Plato and Confucius were fifth round men and our Lord a sixth round man . . .[13]

> . . . the old, very old fact distinctly taught by our Lord . . .[14]

> "The right in thee is base, the wrong a curse," was said by our Lord Buddha for such as she; . . .[15]

> The Devachan, or land of "Sukhavati," is *allegorically* described by our Lord Buddha himself.[16]

In letters from the Mahatma Morya to S. Ramaswamier and from the Mahatma K.H. to C. W. Leadbeater, we find similar references to "our Lord," using the term "Tathāgata," another title of the Buddha:

> . . . decide after counting the whole cost, and may the light of our Lord Tathagata's memory aid you to decide for the best.[17]

> So now choose and grasp your own destiny—and may our Lord's the Tathâgata's memory aid you to decide for the best.[18]

> Let no one know that you are going, and may the blessing of our Lord and my poor blessing shield you from every evil in your new life.[19]

The letters from these Mahatmas also include other passages that specifically identify them as Buddhists:

> . . . our lamas to honour the fraternity of the *Bhikkhus* [Buddhist monks] established by our blessed master himself, . . .[20]

> "Real Adepts like Gautama Buddha or Jesus Christ did not shroud themselves in mystery, but came and talked openly,"

> quoth our oracle. If they did it's news to us—the humble followers of the former.[21]

> . . . he who reads our Buddhist scriptures . . .[22]

> Therefore, we deny God both as philosophers and as Buddhists.[23]

> If it is objected that we too have temples, we too have priests and that our lamas also live on charity . . . let them know that the objects above named have in common with their Western equivalents, but the name. Thus in our temples there is neither a god nor gods worshipped, only the thrice sacred memory of the greatest as the holiest man that ever lived.[24]

They distinguish themselves from other creeds, including even Advaita Vedanta, which is said by Blavatsky to be, along with Buddhism, the closest to the Esoteric Philosophy:

> We are not Adwaitees . . . . / . . . we never were Adwaitees . . . .[25]

They retain this distinction, even though they accept the truths taught in Advaita Vedanta, and have Advaita Vedanta chelas or pupils:

> It is an every day occurrence to find students belonging to different schools of occult thought sitting side by side at the feet of the same Guru. *Upasika* (Madam B[lavatsky]) and Subba Row, though pupils of the same Master, have not followed the same Philosophy—the one is Buddhist and the other an Adwaitee.[26]

The Mahatma Morya wrote to Dr. Franz Hartmann that his becoming a Buddhist will make the path of knowledge easier of access. After H. P. Blavatsky and H. S. Olcott publicly took "Panchashila" at Galle, Ceylon, on May 25, 1880, to formally become Buddhists, the first Westerners known to do so, Hartmann followed suit and became a Buddhist on Dec. 26, 1883. The Mahatma Morya wrote in a letter to him on Feb. 5, 1884:

> Let me give you an advice. Never offer yourself as a chela, but wait until chelaship descends by itself upon you. Above all, try to find yourself, and the path of knowledge will open itself before you, and this so much the easier as you have made a contact with the Light-ray of the Blessed one, whose name you have now taken as your spiritual lode-star. . . . Receive in advance my blessings and my thanks.[27]

It would seem that not only were Blavatsky's Mahatma teachers Buddhists, but so was the trans-Himalayan school of adepts to which they belonged.

> When our great Buddha—the patron of all the adepts, the reformer and the codifier of the occult system, reached first *Nirvana* on earth, . . .[28]

> . . . and philanthropy as preached by our Great Patron—"the Saviour of the World—the Teacher of Nirvana and the Law," . . .[29]

In a letter to Mrs. Sinnett, Blavatsky refers to other Masters or Mahatmas of this school,

> . . . who are pure blooded Mongolian Buddhists.[30]

Indeed, some of the clearest references identifying this school of Mahatmas with Buddhism are found in the words of the Chohan, the teacher of Blavatsky's teachers:

> That *we* the devoted followers of that spirit incarnate of absolute self sacrifice, of philanthropy, divine kindness, as of all the highest virtues attainable on this earth of sorrow, the man of men, Gautama Buddha, should ever allow the Theosophical Society to represent the *embodiment of selfishness*, the refuge of the few with no thought in them for the many, is a strange idea, my brothers.
>
> Among the few glimpses obtained by Europeans of Tibet and its mystical hierarchy of "perfect lamas," there is one which was correctly understood and described. "The incarnations of the Boddisatwa Padma Pani or Avalo-Kiteswara and of Tsong Kapa,

> that of Amitabha, relinquish at their death the attainment of Buddhahood—*i.e.* the summum bonum of bliss, and of individual *personal* felicity—that they might be born again and again for the benefit of mankind." (Rhys Davids). In other words, that they might be again and again subjected to misery, imprisonment in flesh and all the sorrows of life, provided that by such a self sacrifice repeated throughout long and dreary centuries they might become the means of securing salvation and bliss in the hereafter for a handful of men chosen among but one of the many races of mankind. And it is we, the humble disciples of these perfect lamas, who are expected to allow the T.S. to drop its noblest title, that of the Brotherhood of Humanity to become a simple school of psychology? No, no, good brothers, you have been labouring under the mistake too long already.[31]

As clear as these references are to the Mahatmas of this school being the devoted followers of Gautama Buddha, and "humble disciples of these perfect lamas," there yet exists an even more direct statement. This came through unfiltered in a response from the Mahatma Morya to a request from a certain Hindu Theosophist to open up new correspondence. He and other Hindu Theosophists, however, were not prepared to give up caste and their "old superstitions" such as faith in the Gods and God, as had the Hindu Theosophist Damodar Mavalankar. The Mahatma Morya says in his characteristic blunt manner:

> What have we, the disciples of the true *Arhats*, of esoteric Buddhism and of Sang-gyas [Buddha] to do with the *Shastras* and Orthodox Brahmanism? There are 100 of thousands of Fakirs, Sannyasis and Sadhus leading the most pure lives, and yet being as they are, on the path of *error*, never having had an opportunity to meet, see or even hear of us. Their forefathers have driven away the followers of the only true philosophy upon earth from India and now it is not for the latter to come to them but for them to come to us if they want us. Which of them is ready to become a Buddhist, a *Nastika* [one who does not believe in God or Gods] as they call us? None. Those who have believed and followed us have had their reward.[32]

These quotations given above leave little doubt that the Mahatmas behind the Theosophical movement, Blavatsky's teachers, considered themselves to be Buddhists as such, and not only esoteric Buddhists.

The obvious question that now arises is this: Why don't the teachings given out by the Theosophical Mahatmas agree with the known teachings of Buddhism? To merely say that the Mahatmas are esoteric Buddhists does not entirely answer the question. It does not explain the Buddhist part. What makes them esoteric Buddhists rather than esoteric Hindus or esoteric Christians or esoteric anything else? Why should there have ever been any talk of pre-Vedic Buddhism or esoteric Buddhism unless known Buddhism has some direct connection with their teachings? Having investigated this question for many years, my own conclusion is simply and in brief as follows.

Buddhism is the most direct descendant of the Wisdom-Religion now in existence, and in the Buddhist scriptures are preserved more of the Wisdom-Religion's teachings than in any other texts now extant. Thus Blavatsky's Mahatma teachers are even exoterically Buddhists. But, as often repeated by Blavatsky, the commentaries which give the true meanings of the known texts have been withdrawn and are no longer accessible. Thus the teachings of the Mahatmas differ significantly from those of exoteric or known Buddhism. In other words, the texts of the Wisdom-Religion are best preserved in Buddhism, while the true teachings of these texts, long preserved in secret by the Mahatmas, began to be given out to the world as Theosophy.

We may recall that when the Theosophical Society was started, the scriptures of Northern Buddhism were almost all unavailable and untranslated, unlike those of Hinduism that Blavatsky cited frequently. The books on Buddhism that then existed were criticized by the Mahatma K.H. Yet he indicates that even the exoteric Buddhism portrayed in them "is full of the sparkle of our most important esotericism," likening it to diamond mines:

> The more one reads such speculations as those of Messrs. Rhys Davids, Lillie, etc.—the less can one bring himself to believe that

> the unregenerate Western mind can ever get at the core of our abstruse doctrines. . . . Mr. Rhys Davids' *Buddhism* is full of the sparkle of our most important esotericism; but always, as it would seem, beyond not only his reach but apparently even his powers of intellectual perception. . . . He is like the Cape Settlers who lived over diamond mines without suspecting it.[33]

To show this, the Mahatma K.H. then provides Sinnett with the esoteric explanation of an exoteric Buddhist doctrine given in Rhys Davids' book.

> *En passant*, to show to you that not only were not the "races" *invented* by us, but that they are a cardinal dogma with the Lama Buddhists and with all who study our esoteric doctrine, I send you an explanation on a page or two in Rhys Davids' *Buddhism*,—otherwise incomprehensible, meaningless and absurd. It is written with the special permission of the Chohan (*my* Master) and—for your benefit. No Orientalist has ever suspected the truths contained in it, and—you are the first Western man (outside Tibet) to whom it is now explained.[34]

As far as I know, this explanation has not come down to us, as it is not among the Mahatma papers now preserved in the British Library. From a perusal of Rhys Davids' book, we may assume that this explanation was "on a page or two" of his chapter 8, "Northern Buddhism." Specifically, it likely refers to the listing he gives of the five Dhyāni Buddhas, their five Bodhisattvas, and the five corresponding Mānushi (human) Buddhas.[35] K.H. had also in a previous letter spoken of sending an explanation of this material; but if there included, it too has not come down to us. In this letter he appeared anxious that the theosophists give out the right explanation of this seemingly fantastic Buddhist teaching.

> Only, to prove *to you*, if not to him, that we have not *invented* those races, I will give out for your benefit that which has never been given out before. I will explain to you a whole chapter out of Rhys Davids work on Buddhism, or rather on Lamaism, which,

> in his natural ignorance he regards as a *corruption* of Buddhism! Since those gentlemen—the Orientalists—presume to give to the world their *soi-disant* translations and commentaries on our sacred books, let the theosophists show the great ignorance of those "world" pundits, by giving the public the right doctrines and explanations of what they would regard as an absurd, fancy theory.[36]

Fortunately, Sinnett did give out in his *Esoteric Buddhism* what is apparently this right explanation. In chapter 9, entitled "Buddha," Sinnett explains that the five human Buddhas given by Rhys Davids relate to the five races taught by Theosophy. He introduces this topic thus:

> The explanation of this branch of the subject, in plain terms, will not alone be important for its own sake, but will be interesting to all students of exoteric Buddhism, as elucidating some of the puzzling complications of the more abstruse "Northern doctrine."[37]

The listing of the human Buddhas in the Rhys Davids book gives three Buddhas of the remote past, then Gautama the historical Buddha as fourth, and Maitreya the coming Buddha as fifth. Sinnett explains why it is that the fourth Buddha belongs to our fifth race; namely, that at the beginning of the first race appears a teacher he refers to as a Dhyan Chohan, and who is therefore not in this list of five Buddhas. His explanation of this, however, was not altogether clear; and a correspondent questioned it in *The Theosophist* for August, 1884. The editor, H. P. Blavatsky, clarified that:

> . . . *Gautama* was the *fourth Buddha, i.e.*, "enlightened," while he was the *fifth* spiritual *teacher*. The first "teacher" of this "Round" on this planet was a *Dhyan Chohan*. As a *Dhyan Chohan*, he belonged to another System, and was thus far higher than a *Buddha*. As, however, in ordinary language, all spiritual teachers are called "*Buddhas*," Mr. Sinnett speaks of Gautama as the fifth *Buddha*. To be more accurate, it must be said that Gautama was

> the fifth spiritual teacher in this "Round" on this planet, while he was the *fourth* who became a *Buddha*.[38]

With this one example the Mahatma K.H. showed that the hitherto esoteric teachings now given out as Theosophy could explain the known teachings of Buddhism that were otherwise considered fantastic, and at the same time the known teachings of Buddhism could support the newly given out Theosophical teachings that were otherwise considered fantastic.

The many schools of Buddhism, each with its own varying interpretations, all claim to have preserved intact the original teachings, and to have transmitted their correct explanations in an unbroken line. Theosophy, too, makes this claim. As Blavatsky describes to a correspondent:

> But what I do believe in is: (1), the unbroken oral teachings revealed by living *divine* men during the infancy of mankind to the elect among men; (2), that it has reached us *unaltered*; and (3), that the MASTERS are thoroughly versed in the science based on such uninterrupted teaching.[39]

Both Buddhism and Theosophy teach that each person should determine for his or her own self what is true through proper reasoning. If the example given by the Mahatma K.H. be taken as representative, we may reasonably conclude that Buddhism does in fact preserve original teachings of the Wisdom-Religion, and that the correct explanations have indeed been transmitted in an unbroken line to the esoteric school of the Mahatmas, and partially given out to the world as Theosophy.

The Mahatma K.H. had advised Sinnett that to properly study and correctly understand their teachings, a special group should be formed for the express purpose of seeking esoteric knowledge from the Northern Buddhist source:

> It seems necessary for a proper study and correct understanding of our Philosophy and the benefit of those whose inclination leads them to seek esoteric knowledge from the Northern Buddhist Source, . . . that an exclusive group composed of those

> members who desire to follow absolutely the teachings of the School to which we, of the Tibetan Brotherhood, belong, should be formed . . . .[40]

However, the attempt made at that time soon proved abortive; and this remains unaccomplished and still a desideratum. Now that so many of the Northern Buddhist scriptures have become available, the opportunities to study and interpret them in light of Theosophy as sourcebooks of the Wisdom-Religion are very great indeed.

NOTES

1. *Isis Unveiled,* by H. P. Blavatsky, 1st ed., 1877; rev. ed. [by Boris de Zirkoff] (pagination unchanged), Wheaton, Illinois: Theosophical Publishing House, 1972, vol. 2, p. 123.

2. *Isis Unveiled,* vol. 2, p. 169.

3. *Isis Unveiled,* vol. 2, p. 639.

4. *The Path,* vol. 9, March 1895, p. 431; reprinted in *Echoes of the Orient: The Writings of William Quan Judge,* vol. I, compiled by Dara Eklund, San Diego: Point Loma Publications, 1975, p. 453. The word "Buddhists" in the phrase "pre-Vedic Buddhists" is spelled "Budhists" in these publications. I have used "Buddhists" because that is what Blavatsky used at that time, not changing this until years later.

5. *The Mahatma Letters to A. P. Sinnett,* compiled by A. T. Barker, 1st ed., 1923; 3rd rev. ed., Adyar, Madras: Theosophical Publishing House, 1962, p. 392; arranged in chronological sequence by Vicente Hao Chin, Jr., Quezon City, Metro Manila: Theosophical Publishing House, 1993, p. 410.

6. *The Mahatma Letters,* 3rd ed., p. 198; chron. ed., p. 363.

7. *Letters from the Masters of the Wisdom,* compiled by C. Jinarajadasa, First Series, letter no. 38, Adyar, Madras: Theosophical Publishing House, 1st ed., 1919, p. 102; 5th ed., 1964, p. 85; Second Series, letter no. 1, Adyar, Madras: Theosophical Publishing House, 1925, p. 4; Chicago: The Theosophical Press, 1926, p. 11. Both volumes include a transcription of the original French letter, and an English translation. The second volume also includes a facsimile of the original, allowing my corrected spelling "Sang-gyas," rather than the printed "Sangyas."

8. *The Mahatma Letters,* 3rd ed., p. 339; chron. ed., pp. 377-78.

9. *The Mahatma Letters*, 3rd ed., p. 393; chron. ed., p. 410.
10. *The Mahatma Letters*, 3rd ed., p. 134; chron. ed., p. 279.
11. *The Mahatma Letters*, 3rd ed., p. 381; chron. ed., p. 385.
12. *The Mahatma Letters*, 3rd ed., p. 94; chron. ed., p. 186.
13. *The Mahatma Letters*, 3rd ed., p. 83; chron. ed., p. 176.
14. *The Mahatma Letters*, 3rd ed., p. 108; chron. ed., p. 199.
15. *The Mahatma Letters*, 3rd ed., p. 354; chron. ed., p. 442.
16. *The Mahatma Letters*, 3rd ed., p. 97; chron. ed., p. 189.
17. *Letters from the Masters of the Wisdom*, Second Series, letter no. 51, Morya to S. Ramaswamier, Adyar ed., 1925, p. 98; Chicago ed., 1926, p. 110.
18. *Letters from the Masters of the Wisdom*, First Series, letter no. 7, K.H. to C. W. Leadbeater, 1st ed., 1919, p. 35; 5th ed., 1964, p. 30. A facsimile of this letter was published in *The "K.H." Letters to C. W. Leadbeater*, by C. Jinarajadasa, Adyar, Madras: Theosophical Publishing House, 1941, where this passage occurs on p. 11 (incidentally showing the circumflex mark in the word Tathâgata).
19. *Letters from the Masters of the Wisdom*, First Series, letter no. 8, K.H. to C. W. Leadbeater, 1st ed., 1919, p. 36; 5th ed., 1964, p. 30; facsimile in *The "K.H." Letters to C. W. Leadbeater*, pp. 50-51.
20. *The Mahatma Letters*, 3rd ed., p. 58; chron. ed., p. 275.
21. *The Mahatma Letters*, 3rd ed., p. 277; chron. ed., p. 71.
22. *The Mahatma Letters*, 3rd ed., p. 54; chron. ed., p. 271.
23. *The Mahatma Letters*, 3rd ed., p. 52; chron. ed., p. 270.
24. *The Mahatma Letters*, 3rd ed., p. 58; chron. ed., p. 275.
25. *The Mahatma Letters*, 3rd ed., pp. 53, 284; chron. ed., pp. 271, 245.
26. *The Mahatma Letters*, 3rd ed., p. 393; chron. ed., p. 410.
27. *H. P. Blavatsky Collected Writings*, vol. 8, Adyar, Madras: Theosophical Publishing House, 1960, p. 446.
28. *The Mahatma Letters*, 3rd. ed., p. 43; chron. ed., p. 62.
29. *The Mahatma Letters*, 3rd. ed., p. 33; chron. ed., p. 49.
30. *The Letters of H. P. Blavatsky to A. P. Sinnett*, compiled by A. T. Barker, 1st ed., 1925; facsimile edition, Pasadena: Theosophical University Press, 1973, p. 85.
31. *Combined Chronology*, Margaret Conger, Pasadena: Theosophical University Press, 1973, pp. 46-47; *The Mahatma Letters*, chron. ed., appendix II, pp. 479-80; with minor variants, *Letters from the Masters of the Wisdom*, First Series, letter no. 1. The reference attributed to Rhys Davids is actually from Clements R. Markham, ed., *Narratives of the Mission of George Bogle to Tibet and of the Journey of Thomas Manning to Lhasa*, 1st ed., 1876; 2nd ed., London, 1879, p. xlvii. The reference to

securing salvation for a handful of men from but one of the many races of mankind is further explained in an excerpt from a secret book, given by H. P. Blavatsky in "'Reincarnations' of Buddha," *H. P. Blavatsky Collected Writings,* vol. 14, Wheaton, Illinois: Theosophical Publishing House, 1985, p. 405:

> The Seven Ways and the Four Truths were once more hidden out of sight. The Merciful One [Buddha] confined since then his attention and fatherly care to the heart of Bodyul [Tibet], the nursery grounds of the seeds of truth. The blessed "remains" since then have overshadowed and rested in many a holy body of human Bodhisattvas.

32. *The Mahatma Letters,* 3rd. ed., p. 455; chron. ed., p. 95.
33. *The Mahatma Letters,* 3rd. ed., p. 337; chron. ed., p. 376.
34. *The Mahatma Letters,* 3rd. ed., p. 154; chron. ed., p. 315.
35. *Buddhism: Being a Sketch of the Life and Teachings of Gautama, the Buddha,* by T. W. Rhys Davids, 1st ed., 1877; rev. ed., London: Society for Promoting Christian Knowledge, 1886, p. 205; taken from Eugène Burnouf, *Introduction à l'histoire du Buddhisme indien,* Paris, 1844, p. 117.
36. *The Mahatma Letters,* 3rd. ed., p. 182; chron. ed., p. 261.
37. *Esoteric Buddhism,* by A. P. Sinnett, 1st ed., 1883; 5th annotated ed. 1885, reprint, Minneapolis: Wizards Bookshelf, 1973, p. 171.
38. *H. P. Blavatsky Collected Writings,* vol. 6, 1st ed., 1954; 2nd ed., Wheaton, Illinois: Theosophical Publishing House, 1975, p. 267. The Buddhist texts (e.g., the *Bhadra-kalpika Sūtra*) speak of many more than five Buddhas, but only four have so far appeared in our *kalpa,* or eon; with the fifth, Maitreya, next to come in our kalpa. Buddhist texts (e.g., the *Abhidharma-kośa*) describe several kinds of kalpas. One kind of kalpa is, in the Theosophical terminology coined by A. P. Sinnett, a "round." A round is the time period during which seven sequential races or humanities evolve on our planet. The equivalence of this kalpa and "round" is shown in a quotation from a commentary given in *The Secret Doctrine,* by H. P. Blavatsky, 1st ed., 1888; rev. ed. [by Boris de Zirkoff] (pagination unchanged), Adyar, Madras: Theosophical Publishing House, 1978, vol. 1, p. 184:

> The human foetus follows now in its transformations all the forms that the physical frame of man had assumed throughout the three Kalpas (Rounds) during the tentative efforts at plastic formation around the monad by senseless, because imperfect, matter, in her blind wanderings. In the present age, . . .

39. *H. P. Blavatsky Collected Writings*, vol. 11, Wheaton, Illinois: Theosophical Publishing House, 1973, pp. 466-67. Contrast this statement with the popular view repeated again and again by ill-informed writers that Blavatsky's source was psychic communications from "Ascended Masters."

40. *The Mahatma Letters*, 3rd. ed., p. 394; chron. ed., p. 411.

Later addition:
The important series of articles titled, "Some Inquiries Suggested by Mr. Sinnett's *Esoteric Buddhism*," is believed to have been written by three Mahatmas (see: *Blavatsky Collected Writings*, vol. 5, pp. 135, 136, quoted below in notes 5-6 on pp. 63-64). In two of these articles the Mahatma writer again leaves no doubt that he considers himself to be a Buddhist, by his references to "our Lord," etc. These occur, in the *Blavatsky Collected Writings* reprint (vol. 5), as follows:
"Philological and Archaeological 'Difficulties'":
p. 229: ". . . as to the date of our Lord's birth, . . ."
p. 232: ". . . the date of our Lord and Glorified Deliverer . . ."
p. 232: ". . . the date of our Lord Sanggyas' birth, . . ."
p. 240: ". . . Buddhism . . . our religion . . ."
p. 240: ". . . our Lord Gautama . . ."
"Sakya Muni's Place in History":
p. 244: ". . . the prophecy of our Lord that 'a thousand years after he had reached Nirvana, his doctrines would reach the north' . . ."
p. 245: ". . . the great Sramanāchāryas who preceded Him, and were His teachers, their humble successors trying to this day to perpetuate their and His doctrines."
p. 245: ". . . in consequence of a vision of our Lord, . . ."
p. 246 fn.: "When our Lord first sat in it for *Dhyana*, . . ."
p. 247 fn.: ". . . while teaching the mendicants outside, our Lord . . ."
p. 248: ". . . the Buddhist Sacred Annals record certain words of our Lord . . ."
p. 249: ". . . as prophesied by Lokanātha, our Buddha."
p. 250: ". . . prophecy by our Lord; . . ."
p. 250: ". . . our Sakyasinha's prophecies . . ."
In another article, "Was Writing Known before Pānini?" by a Chela:
p. 304: ". . . our Lord Buddha . . ."

[The foregoing article was written by David Reigle, and published in *Fohat*, A Quarterly Publication of Edmonton Theosophical Society, vol. 4, no. 1, Spring 2000, pp. 14-17, 22-23.]

Sāṃkhya and the Wisdom-Religion

The existence of the once universal Wisdom-Religion was made known to the modern world by H. P. Blavatsky, who called its modern form Theosophy. She early on described its original form as "pre-Vedic Buddhism."[1] Today, no one knows of any pre-Vedic Buddhism. Buddhism is thought to have originated with Gautama Buddha around 500 B.C.E., while the Vedas are much older than that. However, some intriguing indications have been found for a "pre-canonical Buddhism." This refers to Buddhist teachings before their formulation into the known Buddhist canons. Those who have postulated the existence of pre-canonical Buddhism do not consider it to be pre-Vedic, since they still trace it to Gautama Buddha. But Buddhist texts speak of previous Buddhas, who when not taken as merely mythological could well have been pre-Vedic. This promising area of research is being pursued by my colleague Robert Hütwohl, and we may expect an article on it from him in due course. There remains, however, a great question.

The Wisdom-Religion has been described as pre-Vedic Buddhism. We have earlier reviewed the considerable evidence linking its present custodians, Blavatsky's teachers, with Tibetan Buddhism.[2] In other words, from earliest to latest, we find the Wisdom-Religion associated with Buddhism. Yet its most basic teaching, presented to us as the first fundamental proposition of the Secret Doctrine, is not the teaching of any known form of Buddhism. Speaking generally, Southern Buddhism ignores any such teaching as that of an "omnipresent, eternal, boundless, and immutable principle," while Northern Buddhism, particularly Tibetan Gelugpa Buddhism, specifically refutes it.[3] And a teaching this major will be hard to recover from the fragmentary remains of pre-canonical Buddhism. So we must ask if there are any other known systems that could possibly lay claim to being pre-Vedic, and that preserve teachings we could possibly consider as being pre-Vedic Buddhism. The answer is yes, there are two such. These are the Jaina religion and the Sāṃkhya philosophy.[4] It is to Sāṃkhya that we must turn to find the primary ramification of the first fundamental proposition of the Secret Doctrine, namely, the teaching that the universe is the result not of God or of spirit, but of matter.

"We Believe in Matter Alone"

The first fundamental proposition established by the Secret Doctrine is "An Omnipresent, Eternal, Boundless, and Immutable PRINCIPLE on which all speculation is impossible, since it transcends the power of human conception."[5] Were we to stop at this, our difficulties would be minimized, since such a principle can be found in many of the Indian scriptures. It can be extracted from the Southern Buddhist Pali canon,[6] and can be found in the Tathāgata-garbha texts of Northern Buddhism.[7] But *The Secret Doctrine* goes on to explain that this one reality is symbolized under two aspects: absolute abstract space, and absolute abstract motion. It further describes these two aspects as pre-cosmic substance and pre-cosmic ideation, the precursors of manifested matter and spirit (or consciousness). We are cautioned not to regard these as two independent realities, but as the two facets or aspects of the one reality. Therefore when the doctrine is later summed up, this omnipresent, eternal, boundless, and immutable principle, the one reality, is called "the One homogeneous divine SUBSTANCE-PRINCIPLE." Blavatsky explains:

> It is called "Substance-Principle," for it becomes "substance" on the plane of the manifested Universe, an illusion, while it remains a "principle" in the beginningless and endless abstract, visible and invisible SPACE. It is the omnipresent Reality: impersonal, because it contains all and everything. . . . It is latent in every atom in the Universe, and is the Universe itself.[8]

Six years earlier, in one of the clearest and most direct statements we have of the doctrines of the Mahatmas, this was summarized by Mahatma K.H. as: "we believe in matter alone." K.H. was explaining to A. O. Hume in a letter that they do not believe in God, and here stated what they do believe in.

> If people are willing to accept and to regard as God our ONE LIFE immutable and unconscious in its eternity they may do so and thus keep to one more gigantic misnomer.[9]

> When we speak of our One Life we also say that it penetrates, nay is the essence of every atom of matter; and that therefore it not only has correspondence with matter but has all its properties likewise, etc.—hence *is* material, is *matter itself.*[10]

> Matter we know to be eternal, *i.e.*, having had no beginning (*a*) because matter is Nature herself (*b*) because that which cannot annihilate itself and is indestructible exists necessarily—and therefore it could not begin to be, nor can it cease to be (*c*) because the accumulated experience of countless ages, and that of exact science show to us matter (or nature) acting by her own peculiar energy, of which not an atom is ever in an absolute state of rest, and therefore it must have always existed, *i.e.*, its materials ever changing form, combinations and properties, but its principles or elements being absolutely indestructible.[11]

> In other words we believe in MATTER alone, in matter as visible nature and matter in its invisibility as the invisible omnipresent omnipotent Proteus with its unceasing motion which is its life, and which nature draws from herself since she is the great whole outside of which nothing can exist.[12]

> The existence of matter then is a fact; the existence of motion is another fact, their self existence and eternity or indestructibility is a third fact. And the idea of pure spirit as a Being or an Existence—give it whatever name you will—is a chimera, a gigantic absurdity.[13]

An important article by the same author written just previously and published at that same time, "What Is Matter and What Is Force?," concludes with the same idea:

> Therefore, whether it is called Force or Matter, it will ever remain the Omnipresent Proteus of the Universe, the one element—LIFE—Spirit or Force at its *negative*, Matter at its *positive* pole; the former the MATERIO-SPIRITUAL, the latter, the MATERIO-PHYSICAL Universe—Nature, Svabhavat or INDESTRUCTIBLE MATTER.[14]

Most people assume that it is spirit that generates matter, not vice versa. A correspondent to *The Theosophist* magazine, where the above-quoted article was published, did so in a letter a few months later. Blavatsky replied:

> Nor do we believe that "Spirit breathed out Matter;" but that, on the contrary, it is *Matter which manifests Spirit.*[15]

In the following months she would return to this topic:

> . . . the Arhat esoteric doctrine teaches that (1) "'Matter and Life are equally eternal and indestructible,' for—they are one and identical; the purely subjective—hence (for physical science) unprovable and unverifiable—matter becoming the ONE life or what is generally termed 'Spirit.'[16]

And again:

> . . . the Eastern Occultists hold that there is but one element in the universe—infinite, uncreated and indestructible—MATTER; which element manifests itself in seven states. . . . *Spirit* is the highest state of that matter, they say, since that which is neither matter nor any of its attributes is—NOTHING.[17]

By the time she wrote *The Secret Doctrine* a few years later, she had come to prefer the term "substance" as being more accurate and less misleading than "matter."

> In strict accuracy—to avoid confusion and misconception—the term "Matter" ought to be applied to the aggregate of objects of possible perception, and "Substance" to *noumena*; . . .[18]

> The Occultists, who do not say—if they would express themselves correctly—that *matter*, but only the *substance* or *essence* of matter, is indestructible and eternal (*i.e.*, the Root of all, *Mūlaprakṛiti*), . . .[19]

As just seen, she also used the Sanskrit equivalent "*mūlaprakṛti*," since this Sāṃkhya term was familiar to many readers, and was more precise than either "matter" or "substance." Her teachers had also used the term "*mūlaprakṛti*" in their letters:

> The One reality is *Mulaprakriti* (undifferentiated Substance)—the "Rootless root," . . .[20]

So when she gave the first fundamental proposition of the Secret Doctrine, she explained its aspects using the terms "precosmic substance" and "*mūlaprakṛti*" rather than "matter." She also used the Vedānta term "*parabrahman*" to refer to the omnipresent, eternal, boundless, and immutable principle as such.[21] It is important to keep in mind that these are not two different things, but that *parabrahman* only refers to *mūlaprakṛti* or cosmic substance in its primary state of abstract potential objectivity.

> During the period of Universal Pralaya [the dissolution of the universe], Cosmic Ideation is non-existent; and the variously differentiated states of Cosmic Substance are resolved back again into the primary state of abstract potential objectivity.[22]

Thus a casual reader, not knowing this, could easily take the following passage of *The Secret Doctrine* as teaching that spirit manifests as matter, which as we have seen above is not the case.

> At the commencement of a great Manvantara [manifestation], Parabrahman manifests as Mūlaprakṛiti and then as the Logos.[23]

Blavatsky goes on in the same passage to again reiterate that matter precedes spirit, here termed force, at the same time pointing out that it is unnecessary to weave too fine a cobweb of subtleties when speaking of the order of succession of cosmic ultimates. This explains why she has not stressed this point in *The Secret Doctrine*, although she had spoken of it earlier.

> Force, then, does not emerge with Primordial Substance from Parabrahmic Latency. . . . Force thus is *not synchronous with the first objectivation of Mūlaprakṛiti.* But as, apart from it, the latter is absolutely and necessarily inert—*a mere abstraction*—it is unnecessary to weave too fine a cobweb of subtleties as to the order of succession of the Cosmic Ultimates. Force *succeeds* Mūlaprakṛiti; but, *minus* Force, Mūlaprakṛiti is for all practical intents and purposes non-existent.[24]

As we have seen, *parabrahman* is the one substance-principle as a principle, and *mūlaprakṛti* is the same substance-principle as substance.

The first fundamental proposition of the Secret Doctrine, an omnipresent, eternal, boundless, and immutable principle, the one reality, and the one homogeneous divine substance-principle, remains a principle in beginningless and endless abstract space, and becomes substance on the plane of the manifested universe. Thus for us, it is "matter alone." In the plain words of a hitherto secret commentary:

> It is Substance to OUR spiritual sight. It cannot be called so by men in their WAKING STATE; therefore they have named it in their ignorance 'God-Spirit.'[25]

The Fundamental Doctrine of Sāṃkhya

This distinctive teaching from the Wisdom-Religion once called pre-Vedic Buddhism and now called Theosophy, that the universe is matter alone, is the fundamental doctrine of the Sāṃkhya system. Of all known systems, only Sāṃkhya teaches this. It is not taught by any school of Buddhism, nor is it taught by other Hindu schools. Indeed, all these schools have found in Sāṃkhya a favored target for their criticisms. Sāṃkhya has been around for so long that, except the system it is paired with, *yoga,* it has been refuted by practically all other Indian systems. For centuries now it has had no adherents of its own to defend it.

So what is Sāṃkhya? Sāṃkhya is now found in Hinduism as one of the six *darśanas,* worldviews, or systems of philosophical thought. It is studied along with the other five *darśanas,* but as just mentioned, for centuries it has had virtually no followers of its own. However, things were not always this way. It was once the prevailing worldview throughout ancient India. It is taken for granted in the epic, *Mahābhārata,* including the *Bhagavad-gītā,* and in the Purāṇas. It is found in the ancient medical work of Caraka. It is shown in the *Buddha-carita* being taught to the young Gautama in his quest for enlightenment. It is considered to be the original *darśana,* and its propounder, the sage Kapila, to be the first knower (*ādi-vidvān*). Although it is not normally considered to be pre-Vedic, its mythological origins could easily place it there. Indeed, the *Yukti-dīpikā* Sāṃkhya commentary, when giving the traditional lineage of the teaching,

> boldly declares in this connection that the Śāstra [Sāṃkhya] was promulgated by Kapila at the beginning (of creation), hence it is not possible like [in] other systems of thought, to enumerate its lineage of teachers even in [a] hundred years.[26]

It has become customary to refer to Sāṃkhya as dualism, since it posits two eternal principles: *prakṛti* or matter, and *puruṣa* or spirit. However, it does not refer to itself as dualism, nor was it called dualism in the fourteenth-century summary of various systems, the *Sarva-darśana-saṃgraha* by Mādhavācārya. Further, Sāṃkhya scholar Gerald Larson points out that it is not dualism in any normal sense of the word, since the whole universe, including intelligence (*buddhi*), self-consciousness (*ahaṃkāra*), and mind (*manas*), all derive solely from *prakṛti* or matter.[27] The role of *puruṣa* or spirit, which he terms pure contentless consciousness, is mere passive presence (*sākṣitva*), since it cannot think or act. Finally, it is well-recognized that we do not have the Sāṃkhya system in its completeness. Its original works such as the *Ṣaṣṭitantra* are referred to in extant texts, but are no longer available. Certain of the extant texts attribute to Sāṃkhya the teaching of *brahman*, which could refer to the unity of *prakṛti* and *puruṣa*.[28]

If Sāṃkhya is indeed a direct teaching from the Wisdom-Religion, as it appears to be, we know that it cannot ultimately be dualistic. The oneness of all life is stressed repeatedly as a basic Theosophical teaching. The Mahatma K.H. specifically refers to the unity of matter and spirit, *prakṛti* and *puruṣa*:

> The conception of matter and spirit as entirely distinct, and both eternal, could certainly never have entered my head, however little I may know of them, for it is one of the elementary and fundamental doctrines of Occultism that the two are one, and are distinct but in their respective manifestations, and only in the limited perceptions of the world of senses.[29]

It is entirely possible to write a treatise on Sāṃkhya, which deals with *prakṛti* and *puruṣa*, completely taking for granted the fact that they are ultimately one, and therefore never mentioning that fact separately. We would assume that this is exactly what Īśvara-kṛṣṇa did in his *Sāṃkhya-kārikā*, the basic textbook of the Sāṃkhya system.[30] As stated in Blavatsky's explanations of the first fundamental proposition of the Secret Doctrine, once we pass in thought from this absolute principle, duality supervenes in the contrast of spirit and matter. It is therefore only to be expected that a system would arise to deal with reality from this standpoint, just as we have another system to deal with reality from the standpoint of ultimate unity.[31]

The Sāṃkhya teaching of *puruṣa*, or spirit, is of course analogous to the Theosophical teaching of cosmic ideation, the other aspect of the one reality. Sāṃkhya posits a plurality of *puruṣas*, spirits or souls. However, in a few places *puruṣa* is said to be one.[32] Modern scholars have considered these to be wrong or unreliable readings. But *The Secret Doctrine* explains that spirit is a compound unity; that is, both one and many:

> . . . *Īśvara* or *Logos* is Spirit; or, as Occultism explains, it is a compound unity of manifested living Spirits, the parent-source and nursery of all the mundane and terrestrial monads, *plus* their *divine* reflection, which emanate from, and return into, the Logos, each in the culmination of its time.[33]

This teaching of spirit as both one and many reaches its logical conclusion in the important doctrine of the Wisdom-Religion: the teaching of the preservation of individuality even when merged in unity.

> . . . I maintain as an occultist, on the authority of the Secret Doctrine, that though merged entirely into Parabrahm, man's spirit while not individual *per se*, yet preserves its distinct individuality in Parinirvana, . . .[34]

The fundamental doctrine of Sāṃkhya is the universe as *prakṛti* or matter. It posits the evolution of the universe from the principle (*tattva*) of *prakṛti*, when in proximity with the inactive *puruṣa* or spirit (as if this were mere polarity). *Prakṛti* then evolves into twenty-three other principles of matter, together comprising the universe. This, the system of Kapila, founder of Sāṃkhya, and the system of Manu, are specifically stated to be the basis of the Theosophical teachings on evolution:

> It has been repeatedly stated that evolution as taught by Manu and Kapila was the groundwork of the modern teachings [of *Esoteric Buddhism*, as opposed to Darwinism], . . .[35]

> Both Occult and Eastern philosophies believe in evolution, which Manu and Kapila give with far more clearness than any scientist does at present.[36]

Although these teachings on matter and on evolution are not found in Buddhism, there do exist similarities between Sāṃkhya and Buddhism. In fact, some of these are so marked that earlier Western scholars long discussed the question of Sāṃkhya influence on Buddhism. For example, the first verse of the *Sāṃkhya-kārikā* states that the reason for undertaking this inquiry, that is, the rationale of the Sāṃkhya system, is suffering (*duḥkha*). This, of course, is the first Noble Truth of Buddhism. The text also indicates that scriptural means are insufficient to get rid of suffering, so it proceeds to use reasoning rather than scriptural authority to determine how to do this. Again, this emphasis on use of reasoning is a distinctive characteristic of Buddhism. It has also been noticed that Gautama Buddha's birthplace is named Kapila-vastu, the place of Kapila (founder of Sāṃkhya). More recently, research on Sāṃkhya has moved away from comparisons with Buddhism. At about the same time that research on pre-canonical Buddhism began, an important book on early or pre-classical Sāṃkhya was published,[37] though it did not attempt to link Sāṃkhya and Buddhism. Sāṃkhya and Buddhism as we now know them are thus seen to have both significant similarities and significant differences.

Conclusion

In conclusion, we do not say that Sāṃkhya is pre-Vedic Buddhism, but we do say that Sāṃkhya is a major piece of the ancient Wisdom-Religion now found nowhere else. It is the only place we find the universe described as matter alone. In accord with the first fundamental proposition of the Secret Doctrine, an omnipresent, eternal, boundless, and immutable principle, the one reality, the one substance-principle, Sāṃkhya teaches the manifested universe as substance. The only way to get this teaching in Buddhism is to understand *śūnyatā*, emptiness, as substance. There is reason for a student of *The Secret Doctrine* to do this,[38] but we do not expect any Buddhists to accept this. Even this would still not give us the doctrine of the evolution of the universe taught in the Wisdom-Religion, and taught in Sāṃkhya. Only in Sāṃkhya do we find the doctrine of *prakṛti*, matter or substance, and its evolution as the universe. So it is to Sāṃkhya that we must turn to trace this distinctive teaching of the Wisdom-Religion, the outcome of its first fundamental proposition.

NOTES

1. *Isis Unveiled,* by H. P. Blavatsky, 1st ed., 1877; rev. ed. [by Boris de Zirkoff] (pagination unchanged), Wheaton, Illinois: Theosophical Publishing House, 1972, vol. 2, pp. 123, 169, 639.

2. "Theosophy and Buddhism," by David Reigle, *Fohat,* vol. 4, no. 1, Spring 2000, pp. 14-17, 22-23; reprinted in this book as chapter 1.

3. There is in Buddhism a famous group of questions pertaining to teachings such as this, that the Buddha refused to answer. These begin, as found in the Pali canon: (1) Is the universe eternal, or (2) is it not eternal? (3) Is the universe finite, or (4) infinite? While a similar group is also found in Northern Buddhism, it seems that the Southern Buddhists took them to heart. They frequently cite the story from the *Cūla Māluṅkya Sutta* of a person wounded by an arrow, who wanted to know what kind of arrow it was, where it came from, who shot it, etc., before being treated for the wound. For the Tibetan Gelugpa direct refutation of an absolute principle or essence, see by Tsong-kha-pa:
Emptiness in the Mind-Only School of Buddhism: Dynamic Responses to Dzong-ka-ba's The Essence of Eloquence: I, by Jeffrey Hopkins, Berkeley, Los Angeles, London: University of California Press, 1999;
The Nature of Things: Emptiness and Essence in the Geluk World, by William Magee, Ithaca, New York: Snow Lion Publications, 1999.

4. On Jainism, see: *Isis Unveiled,* vol. 2, pp. 322-323.

5. *The Secret Doctrine,* by H. P. Blavatsky, 1st ed., 1888; [ed. by Boris de Zirkoff] (pagination unchanged), Adyar, Madras: Theosophical Publishing House, 1978, vol. 1, p. 14.

6. For example, Khuddaka Nikāya, *Udāna,* 81: O monks, there is an unborn, unoriginated, uncreated, uncompounded; and if there were not this unborn, unoriginated, uncreated, uncompounded, no escape would be possible from what is born, is originated, is created, is compounded.

7. For example, *Ratna-gotra-vibhāga,* 80: It is not born, does not die, is not afflicted, and does not grow old, because it is permanent, stable, quiescent, and eternal.

8. *The Secret Doctrine,* vol. 1, p. 273.

9. *The Mahatma Letters to A. P. Sinnett,* compiled by A. T. Barker, 1st ed., 1923; 3rd rev. ed., Adyar, Madras: Theosophical Publishing House, 1962, p. 53; arranged in chronological sequence by Vicente Hao Chin, Jr., Quezon City, Metro Manila: Theosophical Publishing House, 1993, p. 270.

10. *The Mahatma Letters,* 3rd. ed. p. 53; chron. ed. p. 271.

11. *The Mahatma Letters*, 3rd. ed. p. 55; chron. ed. p. 272.

12. *The Mahatma Letters*, 3rd. ed. p. 56; chron. ed. p. 273.

13. *The Mahatma Letters*, 3rd. ed. p. 56; chron. ed. p. 273.

14. *H. P. Blavatsky Collected Writings*, vol. 4, Wheaton, Illinois: Theosophical Publishing House, 1969, p. 226.

15. *H. P. Blavatsky Collected Writings*, vol. 4, p. 298.

16. *H. P. Blavatsky Collected Writings*, vol. 4, p. 452.

17. *H. P. Blavatsky Collected Writings*, vol. 4, p. 602.

18. *The Secret Doctrine*, vol. 1, p. 329.

19. *The Secret Doctrine*, vol. 1, p. 147.

20. *The Mahatma Letters*, 3rd. ed. p. 341; chron. ed. p. 379.

21. *The Secret Doctrine*, vol. 1, pp. 15, 16. See also: *Blavatsky Collected Writings*, vol. 7, pp. 347-348, where she clearly states that she gives the esoteric philosophy of the trans-Himalayan Occultists or Tibetan Arhats in Hindu Brahmanical terms obtained by consulting Brahmans around her, and that therefore these may not always be used correctly. Her use of the Vedānta term *parabrahman* in juxtaposition with the Sāṃkhya term *mūlaprakṛti* is taken from T. Subba Row's lectures on the *Bhagavad-Gītā*, published in *The Theosophist*, 1886-1887. These have been reprinted in book form several times; *e.g.*, *Notes on the Bhagavad Gita*, Pasadena: Theosophical University Press, 1934, 1978.

22. *The Secret Doctrine*, vol. 1, p. 328.

23. *The Secret Doctrine*, vol. 2, p. 24.

24. *The Secret Doctrine*, vol. 2, pp. 24-25.

25. *The Secret Doctrine*, vol. 1, p. 289.

26. *Origin and Development of the Sāṃkhya System of Thought*, by Pulinbihari Chakravarti, Calcutta: Metropolitan Printing and Publishing House, 1951; reprint, New Delhi: Oriental Books Reprint Corporation, 1975; p. 130.

27. *Encyclopedia of Indian Philosophies/Sāṃkhya: A Dualist Tradition in Indian Philosophy*, ed. Gerald James Larson and Ram Shankar Bhattacharya, Princeton: Princeton University Press, 1987, pp. 75-77.

28. *Origin and Development of the Sāṃkhya System of Thought*, pp. 25-28, cites *Mahābhārata* 12.218.14, 12.221.18 (Southern recension); *Buddhacarita* 12.65; *Caraka-saṃhitā* 1.99, 5.19, 5.34; *Yoga-sūtra-bhāṣya* 4.22; etc., giving the teaching of *brahman* in Sāṃkhya. Although Gauḍapāda and others give *brahman* as a synonym of *prakṛti* in their commentaries on *Sāṃkhya-kārikā* 22, we know that these are not always full synonyms. The *Yukti-dīpikā* commentary, like the other texts just cited, explains *brahman* in terms referring to the ultimate stage of unity.

29. *The Mahatma Letters*, 3rd ed. p. 138; chron. ed. p. 282.

30. The classic *Sāṃkhya-kārikā* has for many centuries been the basic textbook of the Sāṃkhya *darśana*, even though we would expect the *Sāṃkhya-sūtras* of Kapila to be. The now extant *Sāṃkhya-sūtras* clearly contain late interpolations. Most scholars have despaired of trying to sort out the undeniably old *sūtras* from this modern collection. It may therefore be useful for readers to know that, according to Udayavira Shastri, there are (besides some small sections) two large sections of interpolated *sūtras*: 1.20-54 and 5.84-115. See his "Antiquity of the Sāṅkhya Sūtras," *Ṛtambharā: Studies in Indology*, Ghaziabad: Society for Indic Studies, 1986, pp. 31-43.

31. This is, of course, the Vedānta system, specifically Advaita Vedānta. We are fully aware of the extensive critique of Sāṃkhya in Śaṅkarācārya's commentary on the *Vedānta-sūtras*, but this is a subject for another paper.

32. For example, *Caraka-saṃhitā* 1.14, 1.84, and 1.155, say *puruṣa* is one. See: "The Sāṃkhya Philosophy in the Carakasaṃhitā," by K. B. Ramakrishna Rao, *Adyar Library Bulletin*, vol. 26, parts 3-4, Dec. 1962, pp. 193-205, especially p. 200. We know that *Sāṃkhya-kārikā* 18 teaches the plurality of *puruṣas*. Gauḍapāda's commentary on *Sāṃkhya-kārikā* 11, even though first using the plural phrase "of all the *puruṣas*" (*sarva-puruṣānāṃ*), says later that: "the manifest is manifold; the unmanifest is one; so also is spirit one" (. . . *tathā pumān apy ekaḥ*). Here the old commentary translated into Chinese by Paramārtha and now found in the Chinese Buddhist canon has that spirit is plural, as does the later commentary of Vācaspati-miśra. But what looks like a mistake and a contradiction by Gauḍapāda may in fact be an intentional statement, in agreement with *Caraka-saṃhitā*, that spirit is both one and many.

33. *The Secret Doctrine*, vol. 1, p. 573.

34. *H. P. Blavatsky Collected Writings*, vol. 7, p. 51.

35. *The Secret Doctrine*, vol. 1, p. 186.

36. *The Secret Doctrine*, vol. 2, p. 259.

37. *Early Sāṃkhya*, by E. H. Johnston, London: Royal Asiatic Society, 1937; reprint, Delhi: Motilal Banarsidass, 1974. This book includes a discussion of *svabhāva* in Sāṃkhya, pp. 67-72. Note, however, that his reading of Gauḍapāda on *Sāṃkhya-kārikā* 27 seems faulty (p. 68). The idea of pre-canonical Buddhism was introduced by Stanislaw Schayer in 1935: "Precanonical Buddhism," *Archiv Orientalni*, vol. 7, pp. 121-132.

38. *Blavatsky's Secret Books*, by David Reigle and Nancy Reigle, San Diego: Wizards Bookshelf, 1999, p. 120; quoting *The Secret Doctrine*, vol. 1, p. 289.

[The foregoing article was written by David Reigle, and published in *Fohat,* A Quarterly Publication of Edmonton Theosophical Society, vol. 4, no. 4, Winter 2000, pp. 84-86, 92-94.]

The First Fundamental Proposition of the Secret Doctrine

There are three fundamental propositions that we are told must be comprehended before we can understand the Secret Doctrine, the once universal Wisdom Tradition, now called Theosophy. They are given in the Proem of H. P. Blavatsky's book, *The Secret Doctrine.* I first read these in December of 1973. I could not understand them. Some time later I read the advice that Blavatsky gave shortly before her death, to Robert Bowen, on how to study *The Secret Doctrine*:

> The first thing to do, even if it takes years, is to get some grasp of the "Three Fundamental Principles" given in the PROEM.[1]

I took this advice to heart, and continued to struggle with them year after year; but it was to little avail. Yesterday, March 17, 2001, more than twenty-seven years later, the light finally came on. I do not know how typical my experience was, yet I cannot help but feel I should write down the results.

The necessity of understanding these fundamental propositions is made clear by Blavatsky when introducing them:

> Before the reader proceeds to the consideration of the Stanzas from the Book of Dzyan which form the basis of the present work, it is absolutely necessary that he should be made acquainted with the few fundamental conceptions which underlie and pervade the entire system of thought to which his attention is invited. These basic ideas are few in number, and on their clear apprehension depends the understanding of all that follows; therefore no apology is required for asking the reader to make himself familiar with them first, before entering on the perusal of the work itself.[2]

The first of the three fundamental propositions established by the Secret Doctrine is stated as:

> An Omnipresent, Eternal, Boundless, and Immutable PRINCIPLE on which all speculation is impossible, since it transcends the power of human conception and could only be dwarfed by any human expression or similitude. It is beyond the range and reach of thought—in the words of *Māṇḍūkya Upanishad,* "unthinkable and unspeakable."[3]

Then follow three pages of explanations of this first fundamental proposition. At the end of these explanations is a summary with four numbered items. This is the crux of the problem. The summary is introduced with these words: "The following summary will afford a clearer idea to the reader." In fact, up to this point, and despite some questions, I thought I could follow the explanations well enough; but this summary, rather than affording me a clearer idea, caused me to doubt my understanding almost entirely.

The problem for me in these explanations of the first fundamental proposition was with the numbers involved. The explanations begin with the one reality. This is symbolized under two aspects. The two aspects of the one reality then make a trinity or metaphysical triad. Then another (fourth?) thing is added to the explanations, Fohat. But the four numbered items in the summary are not the same as the four concepts that were just explained.

Assuming that I was merely getting caught up in the words, I asked my wife Nancy, who is far more intuitive than I am, if she could see how these explanations and the four item summary correlate. When she could not either (and I kept asking her year after year), I knew there was a problem here.

The explanations start by attempting to clarify the above cited statement of the first fundamental proposition.

> To render these ideas clearer to the general reader, let him set out with the postulate that there is one absolute Reality which antecedes all manifested, conditioned, being.[4]

The one absolute reality is there also referred to as the "Infinite and Eternal Cause" (which is, as later clarified, not the "First Cause"), as the "rootless root of 'all that was, is, or ever shall be,'" and as "'Be-ness' rather than Being." So far, so good.

This one reality is then said to be symbolized under two aspects: "absolute abstract Space," and "absolute abstract Motion." The latter of the two aspects represents "Unconditioned Consciousness." This latter aspect is also symbolized as "The Great Breath." The paragraph explaining these two aspects concludes:

> Thus, then, the first fundamental axiom of the Secret Doctrine is this metaphysical ONE ABSOLUTE—BE-NESS—symbolized by finite intelligence as the theological Trinity.[5]

My intelligence may be more finite than that of others, but I did not follow how the two aspects of one thing became a trinity, when this one thing is unmanifested. I can guess that if a person counts the one reality separately, then along with its two aspects there is a trinity. But this is not stated.

Then follows further explanations given to assist the student. Herbert Spencer's "First Cause," we are told, cannot apply to the absolute, because "first" means something "first brought forth," a manifestation, being therefore finite and conditioned. The absolute, then, is not the "First Cause," but rather is the "Causeless Cause."

We next find some Vedānta views and terminology used to explain the first fundamental proposition. The Vedānta term "Parabrahman" is used for "the One Reality, the Absolute." It is described as "the field of Absolute Consciousness, *i.e.*, that Essence which is out of all relation to conditioned existence, and of which conscious existence is a conditioned symbol." Here we must proceed carefully. Blavatsky is now explaining the one reality as such, not its aspect of "absolute abstract Motion representing Unconditioned Consciousness" described earlier. The potential confusion with the word "Consciousness," used for both, is due to the fact that she is here giving the "esoteric and Vedāntin tenet" from "T. Subba Row's four able lectures on the *Bhagavad-Gītā.*" We must know that Advaita Vedānta holds Parabrahman to be absolute consciousness, while Blavatsky and her Mahatma teachers regularly describe the absolute as unconscious. See, for example, Stanza I.8 of the Book of Dzyan: "Alone the one form of existence stretched boundless, infinite, causeless, in dreamless sleep; and life pulsated unconscious in universal space, . . ."

Two more terms are here given for the two aspects described earlier of the one reality: "Spirit (or Consciousness)" and "Matter." "Spirit (or Consciousness)" must correspond to the earlier described "absolute abstract Motion," since this latter was said to represent "Unconditioned Consciousness." This is confirmed in the following paragraphs, but only by putting together the statements that "the Great Breath assumes the character of pre-cosmic Ideation," and that "pre-cosmic Ideation is the root of all individual consciousness," while remembering that absolute abstract motion was earlier said to be symbolized by "the Great Breath." In other words, absolute abstract motion = unconditioned consciousness = the great breath = spirit (or consciousness) = pre-cosmic ideation.

As for "Matter," the other of the two aspects of the one reality, we must assume by default that this corresponds to the earlier described "absolute abstract Space," although this is not stated. Similarly, we must assume that this corresponds to "pre-cosmic root-substance (*Mūlaprakṛiti*)," and "pre-cosmic Substance," used in the following paragraphs. Again, we must know that the term *mūlaprakṛti,* brought in from Subba Row as a Vedānta term, is here used in its Sāṃkhya sense as something real and eternal. It does not have this meaning in standard Advaita Vedānta.[6] Subba Row used it esoterically as a Vedānta term having this meaning. The terms used for this aspect, then, are absolute abstract space = matter = pre-cosmic root-substance (*mūlaprakṛti*) = pre-cosmic substance.

We are cautioned that these two, here called spirit (or consciousness) and matter, are "to be regarded, not as independent realities, but as the two facets or aspects of the Absolute (Parabrahman), . . ." We then read: "Considering this metaphysical triad as the Root from which proceeds all manifestation, . . . " As before, I can only assume that "this metaphysical triad" is the one absolute reality with its two aspects, though we have just been warned not to regard these as independent realities.

At the time of manifestation, she continues, "the Great Breath [or absolute abstract motion] assumes the character of pre-cosmic Ideation," being the "*fons et origo*," source and origin, of all individual consciousness. Likewise the other aspect of the absolute, "pre-cosmic root-substance (*Mūlaprakṛiti*)," is the substratum of all matter in its various grades of differentiation.

After explaining that "the contrast of these two aspects of the Absolute is essential to the existence of the 'Manifested Universe,'" the one being unable to manifest without the other, Blavatsky introduces the idea of Fohat:

> But just as the opposite poles of subject and object, spirit and matter, are but aspects of the One Unity in which they are synthesized, so, in the manifested Universe, there is "that" which links spirit to matter, subject to object.[7]

This is Fohat. The explanation of Fohat concludes with:

> Thus from Spirit, or Cosmic Ideation, comes our consciousness; from Cosmic Substance the several vehicles in which that consciousness is individualized and attains to self—or reflective—consciousness; while Fohat, in its various manifestations, is the mysterious link between Mind and Matter, the animating principle electrifying every atom into life.[8]

Finally, we have the summary that is meant to afford a clearer idea to the reader:

> (1). The ABSOLUTE; the *Parabrahman* of the Vedāntins, or the one Reality, SAT, which is, as Hegel says, both Absolute Being and Non-Being.
>
> (2). The first manifestation, the impersonal, and, in philosophy, *unmanifested* Logos, the precursor of the "manifested." This is the "First Cause," the "Unconscious" of European Pantheists.

(3). Spirit-matter, LIFE; the "Spirit of the Universe," the Purusha and Prakṛiti, or the *second* Logos.

(4). Cosmic Ideation, MAHAT or Intelligence, the Universal World-Soul; the Cosmic Noumenon of Matter, the basis of the intelligent operations in and of Nature, also called MAHĀ-BUDDHI.

The ONE REALITY; its *dual* aspects in the conditioned Universe.[9]

The concluding sentence reiterates that the first fundamental proposition being explained here is the one reality with its two aspects. But I could find no way to correlate the four numbered items of this summary with the one reality and its two aspects, on the basis of the three pages of explanations that had just been given.

Item number (1) is clearly the one reality as such. There is no problem here.

Item number (2), of course, is not the one reality as such; but neither is it either of the two aspects of the one reality. Just what it is was not clear to me from the foregoing three pages. It was not clear how this "first manifestation" could also be the "*unmanifested* Logos, the precursor of the 'manifested.'" The "manifested" proper is apparently one of the following numbered items. Nor was it clear how the "First Cause" comes about from the absolute, described as the "Causeless Cause."

Item number (3) presents another problem. The terms spirit and matter have been used in the preceding explanations as the two aspects of the one reality (*puruṣa* and *prakṛti* are Sāṃkhya terms that correspond to spirit and matter). But they have not been used there hyphenated together, "Spirit-matter." When we find the hyphenated term "Father-Mother" further on, it means these as a unity before their separation into distinct father and distinct mother. Of course, Blavatsky has explained that the one reality is a unity that has two aspects, spirit and matter. But if spirit-matter refers to this unity, how is it different from item number (1), the one reality as such? If it refers to spirit and matter as distinct in manifestation, how is it the "Spirit of the Universe?" Where would the matter of "Spirit-matter" then be? And what of the unexplained epithet "Life" used here? Could this not apply equally well to any of these four items?

Item number (4) seems to be even more problematic. "Cosmic Ideation" (or at least pre-cosmic ideation) has in fact been used for one of the two aspects only, absolute abstract motion, or spirit. But then, where is the other one, cosmic substance, or absolute abstract space, or matter, in this list of numbered items? And how is this one "the Cosmic Noumenon of Matter?" Further, have we not just had the two of them together in item number (3), spirit-matter? "Mahat" or "Mahā-Buddhi" are again Sāṃkhya terms, meaning, as stated here, "Intelligence," as a universal principle (*tattva*). But these are not found in the explanations given on the preceding pages. Then, what about Fohat, which has not yet been accounted for? Are we to understand that this somehow goes here? These were some of the questions that I had.

So I was much better off in understanding the first fundamental proposition before reading this four item summary. Blavatsky undoubtedly had clearly in her mind what she meant here; so that when she concluded, "The ONE REALITY, its *dual* aspects in the conditioned Universe," she thought these four items had clarified this. But unfortunately we do not have spelled out what she meant here; and as this summary stands, it is more confusing than helpful, at least to me. We must now try to make sense out of it.

The first numbered item refers to the omnipresent, eternal, boundless, and immutable principle, the one absolute reality, as such; and as noted above, there is no problem here. This is not the "First Cause"; rather, it is the "Causeless Cause."

The second numbered item refers to the "First Cause," but still the "*unmanifested* Logos." The initial question is, how do we understand the difference between this and the one reality as such, requiring the "First Cause" to be distinguished from the "Causeless Cause," when both are unmanifested. I believe that this is the question alluded to in Blavatsky's explanation of the purport of Stanza II of the Book of Dzyan:

> The stage described in Stanza II is, to a Western mind, so nearly identical with that mentioned in the first Stanza, that to express the idea of its difference would require a treatise in itself. Hence

> it must be left to the intuition and the higher faculties of the reader to grasp, as far as he can, the meaning of the allegorical phrases used.[10]

Here is the problem. If the one reality is in fact immutable, as it is stated to be, it cannot change. So how can it manifest the universe? It cannot transform or evolve into the universe, as this would involve change in the unchangeable. How can there be manifestation or differentiation in the unmanifested and undifferentiated? When this question was raised in the journal she edited, *The Theosophist,* Blavatsky did make an attempt to explain this highly metaphysical conception, and thereby to express the subtle difference between the causeless cause and the unmanifested first cause. In doing so, she also addressed the related question of how the first cause can come about from the causeless cause.

> This Brahma [neuter, the absolute; = Parabrahman] when viewed as the *fons et origo* [source and origin] of the Substance of the Universe is, as has been repeatedly said in these columns, *Mulaprakriti*—a term which, in the poverty of English metaphysical vocabulary, has been translated as "undifferentiated cosmic matter." It has also been said that the *differentiation* of Mulaprakriti produces infinite forms of being. . . .
>
> "Brahma"—our opponents argue,—"the Mulaprakriti, is made to undergo a differentiation, like matter, of which we have a physical conception, to form the visible universe. Therefore, Brahma is subject to change . . . ."
>
> It must not for a single moment be supposed that Mulaprakriti or Brahma (Parabrahm) can ever undergo change of substance (*Parinama*). It is the Absolute Wisdom, the Only Reality, the Eternal Deity—to dissociate the word from its vulgar surroundings. What is meant by the differentiation of Mulaprakriti is that the primordial essence of all forms of existence (*Asat*) is radiated by it, and when radiated by it becomes the centre of energy from which by gradual and systematic processes of emanation or

differentiation the universe, as perceived, springs into existence. It is from our opponents' incapacity to grasp this highly metaphysical conception that all the evil flows. . . .

It is manifest from this that "Mulaprakriti" never differentiates but only emanates or radiates its first born Mahat-tattva . . . .[11]

What we have here, then, is the doctrine of radiance or radiation, which does not involve change in the unchangeable. An analogous doctrine of radiance is found in Advaita Vedānta, and may be called *ābhāsa-vāda.*[12] It is one explanation in Advaita Vedānta for the appearance of diversity. Using this paradigm, we can explain how the universe comes into manifestation as follows. The universe is the radiance (*ābhāsa*) of Parabrahman, the one reality. No change occurs in Parabrahman in order for the universe to appear. This radiance is considered to be a false appearance, like seeing a snake where there is only a rope. The appearance involves only apparent change (*vivarta*), not actual change (*pariṇāma*). The doctrine of only apparent change or false appearance (*vivarta-vāda*) is now the basic teaching of all Advaita Vedānta. Even though this false appearance is illusory, it is held to take on the characteristics of a seed or germ, from which the universe evolves in an orderly manner.[13]

This radiance, which is a false appearance, which takes on the characteristics of a seed, can now be called the first cause, because it can change or evolve into the universe, unlike the changeless Parabrahman, the causeless cause. It is described in Vedānta treatises both as undifferentiated (*avyākṛta*), as it is in the above quotation from Blavatsky, and as unmanifested (*avyakta*), as it is in Blavatsky's four item summary from *The Secret Doctrine.*[14] According to Śaṅkarācārya, it cannot be said to be different from or not different from the absolute Ātman or Brahman or Parabrahman;[15] but we can now distinguish the "First Cause" from the "Causeless Cause," even when both are unmanifested. In this way we can also understand the related question of how the causeless cause can bring about the first cause, without itself undergoing any change. The first cause is merely its radiance.

This second numbered item, then, refers to something that is neither different nor not different from the one reality as such, the immutable causeless cause. It refers to the radiance of the one reality, still unmanifested, as the seed or germ of the universe, the mutable first cause.

Of the four numbered items, this second one was the most difficult. Once it became clear, the others immediately fell into place.

The third numbered item, "Spirit-matter," "the Purusha [spirit] and Prakṛiti [matter]," is explained in a passage of *The Mahatma Letters*:

> The conception of matter and spirit as entirely distinct, and both eternal, could certainly never have entered my head, however little I may know of them, for it is one of the elementary and fundamental doctrines of Occultism that the two are one, and are distinct but in their respective manifestations, and only in the limited perceptions of the world of senses. Far from "lacking philosophical breadth" then, our doctrines show but one principle in nature—spirit-matter or matter-spirit, the third the ultimate Absolute or the quintessence of the two—if I may be allowed to use an erroneous term in the present application—losing itself beyond the view and spiritual perceptions of even the "Gods" or Planetary Spirits. This third principle, say the Vedantic Philosophers—is the only reality, everything else being Maya, as none of the Protean manifestations of spirit-matter or Purusha and Prakriti have ever been regarded in any other light than that of temporary delusions of the senses.[16]

We may therefore conclude that "Spirit-matter" in item number (3) does in fact refer to the unity of spirit and matter, the two aspects of the one reality, before their (at least apparent) separation in manifestation. The difference between this item and item number (1), the one reality as such, is that here we have the one reality, or rather its radiance, the seed or germ of the universe, as polarized into its two aspects, immediately prior to manifestation. The one, while remaining a unity, has become polarized, and therefore potentially two.

The fourth numbered item, "Cosmic Ideation, MAHAT or Intelligence, the Universal World-Soul," is also explained in a passage of *The Mahatma Letters*, once we know that the preceding item is a unity with two aspects, or the simple duality of spirit-matter.

> Pythagoras had a reason for never using the finite, useless figure—2, and for altogether discarding it. The ONE, can, when manifesting, become only 3. The unmanifested when a simple duality remains passive and concealed.[17]

Two in manifestation necessarily become three, because any time there are actually two, there is also the relationship between them as the third. So the moment spirit becomes distinct from matter, their interplay also comes into being. This interplay is cosmic ideation, intelligence, the universal world-soul.

Thus it is only here, with the fourth numbered item, that actual manifestation occurs. The duality of spirit-matter, the third numbered item, must become a triplicity in order to manifest; otherwise, as the *Mahatma Letters* passage continues, "the duality could never tarry as such, and would have to be reabsorbed into the ONE."[18]

Cosmic ideation becomes the basis or noumenon of all manifestation, including manifested physical matter as we know it; thus, "the Cosmic Noumenon of Matter." But as in Sāṃkhya, where the terms *mahat* and *mahā-buddhi* used here come from, cosmic ideation is itself the first manifestation of unmanifested matter, or root substance (*mūlaprakṛti*). Manifestation takes place when unmanifested matter comes into conjunction or proximity with spirit; read esoterically, when the unity acquires polarity. Here as in Sāṃkhya, the first-born cosmic ideation proceeds to evolve into the entire manifested universe, going from subtle to dense, in an orderly and systematic manner.

Here follows a re-statement of the four item summary, incorporating the results discussed above of my rather too protracted inquiry, and including well-attested Sanskrit equivalents whenever these are available.[19]

1. There is an omnipresent (*sarvaga*), eternal (*nitya*), boundless (*ananta*), and immutable (*avikāra*) principle, the one reality. This absolute, like the Parabrahman of Advaita Vedānta, is beyond the range and reach of thought (*agocara*), so is inconceivable (*acintya*) and inexpressible (*nirabhilāpya*). It cannot properly be referred to as "being"; rather, to coin a new term, it is "be-ness." It is without attributes (*nirguṇa*), and is essentially unrelated to manifested, finite being (*avyavahārya*). Yet it is the rootless root (*amūlaṃ mūlam*), the causeless cause, of all that was, is, or ever shall be (*bhūtaṃ bhavad bhaviṣyad iti sarvam*).

2. The radiance (*ābhāsa*) of the one reality becomes a center of energy, a germ (*garbha*), or seed (*bīja*). It is neither different nor not different (*na bhinnaṃ nābhinnam*) from the one reality. Like the one reality, it is unmanifested (*avyakta*) or undifferentiated (*avyākṛta*); but unlike the one reality, it is the cause of manifestation or differentiation. It may therefore be called the first cause. This germ can now transform or evolve (*pariṇāma*) into the manifested universe (*vyakta*).

3. The germ becomes polarized, in this way becoming what we may term "spirit-matter" or "matter-spirit." It is a single thing, still unmanifested, having at one pole spirit (*puruṣa*) and at the other pole matter (*prakṛti*). These are the two aspects of the one reality. The spirit aspect may also be called absolute abstract motion, unconditioned consciousness, and the great breath. The matter aspect may also be called absolute abstract space, and root substance or primordial substance.

4. The interaction of the two poles of spirit and matter produces cosmic ideation, the principle of intelligence in the universe (*mahat*), the universal world-soul (*ālaya-vijñāna* as the lower aspect of the one mind, *eka-citta*). This is the first actual manifestation, although it is the third stage of the manifestation process. It is the basis of the entire manifested universe, from spirit to matter. Like the unmanifested, the manifested also has two poles. The interaction of the two poles of manifested spirit and matter produces cosmic energy or vital force, called Fohat.

The one reality; its dual aspects in the conditioned universe, and the three stages of cosmic manifestation.

This explanation has largely followed the Advaita Vedānta paradigm of *ābhāsa-vāda,* the doctrine of radiance. Blavatsky tells us that she used Vedānta concepts to explain the teachings of the trans-Himalayan esoteric school, since these were more familiar.[20] But her own Mahatma teachers were not Advaita Vedāntins. Their own preferred model was given in late 1881,[21] although it does not seem to have been much followed up on. This model employs a trinity of space (or matter), motion, and duration. Here, motion is the correspondence of the Vedānta radiance. Motion is the *svabhāva,* or inherent nature, of eternal matter, "the one element." Their doctrine may thus be called *svabhāva-vāda.*[22] Speaking of the Svābhāvikas, followers of this doctrine, the Mahatma K.H. writes: "Their plastic, invisible, eternal, omnipresent and unconscious Swabhavat is Force or *Motion* ever generating its electricity which is life."[23] Blavatsky shows that this *svabhāva* is the above discussed radiance:

> Throughout the first two Parts [of vol. I of *The Secret Doctrine*], it was shown that, at the first flutter of renascent life, Svabhavat, "the mutable radiance of the Immutable Darkness unconscious in Eternity," passes, at every new rebirth of Kosmos, from an inactive state into one of intense activity; that it differentiates, and then begins its work through that differentiation.[24]

Using this model, where the inherent nature (*svabhāva*) of eternal matter is motion, the second numbered item could be stated, "The motion of the one element produces a center of energy, a germ, or seed. . . ," etc., etc.

Since the one reality is inconceivable and inexpressible, whatever conceptual model we may use to describe it and its periodic manifestation is still a model; a model that may "lead towards the truth," as Blavatsky says, but is not the truth itself.[25] This does not, however, make such models any less important. The most widespread model of the source and origin of the universe is that of a creator God. According to the Mahatma K.H., "belief in God and Gods" is the cause of two thirds of the evils that pursue humanity.[26] So our conceptual models do make a difference. Such a difference, in fact, that K.H. says about the God-idea, "Our chief aim is to deliver humanity of this nightmare."[27] It is not without importance, then, to refine our understanding of the conceptual models that Blavatsky and her teachers gave in its place.

NOTES

1. "The 'Secret Doctrine' and Its Study," by Robert Bowen, 1932; reprinted in: *An Invitation to The Secret Doctrine*, by H. P. Blavatsky, Pasadena: Theosophical University Press, 1988, p. 2.

2. *The Secret Doctrine*, by H. P. Blavatsky, 1st ed., 1888; *H. P. Blavatsky Collected Writings* edition [edited by Boris de Zirkoff] (pagination unchanged), Adyar, Madras: Theosophical Publishing House, 1978, vol. 1, p. 13.

3. *The Secret Doctrine*, vol. 1, p. 14.

4. *The Secret Doctrine*, vol. 1, p. 14.

5. *The Secret Doctrine*, vol. 1, p. 14.

6. The term *mūlaprakṛti* is not generally used in Advaita Vedānta. When it is, it is taken to mean simply *prakṛti*. In Advaita Vedānta, *prakṛti* is a synonym of *māyā*, illusion. As such, it is temporary rather than eternal. Thus, Subba Row's esoteric view of *mūlaprakṛti* as eternal is not accepted in standard Advaita Vedānta. See, for example, the introduction to the translation of the *Vasudevamanana*, "considered by the Pandits in Southern India as the standard compendium on Advaita philosophy," published in *Lucifer*, vol. 10, 1892, p. 48:

> "T. Subba Row, in his learned *Bhagavad Gītā* lectures, has postulated three eternal principles in the fourth state [Turīya]: viz., Mūlaprakriti; the Logos, or Īshvara, or Nārāyana; and the Light from the Logos, or Daiviprakriti, or Fohat. He also states that Nirvāna, or Moksha, is attained by merging into the Logos, which, as he says, has the veil of Mūlaprakriti between it and Parabrahman. But the Brāhmans in Southern India are loth to accede to this proposition in the light of this and other authorities, on the ground that there can be no Māyā in Nirvāna, whereas, according to T. Subba Row, there is Mūlaprakriti in that state which they consider to be Māyā."

The *Vasudevamanana*, one of the few Advaita Vedānta texts to use the term *mūlaprakṛti*, specifically equates it with *māyā* (illusion), *avidyā* (ignorance), etc. (*Lucifer*, vol. 10, 1892, p. 51). *Māyā* is said in Advaita Vedānta to be indescribable (*anirvacanīya*) as to its existence.

This is because it is without beginning, but it ends, in the case of a practitioner, when Brahman is realized. It is therefore not eternal.

Subba Row's use of *mūlaprakṛti* as the equivalent of the *avyaktam* (the "unmanifested") of the *Bhagavad-Gītā* was criticized by a Hindu Theosophist for giving a Sāṃkhya interpretation to a Vedānta concept ("Criticism on the Late Mr. T. Subba Row's Bhagavad-Gītā," by A. Krishnaswamy Iyer, *The Theosophist*, vol. 17, April 1896, pp. 425-427). But even Subba Row's defender on this issue agrees with standard Advaita Vedānta that *mūlaprakṛti* is a temporary illusion, saying that "Mulaprakriti is simply an illusory veil thrown over Parabrahman," and that Parabrahman was "existing anterior to it," and "does not perish during the Cosmic Pralaya" ("Subba Rao's Avyaktam," by C. R. Srinivasayangar, *The Theosophist*, vol. 17, July 1896, pp. 615-616).

In other words, *mūlaprakṛti* is not viewed in standard Advaita Vedānta, or even by Hindu Theosophists, as being eternal, despite Subba Row's insistence to the contrary. His is an esoteric view of it. Therefore, it can apply as an aspect of the one reality taught in the Secret Doctrine only in its Sāṃkhya meaning; that is, as something real and eternal.

Finally, we may note that the first use of *mūlaprakṛti* by Blavatsky was as a Sāṃkhya term. See "The Septenary Principle in Esotericism," *The Theosophist*, vol. 4, July 1883, pp. 253-256; *H. P. Blavatsky Collected Writings*, vol. 4, 1969, pp. 574-582.

7. *The Secret Doctrine*, vol. 1, p. 16.
8. *The Secret Doctrine*, vol. 1, p. 16.
9. *The Secret Doctrine*, vol. 1, p. 16.
10. *The Secret Doctrine*, vol. 1, p. 21.
11. "Victims of Words," *H. P. Blavatsky Collected Writings*, vol. 6, 1st ed., 1954; 2nd ed., Wheaton, Ill.: Theosophical Publishing House, 1975, pp. 141-143. In this edition, throughout this article, the word "Brahma" is printed incorrectly as "Brahmâ," with a circumflex on the last letter indicating that it is a long vowel. In the original printing in *The Theosophist*, vol. 5, Feb. 1884, p. 117, the word in its first two occurrences and once again later on is printed as "Brahmă," with a breve on the last letter indicating that it is a short vowel; and all other times as "Brahma," with no diacritical mark on the last letter, also indicating that it is a short vowel. The neuter "Brahma" with short vowel is clearly meant here, since its synonym is given as Parabrahman. "Brahma" is the correct declined form of this neuter word, but it is now generally written in its stem form "Brahman," in order to distinguish it from the masculine form "Brahmā" with long vowel. Brahmā or Brahmâ, with

either a macron (as used now) or a circumflex (as used earlier) on the last letter, both indicating that it is a long vowel, is the creator god; while the neuter Brahma or Brahman is the impersonal absolute.

Note that errors like this in the *H. P. Blavatsky Collected Writings*, edited by Boris de Zirkoff, are rare. A great many more are found in the unedited writings of Blavatsky. So serious researchers will always benefit from the painstaking editorial work of Boris de Zirkoff.

12. This Advaita Vedānta doctrine is more commonly known as *pratibimba-vāda*, the doctrine of reflection, as it was developed in the *Vivaraṇa* school of Advaita Vedānta. I purposely refer to it here as *ābhāsa-vāda* in order to emphasize the radiance aspect of the teaching, and to avoid the sectarian controversy between the *pratibimba-vāda* and *avaccheda-vāda* (the doctrine of limitation) followers. On *ābhāsa*, see *Brahma-sūtra* 2.3.50, and Śaṅkarācārya's commentary thereon. On this doctrine in reference to the manifestation of the universe, see *Pañca-pādikā* by Padmapāda, chap. 26, verses 95 ff. For a good example of a brief text following this doctrine, see the *Laghu-vākya-vṛtti* by Śaṅkarācārya.

13. See, for example, Sureśvara's commentary on Śaṅkarācārya's *Pañcī-karaṇa*, verse 2 and following.

14. It is described as *avyakta* in Śaṅkarācārya's *Viveka-cūḍāmaṇi*, verse 108, and as *avyākṛta* in Śaṅkarācārya's *Pañcī-karaṇa*, to give just two examples.

15. See Śaṅkarācārya's *Pañcī-karaṇa*, and also his *Viveka-cūḍāmaṇi*, verse 109.

16. *The Mahatma Letters to A. P. Sinnett*, transcribed and compiled by A. T. Barker, 1st ed., 1923; 3rd rev. ed., Adyar, Madras: Theosophical Publishing House, 1962, p. 138; chronological ed., Quezon City, Metro Manila, Philippines: Theosophical Publishing House, 1993, pp. 282-283.

17. *The Mahatma Letters*, 3rd. ed., p. 341; chron. ed., p. 379.

18. *The Mahatma Letters*, 3rd. ed., p. 341; chron. ed., p. 379. On the necessity of a triplicity for manifestation, see Blavatsky's statement of the three stages of cosmic manifestation found in all theogonies, in *The Secret Doctrine*, vol. 1, p. 437.

19. There are, of course, many possible Sanskrit equivalents for the terms and ideas found in this summary, from various schools of thought. I have tried to choose the more widely used equivalents. Some come from the *Māṇḍūkya Upaniṣad*, which Blavatsky referred to here. From a translation of it by Archibald Edward Gough found in his book, *The Philosophy of the Upanishads and Ancient Indian Metaphysics*

(London: Trübner, 1882, p. 71), she quoted the words, "unthinkable and unspeakable." Since these two words in other contexts have other connotations, I have preferred "inconceivable" and "inexpressible." For the first of these, the equivalent from the *Māṇḍūkya Upaniṣad* is *acintya*, and I have adopted this widely used Sanskrit term. For the second, the *Māṇḍūkya* equivalent is *avyapadeśya*. A much more widely used equivalent, in both Hindu and Buddhist texts, is *nirabhilāpya*. So I have adopted the latter. Note that the term *agocara* means only "beyond the range," and "of thought" must be supplied.

20. See *H. P. Blavatsky Collected Writings*, vol. 7, 1st ed., 1959; 2nd ed., 1975, pp. 347-348; *The Secret Doctrine*, vol. 1, p. 20; vol. 2, p. 308 fn.

21. This model was first outlined in the "Cosmological Notes," given by the Mahatma Morya to A. O. Hume, copies of which were made for A. P. Sinnett and Blavatsky. According to Daniel Caldwell, these were given about October 1881 (not January 1882, the date of the follow-up Mahatma letter no. 13 on the same subject). These were first published as an appendix in *The Letters of H. P. Blavatsky to A. P. Sinnett*, transcribed and compiled by A. T. Barker, 1st ed., 1925; repr., Pasadena, California: Theosophical University Press, 1973. Further material on this model was given in Mahatma letters 15, 10, and 22; and in the important article, "What Is Matter and What Is Force?," *The Theosophist*, vol. 3, Sep. 1882, pp. 319-324; reprinted in *H. P. Blavatsky Collected Writings*, vol. 4, 1969, pp. 208-226.

22. *Svabhāva-vāda* is an ancient and little-known doctrine. *Svabhāva* is listed in the *Śvetāśvatara Upaniṣad*, 1.2, along with five other things that had been proposed in the past as the source of the universe. All are here rejected in favor of Brahman as the source of the universe. There are no extant texts on *svabhāva-vāda*, only stray references such as this one. *Svabhāva* is the "inherent nature" of something; but of what is not clear. In its doctrine as refuted here, *svabhāva* is commonly explained as what makes swans white, for example. So it is understood as the inherent nature of individual things like swans. Early Buddhism in its teaching of individual *dharmas* also says that these have each their own inherent nature or *svabhāva*. But in the model given by the Mahatmas, *svabhāva* is the inherent nature of the one element. This alone produces all apparent diversity.

23. *The Mahatma Letters*, 3rd ed., p. 136; chron. ed., p. 281.

24. *The Secret Doctrine*, vol. 1, pp. 634-635.

25. "The 'Secret Doctrine' and Its Study," by Robert Bowen, p. 3.

26. *The Mahatma Letters*, 3rd ed., pp. 57-58; chron. ed., p. 274.

27. *The Mahatma Letters*, 3rd ed., p. 53; chron. ed., p. 270.

[The foregoing article was written by David Reigle, and published in *Keeping the Link Unbroken: Theosophical Studies Presented to Ted G. Davy on His Seventy-fifth Birthday*, ed. Michael Gomes, [New York]: TRM, an imprint of Theosophical Research Monographs, 2004, pp. 22-38.]

The Original Śaṅkarācārya

The once universal Wisdom Tradition, whose existence was made known to the modern world by H. P. Blavatsky, had been preserved for long ages in the utmost secrecy. So when Blavatsky brought out a portion of it, she was faced with the problem of making these now unheard of teachings plausible. To address this, she attempted to establish the probability of the existence of such a tradition, and to support the correctness of its teachings, by reference to known authors. For this support she drew heavily on the teachings of Śaṅkarācārya. But it would seem that the Śaṅkarācārya referred to by Blavatsky and the Śaṅkarācārya whose writings have conditioned Indian thought for the last dozen centuries or so are not the same person.

Śaṅkarācārya, the preceptor (*ācārya*) Śaṅkara, is regarded by Blavatsky as a great teacher of the Wisdom Tradition, or the Esoteric Philosophy. In her primary work, *The Secret Doctrine*, he is referred to as "the greatest Initiate living in the historical ages,"[1] and as "the greatest of the Esoteric masters of India."[2] The philosophy promulgated by him, the *advaita* or non-dual school of Vedānta, is there called the nearest exponent of the Esoteric Philosophy.[3] This is because the Esoteric Philosophy, the Wisdom Tradition, is non-dual like Śaṅkarācārya's *advaita* school,[4] as opposed to the qualified non-dualism of Rāmānuja's *viśiṣṭādvaita* school, or the dualism of Madhva's *dvaita* school, of Vedānta. So we are led to believe that Śaṅkarācārya, as a great Initiate, was fully versed in the Wisdom Tradition; and that even his public teachings, the non-dual *advaita* school of Vedānta, provide the best available support for its teachings.

This assumption is further strengthened by the amount of attention given to the question of Śaṅkarācārya's date in the important series of articles called, "Some Inquiries Suggested by Mr. Sinnett's *Esoteric Buddhism*."[5] This series is believed to have been written (or caused to be written) by three Mahatmas, or adepts in the Wisdom Tradition.[6] Its importance is that it purports to give replies based on the definite information held by the Mahatmas rather than on speculation. But despite this rare opportunity for direct knowledge, and as predicted by Blavatsky who thought this lengthy series was a colossal waste of the Mahatmas' time,[7] the answers given were not accepted then, nor are they now.

The then prevailing opinion, accepted by both Western scholars and their Indian counterparts, was that Śaṅkarācārya lived in the eighth century C.E.[8] An article in this series, after examining the various speculations of European orientalists on this question, gives the true date of Śaṅkarācārya's birth from the secret records:

> We may perhaps now venture to place before the public the exact date assigned to Sankaracharya by Tibetan and Indian Initiates. According to the historical information in their possession he was born in the year *B.C.* 510 (51 years and 2 months after the date of Buddha's nirvana), . . .[9]

This was published in *The Theosophist* for 1883. The next article to appear in *The Theosophist* on Śaṅkarācārya's date, a detailed three-part study by the Pandit of the Adyar Library published six years later, consciously ignored this information and concluded that "we may not be far from truth if we say that he lived somewhere about the 5th century A.C."[10] Other articles followed in *The Theosophist,* proposing other dates.[11]

Meanwhile, discussion of Śaṅkarācārya's date continued in earnest in the orientalist journals. From 1882 to 2000 more than forty articles and books on this question appeared.[12] K. B. Pathak had in 1882 published a chronogram from an obscure manuscript giving dates corresponding to 788 C.E. for Śaṅkara's birth and 820 for his death.[13] Most of the writings that followed also favored dates in the eighth century C.E., many arguing for 700 or 750 C.E. rather than 788 C.E. A few, however, proposed 509 B.C.E.,[14] in remarkable agreement with the date put forward by the Tibetan and Indian Initiates. This date of 509 B.C.E., moreover, comes from the very sources that one would most expect to find Śaṅkarācārya's date preserved in: the records of the *maṭhas* or monastic centers established by him.

Śaṅkarācārya is said to have founded *maṭhas* at the four cardinal points of India: the Jyotir *maṭha* near Badrinath in the North; the Govardhana *maṭha* at Puri (Jagannath) in the East; the Kālikā *maṭha* (Śāradā *pīṭha*) at Dwaraka in the West; and the Śṛṅgerī *maṭha* (again, Śāradā *pīṭha*) at Sringeri in the South. In addition to these four, he is said to have founded the Śāradā *maṭha* (Kāmakoṭi *pīṭha*) at Kanchi, also in the South. Each of these *maṭhas* has had a succession of pontiffs, who hold the title Śaṅkarācārya, from the time of the original or first (Ādi) Śaṅkarācārya. Their traditional lineage lists (*guru-paramparā*) give the names and usually the dates of each successive pontiff of that particular *maṭha*. The list of the Kālikā *maṭha* in the West gives for the birth of Śaṅkara the date 2631 of the Yudhiṣṭhira era, corresponding to 509 B.C.E.[15] The list of the Śāradā *maṭha* (at Kanchi) in the South gives the date 2593 of the Kali Yuga era, also corresponding to 509 B.C.E.[16] It is significant that two different lineage lists from two widely separated *maṭhas*, having 77 and 68 successors respectively, both go back in an unbroken line to 509 B.C.E.

The list of the Govardhana *maṭha* in the East does not give dates, but has 144 successors, about twice as many as the above two *maṭhas* have.[17] This is due to the circumstance that at this *maṭha* the successors are normally those who have gone through the householder stage of life before becoming renunciants (rather than doing so immediately after the student stage), so are older when they are chosen to become Śaṅkarācāryas.[18] So this list, too, supports the date of 509 B.C.E. The list of the Jyotir *maṭha* in the North has not yet been recovered (except for some recent centuries), since it was lost when this *maṭha* ceased to function between 1776 and 1941 C.E.[19] Even so, this *maṭha* in its current publications accepts the traditional date of 509 B.C.E. The list of the Śṛṅgerī *maṭha* in the South gives for the birth of Śaṅkara the date 3058 of the Kali Yuga era, corresponding to 44 B.C.E.[20] This list, however, having only 35 successors, gives an improbable reign of 785 years for the second successor.[21] It does not seem to be regarded as reliable by this *maṭha,* since their current publications give instead of 44 B.C.E. for Śaṅkara's birth the commonly accepted later date of 788 C.E.[22] Thus the Jyotir *maṭha,* whose lineage list is incomplete, accepts the traditional date of 509 B.C.E., while the Śṛṅgerī *maṭha,* whose lineage list is imperfect, accepts the later date of 788 C.E. The other three *maṭhas,* in accordance with the lineage lists preserved by them, all give the date of Śaṅkara's birth as 509 B.C.E.

There are also other traditional sources that confirm the date of 509 B.C.E. One would next expect to find the date of Śaṅkara in the various biographies of him preserved in India. But the available biographies, written in Sanskrit, have proved to be of little help on this, sometimes giving astrological aspects of his birth, yet strangely, not the year.[23] There are, however, a few inaccessible but more informative ones. Far and away the most important of these is the full *Bṛhat Śaṅkara-vijaya* written by Citsukhācārya.[24] Citsukhācārya was a lifelong companion of Śaṅkara who says he "never departed from Śaṅkara from the time he left his native place until he attained his marvellous Brahmībhāva,"[25] that is, died. In other words, "he was an eye-witness of the life and doings of Śaṅkara from start to finish, and one of his direct disciples."[26] This biography gives full details of Śaṅkara's life, with dates. Although this rare text is not found in libraries, T. S. Narayana Sastry managed to obtain a manuscript of it, from which he brought out material in a book in 1916.[27] Sastry in another place quoted in full its section on Śaṅkara's birth, in the original Sanskrit, and translated this into English. It gives the date 2631 of the Yudhiṣṭhira era, corresponding to 509 B.C.E.[28] Sastry also managed to obtain copies of two other biographies not now found in libraries: the equally rare *Prācīna Śaṅkara-vijaya* by Ānandagiri, and a version of the *Vyāsācalīya Śaṅkara-vijaya* by Vyāsācala. Each of them gives, using different word-numbers, the date 2593 of the Kali Yuga era for his birth, again corresponding to 509 B.C.E.[29]

There is also epigraphic evidence supporting the date of 509 B.C.E. for Śaṅkara's birth. This is a copper plate inscription addressed to Śaṅkara by King Sudhanvan of Dwaraka, dated 2663 of the Yudhiṣṭhira era, corresponding to 477 B.C.E., the year of Śaṅkara's death.[30] Since Śaṅkara died at the age of 32, this places his birth in 509 B.C.E.

This evidence seems quite convincing; yet it is disregarded by modern scholars, who consider it mere myth. For example, leading Indologist Hajime Nakamura in his influential book, *A History of Early Vedānta Philosophy*, devotes forty pages to the question of Śaṅkara's date.[31] Before setting out his own theory that "he probably lived, roughly, 700-750 [C.E.]," Nakamura says he "will carefully go into the theories advanced hitherto on the dates of Śaṅkara," noting that "I think that what is cited below will have exhausted all the important theses."[32] Yet he does not so much as mention the view that Śaṅkara was born 509 B.C.E. His section, "The Traditional Theory of the Śāṅkara School," deals with the 788 C.E. birth date, hardly the traditional theory.

Of course, scholars such as Nakamura are not fools, and there are good reasons for disregarding the date of 509 B.C.E. and for concluding that Śaṅkara must have lived in the eighth century C.E. For example, Śaṅkara's commentary on *Brahma-sūtra* 2.2.18-32 is a refutation of Buddhist doctrines developed in the both the older Sarvāstivāda school and in the newer Vijñānavāda school. A fifty-year gap between the death of the Buddha and the birth of Śaṅkara is not nearly enough time for at least these latter doctrines to have developed. To allow for this, proponents of the 509 B.C.E. date have advocated pushing back the date of the Buddha to 1800 B.C.E.[33] But besides the fact that this conflicts with the time period of the Buddha as found in traditional Southern Buddhist sources and as determined in general by modern scholars, and also the date of the Buddha as given by the Mahatmas, it still does not solve the problem. Śaṅkara in his commentary on these verses of the *Brahma-sūtras* quotes material from the Buddhist writer Dignāga and refers to material from the Buddhist writer Dharmakīrti, who are dated in the fifth and sixth centuries C.E., respectively.[34] Thus Śaṅkara could not have lived before then.

There is an obvious solution to this dilemma, but to my knowledge none of the advocates of the 509 B.C.E. date have yet proposed it (nor has anyone else, for that matter). They take great pains to show that the 788 C.E. date actually refers to one

Abhinava or "new" Śaṅkarācārya, not to the Ādi or "original" Śaṅkarācārya. This Abhinava Śaṅkarācārya was the 38th pontiff of the Śāradā *maṭha* at Kanchi, who achieved wide fame during his lifetime, and the details of his life have been confused with those of the first Śaṅkarācārya.[35] Thus are explained the two conflicting sets of parents, places of birth, and places of death, found in the varying biographies.[36] These advocates even admit, here agreeing with Western scholars, that of the more than four hundred works attributed to Śaṅkarācārya, many must actually have been written by later Śaṅkarācāryas of the various *maṭhas*. But no one, neither Indian nor Western, questions that the commentary (*bhāṣya*) we have on the *Brahma-sūtras* is by the original or Ādi Śaṅkarācārya.[37] This work is taken to define Ādi Śaṅkarācārya. This and the commentaries on the other two of the three pillars of Vedānta (*prasthāna-traya*), namely, on the Upaniṣads and on the *Bhagavad-gītā*, form his major works.

Already in 1888, when Blavatsky gave in *The Secret Doctrine* the esoteric tradition that the Upaniṣads had been greatly abridged at the time of the Buddha, she indicated that we do not have the original commentaries on them by Śaṅkarācārya:

> Śrī Śaṃkarāchārya, the greatest Initiate living in the historical ages, wrote many a *Bhāshya* on the *Upanishads*. But his original treatises, as there are reasons to suppose, have not yet fallen into the hands of the Philistines, for they are too jealously preserved in his *maṭhas* (monasteries).[38]

Then in 1896-1897 some extraordinary articles appeared in *The Theosophist*, written with the collaboration of a blind pandit who could recite from memory a large number of lost Sanskrit texts. One of these articles stated that the now current commentary by Śaṅkarācārya on the *Bhagavad-gītā* is not the genuine one, but rather is by Nāgeśvara Bhaṭṭa. It then gives a quote from the genuine one.[39] In another of these articles the authors offered "to give to the world the genuine commentary, if not precluded by unforeseen and unavoidable events."[40] The "unforeseen and unavoidable events" may have been an allusion to the authors' concern over the lack of acceptance and even antagonism these articles met with among the orthodox readers of *The Theosophist.* Of course, the genuine commentary never came out. In any case, the above indicates that the extant commentaries on the Upaniṣads and on the *Bhagavad-gītā* attributed to Śaṅkarācārya may not be the original and genuine ones.

But it is Śaṅkarācārya's commentary on the *Brahma-sūtras* that modern scholarship, both Eastern and Western, takes as the one unquestionable work of Ādi Śaṅkarācārya. It is used as the standard by which to judge the authenticity of all the other works attributed to him. This work presents us with a dilemma not only because it quotes and refutes Buddhist writers from the fifth and sixth centuries C.E., more than a millennium after Śaṅkara is supposed to have lived, but also in regard to the unique Theosophical teaching of the relationship between Śaṅkara and the Buddha. In brief, this esoteric teaching is that the Buddha's astral remains, i.e., his intermediate principles, provided the middle principles for the *avatāra* Śaṅkara.[41] Thus there was a close relationship between the two of them. It is therefore inexplicable to Theosophists when the Śaṅkara who wrote the extant *Brahma-sūtra* commentary has these choice words to say about the Buddha and his doctrine:

> From whatever new points of view the Bauddha [Buddhist] system is tested with reference to its probability, it gives way on all sides, like the walls of a well dug in sandy soil. It has, in fact, no foundation whatever to rest upon, and hence the attempts to use it as a guide in the practical concerns of life are mere folly.—Moreover, Buddha by propounding the three mutually contradictory systems, teaching respectively the reality of the external world [the Sarvāstivāda system], the reality of ideas only [the Vijñānavāda or Yogācāra system], and general nothingness [the Śūnyavāda or Madhyamaka system], has himself made it clear either that he was a man given to make incoherent assertions, or else that hatred of all beings induced him to propound absurd doctrines by accepting which they would become thoroughly confused.—So that—and this the Sūtra means to indicate—Buddha's doctrine has to be entirely disregarded by all those who have a regard for their own happiness.[42]

The obvious solution is that the *Brahma-sūtra* commentary, taken to be the one definite work of the original Śaṅkarācārya, and the standard by which the authenticity of all the others are judged, was in fact written by a later Śaṅkarācārya. In this way only can be explained how this commentary can quote a fifth century C.E. writer, when Śaṅkarācārya is traditionally supposed to have lived in the fifth century B.C.E. The ramifications of this for the study of the Wisdom Tradition are far-reaching.

Modern Western scholars have subjected Śaṅkarācārya's writings to a type of literary criticism that had never been a part of traditional Indian scholarship. They have minutely surveyed the use of characteristic technical terms in the *Brahma-sūtra* commentary, and compared this usage of technical terms with that found in other writings attributed to him. In this way they have been able to determine that most of the commentaries on the Upaniṣads and the commentary on the *Bhagavad-gītā* were written by the same person who wrote the commentary on the *Brahma-sūtras*, but that virtually all the other writings attributed to Śaṅkarācārya, the many shorter works including the popular *Viveka-cūḍāmaṇi*, "Crest Jewel of Discrimination," were not.[43] For them, this means that only these commentaries are genuine works of the original Śaṅkarācārya. For us, in accordance with the data presented above, this means just the opposite.

The major writings of Śaṅkarācārya now extant, namely his commentaries on the *Brahma-sūtras*, Upaniṣads, and *Bhagavad-gītā*, cannot be relied upon to support the Wisdom Tradition, since they were not written by the original Śaṅkarācārya. These works include important doctrines that are contradictory to the teachings of the Wisdom Tradition, and also contradictory to those of some of his other writings; that is, ones that scholars consider spurious but that we must consider genuine. Thus, Pandit N. Bhashya Charya writes in *The Theosophist* for 1890:

> The other works, such as Apárókshánubhúti, Átmánátmavivéka, Vivékachúdámani and Átmabódha cannot be his works, for they are in many respects in contradiction with philosophical conclusions found in his [Brahma-]Sútra, Upanishad, and Gitá Bháshyas.[44]

It is only some of his shorter works, such as the ones just listed, that can be relied upon to support the Wisdom Tradition, since it is only these that we can assume were actually written by the original Śaṅkarācārya.[45] The *Brahma-sūtra* commentary and the other long commentaries were not yet available in English when Blavatsky drew on Śaṅkarācārya's teachings for this support.[46] Only some of his shorter works were then available in English, such as the *Viveka-cūḍāmaṇi,* translated by Mohini Chatterji and serialized in *The Theosophist,* 1885-1887.[47] It is to some of these shorter works that we must turn to find the original teachings of the original Śaṅkarācārya.

Śaṅkarācārya on God

Of course, the *Brahma-sūtra* commentary and the other long commentaries by the later Śaṅkarācārya would no doubt have been based largely on those of the original Śaṅkarācārya, but with some very important changes. The most important of these involves what is perhaps the greatest question in Indian religion in the last two millenniums: the question of God.

The teaching of a single non-dual reality called Brahman, that includes within it the entire universe, has always been the hallmark of Advaita Vedānta. The universal self of all, called *ātman,* is identified with Brahman. This impersonal principle goes beyond any conception of a personal God, and is therefore described as the *param* or highest Brahman, Parabrahman.

But according to the researches of modern scholarship, the author of the extant *Brahma-sūtra* commentary makes no distinction between the impersonal Brahman and the personal God, Īśvara. He does not even distinguish Parabrahman from Īśvara. In fact, his theistic interpretation is so pronounced that this usage of Īśvara, the personal God, serves to distinguish his writings from those of other Advaita Vedānta writers, even his disciples.

> . . . G. A. Jacob had observed [in 1893] that theistic terms in Śaṅkara's *Brahmasūtrabhāṣya* often appeared in passages where the logic of the system seemed to call for impersonalistic and

> monistic terms, and that Śaṅkara again and again ignored the distinction between *paraṃ brahma* and *īśvara* . . . .
> . . . the theistic basis or background perceptible in Śaṅkara's monistic thought . . . indeed marks a feature which is of major relevance to an evaluation of the great thinker's personality and which distinguishes him from other philosophers of his school.[48]

German Indologist Paul Hacker sums up his landmark study, "Distinctive Features of the Doctrine and Terminology of Śaṅkara," as follows:

> Recapitulating our results so far, we can say that the words (*paraṃ*) *brahma* or *paramātman* are almost always interchangeable with *īśvara*; that *īśvara* can in most places be replaced by (*paraṃ*) *brahma* or *paramātman*; . . .
> This use of language is characteristic of Ś[aṅkara]. Comparisons with his disciples are, however, helpful only insofar as they establish that the word *īśvara* is used very seldom by them, whereas it occurs very frequently in the SBh [Śaṅkara's *Brahma-sūtra-bhāṣya*]. At the same time, the concept does not appear to have had much systematic development for them. But in later Vedānta (*Pañcadaśī*, *Vedāntasāra*) Īśvara is no longer confused with Brahman. He has been given a clearly defined place in the system, namely, He is Brahman associated with *māyā*.
> How is this strange confusion on Ś[aṅkara]'s part to be explained?[49]

From our perspective, it is explained by the fact that this book was not written by the original Śaṅkarācārya, but by a later, theistic, Śaṅkarācārya. This allows us to understand why virtually all modern Advaita Vedāntins are theists, believers in God, when we know that this belief is not a part of the Wisdom Tradition; nor, apparently, was it part of the original teachings of the original Śaṅkarācārya. The Mahatma K.H. writes on this in a letter replying to A. O. Hume:

> In the first [letter] you notify me of your intention of studying Advaita Philosophy with a "good old Swami". The man, no

doubt, is very good; but from what I gather in your letter, if he teaches you anything you say to me, *i.e.*, anything save an impersonal, *non*-thinking and *non*-intelligent Principle they call Parabrahm, then he will not be teaching you the *true spirit* of that philosophy, not from its esoteric aspect, at any rate.[50]

The Mahatma K.H. clearly states the position of the Wisdom Tradition on belief in God in his letters #10 and #22. In brief, this position is as follows:

> Neither our philosophy nor ourselves believe in a God, least of all in one whose pronoun necessitates a capital H.[51]

K.H. continues, specifically differentiating Parabrahman from God, Īśvara:

> Parabrahm is not a God, but absolute immutable law, and Iswar is the effect of Avidya and Maya, ignorance based on the great delusion.[52]

He says that Parabrahman is the one life taught by them:

> We are not Adwaitees, but our teaching respecting the one life is identical with that of the Adwaitee with regard to Parabrahm.[53]

He reiterates that the one life, or Parabrahman, is not God:

> If people are willing to accept and to regard as God our ONE LIFE immutable and unconscious in its eternity they may do so and thus keep to one more gigantic misnomer.[54]

He says it does matter whether or not we think of this principle as God:

> You say it matters nothing whether these laws are the expression of the will of an intelligent conscious God, as you think, or constitute the inevitable attributes of an unintelligent, unconscious "God," as I hold. I say, it matters everything, . . .[55]

A Hindu Adept affirms that Parabrahman is to be understood as an abstract principle rather than as God:

> Moreover, I assert that the PARABRAHM of the Vedantins and the "Adi-Buddha" of the northern Buddhists are identical. Both are *Abstract Principles*, or—*non*-entities; . . .[56]

How important is this question of God? In one Indian's view, the introduction of the concept of a supreme almighty God into India from the West and its thorough establishment there by Śaṅkarācārya, both in the eighth century C.E., brought about the ruin of India. He holds that India's effeteness in the past twelve hundred years, when it was ruled first by the Muslims and then by the British, is due to this theism, which had been so effectively promulgated there by Śaṅkarācārya. Of course, this refers to who we would consider to be the later Śaṅkarācārya. This author, Phulgenda Sinha, explains how through historical research he arrived at this startling conclusion:

> Considering the whole history of India from the most ancient to the contemporary period, I found a distinct dividing line in the literary and philosophical heritage of the country, making it appear as if there were two Indias—one which existed from ancient times to 800 A.D., and another which came after 800 A.D. . . .
>
> India prior to 800 A.D. produced philosophers and writers who accepted Man as the supreme being. They talked about two main entities: *Purusha* (Man) and *Prakriti* (Nature). . . . Man can liberate himself from *dukha* [sorrow or unhappiness] and can attain *sukha* (happiness) by acquiring proper knowledge, mastering certain teachings, following certain practices, and by working according to the Samkhya-yoga theory of action.
>
> India after 800 A.D. adopted quite a different outlook. The ideas proposed by writers and commentators were now mostly matters of belief and faith, colored by religion, mysticism, and caste. Not Man but God was held to be supreme. Man could do only what was predestined by God.[57]

He continues further on, after saying that religious tolerance held sway in India until about the eighth century C.E.:

> However, this condition changed when the Brahmans accepted monotheism and began interpreting the whole religious history of India, from Vedas to Upanishads, in a completely new way. The most interesting points in this interpretation were that the status of Brahmans as a caste and class was strengthened, all the gods and goddesses of Vedas were superseded by a single Almighty God, and religious persecution began with a sense of crushing the enemies. It happened with the coming of Shankaracharya.[58]

He begins his section, "An Appraisal of Shankaracharya," with:

> Shankaracharya was the first Indian to openly accept, propagate, and expound the concept of monotheism as a part of Hindu religion.[59]

He concludes his appraisal with this verdict:

> India entered into a dark age with the coming of Shankaracharya.[60]

When reading at a distance Śaṅkarācārya's philosophical treatises on non-dualism, we are apt to remain unaware of the reality of just how theistically they are understood in India, and just how pervasive the God idea is there. In his 1983 study of the modern Śaṅkarācāryas and their followers, William Cenkner reports:

> Worship is the most significant duty encouraged by the Śaṅkarācāryas; daily *pūjā* is their consistent advice. . . . The observer frequently notes the worship of personal gods even among ascetics of the Śaṅkara orders today; the practice, it is believed, was part of Ādi Śaṅkara's renovation of ascetical life.[61]
>
> The popular eclectic worship is based upon the tradition that Ādi Śaṅkara revived and gave stability to the six alternate ways of

> worship, the *ṣaṇmata*-s [i.e., of the six Gods]. Ascetics from the Śaṅkara orders have consistently worshipped personal gods. Śaṅkara in his commentary on the *Gītā* speaks of the six attributes of God that correspond to the six Gods, Śiva, Viṣṇu, Śakti, Sūrya, Gaṇapati and Kumāra.[62]

T. M. P. Mahadevan, well-known scholar and exponent of Advaita Vedānta, explains that this sixfold worship came about at the request of six of Śaṅkara's disciples.

> Admitting the non-duality of the Absolute Spirit, they had their own preference in regard to the form of the Personal Godhead.[63]

After stressing the importance of God in Advaita Vedānta, he says that this importance is because, according to Śaṅkara's commentary on *Brahma-sūtra* 2.3.41:

> . . . it is by gaining knowledge that comes through God's grace that one gets released from bondage.[64]

Thus, Śaṅkarācārya is understood in India to have widely propagated the worship of a personal God, since the grace of a personal God is required for liberation. The prevalence of this teaching largely coincided with the difficult period in Indian history of foreign domination. However one may choose to judge the effects of belief in God seen in India over the past twelve hundred years, this belief is certainly due in large part to the theistic interpretation of Vedānta by the later Śaṅkarācārya. It would seem that the pure Advaita teaching of the original Śaṅkarācārya has now become thoroughly overlaid with theism, as a result of the additions made to that teaching by the Śaṅkarācārya who wrote the extant commentaries on the three pillars of Vedānta. But this theism, according to the Wisdom Tradition, is not the teaching of Vedānta as expounded by the original Śaṅkarācārya.

The most fundamental teaching of Vedānta is that of the existence of Brahman, the one reality, and of the identity of *ātman*, the self of all, with Brahman. The original Śaṅkarācārya promulgated the Advaita, or non-dual, understanding of this ultimate principle, in direct accordance with the teachings of the Wisdom Tradition. This non-dual principle, the one life, is the most essential teaching of the hidden Wisdom Tradition. For bringing this teaching out, the world is indebted to the original Śaṅkarācārya.[65] Nowhere else in all the world's sacred writings was this taught in its fullness and its purity. The task now before the student of the Wisdom Tradition is to separate this original teaching of the original Śaṅkarācārya from its later accretions, which go under the same name.

NOTES

1. *The Secret Doctrine*, by H. P. Blavatsky, 1st ed., 1888; [ed. by Boris de Zirkoff] (pagination unchanged), Adyar, Madras: Theosophical Publishing House, 1978, vol. 1, p. 271.
2. *The Secret Doctrine*, vol. 1, p. 86.
3. *The Secret Doctrine*, vol. 1, p. 55.
4. See, for example, the advice given by Blavatsky to Robert Bowen on how to study *The Secret Doctrine*, where she gives as the first idea the mind must hold fast to: "The FUNDAMENTAL UNITY OF ALL EXISTENCE. This unity is a thing altogether different from the common notion of unity—as when we say that a nation or an army is united; or that this planet is united to that by lines of magnetic force or the like. The teaching is not that. It is that existence is ONE THING, not any collection of things linked together. Fundamentally there is ONE BEING." This advice is found in an article, "The 'Secret Doctrine' and Its Study," which has been reprinted several times. I here cite the above from *An Invitation to The Secret Doctrine*, by H. P. Blavatsky, Pasadena: Theosophical University Press, 1988, p. 3.
5. This series of articles was published in *The Theosophist*, vols. 4, 5, Sep., Oct., Nov., 1883. It was reprinted in *Five Years of Theosophy*, 1885; 2nd ed. 1894. It was also reprinted in *H. P. Blavatsky Collected Writings*, vol. 5, Los Angeles: Philosophical Research Society, 1950, pp. 129-275. I use this latter edition because of the careful editorial work done in it by the compiler, Boris de Zirkoff (see p. 275).
6. This series consists of twelve parts, ten of which are unsigned, and two of which are signed by T. Subba Row, a Hindu chela (pupil) of one of the three Mahatmas who are believed to have written them.

Subba Row writes: "The 'Replies'—as every one in our Society is aware of—were written by three 'adepts' as Mr. Maitland calls them—none of whom is known to the London Lodge, with the exception of one—to Mr. Sinnett." (Cited from "Introductory Remarks by the Compiler," Boris de Zirkoff, to this series of articles reprinted in *Blavatsky Collected Writings*, vol. 5, p. 135.) Blavatsky writes in a letter to A. P. Sinnett: "It is my Boss and two others you do not know." (*Blavatsky Collected Writings*, vol. 5, p. 136.) In the case of the two articles signed by Subba Row, one of which is "Sri Sankaracharya's Date and Doctrine," this apparently means that he was given certain information, such as the correct date of Śaṅkarācārya, and wrote the rest based on his own knowledge.

7. This may be seen in the following excepts from *The Letters of H. P. Blavatsky to A. P. Sinnett* (1925): "Where's the necessity of writing three pages for every line of the question and explaining things that after all none of them except yourself, perhaps, will understand. . . . and who is Mr. Myers that my big Boss should waste a bucket full of his red ink to satisfy *him*? And He won't; see if he does. For Mr. Myers will *not* be satisfied with negative proofs and the evidence of the failings of European astronomers and physicists" (p. 46). "I say that these *Replies* to 'An English F.T.S.' are time lost; they will not accept the truth, and they occupy half of every number of the *Theosophist* that comes out, crowding off other matter. . ." (p. 59). "I am really sorry for these *Replies* that appear in the *Theosophist*. It does seem wisdom thrown out of the window. Well—*Their* ways *are* mysterious" (p. 63). "And I always said it was useless and time lost for no one will believe and very few will understand, *I don't*" (p. 68). "What does Mr. Myers say to the *Replies*? *Disgusted* I suppose? I thought as much. Well that's all the Adepts will get for their trouble" (p. 73).

8. As summed up by Kashinath Trimbak Telang (translator of the *Bhagavadgītā* for the Sacred Books of the East series) in his article, "The Life of Sankaracharya, Philosopher and Mystic," *The Theosophist*, vol. 1, Dec. 1879, p. 71: "Most modern scholars agree in locating him in the eighth century of the Christian era; and, since we have for this opinion the concurrent authority of Wilson, Colebrooke, Rammohan Roy, Yajnesvar Shastri, and Professor Jayanarayan Tarkapanchanam, the Bengali editor of Anandagiri's *Sankara Vijaya*, . . . we may as well accept that decision without debate."

9. "Sri Sankaracharya's Date and Doctrine," by T. Subba Row, *The Theosophist*, vol. 4, no. 12, Sep. 1883, p. 310; reprinted in *H. P. Blavatsky Collected Writings*, vol. 5, p. 197. Note that the "51 years and 2 months after the date of Buddha's nirvana" does not quite match the date of

this given elsewhere in this series of articles. *Blavatsky Collected Writings*, vol. 5, p. 256, gives the date of the Buddha's *nirvāṇa* as 2544 of the Kali Yuga era. This corresponds to 558 B.C.E. See note 33 below.

It may be further noted that there is a question of interpretation in regard to another of Subba Row's statements found in this article. He writes: "It is generally believed that a person named Govinda Yogi was Sankara's guru, but it is not generally known that this Yogi was in fact Patanjali—the great author of the *Mahabhashya* and the *Yoga Sutras*—under a new name. . . . But it is quite clear from the 94th, 95th, 96th and 97th verses of the 5th chapter of Vidyaranya's *Sankara Vijaya* that Govinda Yogi and Patanjali were identical. According to the immemorial custom observed amongst initiates Patanjali assumed the name of Govinda Yogi at the time of his initiation by Gaudapada" (*Blavatsky Collected Writings*, vol. 5, pp. 192-193).

In fact, the generally accepted understanding of these verses is that Govinda was an incarnation of Patañjali, not Patañjali himself. Compare: *The Theosophist*, vol. 11, p. 106, fn. 3, where Pandit N. Bhashya Charya writes: "Mr. T. Subba Row makes him *identical* with Patanjali, and says that Sri Sankarāchārya was a disciple of Patanjali. We believe he said so on the authority of this verse. In that case, the verse itself and the commentary thereon are quite sufficient to show that he is wrong and that Patanjali himself lived long before the time of Govindayogi." See also: vol. 10, p. 738, fn. 1. Patañjali himself was supposed to have been the guru of Gauḍapāda, who was the guru of Govinda. In any case, a difference of two generations does not affect Subba Row's basic argument in this article, that the date of Patañjali is a determining factor for the date of Śaṅkara.

10. "The Age of Srī Sankarāchārya," by Pandit N. Bhashya Charya, *The Theosophist*, vol. 11, Nov. 1889, pp. 98-107; Jan. 1890, pp. 182-185; Feb. 1890, pp. 263-272. The quotation is from p. 270. I say that he consciously ignored the date of 510 B.C. because he twice refers to the article it is found in (on p. 102, fn. 1, and on p. 106, fn. 3), citing page numbers from both *The Theosophist* and its reprint in *Five Years of Theosophy*, but nowhere even mentions this date. This is despite the fact that he examines the various traditions of Śaṅkarācārya's date, giving eight others ranging from about 56 B.C. to 1349 A.C.

11. "Śri Śankara's Date" (in Correspondence section), letter by Charles Johnston, reply by S. E. Gopalacharlu, *The Theosophist*, vol. 14, Jan. 1893, pp. 253-256. This reproduces the lineage list of the Śṛṅgerī *maṭha*, and gives equivalent Western dates, giving 43 B.C. for Śaṅkara's birth. See note 20 below. Gopalacharlu, however, rejects this date, and

states at the end that "it is impossible to maintain the theory that Sankarāchārya flourished *before* 56 B.C." (p. 256).

"The Date of Shankarāchārya," by Govinda-dāsa, *The Theosophist*, vol. 16, Dec. 1894, pp. 163-168. This gives the lineage list of the *maṭha* at Dwaraka, with its dates in the Yudhiṣṭhira era. See note 15 below. The date of Śaṅkara's birth is given as 2631 of this era. This era "is said to have lasted 3050 years, after which began *Vikrama's* Era, now [1894] in its 1951st year" (p. 164).

"The Date of Shankarāchārya," by J. S. Gadgil, *The Theosophist*, vol. 16, Feb. 1895, pp. 292-296. This cites several dates, and from them proposes three different Śaṅkarācāryas. It cites nine verses from the *Jina-vijaya*, giving the date of Śaṅkara's birth as 2157 Yudhiṣṭhira era. From this, Śaṅkara "lived about 2,838 years ago, counting back from the present year [1895]" (p. 294). This accepts that the Yudhiṣṭhira era lasted 3,044 years; but according to Narayana Sastry, this era is reckoned by Jaina writers as lasting less than that. See note 30 below.

"The Date of Sri Sankaracharya," by Siva, *The Theosophist*, vol. 21, June 1900, pp. 561-562. This cites the chronogram giving the date of Śaṅkara's birth as 788 A.D. (see note 13 below), and also cites the date of 510 B.C. given by Subba Row. It then asks if the exact date can be calculated by some astronomer from the horoscope data given in the verse he quotes from the Śaṅkara-vijaya by Vidyāraṇya (i.e., Mādhava). See notes 23 and 29 below.

"Śrī Śankarācārya: His Date, Life-Work and Teachings," by B. S. Ramasubbier, *The Theosophist*, vol. 56, Dec. 1934, pp. 293-297. This cites the date of 509 B.C. for Śaṅkara's birth, from T. S. Nārāyana Sastri, following Citsukhācārya. See note 24 below. Further on, it says: "A fragment of Citsukha's life of Śankara, in the archives of the Adyar Library, . . ." (pp. 293-294). This biography is otherwise unavailable. See note 27 below. In reply to my inquiry, the Adyar Library informed me that this fragment is a printed pamphlet in devanāgarī script, of eight pages, having no date or place of publication, with the heading, *Śrī-maṭhāmnāyaḥ*. I was able to obtain a photocopy of it from them, and its colophon indeed identifies it as a section of Citsukhācārya's *Bṛhat Śaṅkara-vijaya*. As its name implies, it concerns the *maṭhas* founded by Śaṅkarācārya, five in all, their founding and their allotted disciplines of spiritual practice.

12. These are here listed in chronological order, followed by a brief statement (in parentheses) of their position on Śaṅkarācārya's date:

"The Date of Śamkarāchārya," by K. B. Pathak, *Indian Antiquary*, vol. 11, 1882, pp. 174-175 (cites a Sanskrit manuscript giving 3889 of the Kali Yuga era for his birth, corresponding to 788 C.E., and 3921 for his death, or 820 C.E.)

"The Date of Śaṃkarāchārya," by Editor [James Burgess], *Indian Antiquary*, vol. 11, 1882, p. 263 (notes that Tiele had in 1877 given 788 C.E. for his birth)

"The Date of Śaṅkarāchārya," by K. T. Telang, *Indian Antiquary*, vol. 13, 1884, pp. 95-103 (rejects 788-820 C.E., and proposes the latter half of the sixth century C.E., no later than 590 C.E.)

"A Note on the Date of Samkaracharya," by J. F. Fleet, *Indian Antiquary*, vol. 16, 1887, pp. 41-42 (suggests circa 630-655 C.E., with a ten or twenty year margin of error)

"The Date of Samkaracharya," by W. Logan, *Indian Antiquary*, vol. 16, 1887, pp. 160-161 (cites evidence to support the first quarter of the ninth century C.E.)

"Dharmakīrti and Śaṃkarāchārya," by K. B. Pathak, *Journal of the Bombay Branch of the Royal Asiatic Society*, vol. 18, 1890-1894 (read Apr. 13, 1891), pp. 88-96 (says he flourished in the eighth century C.E., since he refers to and quotes Dharmakīrti as a classical authority)

"Bhartṛihari and Kumārila," by K. B. Pathak, *Journal of the Bombay Branch of the Royal Asiatic Society*, vol. 18, 1890-1894 (read June 28, 1892), pp. 213-238 (this continues the article listed immediately above, giving more evidence for the eighth century C.E.)

"Can We Fix the Date of Śaṃkarāchārya More Accurately?," by D. R. Bhandarkar, *Indian Antiquary*, vol. 41, 1912, p. 200 (supports the latter part of the eighth century C.E.)

"The Date of Śankarāchārya," by S. V. Venkatesvaran, *Indian Antiquary*, vol. 43, 1914, p. 238 (proposes the earlier half of the ninth century C.E., around 825 C.E.)

"The Date of Sankaracharya," by S. V. Venkateswara, *Journal of the Royal Asiatic Society*, 1916, pp. 151-162 (utilizing astronomical and other evidence, gives 805-897 C.E.)

"The Date of Sarvajñātma and Śaṅkarāchārya," by A. Balakrishna Pillai, *Indian Antiquary*, vol. 50, 1921, pp. 136-137 (proposes the middle of the ninth century C.E.)

"The Date of Sankara," in *Sankaracharya the Great and His Successors in Kanchi*, by N. Venkata Raman, Madras: Ganesh & Co., 1923, pp. 17-22 (after reviewing the chronologies of the various *maṭhas* in the preceding pages, suggests the latter half of the first century C.E.)

"The Probable Date of Śaṃkara," by B. V. Kamesvar Iyer, *Proceedings and Transactions of the Fourth Oriental Conference*, Allahabad, 1926, Summaries of Papers, pp. 38-40 (seems to favor circa 600 C.E.)

"Śaṅkara: His Life and Times," in *Shree Gopal Basu Mallik Lectures on Vedānta Philosophy*, by S. K. Belvalkar, Poona: Bilvakuñja Publishing House, 1929, pp. 209-215 (gives evidence in support of 788-820 C.E.)

"The Date of Śrī Śaṅkarācārya and Some of His Predecessors," by T. R. Chintamani, *Journal of Oriental Research*, Madras, vol. 3, 1929, pp. 39-56 (proposes 655-687 C.E.)

"The Date of Śaṅkarācārya," by Vidhusekhara Bhattacharya, *Indian Historical Quarterly*, vol. 6, 1930, p. 169 (says he cannot be earlier than the fifth century C.E., because he quotes Digṅāga)

"A Note on the Date of Samkara," by S. Srikantha Sastri, *Quarterly Journal of the Mythic Society*, Bangalore, n.s., vol. 20, 1930, pp. 313-316 (gives the latter half of the sixth and former half of the seventh century C.E., i.e., between 568 and 640 C.E.)

"Śaṅkarācārya and Dharmakīrtti," by Vidhushekhara Bhattacharya, *Indian Historical Quarterly*, vol. 9, 1933, pp. 979-980 (says he cannot be earlier than circa 635-650 C.E., because he quotes Dharmakīrti)

"The Age of Śaṃkara," by S. Srikanta Sastri, *Proceedings and Transactions of the Eighth All-India Oriental Conference*, 1935, pp. 563-572 (gives 625 C.E.)

"A Note on the Date of Śaṅkara," by K. A. Nilakantha Sastri, *Journal of Oriental Research*, Madras, vol. 11, 1937, pp. 285-286 (calls attention to a Cambodian inscription from between 878 and 887 C.E. by Śivasoma, who describes himself as a pupil of Śaṅkara)

"Śrī Śaṃkara in Cambodia?" by S. Srikantha Sastri, *Indian Historical Quarterly*, vol. 18, 1942, pp. 175-179 (says the Cambodian reference cannot be to Ādi Śaṅkara, who lived towards the close of the sixth and beginning of the seventh century C.E.)

"The Date of Ādya Śamkarācārya (The 1st Century A.D.)," by V. B. Athavale, *Poona Orientalist*, vol. 19, 1954, pp. 35-39 (gives first century C.E.)

"Date of Sri Samkaracarya," by S. Srikantaya, *Quarterly Journal of the Mythic Society*, vol. 46, 1956, pp. 300-305 (accepts 789-820 C.E.)

"On the Date of Śaṃkarācārya and Allied Problems," by K. Kunjunni Raja, *Adyar Library Bulletin*, vol. 24, 1960, pp. 125-148 (says his works must have been composed towards the close of the eighth century C.E.)

"The Pīṭhas and the Date of Śankara," by P. Sastri, *Indian Historical Quarterly*, vol. 39, 1963, pp. 160-184 (this is not a study of the lineage lists of the various *pīṭhas*, as the title might imply; based on other evidence, it places him in the fourth century C.E., apparently favoring a birth date of 333 C.E.)

"Date of Life of Śaṅkara," by S. Radhakrishnan, *Sringeri Souvenir*, Madras, 1965, pp. 38-39 (cites opinions of other scholars, but does not give his own here; elsewhere he apparently accepts 788-820 C.E.)

"Age of Śamkara and the Social Conditions of the Times," by O. Ramachandraiya, *Sringeri Souvenir*, Srirangam, 1970, pp. 22-24 (accepts 788-820 C.E.)

"The Dates of Maṇḍana Miśra and Śaṃkara," by Allen Wright Thrasher, *Wiener Zeitschrift für die Kunde Südasiens*, vol. 23, 1979, pp. 117-139 (assigns him to 700 C.E. or slightly before)

"Date of Sankara," by V. G. Ramachandran, *The Voice of Śaṅkara*, Madras, vol. 6, 1981, pp. 77-88 (cites evidence in support of his birth date as 509 B.C.E.)

Shankara's Date, by R. M. Umesh, Madras: R. M. Umesh, [1981], iv + 301 pp. (gives seventh century C.E.)

"Historicity of Sankaracharya in the Light of Kerala Traditions and Tamil Epigraphic Records," by Swami Sakhyananda, in *Studies in Religion and Change*, ed. Madhu Sen, New Delhi: Books & Books, 1983, pp. 73-78 (accepts 508 B.C.E. for the birth of Ādi Śaṅkarācārya, and gives 805 C.E. for the birth of a later Śaṅkarācārya at Kaladi in Kerala, different from Abhinava Śaṅkarācārya who lived 788-840 C.E.)

"On the Date of Maṇḍana Miśra and Śaṅkara and Their Doctrinal Relation," by Fernando Tola, *Annals of the Bhandarkar Oriental Research Institute*, vol. 70, 1989, pp. 37-46 (holds that it is not possible to place Śaṅkara more precisely than between the middle of the seventh and the end of the eighth centuries C.E.)

"On the Dates of Śaṃkara and Maṇḍana," by K. Kunjunni Raja, *Adyar Library Bulletin*, vol. 55, 1991, pp. 104-116 (supports circa 750-800 C.E.)

"Date of Śrī Śaṅkara," in *Śrī Śaṅkara: His Life, Philosophy and Relevance to Man in Modern Times*, by S. Sankaranarayanan, Adyar, Madras: The Adyar Library and Research Centre, 1995, Appendix I, pp. 269-287 (while not fixing a definite date, proposes that he lived much earlier than the seventh-eighth centuries C.E.)

"Date of Śrī Śaṅkara—A New Perspective," by S. Sankaranarayanan, *Adyar Library Bulletin*, vol. 59, 1995, pp. 132-176 (offers a working hypothesis that he might have flourished earlier than 500 C.E.)

"A Note on Śaṃkara's Date," by K. Kunjunni Raja, *Adyar Library Bulletin*, vol. 59, 1995, p. 177 (briefly counters Sankaranarayanan's article, listed immediately above)

See also note 14 below for six more listings.

13. K. B. Pathak, "The Date of Śamkarāchārya," *Indian Antiquary*, vol. 11, 1882, pp. 174-175. The birth date of 788 C.E. had been given earlier by C. P. Tiele in his book, *Outlines of the History of Religion, to the Spread of the Universal Religions*, London: Trübner & Co., 1877, p. 140. Although not stated, this apparently was taken from Albrecht Weber's *Indische Studien*, vol. 14, Leipzig: F. A. Brockhaus, 1876, p. 353. Weber had cited this date from "Āryavidyāsudhānidhi, p. 226." This, in fact titled *Āryavidyāsudhākaraḥ*, is a modern book in Sanskrit written in 1866 by Yajñeśvara Cimaṇa Bhaṭṭa, Bombay: Gaṇpat Kṛṣṇaji's Press, 1868. The relevant passage from this now rare book is quoted and translated by Paul Deussen in his *Das System des Vedānta*, Leipzig: F. A. Brockhaus, 1883, pp. 37-38 fn.; this book translated into English by Charles Johnston as *The System of the Vedānta*, Chicago: Open Court Publishing Company, 1912, pp. 35-36 fn.

14. The books proposing 509 B.C.E. as Śaṅkara's date of birth that were primarily used in this article are:

Narayana Sastry, T. S., *The Age of Śankara*, 2nd enlarged edition, edited by T. N. Kumaraswamy, Madras: B. G. Paul & Co., 1971 (1st ed., Madras: 1916, with the spelling Sastri). This is the only biography to use Citsukhācārya's *Bṛhat Śaṅkara-vijaya*, which is the only traditional biography that is a firsthand account, that gives dates, and that is not embellished with myth. Sastry's book was to have additional parts, but these were never published due to the death of the author.

Kuppūswāmī, A., *Śrī Bhagavatpāda Śaṅkarācārya*, Chowkhamba Sanskrit Studies vol. 89, Varanasi: Chowkhamba Sanskrit Series Office, 1972. This biography utilizes all available sources, and cites them all when their views on various aspects of Śaṅkara's life differ.

Udayavir Shastri, *The Age of Shankara*, translated into English by Lakshmi Datta Dikshit, Gaziabad: Virjanand Vedic Research Institute, 1981 (originally written in Hindi, apparently in 1968, and though not stated, this is presumably part of *Vedāntadarśana kā Itihāsa*, published circa 1970). This book includes all the available lineage lists of the Śaṅkarācāryas of the various *maṭhas*. I have used it primarily for this.

Other books proposing 509 B.C.E. as Śaṅkara's date of birth that were consulted are:

Nataraja Aiyer, A., and Lakshminarasimha Sastri, S., *The Traditional Age of Sri Sankaracharya and the Maths*, Madras: Thompson & Co., 1962.

Ramachandran, V. G., *Date of Adi Sankara*, Madras: International Society for the Investigation of Ancient Civilizations, 1985.

S. D. Kulkarni, ed., *Adi Sankara: The Saviour of Mankind*, Bombay:

Shri Bhagavan Vedavyasa Itihasa Samshodhana Mandira (Bhishma), 1987, Part II, "Date of Śaṅkara," pp. 275-294.

15. The lineage list of the Kālikā *maṭha* (Śāradā *pīṭha*) at Dwaraka is given by Udayavir Shastri, op. cit., pp. 33-35. Its date 2631 has sometimes been wrongly taken as being of the Kali Yuga era. See on this: Udayavir Shastri, pp. 36-38; see also: Narayana Sastry, op. cit., p. 236. The list itself, however, specifies the Yudhiṣṭhira era, which began in 3139 or 3140 B.C.E., 37 or 38 years before the Kali Yuga began in 3102 B.C.E. There is a possible one year difference in converting an Indian date to a B.C.E. date, depending on whether the Indian era it is given in is counted in current or in elapsed years (normally the latter), and also depending on whether that era starts at some point within the corresponding B.C.E. year, such as in July.

16. The lineage list of the Śāradā *maṭha* (Kāmakoṭi *pīṭha*) at Kanchi is given by Udayavir Shastri, op. cit., pp. 38-40; and by Narayana Sastry, op. cit., pp. 194-197. The Kali Yuga era began Feb. 18, 3102 B.C.E.

17. The lineage list of the Govardhana *maṭha* at Puri is given by Udayavir Shastri, op. cit., pp. 41-43. The numbers of successors of the various *maṭhas* cited here are as of the date this book was originally written (in Hindi), 1968.

18. See on this: Udayavir Shastri, op. cit., pp. 40-41, 43; see also: Cenkner, William, *A Tradition of Teachers: Śaṅkara and the Jagadgurus Today*, Delhi: Motilal Banarsidass, 1983; reprint 1995, pp. 125, 157.

19. On the break in lineage of the Jyotir *maṭha* near Badrinath, see: Udayavir Shastri, op. cit., pp. 45-46; Cenkner, op. cit., pp. 111, 126. Its partial lineage list, from 1443 or 1497 C.E. to 1776, is given by Udayavir Shastri, op. cit., pp. 44-45.

20. The lineage list of the Śṛṅgerī *maṭha* (Śāradā *pīṭha*) at Sringeri is given by Udayavir Shastri, op. cit, pp. 59-60; and by Narayana Sastry, op. cit., pp. 200-201. An attempt to explain how the date 3058 of the Kali Yuga era, corresponding to 44 B.C.E., arose as a confusion of the real date is made by Narayana Sastry, pp. 208-212, 235-237.

21. The reign of 785 years is according to the lineage list given by Narayana Sastry (see note 20); Udayavir Shastri, op. cit., pp. 61-62, gives this reign as 725 years. The Śṛṅgerī *maṭha* lineage list published in *Mysore and Coorg: A Gazetteer Compiled for the Government of India*, by Lewis Rice, vol. I, Bangalore: Mysore Government Press, 1877, p. 380, seems to have given this reign as 800 years, as may be deduced from Rice's footnote. The Śṛṅgerī *maṭha* lineage list published by S. E. Gopalacharlu in *The Theosophist*, vol. 14, 1893, p. 255, also gives this reign as 800 years. A lineage list having 56 successors with their dates,

filling in the gap of 700 plus years, was "procured from the records of Śṛingerī" by Janārdan Sakhārām Gāḍgil and published in "A Note on the Age of Madhusūdana Sarasvatī," by Kāshināth Trimbak Telang, *Journal of the Bombay Branch of the Royal Asiatic Society*, vol. 10, no. 30, 1874, pp. 368-377. The same list was also published in "Gurus of the Sringeri Math," by A. Siva Row, *The Theosophist*, vol. 14, no. 7, April 1893, pp. 446-448. However, this is actually the lineage list of the Kudalī *maṭha*, and not of the Śṛṅgerī *maṭha*, with which it is affiliated. Compare the lineage list of the Kudalī *maṭha* given by Udayavir Shastri, op. cit., pp. 62-63. Still, there is some possibility that this list does preserve the Śṛṅgerī lineage for this 700 plus year period, since the history of these two *maṭhas* as distinct from each other during that time is obscure. Extracts from a *Guru-paramparā-stotra*, apparently of the Kudalī *maṭha*, were published in *Reports on Sanskrit Manuscripts in Southern India*, by E. Hultzsch, no. III, Madras: Government Press, 1905, as no. 2146i, on pp. 133-135. This lineage hymn is noteworthy for saying that Śaṅkara died at Kanchi. See note 36 below.

22. See on this: Kuppūswāmī, op. cit., p. 22. See also, for example: *The Greatness of Sringeri*, Bombay: Tattvaloka, 1991, pp. 4, 38, giving the date of Śaṅkara's birth as 788 C.E. The Śṛṅgerī lineage list published therein, p. 123, incorporates the dates 788-820 C.E. for Śaṅkarācārya, as does the lineage list published in the *Sringeri Souvenir*, Madras, 1965, pp. 96-97. The Śaṅkarācārya of Śṛṅgerī said in a 1989 interview, "It can be accepted that Śaṅkara was born twelve or so centuries ago." This statement is found in: Bader, Jonathan, *Conquest of the Four Quarters: Traditional Accounts of the Life of Śaṅkara*, New Delhi: Aditya Prakashan, 2000, p. 334; see also p. 19, fn. 6.

23. The most widely known Sanskrit biography of Śaṅkara is that by Mādhava, now popularly called the *Śaṅkara-dig-vijaya*. It gives some horoscope data, but no year. The next most widely known biography of Śaṅkara is the *Śaṅkara-vijaya* commonly attributed to Ānandagiri, but actually by Anantānandagiri. It gives no information on the time of his birth. Narayana Sastry, op. cit., pp. 32-33, lists ten Śaṅkara-vijayas, or biographies, that he collected, and gives the data relating to Śaṅkara's birth from all of them. The data from the seven which do not give Śaṅkara's date is found on pp. 237-263. Kuppūswāmī, op. cit., pp. 9-15, lists eleven biographies, including four not used by Narayana Sastry. These four do not give Śaṅkara's date either. Bader, *Conquest of the Four Quarters*, p. 24, lists eight biographies, including two not used by Narayana Sastry. These two likewise do not give his date. Current bibliographical information on these eight is given on pp. 357-358.

24. On Citsukhācārya and his *Bṛhat Śaṅkara-vijaya*, see: Narayana Sastry, op. cit., pp. 39-40 fn., 224-226 fn. On pp. 271-282 is given from it in Sanskrit and English the whole chapter on Śaṅkara's birth. Narayana Sastry then concludes: "Such is the simple account of the birth of Sankara as narrated by Chitsukhacharya in his biography of Sri Sankaracharya known as Brihat Sankara Vijaya. The life history of the Great Guru as depicted by him is throughout natural and unexaggerated, and clearly bears the unmistakable impress of an eye-witness and a contemporary writer. Chitsukha has, indeed, the highest regard for Sankara, . . . and yet he dealt with him only as a man. . . . He certainly does not go to the length of deifying him and his disciples and contemporaries as various incarnations of gods, nor does he colour his life with supernatural incidents and divine interferences, with which later Sankara Vijayas, including that of Anandagiri, are replete. . . .

"The incidents of the Gods including Brahmadeva going to Mount Kailasa and praying to God Sadasiva for giving a quietus to the warring faiths and creeds in Bharata varsha, His solemn promise to the Gods that He would be born as Sri Sankaracharya on the earth to put down the wicked creeds and teachings prevalent among men, His graceful presence before the pious couple, Aryamba and Sivaguru, asking them to choose between one short-lived omniscient son and one hundred long-lived idiots and His appearance before Aryamba at the time of his birth in the form of the Great God Siva Himself, with four hands, three eyes and a head wearing the crescent of the Moon as the diadem of His Crown are all later additions, of which incidents there is absolutely no reference in the great work of Chitsukhacharya" (pp. 281-283).

25. Narayana Sastry, op. cit., p. 40 fn. Brahmībhāva means identity with Brahman (Narayana Sastry, p. 180). The original Sanskrit of this or a similar sentence is quoted in the *Suṣumā* commentary on the *Guru-ratna-mālikā* of Sadāśiva Brahmendra, and given by W. R. Antarkar in his article, "Bṛhat-Śaṅkara-Vijaya of Citsukhācārya and Prācīna-Śaṅkara-Vijaya of Ānandagiri a/s Ānanda-jñāna," *Journal of the University of Bombay*, vol. 29 (n.s.), 1960, p. 114 fn. On p. 115, Antarkar says: "It is also worth noting that Citsukha's version of Śaṅkara's life as given by Mr. Śāstrī [Narayana Sastry], which differs from the versions of the same in all the other biographies in Sanskrit, eminently agrees with the one as culled from the quotations from Br[hat]. Ś[aṅkara]. V[ijaya]. in Suṣumā." *Suṣumā* was published in *Vedāntapañcaprakaraṇī*, Sadāśivendra Sarasvatī, Kumbhakonam: Śrī Vidyā Press, 1813 [1891].

26. Narayana Sastry, op. cit., p. 40 fn.

27. *The Age of Śankara*; see note 14. The manuscript of the *Bṛhat Śaṅkara-vijaya* used by Narayana Sastry seems to have disappeared when he died in 1918 at age 48. His son writes in the preface to the 2nd ed. of *The Age of Śankara*, "Death overtook him at the prime of life and prevented him from fulfilling his intentions. The manuscripts containing valuable matter were lost, leaving no trace behind." This refers to manuscripts of the promised remaining parts of *The Age of Śankara*, as well as to the Sanskrit manuscripts he used. Bader, *Conquest of the Four Quarters*, p. 347 fn., reports that: "W. R. Antarkar has informed me that he met the author's son but was unable to trace this sole MS. of the work." Antarkar, in his article cited in note 25 above, says that the *Bṛhat Śaṅkara-vijaya*, as well as the *Prācīna Śaṅkara-vijaya*, "did not become available to me even after an intensive search for them throughout India" (p. 113). Still, after giving other evidence, he closes this article as follows: "It, therefore, can be concluded that there did exist till recently two such works as Br. Ś.V. [*Bṛhat Śaṅkara-vijaya*] of Citsukhācārya and Pr. Ś.V. [*Prācīna Śaṅkara-vijaya*] of Ānandajñāna a/s Ānandagiri though none of them is available to us today and that they are not mere names, as believed by some" (p. 129).

28. Narayana Sastry, op. cit., pp. 273, 278, verses 12-13. This is from his book, *Successors of Śaṅkarāchārya*, 1916, reprinted in the 2nd ed. of *The Age of Śankara* as appendix III, pp. 193-288.

29. On the *Prācīna Śaṅkara-vijaya* by Ānandagiri, not to be confused with the published *Śaṅkara-vijaya* attributed to Ānandagiri but actually by Anantānandagiri, see: Narayana Sastry, op. cit., pp. 227-228 fn. On pp. 264-270 the data from it on Śaṅkara's birth is given. More than 800 verses from this otherwise lost *Prācīna Śaṅkara-vijaya* are quoted in the commentary by Dhanapatisūri on the *Śankara-dig-vijaya* of Mādhava. These have all been conveniently collected in an appendix to the *Śrī Śaṅkaravijaya of Anantānandagiri*, edited by N. Veezhinathan, Madras: University of Madras, 1971.

On the *Vyāsācalīya Śaṅkara-vijaya*, a *Śaṅkaravijaya* by Vyāsācala was published in 1954, edited by T. Chandrasekharan, in the Madras Government Oriental Manuscripts Series, no. 24; but again, as with other extant Śaṅkara-vijayas, the date references were no longer to be found in the six manuscripts this edition was based on. Narayana Sastry, too, at first had only such a manuscript to work from. In his comments on this book, op. cit., pp. 228-229 fn., he writes: "I had only an imperfect copy of this valuable Sankara Vijaya of Vyasachala, but thanks to the Kumbhakonam Mutt, I have recently secured a complete copy of the said book, . . ." From it, he cites nine verses in Sanskrit giving the place and date of Śaṅkara's death, with English translation, pp. 228-235, and two verses on Śaṅkara's birth, pp. 245-249. The first of these two verses gives the year, month, and day; while the second adds astrological data, being the very same verse as that found in the popular *Śaṅkara-vijaya* by Mādhava. See notes 23 above and 36 below. Thus when Mādhava adopted verses from Vyāsācala, he left out the verse giving Śaṅkara's date, and kept only the verse giving astrological data, from which no date could be deduced.

30. See: Narayana Sastry, op. cit., pp. 217-221. On pp. 220-221 fn. is given the full Sanskrit text of this inscription. See also pp. 33, 153 ff. This copper plate inscription was first published by Śrī Rājarājeśvara Śaṅkarāśrama, the Śaṅkarācārya of the *maṭha* at Dwaraka from 1878 to 1900, in his Sanskrit book, *Vimarśa*, Varanasi: Rājarājeśvarīyantrālaya, Vikrama Saṃvat 1955 [1898 C.E.], p. 29 (not seen by me). This copper plate was said to be in the possession of the *maṭha* at Dwaraka until about 1903-1904, at which time it was turned over to a court of law, and never received back. For much information on it, its text from the *Vimarśa*, and also a critique of its authenticity, see: "The Sudhanvan Copper-plate—A Dispassionate Reappraisal," by V. Venkatachalam, in *Śrī Sureśvarācārya Adhiṣṭhāna Jīrnoddhāraṇa Kumbhābhiṣekam: Sringeri. Souvenir*, May 10, 1970, pp. 86-110. On King Sudhanvan, independent information is found in a Jaina source, the *Jina-vijaya*. See Narayana Sastry, op. cit., pp. 149 fn., 152-153 fn., quoting this from the Sanskrit journal, *Saṃskṛta-Chandrikā* (Kolhapur), vol. 9, p. 6.

The *Jina-vijaya*, a biographical poem on the life of Mahāvīra, also provides independent evidence taken to support the date of 509 B.C.E. for Śaṅkara. The date 2157 of the Yudhiṣṭhira era is given in it for Śaṅkara, understood by Narayana Sastry to mean for his death. The verses from the *Jina-vijaya* pertaining to this are cited by Narayana Sastry, op. cit., pp. 149-153 fn., 232-234 fn. According to Narayana Sastry, the Yudhiṣṭhira era used by Jainas and Buddhists and other non-Hindus is different than that used by Hindus. This Yudhiṣṭhira era began 468 years after the Kali Yuga era began, or in 2634 B.C.E.; see on this: pp. 22, 149 fn., 235. Using this era, the date 2157 given in the *Jina-vijaya* corresponds to 477 B.C.E., the date of Śaṅkara's death. Kuppūswāmī, op. cit., pp. 30-31, also cites this same *Jina-vijaya* verse on the date of Śaṅkara, again taking it for that of his death, though wrongly stating that the era starting in 2634 B.C.E. is the Jina Era. We must note, however, that the nine verses from the *Jina-vijaya* cited by Gadgil in *The Theosophist* (see note 11 above), of which this is the first, present this date 2157 as that of his birth, and later give the date 2189 as that of his death. These nine verses were cited from the book, *Bhāratavarshīya Arvāchīna Kosha,* by Raghunāth Bhāskar Godbole of Poona. Further, these verses confuse some of the details of Ādi Śaṅkarācārya's life with those of Abhinava Śaṅkarācārya, as do the various Śaṅkara-vijayas, even though the *Jina-vijaya* distinguishes these two Śaṅkarācāryas, while the Śaṅkara-vijayas do not. See notes 35 and 36 below. The information from the yet unpublished *Jina-vijaya,* when sorted out, will provide valuable independent evidence on the date of Śaṅkara.

The *Jina-vijaya* is, moreover, not a sympathetic source; as it was the Jainas, not the Buddhists, who were in conflict with Hinduism in Śaṅkara's time. Popular accounts say repeatedly that Śaṅkara came to destroy Buddhism and restore Hinduism. But according to Narayana Sastry, who had access to the genuine biographies of Śaṅkara, this is not the case. The famous Hindu teacher Kumārila Bhaṭṭa, who was on his deathbed when Śaṅkara met him, had been a strong opponent of the Jainas. Later biographies confused the Jainas with the Buddhists, and attributed to Śaṅkara an opposition toward them like that shown by Kumārila. Narayana Sastry, pp. 148-149 fn., writes: "One thing is quite clear from a careful perusal of these various Śaṅkara Vijayas, that the later biographers have invariably confounded the Jainas with the Bauddhas, by considering them for all practical purposes as one sect. . . . But Chitsukha distinctly says that Kumārila's opponents were Mahāvīra and his followers called the Jainas, and that he directed his energies against the Jains alone who under their founder Mahāvīra Vardhamāna, began to undermine the Vedic Brāhmanism in his day." Narayana Sastry cites 28 verses in Sanskrit from Citsukhācārya's *Bṛhat Śaṅkara-vijaya* showing this, pp. 146-148 fn. The research of W. R. Antarkar adds to this, saying about these 28 verses of Citsukhācārya: "Sadānanda and Cidvilāsa repeat, in the same context, many of these stanzas almost verbatim, of course omitting many and making small but very important changes in those they have adopted. The most important alteration is that the Jainas and Vardhamāna Mahāvīra in Citsukha's version have been replaced in both by Bauddhas and a Bauddha Guru" (from his article, "Bṛhat-Śaṅkara-Vijaya . . . ," p. 116; see note 25 above).

31. Nakamura, Hajime, *A History of Early Vedānta Philosophy,* Part One, Delhi: Motilal Banarsidass, 1983, pp. 48-88.

32. Nakamura, *History of Early Vedānta Philosophy,* pp. 87, 48.

33. Narayana Sastry, op. cit., pp. viii, 12, 119 fn., 137, 145 fn., gives

the date of the Buddha as 1862 to 1782 B.C., based on the Purāṇas and Itihāsas. This calculation was to be given in his Appendix B, but this was never published. Udayavir Shastri, op. cit., pp. 137, 139, 158, 162, gives the date of the Buddha as "about 1800 B.C.," based on the *Rāja-taraṅgiṇī* of Kalhaṇa. While the Wisdom Tradition teaches that there were previous Buddhas, and therefore that Buddhism existed before Gautama Buddha, for this Buddha it supports the traditional date of his death given in Ceylon chronology as 543 B.C.E. It adds, however, that he lived for a little more than twenty years after his *nirvāṇa*, thus placing his birth in 643 B.C.E. See: "Sakya Muni's Place in History," *Blavatsky Collected Writings*, vol. 5, pp. 241-259. These dates are said to be correct according to *bārhaspatya-māna* reckoning, from which we may deduce that they actually correspond with 637 to 537 B.C.E. See: "Inscriptions Discovered by General A. Cunningham," by T. Subba Row, *Blavatsky Collected Writings*, vol. 5, pp. 259-262.

34. The fact that half a verse from Dignāga's *Ālambana-parīkṣā* is quoted in Śaṅkara's commentary on *Brahma-sūtra* 2.2.28 was first noted by Durga Charan Chatterjee, and published in a brief article by his teacher Vidhusekhara Bhattacharya, "The Date of Śaṅkarācārya," *Indian Historical Quarterly*, vol. 6, 1930, p. 169. On the material from Dharmakīrti that Śaṅkara refers to, also in his commentary on *Brahma-sūtra* 2.2.28, see: Vidhushekhara Bhattacharya, "Śaṅkarācārya and Dharmakīrtti," *Indian Historical Quarterly*, vol. 9, 1933, pp. 979-980. Earlier, S. V. Venkateswara in his article, "The Date of Sankaracharya," *Journal of the Royal Asiatic Society*, 1916, p. 154, had pointed out that: "Sureśvarāchārya, a disciple of Śaṇkara's, has written a *vārṭika* to the latter's poem *Upadeśa Sāhasri*. In the *vārṭika*, Sureśvara remarks that the Āchārya has borrowed a verse from Kīrti (*kīrter idaṃ*). This Kīrti could be no other than Dharma Kīrti who, as we know, flourished in the seventh century." Apparently unknown to Venkateswara, already in 1891 K. B. Pathak had shown that it is Dharmakīrti who Śaṅkara refutes in his commentary on the *Bṛhad-āraṇyaka Upaniṣad*, and from whom he borrows a verse in his *Upadeśa-sāhasrī*. Pathak in his paper, "Dharmakīrti and Śaṃkarāchārya," *Journal of the Bombay Branch of the Royal Asiatic Society*, vol. 18, 1890-1894 (read Apr. 13, 1891), pp. 88-96, writes: "This inference is confirmed by a long and interesting passage which I have discovered in the Bṛhadāraṇyakavārtika and in which Sureśvarāchārya, the disciple and contemporary of Śaṃkarāchārya, actually names and attacks Dharmakīrti" (p. 90). After citing this whole passage in Sanskrit and translating it, Pathak goes on to show that Śaṅkara quotes a verse from Dharmakīrti in his *Upadeśa-sāhasrī*.

The date of Dignāga is given as circa 480-540 C.E. by Erich Frauwallner in "Landmarks in the History of Indian Logic," *Wiener Zeitschrift für die Kunde Süd- und Ostasiens*, vol. 5, 1961, pp. 134-137. Masaaki Hattori had independently arrived at 470-530 C.E. See his: *Dignāga, On Perception*, Cambridge, Mass.: Harvard University Press, 1968, pp. 4-6. The date of Dharmakīrti is given as circa 600-660 C.E. by Frauwallner, pp. 137-139. This has been modified to 530-600 C.E. by Chr. Lindtner. See his two articles: "Apropos Dharmakīrti—Two New Works and a New Date," *Acta Orientalia*, vol. 41, 1980, pp. 27-37; and "On the Date of Dharmakīrti Etc.," *Adyar Library Bulletin*, vol. 56, 1992, pp. 56-62. These dates for Dignāga and Dharmakīrti are supported by traditional Buddhist sources in so far as the latter place the brothers Asaṅga and Vasubandhu 900 years after the death of the Buddha, and say that Dignāga was a pupil of Vasubandhu, and that Dharmakīrti was a pupil of a pupil of Dignāga. See: *History of Buddhism (Chos-ḥbyung) by Bu-ston*, trans. E. Obermiller, 2 vols., Heidelberg, 1931, 1932; and *Tāranātha's History of Buddhism in India*, trans. Lama Chimpa and Alaka Chattopadhyaya, Calcutta: K. P. Bagchi & Company, 1970.

35. On Abhinava Śaṅkara, see: Narayana Sastry, op. cit., pp. ix, 31, 33, 109, 199, 237, 244-245; Kuppūswāmī, op. cit., pp. 33-35. Udayavir Shastri, op. cit., pp. 56-58, believes that 788 C.E. is the date of Abhinava Śaṅkara's installation as Śaṅkarācārya of the *maṭha* at Kanchi rather than the date of his birth. Abhinava Śaṅkara is also distinguished from Ādi Śaṅkara in the *Jina-vijaya*. See on this: J. S. Gadgil, *The Theosophist*, 1895, article listed in note 11 above.

36. The widely known Śaṅkara-vijaya by Mādhava (often confused with Mādhava Vidyāraṇya), accepted by the *maṭha* at Sringeri as the most authoritative Śaṅkara biography, states that Śaṅkara was born at the town of Kalati in Kerala state, his father was Śivaguru and his mother was Āryāmbā, and he died at Kedarnath in the Himalayas. The other widely known Śaṅkara-vijaya, written by Anantānandagiri (often confused with Ānandagiri), accepted by the *maṭha* at Kanchi as the most authoritative Śaṅkara biography, states that Śaṅkara was born at the town of Chidambaram in Tamil Nadu state, his father was Viśvajit and his mother was Viśiṣṭā, and he died at Kanchi in Tamil Nadu. A new edition of this biography came out in 1971 (see note 29 above) that adopted different readings than those of the earlier two editions, in agreement with seven of the sixteen manuscripts used, giving his birthplace as Kalati (Kālaḍi) and his father as Śivaguru. This is as given in the biography by Mādhava. It retained, however, Śaṅkara's place of death as Kanchi, in agreement with all the manuscripts.

Comparison with the several other Śaṅkara biographies provides an overwhelming preponderance of evidence that Śaṅkara was born at Kalati, his parents were Śivaguru and Āryāmbā, and his place of death was Kanchi. This would be Ādi Śaṅkara. Abhinava Śaṅkara, then, was born at Chidambaram, his parents were Viśvajit and Viśiṣṭā, and he died at Kedarnath. The confusion of these basic facts in the two major biographies does not inspire confidence in whatever other statements they may make.

Subba Row in his article on Śaṅkarācārya's date had pointed out the unreliability of the Śaṅkara-vijaya attributed to Ānandagiri (but actually by Anantānandagiri). However, he goes on to say that the one by Vidyāraṇya or Sāyaṇācārya (our Mādhava, above) is "decidedly the most reliable source of information as regards the main features of Sankara's biography" (*Blavatsky Collected Writings*, vol. 5, p. 192). This view was no doubt due to his connections with the *maṭha* at Sringeri, as this is the biography that they regard as authoritative. He says that "its authorship has been universally accepted," referring to the fact that Vidyāraṇya or Sāyaṇācārya was a great commentator on the Vedas and a famous head of the *maṭha* at Sringeri. Actually, this authorship has been strongly questioned, and now proven beyond doubt to be false. The Mādhava who wrote it was not Mādhava Vidyāraṇya, as assumed by the *maṭha* at Sringeri and also by Subba Row.

The Śaṅkara-vijaya by Mādhava, as has now been shown, is a composite work, consisting mostly of verses taken directly from other Śaṅkara-vijayas. One of these, the *Śaṅkarābhyudaya* by Rājacūḍāmaṇi-Dīkṣita, was written in the 1600s C.E., as we know from the fact that this author gives the date corresponding to 1636 C.E. in another of his works. This is three centuries after Mādhava Vidyāraṇya lived. The composite nature of Mādhava's book was pointed out by Narayana Sastry, op. cit., pp. 155-167 fn., 245-253; detailed by W. R. Antarkar in his unpublished thesis, "Śaṅkara-Vijayas: A Comparative and Critical Study," University of Poona, 1960, and in his published article, "Saṅkṣepa Śaṅkara Jaya of Mādhavācārya or Śāṅkara Digvijaya of Śrī Vidyāraṇyamuni," *Journal of the University of Bombay*, vol. 41 (n.s.), 1972, pp. 1-23; and again by Bader, *Conquest of the Four Quarters*, pp. 53-62, 351-356. Mādhava's incorrect placing of Śaṅkara's death at Kedarnath in the Himalayas rather than at Kanchi in south India is apparently due to the dispute which arose in the early 1800s between followers of the *maṭhas* at Sringeri and Kanchi. The former do not think Kanchi is a legitimate *maṭha*. If Śaṅkara died at Kanchi, that fact would lend credence to its legitimacy as a *maṭha*. The evidence on his place of death from each of the many traditional sources may be found in Kuppūswāmī, op. cit., pp. 130-141. The evidence on this from several sources may also be found in "The Last Days of Śrī Śaṅkarācārya," by N. K. Venkatesan, *Journal of Oriental Research*, Madras, vol. 1, part 4, Oct. 1927, pp. 330-335.

The biography of Śaṅkara by Mādhava is the only one of these Śaṅkara-vijayas that has been translated into English. This has been translated twice: first by Swami Tapasyananda, *Sankara-Dig-Vijaya: The Traditional Life of Sri Sankaracharya*, Madras: Sri Ramakrishna Math, 1978; and then by K. Padmanaban, *Srimad Sankara Digvijayam*, 2 vols., Madras: K. Padmanaban, 1985, 1986 (includes original Sanskrit text). Both these translators also attribute this book to Mādhava Vidyāraṇya. Swami Tapasyananda in his Introduction rejects the information from Narayana Sastry's book, which is based on the biography of Śaṅkara by Citsukhācārya, since the latter is not available. He makes much of the fact that Narayana Sastry described the manuscript he had of it as a "mutilated copy." Actually, this refers to the circumstance that this copy was missing the first part, on the predecessors of Śaṅkara, and the last part, on the successor Sureśvara. See: Narayana Sastry, op. cit., pp. 40 fn., 226 fn., 271 fn. It was the middle part that gave the life of Śaṅkara, and this is the part that Narayana Sastry had. His quotations of lengthy sections from it show that the leaves he had were intact. Based on comparison of this and other Śaṅkara-vijayas with that of Mādhava, Narayana Sastry became a harsh critic of the latter.

37. See, for example: Narayana Sastry, op. cit., pp. 31, 83-85: "There are innumerable works, large and small, which go under the name of Śaṅkarāchārya, and it is really impossible at this distant period of time to determine with certainty which of them were the handworks of Ādi Śaṅkarāchārya, and which were written by his successors. But it is really fortunate that all scholars should uniformly agree in ascribing the Bhāshyas on the Prasthāna-Traya to the First Śaṅkarāchārya . . . ." "Whole hosts of commentators have commented upon the Brahma Sūtras but they all want the boldness, depth, originality and simplicity of Śaṅkara. In fact Śaṅkara's Bhāshya is not only the most important, but also the oldest of the commentaries extant on the Brahma Sūtras. As a piece of philosophical argumentation, it occupies the highest rank among the numerous commentaries on the Vedānta Sūtras."

As for Western scholars, see, for example, Paul Deussen's *The System of the Vedanta* (trans. by Charles Johnston from German), p. 37: "His master-piece is the Commentary on the Brahmasūtra's, . . . which gives a substantially complete and sufficient picture of his system, and from which alone we draw our exposition of it, in order in this way to form a safe standard by which the genuineness of the other works attributed to Śaṅkara, the minor writings, as well as the Commentaries to the Upanishad's, may subsequently be tested."

38. *The Secret Doctrine*, vol. 1, p. 271.

39. This article is: "Dhritarāshtra," by Purmeshri Dass and Dhanraj, *The Theosophist*, vol. 18, Sep. 1897, pp. 749-750.

40. See: "Genuineness of Commentaries," by Purmeshri Dass and Dhauaraj, *The Theosophist*, vol. 19, Nov. 1897, pp. 110-111.

41. See: "The Mystery of Buddha," by H. P. Blavatsky, *H. P. Blavatsky Collected Writings*, vol. 14, Wheaton, Illinois: Theosophical Publishing House, 1985, pp. 388-399. See also note 65 below.

42. *The Vedānta Sūtras of Bādarāyaṇa, with the Commentary by Śaṅkara*, translated by George Thibaut, Part I, Oxford: Clarendon Press, 1890, Sacred Books of the East vol. 34, pp. 427-428; from the commentary on verse 2.2.32. It has been reprinted several times. I quote from this translation, as it is the most widely available. Another good translation of this book is: *Brahma-Sūtra-Bhāṣya of Śrī Śaṅkarācārya*, translated by Swami Gambhirananda, Calcutta: Advaita Ashrama, 1965. Note that *Vedānta-sūtras* and *Brahma-sūtras* are alternate titles for the same book.

43. Paul Hacker provided the basis for this study with his article, "Eigentümlichkeiten der Lehre und Terminologie Śaṅkaras: Avidyā, Nāmarūpa, Māyā, Īśvara," *Zeitschrift der Deutschen Morgenländischen Gesellschaft*, vol. 100, 1950, pp. 246-286; now translated into English as "Distinctive Features of the Doctrine and Terminology of Śaṅkara: Avidyā, Nāmarūpa, Māyā, Īśvara," in *Philology and Confrontation: Paul Hacker on Traditional and Modern Vedānta*, edited by Wilhelm Halbfass, Albany: State University of New York Press, 1995, pp. 57-100.

Sengaku Mayeda then utilized this criteria in a series of articles:

"The Authenticity of the Upadeśasāhasrī Ascribed to Saṅkara," *Journal of the American Oriental Society*, vol. 85, 1965, pp. 178-196.

"The Authenticity of the Bhagavadgītābhāṣya Ascribed to Śaṅkara," *Wiener Zeitschrift für die Kunde Süd- und Ostasiens*, vol. 9, 1965, pp. 155-197.

"On Śaṅkara's Authorship of the Kenopaniṣadbhāṣya," *Indo-Iranian Journal*, vol. 10, 1967, pp. 33-55.

"On the Author of the Māṇḍūkyopaniṣad- and the Gauḍapādīya-bhāṣya," *Adyar Library Bulletin*, vols. 31-32, 1967-68, pp. 73-94.

Daniel H. H. Ingalls rejected Śaṅkara's authorship of the *Viveka-cūḍāmaṇi* in his article, "The Study of Śaṃkarācārya," *Annals of the Bhandarkar Oriental Research Institute*, vol. 33, 1952, pp. 1-14. Since this journal is not readily available to all readers, I here quote the relevant portion in full, giving his reasons for this (p. 7):

"Thus, to come to a specific instance, it is improbable that Śaṃkara wrote the *Viveka-cūḍāmaṇi.* The improbable becomes impossible when we pass from this question of general emphasis to specific theories. The author of the *Viveka-cūḍāmaṇi* makes an absolute equation of the waking and dream states after the fashion of Gauḍapāda. Śaṃkara may liken the two to each other, but he is careful to distinguish them. Again, and most decisive of all, the *Viveka-cūḍāmaṇi* accepts the classical theory of the three truth values, the existent, the non-existent and that which is *anirvacanīya,* indescribable as being either existent or non-existent. The workaday world according to the classical theory is *anirvacanīya.*

"Now, Paul Hacker has pointed out that when Śaṃkara uses the word *anirvacanīya,* he uses it in a sense quite different from that of the classical theory. He uses the term in connection with his theory of creation. Before creation primary matter, which he calls *nāmarūpe,* was in a state of *anirvacanīyatva.* It was an indistinguishable mass—*tattvānyatvābhyām anirvacanīya,* a mass in which one could describe nothing as being a this or a that. There is no implication here as to the state of its existence."

Robert E. Gussner later confirmed Ingalls' rejection of Śaṅkara's authorship of the *Viveka-cūḍāmaṇi* by a detailed word-frequency study, comparing it with Śaṅkara's *Upadeśa-sāhasrī,* which had previously been shown to be by the same Śaṅkara who wrote the *Brahma-sūtra* commentary. This study is: "Śaṅkara's Crest Jewel of Discrimination: A Stylometric Approach to the Question of Authorship," *Journal of Indian Philosophy,* vol. 4, 1977, pp. 265-278.

Earlier, before this type of study had been started with Hacker's 1950 article, S. K. Belvalkar had rejected Śaṅkara's authorship of the *Viveka-cūḍāmaṇi* on other grounds. He writes in his *Shree Gopal Basu Mallik Lectures on Vedānta Philosophy,* (delivered December, 1925), Part 1: Lectures 1-6, Poona: Bilvakuñja Publishing House, 1929, p. 225: "A large majority of these texts can be declared as unauthentic, especially when we find them to . . . or to advocate ideas* like—'Anāder api vidhvaṃsaḥ Prāgabhāvasya vīkṣitaḥ' (where the Nyāya-Vaiśeṣika division into different kinds of Negations—against which Śaṅkara has expressed himself so emphatically in the Br[ahma]. S[ūtra]. Bhāṣya *apud* II.i.18—is tacitly assumed). *Compare Viveka-cūḍāmaṇi, st. 202." Thus there is considerable evidence that the *Viveka-cūḍāmaṇi* was not written by the same Śaṅkara who wrote the extant commentaries. For us, this is evidence that it was written by the original Śaṅkarācārya.

Belvalkar, in the lecture just cited, provided the first and still the only comprehensive evaluation of the authenticity of virtually all the works attributed to Śaṅkarācārya. Belvalkar utilized for this "a careful compilation of the data deducible from all the minor and major works attributed to Śaṅkarācārya made by my student, friend and colleague, Mr. R. D. Vadekar" (see his preface, p. v). On the basis of Aufrecht's *Catalogus Catalogorum*, the descriptive catalogues of the Government Oriental Library, Madras, and the various published editions of his collected writings, they were able to enumerate 408 works attributed to Śaṅkarācārya. Of these, Belvalkar accepted 24 as genuine, 26 as questionable, and 358 as not genuine works of Śaṅkarācārya. Among the 24 genuine ones, he included the commentaries on the *Brahma-sūtras*, on nine of the Upaniṣads, and on the *Bhagavad-gītā*, as well as eight hymns (*stotras*), and five shorter works (*prakaraṇas*). For the hymns and shorter works he used such criteria as whether there exist traditional commentaries on them.

At about this same time, Vidhusekhara Bhattacharya evaluated the authenticity of Śankara's authorship of the various commentaries on the various Upaniṣads in his paper, "Śaṅkara's Commentaries on the Upaniṣads," published in *Sir Asutosh Mookerjee Silver Jubilee Volumes*, vol. 3, Calcutta: Calcutta University, 1925, pp. 101-110. Here he rejects Śaṅkara's authorship of those on the *Kena* (*vākya-bhāṣya*), *Śvetāśvatara*, *Māṇḍūkya*, and *Nṛsiṃhapūrvatāpanīya* Upaniṣads, although he accepts Śaṅkara's authorship of the *Kena pada-bhāṣya*. On the *Kena Upaniṣad*, note that Śaṅkara's authorship of both the *pada-bhāṣya* and the *vākya-bhāṣya* are accepted by Mayeda in his 1967 article cited above. Sangam Lal Pandey agrees with Bhattacharya in accepting that of only the *Kena pada-bhāṣya* in his article, "Authentic Works of Śaṃkarācārya," *Journal of the Ganganatha Jha Research Institute*, vol. 24, 1968, pp. 161-177, but disagrees with him on Śaṅkara's authorship of the *Māṇḍūkya Upaniṣad* commentary. Pandey, like Mayeda in his 1967-68 article cited above, accepts Śaṅkara's authorship of this commentary. Most scholars , both Indian and Western, would agree with Pandey's conclusion that the genuine works of Śaṅkara are his commentaries on *Brahma-sūtras*, on the ten principal Upaniṣads, and on the *Bhagavad-gītā*, and besides these commentaries, only the *Upadeśa-sāhasrī*. This of course, from our perspective, would be the later Śaṅkarācārya.

Śaṅkara's authorship of the commentary on the *Bhagavad-gītā* attributed to him has been discussed by several Indian scholars. B. N.

Krishnamurti Sarma accepts it in his article, "Śaṃkara's Authorship of the Gītā-bhāṣya," *Annals of the Bhandarkar Oriental Research Institute*, vol. 14, 1932-33, pp. 39-60. R. D. Karmarkar rejects it in his article, "Did Śaṅkarācārya Write a Bhāṣya on the Bhagavadgītā?," in the same journal, vol. 39, 1958, pp. 365-371. W. R. Antarkar in turn accepts it in his article, "Śri Śaṅkarācārya's Authorship of the Gītā-Bhāṣya," *Oriental Thought*, vol. 6, no. 2, June 1962, pp. 1-26. At this point comes Sengaku Mayeda's 1965 article on this, cited above, which also accepts it. Then Indian scholar Anam Charan Swain, citing Hacker but not Mayeda, again doubts it in his article, "Authenticity of the *Bhagavadgītābhāṣya* Attributed to Śaṃkarācārya," *Mysore Orientalist*, vol. 2, no. 1, March 1969, pp. 32-37. Nonetheless, the great consensus of Indian scholars is to accept its authenticity; i.e., that it is by the same Śaṅkara who wrote the commentary on the *Brahma-sūtras*.

As to the shorter works attributed to Śaṅkarācārya, we may note that some of these have been shown to be wrongly attributed to him. When the *Sarva-siddhānta-saṃgraha* was first published in 1909, the editor and translator, M. Rangacharya, in his introduction defended Śaṅkara's authorship of it. This was countered by B. N. Krishnamurti Sarma in his article, "A Note on the Authorship of Sarvasiddhānta-Saṃgraha," *Annals of the Bhandarkar Oriental Research Institute*, vol. 12, 1930-31, pp. 93-96, who said it must have been written by a post-Śaṅkara Advaitin. This has been shown to be the case with at least three other works. The *Prabodha-sudhākara* attributed to Śaṅkara was shown by V. Raghavan to have actually been written by Daivajña Sūrya Paṇḍita. He showed this on the basis of manuscript colophons, etc., in his article, "The Nṛsimha Campū of Daivajña Sūrya Paṇḍita and the Nṛsimhavijñāpana of Śrī Nṛsimhāśramin," *Adyar Library Bulletin*, vol. 1, part 1, Feb. 1937, pp. 42-47 (see p. 44). Raghavan similarly showed on the basis of colophons that the *Sarva-vedānta-siddhānta-sāra-saṃgraha* attibuted to Śaṅkara was actually written by Sadānanda in his article, "Minor Works Wrongly Ascribed to Ādi Śankara," *Annals of Oriental Research*, University of Madras, vol. 6, part 1, 1941-42, pp. 5-8. Then in a note in W. Norman Brown's *The Saundaryalaharī or Flood of Beauty*, traditionally ascribed to Śaṅkarācārya (Harvard Oriental Series, 43; 1958, pp. 29-30), V. Raghavan reports a manuscript colophon saying that the author of this work is Śaṅkarācārya, head of the Sarasvatīpīṭha at Srividyānagara; in other words, a later Śaṅkarācārya.

44. "The Age of Srī Sankarāchārya," *The Theosophist*, vol. 11, Feb. 1890, pp. 263-264 (see note 10 above).

45. Of course, not all the shorter works attributed to Śaṅkarācārya

were actually written by the original Śaṅkarācārya. But there is good evidence that many were. Citsukhācārya in his *Bṛhat Śaṅkara-vijaya* not only names but also gives in full many of these. Narayana Sastry often cites their opening and closing verses from Citsukhācārya in his notes, which describe more than forty shorter works. He notes when printed editions or manuscripts of these works exist. It is clear that the extant versions match those given by Citsukhācārya. Interestingly, Narayana Sastry also notes that although Citsukhācārya names Śaṅkara's *bhāṣyas* or commentaries on the *Brahma-sūtras*, Upaniṣads, and *Bhagavad-gītā*, he does not cite them: "Excepting the Bhāshyas which are simply referred to, almost all the minor works of Śaṅkara are collected and given in his work with the occasion on which they were composed" (op. cit., p. 40 fn.). So for the commentaries we have nothing to check the extant versions against. Also noteworthy is the fact that Narayana Sastry makes no mention of the *Upadeśa-sāhasrī*, the one verse work that modern scholars agree on as being genuine, i.e., as being by the same Śaṅkara who wrote the extant commentaries. This supports our view that these works were not written by the original Śaṅkarācārya.

46. The first English translation of the *Brahma-sūtra* commentary of Śaṅkarācārya was that by George Thibaut published in the Sacred Books of the East series, vols. 34 and 38, 1890 and 1896 (see note 42). This had been preceded by a German translation in 1887, done by Paul Deussen. As for Śaṅkara's Upaniṣad commentaries, the first chapter only of that on the *Bṛhad-āraṇyaka Upaniṣad* was translated by E. Röer and published in the Bibliotheca Indica series, no. 2, vol. 3, 1856. It was not until 1934 that the first complete translation of this commentary was published, done by Swami Madhavananda. Most of Śaṅkara's other Upaniṣad commentaries were first published in 5 vols. from 1898 to 1901, translated by S. Sitarama Sastri and Ganganath Jha. These are on the *Īśa, Kena, Kaṭha, Praśna, Muṇḍaka, Taittirīya, Aitareya,* and *Chāndogya Upaniṣads*. That on the *Māṇḍūkya Upaniṣad*, along with Gauḍapāda's *Kārikā*, had been published in 1894, translated by Manilal N. Dvivedi. Śaṅkara's commentary on the *Bhagavad-gītā* was first translated by A. Mahadeva Sastri and published in 1897.

47. "The Crest-Jewel of Wisdom," trans. by Mohini M. Chatterji, *The Theosophist*, vol. 7, 1885-86, pp. 65-68, 253-258, 385-390, 661-665, 724-732; vol. 9, 1887-88, pp. 23-35, 124-128, 158-162. This was published in book form, with added Sanskrit text, as *Viveka-chūdāmaṇi, or Crest-Jewel of Wisdom*, Adyar, Madras: Theosophical Publishing House, 1st ed., 1932; several reprintings, with the spelling, *Viveka-cūḍāmaṇi*. Another translation by Charles Johnston appeared in the *Oriental Department*

Papers of the Theosophical Society in America, 1894-1897; published in book form as *The Crest Jewel of Wisdom (Vivekachudamani)*, New York: Quarterly Book Department, 1925; again in *The Crest-Jewel of Wisdom and Other Writings of Śankarāchārya*, Covina, California: Theosophical University Press, 1946; this book reprinted, San Diego: Point Loma Publications, 1993. For Sanskrit students, the translation by Swami Madhavananda usually follows the Sanskrit more closely than the two above do: *Vivekachudamani*, Mayavati: Advaita Ashrama, 1921; several reprintings from Calcutta, with the spelling, *Vivekacūḍāmaṇi*.

Four other short works of Śaṅkarācārya were published in *The Theosophist* while Blavatsky was living:

[*Ātmānātma-viveka*] "Discrimination of Spirit and Not-Spirit," trans. by Mohinee M. Chatterjee, vol. 4, Nov. 1882, pp. 30-31; vol. 5, Dec. 1883, pp. 70-72.

[*Ātma-bodha*] "The Atma Bodh, of Srimat Sankaracharya," trans. by B. P. Narasimmiah, vol. 6, Nov. 1884, p. 36; Feb. 1885, pp. 101-106.

[*Praśnottara-ratna-mālikā*] "Prasnottarararatnamalika (A Necklace of Gem-like Questions and Answers)," trans. not stated, vol. 9, Jan. 1888, pp. 249-257.

[*Advaita-pañca-ratna*, or *Advaita-pañcaka*, or *Ātma-pañcaka*] "Ode on Self," trans. by A. G., vol. 9, Mar. 1888, p. 374 (here called "Atma-Khatak," and having six rather than five verses).

Five works of Śaṅkarācārya were reprinted in: *A Compendium of the Raja Yoga Philosophy, Comprising the Principal Treatises of Shrimat Sankaracharya and Other Renowned Authors*, published by Tookaram Tatya, Bombay: Bombay Theosophical Publication Fund, 1888. These are: *Aparokṣānubhūti*, trans. Manilal Nab[h]ubhai Dvivedi; *Ātmānātma-viveka*, Mohinee M. Chatterjee; *Ātma-bodha*, B. P. Narasimmiah; *Viveka-cūḍāmaṇi*, Mohini M. Chatterji (incomplete, stops with verse 450; the remaining 133 verses, from the last two installments of *The Theosophist*, were left out); *Carpaṭa-pañjarī* (or *Moha-mudgara*, or *Bhaja-govindam*), J. N. Parmanand.

The *Aparokṣānubhūti* had been published in: *Rája Yoga, or The Practical Metaphysics of the Vedánta: Being a Translation of the Vákyasudhá or Drigdrishyaviveka of Bháratitirtha, and the Aparokshánubhuti of Shri Shankaráchárya*, by Manilal Nabhubhai Dvivedi, Bombay: "Subodha-Prakasha" Printing Press, 1885. Note that the *Vākya-sudhā* is sometimes attributed to Śaṅkarācārya.

Four more short works of Śaṅkarācārya were published in *The Theosophist* shortly after Blavatsky's death, all of them translated by B. P. Narasimmiah:

"Sri Sankaracharya's Mahavakyadarpanam, or The Mirror of Mystic Expressions," vol. 13, May, June, Aug. 1892, pp. 503-508, 527-530, 679-683; vol. 14, Oct., Nov. 1892, pp. 16-20, 88-94.

"Srí Sankarácháryá's Harimídastotram, or The Hymn Praising Vishnu," vol. 14, Mar. 1893, pp. 359-367.

"Sri Sankarácháryá's Swátmánirúpanam, or (The Description of One's Own Átmá)," vol. 14, Apr.-July 1893, pp. 403-407, 495-498, 558-562, 618-622.

"Śrí Śankaráchárya's Tatva Bodh," vol. 14, Sep. 1893, pp. 735-740. The *Tattva-bodha* is like a catechism of Advaita Vedānta.

48. Paul Hacker, "Relations of Early Advaitins to Vaiṣṇavism," in Halbfass, ed., *Philology and Confrontation*, p. 33. The wording used here differs slightly from that found in its first publication, *Wiener Zeitschrift für die Kunde Süd- und Ostasiens*, vol. 9, 1965, p. 147. This is due to the fact that "a few minor stylistic changes were made in Hacker's English texts" by the 1995 editor, Wilhelm Halbfass (see p. 352). I agree that these changes only put the passage into better and clearer English, and did not at all alter the author's meaning.

49. Halbfass, ed., *Philology and Confrontation*, p. 94. See note 43 above.

50. This letter was first published in "Echoes from the Past," *The Theosophist*, vol. 28, June 1907, quotation from p. 702 (this printing has "impressional" for "impersonal"); reprinted in *Letters from the Masters of the Wisdom*, compiled by C. Jinarajadasa, [First Series,] Adyar, Madras: Theosophical Publishing House, 1919, no. XXX, p. 79; 5th ed., 1964, p. 66. Corrections were made in the third edition, where this letter was now "transcribed from the original at Adyar." In the 1907 printing it is dated 1881. Jinarajadasa says its date is probably 1882.

51. *The Mahatma Letters to A. P. Sinnett*, transcribed and compiled by A. T. Barker, 1st ed., 1923; 3rd rev. ed., Adyar, Madras: Theosophical Publishing House, 1962, p. 52; chronological ed., Quezon City, Metro Manila, Philippines: Theosophical Publishing House, 1993, p. 269.

52. *The Mahatma Letters*, 3rd ed., p. 52; chron. ed., p. 270. *Avidyā* means ignorance, and *māyā* means the great delusion, or illusion. Īśvara, God, is defined in standard Advaita Vedānta works as Brahman associated with ignorance (*avidyā*), or with illusion (*māyā*). See, for example: *Pañcadaśī* 1.16, 3.37; and *Vedāntasāra* 37, 142.

53. *The Mahatma Letters*, 3rd ed., p. 53; chron. ed., p. 271.

54. *The Mahatma Letters*, 3rd ed., p. 53; chron. ed., p. 270.

55. *The Mahatma Letters*, 3rd ed., pp. 139-140; chron. ed., p. 284.

56. From a letter published under the title, "A Mental Puzzle,"

signed, "One of the Hindu founders of the parent Theosophical Society. Tiruvallam Hills, May 17." *The Theosophist*, vol. 3, June 1882, Supplement, p. 7.

57. *The Gita As It Was: Rediscovering the Original Bhagavadgita*, by Phulgenda Sinha, La Salle, Illinois: Open Court, 1986, p. xiv. In this book, Sinha eliminates as not original all the verses of the *Bhagavad-gītā* that he considers to be theistic, thus reducing its 700 verses to 84. This, however, from the standpoint of the Wisdom Tradition, is not necessary. All we need are the original commentaries on it, to explain these verses properly. On Indian history, Sinha's overall thesis of the early greatness and later decline is largely corroborated in the classic work, *The Wonder That Was India: A Survey of the Culture of the Indian Sub-Continent before the Coming of the Muslims*, by A. L. Basham, New York: Macmillan, 1954.

58. Sinha, *The Gita As It Was*, p. 93.

59. Sinha, *The Gita As It Was*, p. 95.

60. Sinha, *The Gita As It Was*, p. 101.

61. Cenkner, *A Tradition of Teachers*, pp. 139-140.

62. Cenkner, *A Tradition of Teachers*, p. 116.

63. *Sankaracharya*, by T. M. P. Mahadevan, New Delhi: National Book Trust, India, 1968, p. 54.

64. Mahadevan, *Sankaracharya*, p. 64.

65. In "The Mystery of Buddha" (*Blavatsky Collected Writings*, vol. 14, pp. 388-399), we are told that Gautama Buddha, due to compassion on the one hand and his vows of secrecy on the other, had given out partial truths, and that this resulted in their being misunderstood. Therefore part of him, his intermediate principles, came back with the incarnation of Śaṅkarācārya in order to rectify this problem. It is not hard to deduce that what the Buddha left out, and what Śaṅkara brought out, is the teaching of the one life. Blavatsky writes:

"Gautama had sworn inviolable secrecy as to the Esoteric Doctrines imparted to Him. In His immense pity for the ignorance—and as its consequence the sufferings—of mankind, desirous though He was to keep inviolate His sacred vows, He failed to keep within the prescribed limits. While constructing His Exoteric Philosophy (the 'Eye-Doctrine') on the foundations of eternal Truth, He failed to conceal certain dogmas, and trespassing beyond the lawful lines, caused those dogmas to be misunderstood. . . .

"His new doctrine, which represented the outward dead body of the Esoteric Teaching without its vivifying Soul, had disastrous effects: it was never correctly understood, and the doctrine itself was rejected by the Southern Buddhists. Immense philanthropy, a boundless love and charity for all creatures, were at the bottom of His unintentional mistake; but Karma little heeds intentions, whether good or bad, if they remain fruitless. If the 'Good Law,' as preached, resulted in the most sublime code of ethics and the unparalleled philosophy of things external in the visible Kosmos, it biassed and misguided immature minds into believing there was nothing more under the outward mantle of the system, and its dead-letter only was accepted. . . . (p. 388)

"Thus, fifty odd years after his death 'the great Teacher' having refused full Dharmakāya and Nirvāṇa, was pleased, for purposes of Karma and philanthropy, to be reborn. . . . He was reborn as Śaṃkara, the greatest Vedāntic teacher of India, whose philosophy—based as it is entirely on the fundamental axioms of the eternal Revelation, the Śruti, or the primitive Wisdom-Religion, as Buddha from a different point of view had before based His—finds itself in the middle ground between the too exuberantly veiled metaphysics of the orthodox Brāhmans and those of Gautama, which, stripped in their exoteric garb of every soul-vivifying hope, transcendental aspiration and symbol, appear in their cold wisdom like crystalline icicles, the skeletons of the primeval truths of Esoteric Philosophy" (p. 389).

This clearly relates to (I do not say counters) the doctrine of *anātman*, "no self," found throughout Buddhism, and the doctrine of *śūnyatā*, "emptiness," found in Northern Buddhism. This latter, the Madhyamaka doctrine, is commonly understood as teaching nothingness, or nihilism, despite the insistence of its adherents that it is the "middle way" between eternalism and nihilism. Not only do modern Western writers sometimes understand it as nihilism, but also past Hindu and Jaina writers. M. Hiriyanna, in his *Outlines of Indian Philosophy* (London: George Allen & Unwin, 1932), says in his Preface:

"The view taken here of the Mādhyamika school of Buddhism is that it is pure nihilism, but some are of the opinion that it implies a positive conception of reality. The determination of this question from Buddhistic sources is difficult, the more so as philosophic considerations become mixed with historical ones. Whatever the fact, the negative character of its teaching is vouched for by the entire body of Hindu and Jaina works stretching back to times when Buddhism was still a power in the land of its birth. The natural conclusion to be drawn from such a consensus of opinion is that, in at least one important stage of its development in India, the Mādhyamika doctrine *was* nihilistic; and it was not considered inappropriate in a book on Indian philosophy to give prominence to this aspect of it" (pp. 7-8).

To offset the nihilism resulting from his teachings, Buddha in part returned in Śaṅkara to teach the one life. When we know this, some of Śaṅkara's words take on new meaning. The First Noble Truth taught in Buddhism is that of suffering, *duḥkha*. Suffering is said to arise because of the conception of a permanent self, *ātman*. The three defining teachings which characterize all of Buddhism are therefore: suffering (*duḥkha*), impermanence (*anitya*), and no self (*anātman*). The original Śaṅkarācārya says in his *Viveka-cūḍāmaṇi*, verse 379: "Abandoning the thought of no self (*anātman*), which is base and the cause of suffering (*duḥkha*), think of the self (*ātman*), whose nature is bliss, and which is the cause of liberation." Further, the teaching that everything is empty, *śūnya*, was added in Northern Buddhism to the first three. Compare another Advaita Vedānta text, *Aparokṣānubhūti*, verse 29: "It is established that in your own body and yet beyond the body is the lustrous, existing self called the *puruṣa*. Why, O foolish one, do you make the self (*ātman*) empty (*śūnya*) [i.e., non-existent]?"

Śaṅkarācārya came and brought out the teaching of a non-dual reality, of *ātman*, the self of all, as identical with Brahman; in other words, the one life. According to what we have just seen, this was to fill in a big gap in the wisdom teachings brought out by the Buddha. But this, too, had its problems, falling into theism. And it is the Buddhist teachings which in return counter this problem.

ADDENDA
February 2007

Here listed are some important materials obtained after the foregoing article was written:

Antarkar, W. R. "The Date of Śaṅkarācārya." *Journal of the Asiatic Society of Bombay*, n.s., vols. 67-68, 1992-93, pp. 1-20.

Antarkar, W. R. "The Place of Śaṅkara's Final Disappearance." *Journal of the Asiatic Society of Bombay*, n.s., vol. 71, 1996, pp. 1-22.

Gokhale, Malati. "Authorship of the Balabodhini Ascribed to Samkaracarya." *Bulletin of the Deccan College Research Institute*, vol. 18, 1957, pp. 186-191.

Gussner, Robert E. "A Stylometric Study of the Authorship of Seventeen Sanskrit Hymns Attributed to Śaṅkara," *Journal of the American Oriental Society*, vol. 96, no. 2, 1976, pp. 259-267.

Mishra, Parmeshwar Nath. *Era of Adi Shankaracharya: 507 BC - 475 BC.* Howrah: Samskriti Rakshak Parishad, 2003.

* * *

We have prepared two relevant bibliographic guides after this article was written, available at www.easterntradition.org:

Works of the Original Śaṅkarācārya (2005, 2007, 40 pp.).

Śaṅkarācārya's Collected Works: An Annotated Bibliography of Published Editions in Sanskrit (2005, 16 pp.).

[The foregoing article was written by David Reigle, and published in *Fohat*, A Quarterly Publication of Edmonton Theosophical Society, vol. 5, no. 3, Fall 2001, pp. 57-60, 70-71, without the notes.]

God's Arrival in India

Ancient India is considered to be the spiritual motherland of our planet. According to *The Secret Doctrine,* it was the home of the once universal Wisdom Tradition. From ancient India, called Āryāvarta, the wisdom teachings went forth into all the religions and philosophies of the world. H. P. Blavatsky writes:

> For Āryāvarta, the bright focus into which had been poured in the beginning of time the flames of Divine Wisdom, had become the center from which radiated the "tongues of fire" into every portion of the globe.[1]

The one Wisdom Tradition thus took various forms for various peoples. In time these varying forms became religious dogma. But all had their origin in the sacred land of Āryāvarta.

> But all such dogma grew out of the one root, the root of wisdom, which grows and thrives on the Indian soil. There is not an Archangel that could not be traced back to its prototype in the sacred land of Āryāvarta.[2]

It is to ancient India, home of the Wisdom Tradition, that we must turn to find the one truth behind the various religions of the world, and the key to the great mysteries of humanity.

> . . . we affirm that, if Egypt furnished Greece with her civilization, and the latter bequeathed hers to Rome, Egypt herself had, in those unknown ages when Menes reigned, received her laws, her social institutions, her arts and her sciences, from pre-Vedic India; and that, therefore, it is in that old initiatrix of the priests—the adepts of all the other countries—we must seek for the key to the great mysteries of humanity.[3]

The most central truth behind the various religions of the world is generally thought to be that of the existence of God. Finding the key to the great mysteries of humanity, then, would depend on knowing that the various names for God found in the various religions of the world all refer to the same reality. But is God a reality? Although the Theosophical movement, in its efforts to promote the universal brotherhood of humanity, has had to act as if the answer to this question is yes, the teachers behind the Theosophical movement have answered it with an unequivocal no.

Belief in God is so central to modern ideas of spirituality, that it is hardly possible to conceive of a true spiritual tradition without God. A. O. Hume could not imagine that the Wisdom Tradition lacked God; so in his exposition of it written on the basis of correspondence with the Theosophical Mahatmas, he drafted a chapter on God. The Mahatma K.H. responded with one of the clearest and most unmistakable statements we have of their doctrine, saying:

> Neither our philosophy nor ourselves believe in a God. . . . Our philosophy . . . is preeminently the science of effects by their causes and of causes by their effects. . . . Our doctrine knows no compromises. It either affirms or denies, for it never teaches but that which it knows to be the truth. Therefore, we deny God both as philosophers and as Buddhists. We know there are planetary and other spiritual lives, and we know there is in our system no such thing as God, either personal or impersonal. . . . The word "God" was invented to designate the unknown cause of those effects which man has either admired or dreaded without understanding them, and since we claim and that we are able to prove what we claim—i.e., the knowledge of that cause and causes—we are in a position to maintain there is no God or Gods behind them.[4]

In another letter, K.H. said that if Hume publishes his account,

> I will have H.P.B. or Djual Khool deny the whole thing; as I cannot permit our sacred philosophy to be so disfigured.[5]

Nonetheless, after H. P. Blavatsky's death, this position ceased to be upheld, so that at present the vast majority of members of the Theosophical Society are believers in God. Similarly, other teachings with roots in Theosophy that arose later, such as the Djual Khool/Alice Bailey books, utilized the God idea.[6]

The sincere and intelligent modern student of the ancient and Ageless Wisdom Tradition, then, often takes for granted that the idea of God in some form or other is necessarily found in all religions. Now that Buddhism has become more widely known, its noble teachings of compassion have impressed many such students. Like Hume in regard to Theosophy, they cannot imagine that a tradition so noble could be Godless. They then assume that the idea of God must be there under some other name or concept, since they know that this belief is universal. But is it? The Mahatma K.H. tells us that, "the idea of God is not an innate but an acquired notion."[7] If this is true, and the notion of God was in fact never part of the Wisdom Tradition, but was acquired as these truths went forth from their home in ancient India, history should show this.

There are three religions of ancient India, those now called Buddhism, Hinduism, and Jainism. Neither Buddhism nor Jainism have ever taught the existence of God. They are non-theistic. Hinduism presently teaches the existence of God. It is now theistic. However, there is considerable evidence that none of the various schools of Hinduism originally taught the existence of God. In other words, all of ancient India, home of the Wisdom Tradition, was once non-theistic. To show this, we will here attempt to trace God's arrival in India.

Jainism and Buddhism—Religions without God

Jainism is the religion of the Jinas, the Conquerors, those who have conquered their passions and thus achieved liberation. They have done this without the help of God; for indeed, God is not to be found in their worldview. The worldview taught by the Jinas is described in the authoritative *Tattvārthādhigama-sūtra.*[8] This text is a compendium of the teachings of the 24th and last Jina of our time-cycle, called Vardhamāna Mahāvīra, who in turn only re-established the teachings of the previous Jinas, going back in time without beginning.

In the Jaina worldview, karma takes the place of God. No one punishes us but ourselves, through our own former actions; and no one rewards us but ourselves, again through our own actions. The working of karma requires no intelligence to guide it nor power to implement it. It is simply the way things are, an inherent part of the eternal fabric of our universe. The universe has not been created, nor will it end. Matter is eternal and souls are eternal. Souls must through asceticism free themselves from the karmic bondage of matter. In this universe there is no place for God, nor any function for such a being to perform.

The religion of the Jinas is the religion of harmlessness, *ahiṃsā*. Its first principle is to not harm any living thing. This also means no retaliation. The karmic cycle of violence will not stop until it stops with us. For ages, Jainas made harmlessness the guiding principle of their lives. With no help from God, Jainism shares with Buddhism the distinction of having the best record on nonviolence of all religions known to history.

Buddhism is the religion of the Buddhas, the Awakened Ones, those who have awakened to truth or reality and thereby achieved liberation. They, too, have done this without the help of God; for God is not to be found in their worldview either. The basic worldview taught by the Buddhas is described in the authoritative *Abhidharma-kośa*.[9] This text is a compendium of the teachings of the last Buddha, called Gautama or Śākyamuni. While modern writers recognize only this Buddha, the Buddhist texts speak of many previous Buddhas, extending back into the night of time.

In the Buddhist worldview, as in the Jaina, karma takes the place of God. How karma works is understood differently in Buddhism than it is in Jainism, but the results are the same. We make our own destiny through our own actions. The universe and everything in it operates by its own laws, in the sense that science gives to the law of gravity. These require no lawgiver, and function without the need of God. As the present Dalai Lama of Tibet once said to a priest at an ecumenical meeting, "your business is God, my business is karma."

The religion of the Buddhas is the religion of compassion, *karuṇā*. In Tibet, Buddhist monks begin their meditations by generating compassion toward all living beings. This includes especially those who have wronged or harmed them. Thus after the brutal Chinese Communist takeover of Tibet, the Buddhist response was one of nonviolence. This was recognized worldwide when in 1989 the Dalai Lama won the Nobel Peace Prize for his thirty years of efforts to regain his homeland, during which violence was never considered an option. What country that calls upon God to bless it can boast such an example?

Both Jainism and Buddhism teach that each one of us can become perfected, through our own efforts, and be liberated from the compulsory round of rebirth. To do this requires the will power to follow the path taught by the Jinas or the Buddhas in face of all obstacles, as did Mahāvīra and Śākyamuni. This way of self-reliance is in direct contrast with the way of surrender to God taught in theistic religions.

Some modern writers have attempted to find in Buddhism an equivalent for God, or Godhead, and have found this in the Buddhist idea of *nirvāṇa*. Thus, Huston Smith in his deservedly popular book, *The World's Religions*, writes:

> We may conclude with Conze that *nirvana* is not God defined as personal creator, but that it stands sufficiently close to the concept of God as Godhead to warrant the name in that sense.[10]

This refers to Edward Conze's 1951 book, *Buddhism: Its Essence and Development*, which in turn refers to Aldous Huxley's 1944 classic, *The Perennial Philosophy*, on the difference between God and Godhead. According to Huxley, the Perennial Philosophy has at all times and in all places taught a divine Ground of all existence, a spiritual Absolute, or Godhead. This has a personal aspect, who has form, activity, and attributes such as mercy; and this is God. In this philosophy, the two go together; you cannot have one without the other. In order to fit Buddhism into this scheme, Huxley had to make Godhead and God correspond to two of the three bodies of a Buddha. Thus he made the second body of a Buddha, the Sambhoga-kāya, correspond "to Isvara or the personal God of Judaism, Christianity and Islam,"[11] an equation that few Buddhists would accept. God is simply not found in Buddhism.

In making the *nirvāṇa* comparison, Smith distinguished God as Godhead from the personal creator God. The idea of an impersonal Godhead, "the God-without-form of Hindu and Christian mystical phraseology,"[12] is, however, invariably linked with the idea of a personal God. Godhead must be able to think and act, even if through God. Were it possible to conceive of Godhead without God, that is, without any of the qualities that normally define God—those of being all-knowing, all-powerful, ruler of all, or even of merely being conscious—then why call it Godhead, or God as Godhead?

When A. O. Hume wished to describe the One Life taught in the Wisdom Tradition as God, the Mahatma K.H. replied:

> If people are willing to accept and to regard as God our ONE LIFE immutable and unconscious in its eternity they may do so and thus keep to one more gigantic misnomer. But then they will have to say with Spinoza that there is not and that we cannot conceive any other substance than God; . . . —and thus become Pantheists. . . . If we ask the theist is your God vacuum, space or matter, they will reply no. And yet they hold that their God penetrates matter though he is not himself matter. When we speak of our One Life we also say that it penetrates, nay is the essence of every atom of matter; and that therefore it not only has correspondence with matter but has all its properties likewise, etc.—hence *is* material, is *matter itself*. . . . We deny the existence of a thinking conscious God, on the grounds that such a God must either be conditioned, limited and subject to change, therefore *not* infinite, or if he is represented to us as an eternal unchangeable and independent being, with not a particle of matter in him, then we answer that it is no being but an immutable blind principle, a law. . . . The existence of matter then is a fact; the existence of motion is another fact, their self existence and eternity or indestructibility is a third fact. And the idea of pure spirit as a Being or an Existence—give it whatever name you will—is a chimera, a gigantic absurdity.[13]

Nirvāṇa is described in the Buddhist texts as the extinction of thirst (i.e., desire), or the cessation of suffering. It is also called the ultimate truth. It is what the Buddhas attain when liberated. It is the one thing taught by all Buddhist schools as unconditioned (*asaṃskṛta*). Helmuth von Glasenapp says about *nirvāṇa* in his major study, *Buddhism—A Non-Theistic Religion*:

> It does not belong to the world, has no relationship with it, nor does it affect it. It might best be called the 'totally other'; this is, indeed, a much more suitable expression for Nirvāna than it is for the Christian God who, though being above the world, yet governs it and is thus in constant touch with it. If God were the 'totally other', he could never be the 'good friend' of the soul, and neither could the soul establish a relationship with him.[14]

As something "totally other," *nirvāṇa* has no relationship with the world, and plays no role in the life of an individual. It does not think or act. This is not God in any normal sense of the word. Certain epithets used to describe *nirvāṇa*, such as "peace," caused it to be equated with God as Godhead by those who sought to find the idea of God in all religions. This was based on the conception of Godhead and God, explained as the twofold *brahman* found in the Vedānta system of Hinduism: the absolute *brahman* without attributes (*nirguṇa*), and the conditioned *brahman* with attributes (*saguṇa*), now also called God-without-form and God-with-form in modern Hinduism. God-with-form includes the ideas of Īśvara, the ruler of all, and Brahmā, the creator. Buddhism has always refuted these ideas of God. The Buddha is depicted as refuting the idea of Brahmā the creator in the *Brahma-jāla Sutta*;[15] Nāgārjuna is credited with a treatise refuting the idea of Īśvara;[16] and so on throughout Buddhist history. The Buddhist attitude toward the idea of God is pointedly summed up in the *Encyclopaedia of Buddhism*:

> The Buddha and his followers borrowed the name [Brahmā = God] from their Brahmanical counterparts in order to refute, not only their theology but the basis of all theologies: the idea of God.[17]

Religion had been defined in terms of God. When scholars began to study Buddhism seriously, they first suggested that it cannot be a religion, because it does not have a God. It instead could only be a philosophy. But since Buddhism obviously is a religion, with temples, a priesthood, scriptures, etc., scholars had to re-define religion, allowing that there could be religion without God. This, of course, applies equally to Jainism. Now that religions without God are recognized, scholars prefer to refer to them as non-theistic, rather than atheistic, since the term atheistic has other connotations in our society.

The above serves to illustrate just how difficult it is for us in the West to even conceive of a Godless religion. Conversely, it was likewise difficult for the Mahatma K.H. to conceive of the theistic ideas prevalent in the West, as they were so illogical to him. Some passages from his letters to A. O. Hume illustrate the difficulties faced by teachers when trying to communicate the teachings of the Wisdom Tradition to a theistic audience.

> Then for a man endowed with so subtle a logic, and such a fine comprehension of the value of ideas in general and that of words especially—for a man so accurate as you generally are to make tirades upon an "all wise, powerful and love-ful God" seems to say at least strange. I do not protest at all as you seem to think against your theism, or a belief in an abstract ideal of some kind, but I cannot help asking you, how do you or how can you know that your God is all wise, omnipotent and love-ful, when everything in nature, physical and moral, proves such a being, if he does exist, to be quite the reverse of all you say of him? Strange delusion and one which seems to overpower your very intellect.[18]

> And now to your extraordinary hypothesis that Evil with its attendant train of sin and suffering is not the result of matter, but may be perchance the wise scheme of the moral Governor of the Universe. Conceivable as the idea may seem to you, trained in the pernicious fallacy of the Christian,—"the ways of the Lord are inscrutable"—it is utterly inconceivable for me. Must I repeat again that the best Adepts have searched the Universe during millenniums and found nowhere the slightest trace of such a

Machiavellian schemer—but throughout, the same immutable, inexorable law. You must excuse me therefore if I positively decline to lose my time over such childish speculations. It is not "the ways of the Lord" but rather those of some extremely intelligent men in everything but some particular hobby, that are to me incomprehensible.[19]

You say it matters nothing whether these laws are the expression of the will of an intelligent conscious God, as you think, or constitute the inevitable attributes of an unintelligent, unconscious "God," as I hold. I say, it matters everything, and since you earnestly believe that these fundamental questions (of spirit and matter—of God or no God) "are admittedly beyond both of us"—in other words that neither I nor yet our greatest adepts can know any more than you do, then what is there on earth that I could teach you?[20]

Theism, of course, is not limited to the West. It is now the norm in India as well. Buddhism had been driven out of India a thousand years ago, and Jainism at present makes up less than one percent of its population. Today, virtually all of Hinduism is theistic. But it was not always this way.

Hinduism and God—Earlier and Later

The Vedas are the oldest religious compositions of India, and indeed are thought to be the oldest religious texts in the world having a continuous tradition of use up to the present. They will not provide us with the help we might expect from them in our attempt to trace God's presence in ancient India, however, for the simple reason that we do not know for certain how they were understood in ancient India. They require the help of a commentary to be properly understood, and the only commentaries now extant are comparatively modern. The age of the Vedas is not known, but they are estimated by modern scholarship to date from circa 1500-1000 B.C.E., while Indian tradition makes them considerably older than that. Yet for long, the only commentaries known were those of Sāyaṇa, dating from the 14th century C.E.[21] This is well within what we may call the theistic period of Indian history, and at least two thousand years removed from the Vedas themselves. The strange fact that we have only late commentaries on India's oldest texts provides weighty evidence for the Wisdom Tradition's assertion that the genuine commentaries have all been withdrawn.[22]

The Vedas are to all appearances polytheistic, since they are made up of hymns addressed to a number of different "gods," or "deities." But as everyone knows, appearances can be deceiving. When Western scholars approached the Vedas, they of course did so presupposing their own worldview, wherein what is ancient is necessarily primitive, and primitive religion is polytheistic, arising through the deification of various natural phenomena such as the sun and rain. Seeing in the Vedas the personified sacrificial fire (Agni), sky (Indra), sun (Sūrya), etc., they took the Vedas at face value, that is, as being polytheistic. India was at that time under British rule, and institutions of higher learning in India followed a European model. So Indian scholars also took up the view that the Vedas are polytheistic. Thus today, most books by both Western and Indian scholars present this view.

The traditional Indian worldview differs from the modern Western one, holding sometimes opposite presuppositions. In this worldview, whatever is ancient is not of necessity primitive, but on the contrary comes down to us from a spiritually more advanced Age of Truth, or Golden Age as it is called in other traditions around the world. The seers (*ṛṣi*) of the Vedic hymns were not rustics wondering at the awe-inspiring forces of nature they saw around them, but rather were highly advanced sages whose insight far surpasses our own. This is why the Vedas are so revered in Hinduism. The Vedic revelation (*śruti*) includes two parts. The hymns addressed to various deities are found in the first part, on works (*karma-kāṇḍa*). The last part, on knowledge (*jñāna-kāṇḍa*) comprises the Upaniṣads. It is to these texts that Hinduism has traditionally turned for the philosophy of the Vedas, rather than to the hymns themselves. This is because the hymns, consisting of mantras, are liturgical formulae that are considered to be of limited use in determining philosophical issues, such as the question of Vedic polytheism. As pointed out by Ananda K. Coomaraswamy:

> It is precisely the fact that the Vedic incantations are liturgical that makes it unreasonable to expect from them a systematic exposition of the philosophy they take for granted; if we consider the *mantras* by themselves, it is as if we had to deduce the Scholastic philosophy only from the libretto of the Mass.[23]

Thus we find that Hinduism in general adopted the view taught in the Upaniṣads of the one universal *brahman*, and found no contradiction between this and the fact that the Vedas spoke of the many gods. This characteristic Indian attitude is explained by Shrimat Anirvan in his chapter, "Vedic Exegesis," from *The Cultural Heritage of India*:

> . . . in the spiritual idiom of the Vedic seers, gods are *born* as One and Many and All. The same phenomenon of expanding consciousness (*brahma*) is described objectively in a symbolic language by the Vedas, and subjectively in an intellectual language by the Upaniṣads. They speak of a metaphysical realism in which One and Many do not clash either in form or in substance; and their theory of gods cannot be exclusively labelled as monotheism, polytheism, or pantheism, because it is an integrated vision in which all these isms harmonize. Since this was the vision at the root of all forms of Ārya mysticism, a Buddhist nihilism or a Vedāntic monism (which are not to be confounded with a-theism or mono-theism) found nothing to quarrel with in a theory of many gods. This is a phenomenon which very naturally mystifies the western mind, which will see in it nothing but a condescension to an ineradicable superstition. From the Vedic age to the present times, the vision of One Existence and many gods have lived harmoniously in the spiritual realizations of India's greatest seers; . . .[24]

Early on, pioneer Vedic scholar F. Max Müller had noticed that the alleged Vedic polytheism was no ordinary polytheism, since each god may in turn be addressed as if the highest one. This is unlike polytheism found elsewhere, as for example in Greece, where Zeus is always the highest. Thus he coined new terms for this, henotheism and kathenotheism. This observation fits in nicely with the idea from the Upaniṣads of the one and the many. Nonetheless, scholars did not apply this idea of the one and the many to the Vedas, because the Upaniṣads are regarded by them as being a later development. So Western scholars, and now Indian scholars following them, continue to regard the Vedas as being polytheistic, in spite of Hindu tradition on this. As far as can be traced, Hindu tradition has looked upon the Vedas in terms of the one and the many for a very long time.

Already in the Vedas proper, in hymn 1.164 of the *Ṛg-veda,* and repeated in hymn 9.10 of the *Atharva-veda,* we find a verse explicitly stating this idea. Here is this verse, numbered 46 or 28 respectively, translated by Vasudeva S. Agrawala:

> They call him Indra, Mitra, Varuṇa, Agni, and he is the heavenly Winged Bird. The sages speak of the One by many names: they call it Agni, Yama, Mātariśvan.[25]

Modern scholars do not deny the obvious meaning of this verse, but dismiss the hymns it is found in as being "late"; that is, as approaching the time of the Upaniṣads, where such an idea is stated repeatedly. Their presupposition of development from more primitive to less primitive is, however, the very criterion on which these hymns are judged to be late. None of the three religious traditions of ancient India accept this presupposition, and neither does the Wisdom Tradition. Hindu writers down through the ages have quoted this verse as the expression of what the Vedas have always taught.

Although no ancient Vedic commentaries are extant, we do have a very old and authoritative text that gives exegetical comments on selected Vedic passages. This is Yāska's *Nirukta,* estimated by scholars to date from circa 700-500 B.C.E. The *Nirukta* is the "limb" or auxiliary of the Vedas (Vedāṅga) that deals with etymology and related topics. In its section on deities, it quotes the above-cited verse to explain Agni, the first of the Vedic deities, who is said to be all the deities.[26] It had brought up the idea of the one and the many earlier in this section. There Yāska explained that the one is the one *ātman*, the "self," which the Upaniṣads had taught as being identical with the one universal *brahman*. We here cite this passage as introduced and translated by Ananda K. Coomaraswamy, slightly adapting his translation in accordance with that of Lakshman Sarup:

> Modern scholarship for the most part postulates only a gradual development in Indian metaphysics of a notion of a single principle, of which principle the several gods (*devāḥ*, *viśve devāḥ*, etc.) are, as it were, the powers, operative aspects, or personified attributes. But as Yāska expresses it, "It is because of the great divisibility (*mahā-bhāgyāt*) of the deity (*devatā*) that the One Spirit (*eka ātmā*) is praised in various ways. Other gods (*devāḥ*) come to be (*bhavanti*) submembers (*pratyaṅgāni*) of the One Spirit. . . . Their becoming is a birth from one another, they are of one another's nature; they originate in function (*karma*); the Spirit is their origin. . . . Spirit (*ātman*) is the whole of what a god is" (*Nirukta* VII.4).[27]

Lakshman Sarup, who dedicated many years of his life to the editing and translating of Yāska's *Nirukta*, notes here:

> This is Yāska's rejoinder to the objection that non-deities are praised like deities. The so-called non-deities, says Yāska, are but different manifestations of the same single soul [*ātman*]. In other words, Yāska here propounds the doctrine of pantheism.[28]

Yāska's *Nirukta* is the oldest text we have giving exegetical comments on the Vedas, dating from at least 500 B.C.E. Yāska refers to many teachers before him, so he was quite familiar with the ancient schools of Vedic exegesis. He understands the Vedas as teaching the one and the many; and he understands the one as referring to the one universal *ātman*, or *brahman*. This is the earliest available interpretation.

The standard Vedic commentaries now known are those of Sāyaṇa, written in the 14th century C.E., nearly two millenniums later than Yāska. In the preface to Sāyaṇa's commentary on the *Ṛg-veda*, the same above-cited Vedic verse that was quoted by

Yāska is again quoted to explain the many Vedic gods. Here is Sāyaṇa's passage, translated by Peter Peterson:

> Although Indra and the other gods are invoked in many texts there is no contradiction, inasmuch as these are only the Supreme God in the form of Indra and other such gods. And so it is said in another text, "They call Agni, Indra, Mitra, Varuṇa and he is the strong-winged divine Garutman: He is one, but wise men call Him by many names, and call Agni, Yama, Mātariśvan." . . . In this way it is the Supreme God and no other who is invoked of all men.[29]

Thus Sāyaṇa, like Yāska nineteen centuries earlier, understands the Vedas as teaching the one and the many. Now, however, the one is no longer understood to refer to the one universal *ātman* or *brahman*, but instead to the Supreme God (Parama Īśvara). The Supreme God is considered by Sāyaṇa to be an anthropomorphic (*pauruṣeya*), corporeal being (*śarīra-dhāri-jīva*),[30] in other words, a personal God. So somewhere between 500 B.C.E. and 1400 C.E. the idea of the one as an impersonal principle was displaced by the idea of the one as a personal God.

The move to monotheism in Vedic exegesis continued up to modern times, reaching its culmination in the work of Swami Dayananda Saraswati, founder of the Arya Samaj. Although Sāyaṇa believed in a Supreme God behind the many Vedic gods, his primary concern was with Vedic ritual, not with God. Further, his brother Mādhava was a leading exponent of the Advaita Vedānta system, which by then allowed the coexistence of the impersonal *brahman* and the personal God, Īśvara. For Dayananda, there was only the personal God, Īśvara, the one Lord and Ruler of all. The many Vedic gods were in name only; they were not forms of God, but were all simply names of the one God. Thus translations of the Vedas produced by the Arya Samaj replace the names Agni, Indra, etc., with the word God. Nor was there room in Dayananda's view for any impersonal principle such as the *brahman* taught in the Upaniṣads. Thus he demoted the Upaniṣads from their status as revelation (*śruti*), a status they had always held in Hindu tradition.[31]

Dayananda was a Hindu reformer and great champion of the Vedas. This is what led to a brief alliance between his Arya Samaj and the Theosophical Society. It was his monotheism that led to their parting of the ways. Blavatsky and Olcott, founders of the Theosophical Society, had understood from their teachers that an impersonal principle was taught in the Vedas. So they thought that when Dayananda was promoting the Vedas, he was promoting this idea. Dayananda thought that when Blavatsky and Olcott were extolling the Vedas, they were extolling his monotheistic view of them. Neither party could speak the other's language. When they parted ways, a letter was printed pertaining to this from "One of the Hindu Founders of the Parent Theosophical Society," Tiruvallam Hills, considered to be a Mahatma. It is important because it states clearly the position of the Wisdom Tradition in regard to Vedic theism.

> It was in September, 1880,—more than 20 months ago—that the Pandit Dayanand Saraswati was told plainly the truth (as he had been told before, and even written to, from America, when the Society had at last learned what kind of God was the *Iswar* preached by him)—to wit: that the Founders neither then believed, nor ever had believed, in a *personal* God. The Swami . . . endows *his* "Iśwar" with all the finite attributes of the Jewish Jehovah.
>
> The Founders maintain that they *do* believe in the very Divine PRINCIPLE taught in the Vedas; in that *Principle* which is described at the outset in the *Rigveda Sanhita* (Man. X., R. 129) as *nāsad āsīt na [no] sad āsīt*—which is "neither entity nor non-entity," but an ABSTRACT ENTITY, which is *no* entity, liable to be described by either words or attributes. And, as they entirely fail to recognize this eternal, All-Pervading Principle in the "Iśwar" of the Arya Samajists—they turn away from it.[32]

Although we cannot trace in the Vedic commentaries how the one impersonal principle came to be thought of as God, since we lack these, we can see very clearly from the *darśana* texts the arrival of the God idea in India. The *darśanas* are the six systems of Hindu philosophy. According to Hindu tradition, they are based on the Vedas; that is, they have formulated the teachings of the Vedas into systems of philosophical thought. We have texts extant from these six systems that are much older than the extant Vedic commentaries. So they will provide us with considerable help in our attempt to trace God's presence in ancient India.

As is the norm with historical matters in India, we have no definite dates for these texts. The Sāṃkhya system, however, is regarded by Hindu tradition as the oldest *darśana*, taught by the first knower (*ādi-vidvān*), Kapila, so we will begin with it. The Sāṃkhya system, like Buddhism and Jainism, does not teach the existence of God. It instead explains the world and everything in it in terms of the interaction of two self-sufficient principles, *puruṣa* and *prakṛti*. The world is explained as the evolution of eternal substance, *prakṛti*, when in contact with *puruṣa*, what we may call spirit, soul, or life. This latter is not God, since it is a purely passive principle, incapable of thinking or acting. The fact that there is no place for God in what Hindus themselves regard as their oldest *darśana* is a very telling piece of evidence on the question of God's presence in ancient India.

As we have seen before in regard to the Wisdom Tradition and to Buddhism, it is hard for those who have grown up within a theistic worldview to accept that there can be a true religious tradition having no place for God. This is also the case in regard to Sāṃkhya. The *Sāṃkhya-sūtra* is generally understood to refute God. Its verse 1.92, among others,[33] specifically says that God is not proved (*īśvara asiddeḥ*). But the 16th century commentator Vijñāna Bhikṣu, and some modern translators following him, understand this as only saying that God cannot be proved, not that God does not exist.[34] This is very much like the agnostic position, that we cannot know whether or not God exists. The attribution of the agnostic position to the Wisdom Tradition was forcefully refuted by the Mahatma K.H.[35] He points out that when a system fully and completely describes the operation of the cosmos on its own principles, without God, it is absurd to say there might still be room in it for a God it does not know about or cannot prove. Such a God would be a non-entity, something that can and does do absolutely nothing.[36] The attribution of agnosticism to Buddhism, made by certain Buddhist scholars, may be refuted in a similar manner.[37] Likewise, Sāṃkhya gives a full account of the origin and operation of the cosmos, that leaves no room for God in its worldview.[38]

The Yoga *darśana* presupposes the Sāṃkhya worldview. It provides a system of practice based on this worldview. The means of practice it teaches is meditation, which culminates in the state of *samādhi*. If the practitioner cannot attain *samādhi* by means of meditation, it offers an alternative: devotion to *īśvara*. Thus *īśvara* is found in this system, though in a peripheral role. Since the Yoga system accepts the Sāṃkhya worldview wherein God plays no part, there is little else for this *īśvara* to do. Just how *īśvara* is to be understood in the Yoga system is not fully explained in the extant texts. The word *īśvara* occurs only five times in the *Yoga-sūtra* of Patañjali, the textbook of the system.[39] Its earliest commentary is that of Vyāsa. The first person to translate this difficult commentary, Ganganatha Jha, suggested the following to explain *īśvara*'s role in the Yoga system:

> He is nowhere spoken of as the 'creator'; nor even as the 'Consciousness' permeating through all existence. He is spoken of only as an object of devotion, devotion to whom leads to highest results. In this respect the 'god' of the *Yogin* appears to hold the same position, as the 'devatā' of the *Mīmāṃsaka*, who posits the 'devatā' only as one to whom the prescribed sacrifices can be offered. He has no other function.[40]

The fact that *īśvara* is found in the Yoga system at all is seen by some scholars as a concession to growing theism. This only got stronger. The commentaries coming after Vyāsa's, such as those of Vācaspati Miśra (9th century C.E.), and especially of Vijñāna Bhikṣu (16th century C.E.), give increasing importance to *īśvara* as God.

There is a question as to whether *īśvara* means God in Patañjali's *Yoga-sūtra*. M. D. Shastri's important study, "History of the Word 'Īśvara' and Its Idea,"[41] shows that *īśvara* did not mean God in any of India's oldest texts, including not only the

Vedic corpus, but also such works as Pāṇini's *Aṣṭādhyāyī* and Patañjali's *Mahā-bhāṣya.* It instead only meant a ruler, master, administrative head (*rājā*) or king, and competent or capable of. If the same Patañjali wrote both the *Yoga-sūtra* and the *Mahā-bhāṣya,* as assumed by Hindu tradition, but doubted by Shastri, *īśvara* would refer to some sort of administrative head (*rājā*) rather than God in the *Yoga-sūtra.* This makes no sense in the context of Yoga (even though Patañjali's system is known as Rāja Yoga, apparently because in it one learns to rule one's mind), so no one has pursued this angle. At least, it made no sense before the Wisdom Tradition became known.

The Secret Doctrine brought out the teaching of the *mānasa-putras,* the "sons of mind," also called solar *pitṛs* ("fathers"), or solar angels. They are an advanced class of beings, the perfected humanity of a previous *manvantara* or life-cycle, that endowed our present humanity with the spark of mind. In a specific sense they are our higher selves, and thus our rulers or administrative heads (*rājā*). The statements about *īśvara* made by Patañjali, that *īśvara* is a particular spirit (*puruṣa*), etc. (verses 1.24-26), and also those made by the ancient commentator Vyāsa, could apply to these. So could the statements from the *Sāṃkhya-sūtra* describing an *īśvara* of such kind (*īdṛśa*), which is different from the *īśvara* as God that it refutes. This *īśvara* is defined in verse 1.95 as a liberated self (*mukta ātman*), or perfected one (*siddha*), and described in verses 3.54-57 as one who after dissolution into primary substance (*prakṛti*) in a previous life-cycle has arisen in the present one with full knowledge and full action capacity. Devotion to this *īśvara* as a means to achieve *samādhi* would then make sense. The explanation of *īśvara* as a solar *pitṛ* rather than as God would make sense of *īśvara*'s role in the Yoga system.

In either case, *īśvara* as God plays at best a marginal role in the Yoga system, while he plays no role in the Sāṃkhya system. We will next take up the other avowedly non-theistic *darśana,* the Pūrva Mīmāṃsā system.

The Pūrva Mīmāṃsā system is the most orthodox *darśana,* since it is the one that deals with the Vedas proper, the hymns addressed to the many gods. Yet it, like Sāṃkhya, has no place for God. This rather unexpected (at least in later Hinduism) combination of ultra-orthodoxy and non-theism led T. M. P. Mahadevan, modern exponent of Advaita Vedānta, to remark:

> It is rather strange that the most orthodox of systems should turn out to be atheistic.[42]

Not only does it not accept God, even the gods it deals with are not considered real. Its view of the Vedic deities is described by Ganganatha Jha, the foremost translator of Mīmāṃsā texts:

> The deity to whom sacrifices are offered is, for the Mīmāmsaka, a purely hypothetical entity, posited for the sake of the accomplishment of a Sacrifice. . . . this is very clearly brought out in Mīm[āṃsā] Sū[tra] IX—i—6-10; in which connection the *Bhāṣya* explains that the Deity has no body, it does not eat anything, it cannot be either pleased or displeased; nor can it award prizes or punishments, as results of sacrifices. . . .[43]

So the only *darśana* that deals with the Vedas proper regards the Vedic deities as purely hypothetical entities. This fact provides weighty evidence that the Vedas never were polytheistic. As to God, he finds no place in the Pūrva Mīmāṃsā system because the Vedas, the all in all of this system, are eternal.

The Vedas are *śruti*, that which is heard. Even though *śruti* is often translated as revelation, this does not mean, like in other religions, that it is the word of God. What the seers (*ṛṣi*) heard and recorded as the Vedas is something that has always existed: the eternal sound that is believed in Hindu tradition to uphold and order the cosmos. The Vedic hymns are these sound sequences, embodying the cosmic order (*ṛta*). If these sequences of sound were the word of God, there would be a time when they did not exist, before God spoke them. But they are eternal, so they cannot be the word of God. Nor does God play any part in running the cosmos.

It is by the principle of cosmic order (*ṛta*) rather than by the will of God that the cosmos operates. Hence this principle can be said to take the place of God in the Vedic worldview. The idea of *ṛta* or cosmic order when applied to the human sphere became the idea of *dharma* or duty, what it is necessary for us to do simply because it is the eternal way of things. These are the actions (*karma*) enjoined in the Vedas; and this is the sphere of Pūrva Mīmāṃsā. The results of these actions are brought about by an inherent unseen potency (*apūrva*), not by God. Thus in the Pūrva Mīmāṃsā system, God is not the author of the Vedas; God did not create the cosmos; God does not run the cosmos; God did not lay down human duty; God does not reward or punish; God does not bring about the results of actions. Here as in the Sāṃkhya system, God is left with no role to play in the cosmos. So the existence of God is denied in Pūrva Mīmāṃsā, the most orthodox Hindu *darśana*.

Just as Pūrva Mīmāṃsā deals with the Vedas proper, the former (*pūrva*) part of the *śruti*, so Uttara Mīmāṃsā deals with the latter (*uttara*) part of the *śruti*, namely, the Upaniṣads. Thus the one universal principle known as *brahman* or *ātman* taught in the Upaniṣads is the province of the Uttara Mīmāṃsā system, better known as Vedānta, the "end (*anta*) of the Vedas." The *Brahma-sūtra* is the textbook of this system, obviously dealing with *brahman*. There is, however, no mention in this book of *saguṇa brahman*, the conditioned *brahman* with attributes, also called *īśvara*, God; nor is this phrase found in the ten principal Upaniṣads. Neither is the word *īśvara* found in the *Brahma-sūtra*, nor is it found in eight of the ten principal Upaniṣads. *Īśvara* is found in three places in the *Bṛhad-āraṇyaka Upaniṣad*.[44] In two of these, as noted in M. D. Shastri's above-cited study of the word *īśvara*, "it is unambiguously used only in the sense of 'capable of.'"[45] In the third place it is found in the compound *sarveśvara*, "ruler of all," used as an adjective describing *ātman*. It is also found once in the *Māṇḍūkya Upaniṣad*, in the same compound, used as an adjective describing the third quarter of *brahman* or *ātman*. The related word *īś* is found in the *Īśā Upaniṣad*, where according to Shastri, "it becomes clear that the word *Īś* has been used here more in the sense of Paramātman, the supreme self (or Brahman), than in the sense of Parameśvara or supreme God."[46] The word *īś* is also found in the *Muṇḍaka Upaniṣad*, in the same sense, reports Shastri.[47] So the God idea is not found in the primary sources of the Vedānta system, the ten principal

Upaniṣads, nor in its textbook, the *Brahma-sūtra*. Someone had to bring it in, and do so in a decisive and convincing manner. That someone was Śaṅkarācārya.

Śaṅkarācārya is the founder of the Advaita or "non-dual" school, the oldest school of Vedānta. He wrote very influential commentaries on the Upaniṣads and on the *Brahma-sūtra*. In these he repeatedly brought in the idea of *īśvara*, God, usually making no distinction between *īśvara* and the one universal *brahman* or *ātman*.[48] In his emphasis on *īśvara*, he differed from even his own disciples, who very seldom use the word *īśvara* in their writings.[49] The disciples he differed from, however, may not in fact be his. Substantial evidence that the author of the extant commentaries was not the original Śaṅkarācārya from the 5th century B.C.E., but was a later Śaṅkarācārya from the 8th century C.E., has been provided elsewhere.[50] From what we can deduce, the teachings of the original Śaṅkarācārya must differ significantly from the teachings of the later Śaṅkarācārya. The Mahatma K.H. writes in a letter replying to A. O. Hume:

> In the first [letter] you notify me of your intention of studying Advaita Philosophy with a "good old Swami". The man, no doubt, is very good; but from what I gather in your letter, if he teaches you anything you say to me, *i.e.*, anything save an impersonal, *non*-thinking and *non*-intelligent Principle they call Parabrahm, then he will not be teaching you the *true spirit* of that philosophy, not from its esoteric aspect, at any rate.[51]

In contrast to this, the main theme of the extant *Brahma-sūtra* commentary of Śaṅkarācārya is to prove that *paraṃ brahman* is conscious, is a thinking, intelligent entity. This is as opposed to the non-conscious primary substance (*pradhāna*) taught in the Sāṃkhya system, then apparently equivalent to *brahman*.[52] This Śaṅkarācārya made *brahman* equivalent to *īśvara*.

The idea of *īśvara*, the God idea, is universally accepted in Advaita Vedānta today. It exists alongside the ancient idea from the Upaniṣads of the one impersonal principle, *brahman*. In this way it is not the same as the God idea in monotheistic religions. Nonetheless, *īśvara* has many of the characteristics of the God of monotheism. As described by T. M. P. Mahadevan, the God of Advaita Vedānta is omniscient, omnipotent, the intelligent controller of the operation of the law of karma, the dispenser of justice, the moral governor, both the Law-Giver and the Law, the bestower of grace on his devotees, the object of adoration, the giver of prosperity, the grantor of liberation, etc.[53]

In the major Vedānta schools that arose after the Advaita school, such as the Viśiṣṭādvaita or "qualified non-dual" school of Rāmānuja, 11th century C.E., and the Dvaita or "dual" school of Madhva, 13th century C.E., the once impersonal *brahman* was progressively transformed into a full-blown personal God. Since the 8th century C.E., the time of the later Śaṅkarācārya, Vedānta in all its schools has been a major force in promoting the God idea in India.

We now take up the *darśana* that has been for more than a millennium the great defender of the God idea in India. This is the Nyāya system. Nyāya is usually translated as logic.[54] All three religions of ancient India, Jainism, Buddhism, and Hinduism, utilize reasoning to explain their tenets, in contradistinction to the three Abrahamic religions, Judaism, Christianity, and Islam. In each of the three Indian religions, separate schools of logic developed, even though reasoning is used in all their systems. The schools of logic found in Jainism and Buddhism, of course, use logic to refute the idea of God. But the Nyāya system found in Hinduism uses logic to prove the existence of God. Indeed, the use of logic to prove God reached its culmination in a work of this system, the *Nyāya-kusumāñjali*, written in the 11th century C.E. by the great champion of the God idea, Udayana. About this highly influential work Karl Potter writes in his *Encyclopedia of Indian Philosophies*:

> This work contains by general acclaim the definitive treatment of the question of how to prove God's existence.[55]

Ironically, this turns out to be a reversal of the position of the system's founder, Gautama. The original textbook of the system is Gautama's *Nyāya-sūtra*. The oldest extant commentary on it is the *bhāṣya* by Vātsyāyana. The next oldest commentary on it is the *vārttika* by Uddyotakara. These three highly complex texts were first translated into English by Ganganatha Jha and published serially from 1912-1919. In November of 1919 Jha presented at the All-India Oriental Conference a paper titled, "The Theism of Gautama, the Founder of 'Nyāya,'" in which he brought out the fact that Gautama's position on God had been reversed by the commentators. The one and only place in Gautama's *Nyāya-sūtra* that *īśvara* is found, 4.1.19, is in a section giving the views of others, not those of Gautama, that Gautama cites and then refutes. It took all the ingenuity of the theistic commentators to turn this around. Ganganatha Jha writes:

> A study of the commentators however sheds a lurid light upon this device of the Vārtikakāra; and shows how hopelessly confused is the entire attempt to fasten this doctrine on Gautama.[56]

A few decades later, Harvard professor Daniel Ingalls took up this same topic in his paper titled, "Human Effort Versus God's Effort in the Early Nyāya (*NS.* 4. 1. 19-21)," apparently independently of Jha, since Jha's paper is not cited. Here Ingalls observes, as had Jha earlier:

> The general movement of Nyāya opinion throughout this period may be judged from one observation: the later the commentator the greater the importance which he assigns to God . . .[57]

Ingalls shows the progressive stages this theism went through at the hands of the commentators, beginning with Vātsyāyana, who started it all with what is characterized by Ingalls as a "bold aboutface (volte face)."

Since then, other studies have further clarified the non-theistic position of early Nyāya.[58] From the various available sources we get the following picture.

The Nyāya system as described by its founder, Gautama, in his 528-verse *Nyāya-sūtra*, has no place for God. Gautama did, however, bring up the hypothesis of God, in order to reject it in favor of human effort or action (*karma*). Some centuries later, Vātsyāyana, the author of the oldest commentary now extant, although acknowledging that Gautama's verse on *īśvara* is the view of another, inexplicably treated it as if it were Gautama's own view.[59] Vātsyāyana thereby put God's foot in the door of the Nyāya system by allowing God to play a role in the working of karma. A few centuries after that, Uddyotakara, the author of the next oldest commentary, opened the door wide for God, by making God stand above the law of karma, and by giving the first Nyāya proof of God's existence. The next commentator, Vācaspati Miśra, seeing that Gautama's verse on *īśvara* was in fact the view of another, so that the position of the previous two commentators who treated it as Gautama's own view could not be maintained, took a new leap for God. Rather than accepting the fact that Gautama here rejects the view that God is the cause of the world, Vācaspati Miśra has Gautama only rejecting the view that God is the material cause (*upādāna*) of the world, and thereby proving that God is the efficient cause (*nimitta kāraṇa*) of the world. The proof that Vācaspati Miśra put forth on behalf of Gautama became the standard Nyāya proof for the existence of God. This proof was taken up in a fourth commentary, and the proof of God was made eloquent in the *Nyāya-kusumāñjali*, both by God's great champion, Udayana, which put God firmly in control in the Nyāya system.

We have now come full circle from where we started. From all the available evidence, it would seem that the original Nyāya system of Gautama, like Jainism and like Buddhism, believed in karma alone as the sole regulator of the cosmos. God was not yet involved.

Just as the Sāṃkhya system is paired with the Yoga system, with Sāṃkhya providing the basic worldview for both, so the Nyāya system is paired with the Vaiśeṣika system, with Vaiśeṣika providing the basic worldview for both. The basic worldview provided by the Vaiśeṣika system is one of eternal atoms. Like in Nyāya, where God has taken over the operation of karma, so in Vaiśeṣika, God has taken control of the eternal atoms. Thus the joint Nyāya-Vaiśeṣika system is seen in India as the staunchest upholder of the idea of God. This is despite the fact that the original Vaiśeṣika textbook, Kaṇāda's *Vaiśeṣika-sūtra*, does not even mention *īśvara*. How, then, did God get there?

Again, as in Nyāya, God found his way into the Vaiśeṣika system only gradually. None of the ancient commentaries on the *Vaiśeṣika-sūtra*, such as the *bhāṣya* by Rāvaṇa, are extant.[60] From what we know of the commentary by Rāvaṇa, it, like the *Vaiśeṣika-sūtra* itself, did not refer to God.[61] The basic worldview of the *Vaiśeṣika-sūtra* as explained in an ancient commentary, probably Rāvaṇa's, was summarized by Śaṅkarācārya in the 8th century C.E., when this was still available.[62] The eternal atoms come together under the impetus of *adṛṣṭa*, unseen potency, to form the visible cosmos. *Adṛṣṭa* is the unseen potency arising from human actions (*karma*) that brings about their fruition, even if in another lifetime, or even in the next periodic cosmos. *Adṛṣṭa* explains how karma works. Thus in early Vaiśeṣika, as was practically universal in ancient India, it is karma that operates the cosmos rather than God. Only later was God brought in to take over *adṛṣṭa* as the efficient cause of the world, that impels the eternal atoms, the material cause.

The oldest available Vaiśeṣika text after the *Vaiśeṣika-sūtra* is the *Daśa-padārtha-śāstra*, which was translated into Chinese about the 5th century C.E.[63] It, too, nowhere mentions *īśvara*. God first appears in the Vaiśeṣika system in the *Padārtha-dharma-saṅgraha* of Praśasta-pāda, about the 6th century C.E. In this text, *īśvara*, who impels *adṛṣṭa*, is responsible for the creation of the world.[64] The teaching of God was attributed to the *Vaiśeṣika-sūtra* from this time onward. A commentary by Candrānanda from perhaps the 7th century C.E. explains a pronoun in verse 3 of the *Vaiśeṣika-sūtra* as referring to *īśvara*.[65] The commentary by Śaṅkara Miśra from the 15th century C.E., for long the only one known, also explains this pronoun as referring to *īśvara*, but adds that it could refer to the more obvious *dharma*, the subject of the preceding two verses.[66] Interestingly, in a commentary by Bhaṭṭa Vādīndra from the 13th century C.E., although theistic, this pronoun is explained entirely differently, as referring to heaven and liberation (*svargāpavargayoḥ*).[67] This diversity of interpretation is made possible by the terse *sūtra* style. Taking advantage of this terseness, *īśvara* is brought in at several other places in the *Vaiśeṣika-sūtra* by the commentators, who made sure that God was here to stay in the Vaiśeṣika system.

The history of the development of the God idea in the Vaiśeṣika system has formed the subject of extensive research conducted over many years by George Chemparathy. In 1965 he published an article in which he brought out a statement from an early commentator specifically saying that God had been imported into the Vaiśeṣika system. The *Yukti-dīpikā*, an early Sāṃkhya commentary that was only lately discovered and first published in 1938, describes in its discussion of the *īśvara* doctrine two systems: the Pāśupata and the Vaiśeṣika. It says that the original Vaiśeṣika system did not admit the existence of *īśvara*, but that the later Vaiśeṣikas accepted this doctrine from the Pāśupatas. It calls this an innovation or invention. Here is this statement from the *Yukti-dīpikā*, concluding its discussion of the *īśvara* doctrine, translated by Chemparathy:

> This (doctrine of Īśvara) is wrongly attributed to the Ācārya [Kaṇāda, author of the *Vaiśeṣika-sūtra*] in order to put a share of your fault on him, but (in truth) it is not his view. Thus (the doctrine) of the followers of Kaṇāda, that there exists an Īśvara, is an invention (*upajñam*) of the Pāśupatas.[68]

The Pāśupatas may be thought of as Śaivas, those who worship Śiva or some form of Śiva such as Paśupati. There is no doubt that popular movements such as this, not only Śaivism but also Vaiṣṇavism, contributed greatly to God's arrival in India.

In summary, of the six philosophical systems of Hinduism, the oldest, Sāṃkhya, and the most orthodox, Pūrva Mīmāṃsā, are avowedly non-theistic; they do not teach the existence of God. The Yoga system includes *īśvara*, but in a peripheral role, and this *īśvara* may not be God. Vedānta originally taught only the impersonal principle called *brahman*; the idea of a personal God, *īśvara*, was brought in later. Nyāya originally denied God, but this was later turned around and made into the definitive proof of God. Vaiśeṣika originally lacked God, but God was later imported from the Pāśupatas. So philosophical Hinduism did not originally accept God. Nor can a single, all-powerful God be found in the Vedas. All this shows beyond reasonable doubt that early Hinduism, like Jainism and Buddhism, was non-theistic.

Therefore, all of ancient India, home of the Wisdom Tradition, was once non-theistic. God was not a part of the teachings of the Wisdom Tradition.

The Problem with God

The Mahā-Chohan, who is regarded as the teacher of the teachers behind the Theosophical movement, and therefore as the foremost authority of our time on the Wisdom Tradition, is recorded as making this remarkable statement:

> The world in general and Christendom especially, left for two thousand years to the regime of a personal God as well as its political and social systems based on that idea, has now proved a failure.[69]

Perhaps a big failure. The Mahatma K.H. said that their own philosophy "is preminently the science of effects by their causes and of causes by their effects."[70] He asked Hume to work out the causes of evil in the world. After enumerating the human vices that one would expect as the causes of evil, K.H. continued:

> Think well over these few words; work out every cause of evil you can think of and trace it to its origin and you will have solved one-third of the problem of evil. And now, after making due allowance for evils that are natural and cannot be avoided,—and so few are they that I challenge the whole host of Western metaphysicians to call them evils or to trace them directly to an independent cause—I will point out the greatest, the chief cause of nearly two thirds of the evils that pursue humanity ever since that cause became a power. It is religion under whatever form and in whatsoever nation. It is the sacerdotal caste, the priesthood and the churches; it is in those illusions that man looks upon as sacred, that he has to search out the source of that multitude of evils which is the great curse of humanity and that almost overwhelms mankind. Ignorance created Gods and cunning took advantage of the opportunity. Look at India and look at Christendom and Islam, at Judaism and Fetichism. It is

> priestly imposture that rendered these Gods so terrible to man; it is religion that makes of him the selfish bigot, the fanatic that hates all mankind out of his own sect without rendering him any better or more moral for it. It is belief in God and Gods that makes two-thirds of humanity the slaves of a handful of those who deceive them under the false pretence of saving them. Is not man ever ready to commit any kind of evil if told that his God or Gods demand the crime?; voluntary victim of an illusionary God, the abject slave of his crafty ministers. The Irish, Italian and Slavonian peasant will starve himself and see his family starving and naked to feed and clothe his padre and pope. For two thousand years India groaned under the weight of caste, Brahmins alone feeding on the fat of the land, and to-day the followers of Christ and those of Mahomet are cutting each other's throats in the names of and for the greater glory of their respective myths. Remember the sum of human misery will never be diminished unto that day when the better portion of humanity destroys in the name of Truth, morality, and universal charity, the altars of their false gods.[71]

The custodians of the Wisdom Tradition, being committed to the upliftment of humanity, have traced the cause of two thirds of humanity's suffering. This cause, theistic religion and the God idea, is something they aim to deliver humanity from.

> The God of the Theologians is simply an imaginary power. . . . Our chief aim is to deliver humanity of this nightmare, to teach man virtue for its own sake, and to walk in life relying on himself instead of leaning on a theological crutch, that for countless ages was the direct cause of nearly all human misery.[72]

To deliver humanity from the God idea, their chief aim, is no small task. According to *The Secret Doctrine*, theism has been around for many ages.

> Thus the first Atlantean races, born on the Lemurian Continent, separated from their earliest tribes into the righteous and the unrighteous; into those who worshipped the one unseen

> Spirit of Nature, the ray of which man feels within himself—or the Pantheists, and those who offered fanatical worship to the Spirits of the Earth, the dark Cosmic, anthropomorphic Powers, with whom they made alliance. . . .
>
> Such was the secret and mysterious origin of all the subsequent and modern religions, especially of the worship of the later Hebrews for their tribal god.[73]

This explains the Mahatma K.H.'s statement cited earlier that "the idea of God is not an innate but an acquired notion." In our own age, the God idea was acquired by the Hebrews as the teachings of the Wisdom Tradition went forth from their home in ancient India, and acquired from the Hebrews by the Christians and Muslims. Abraham is the patriarch of the three monotheistic faiths, Judaism, Christianity through his son Isaac, and Islam through his son Ishmael. Thus Abraham is hailed as the father of monotheism. *The Secret Doctrine* explains Abram, Abraham's original name before God changed it (see Genesis 17.5), as "A-bram," meaning a non-Brahman (the prefix "a" is a negative in Sanskrit). The Brahmans are India's priestly caste, originally the keepers of the wisdom teachings.

> The Semites, especially the Arabs, are later Āryans—degenerate in spirituality and perfected in materiality. To these belong all the Jews and the Arabs. The former are a tribe descended from the Chaṇḍālas of India, the outcasts, many of them ex-Brahmans, who sought refuge in Chaldea, in Sind, and Āria (Iran), and were truly born from their A-bram (no-Brāhman) some 8000 years B.C.[74]

Abraham is the symbolic non-Brahman who does not keep the wisdom teachings in their purity, and thus he becomes the first monotheist. For this he is celebrated in the world. Through the three Abrahamic religions, monotheism now has become the faith of half the population of the world. From the standpoint of the Wisdom Tradition, what Abraham did with its teachings outside of India, in bringing in the God idea, brought about a major world problem. If India is the spiritual motherland of the world, it is to her that the world must turn to solve this problem. But the God idea has now infiltrated India, too. Even karma, which had once taken the place of God, has now been taken over by God. God's arrival in India, it would seem, has brought about an even more serious problem for the world than did the acquisition of the God idea outside of India.

The Mahā-Chohan, whose statement opened this section, also made another statement at the same time, in 1881:

> Oh, for the noble and unselfish man to help us *effectually* in India in that divine task. All our knowledge past and present would not be sufficient to repay him.[75]

I had long wondered about the meaning of this statement. The divine task he refers to is that of propagating the idea of the brotherhood of humanity. This is, of course, the first object of the Theosophical Society. Were there not already noble and unselfish people to help in this? What was so important about doing this effectually in India?

What the Mahā-Chohan here alludes to, I now think, is the problem of theism in India. By the end of the first millennium C.E., Hinduism had acquired the God idea, Buddhism had left India for other lands, and India had fallen under foreign rule, which was to last until 1947. India under God is not in a position to fulfill its dharma as the source of the wisdom teachings, the teachings that alone can solve the world's greatest problem, the problem of God. To deliver India from the God idea, and thereby ultimately deliver humanity from the God idea, the only realistic course then available was to promote the idea of the brotherhood of humanity. Attempting to directly promote non-theism would only have fostered the very thing the God idea was responsible for in the first place: intolerance of the beliefs of others and hatred of everyone outside one's own sect; in brief, religious persecution. This was not an option.

The Theosophical movement was successful, I believe, in establishing the idea of brotherhood in the consciousness of humanity. It also spread the idea of karma around the world, which must someday take the place of God, as it did in ancient

India. "Replace the word 'God' by that of *Karma* and it will become an Eastern axiom," says *The Secret Doctrine*.[76] Knowledge of the ways of karma, affirms *The Secret Doctrine*, would eliminate the cause of two thirds of the world's evil, i.e., the God idea.

> Nor would the ways of Karma be inscrutable were men to work in union and harmony, instead of disunion and strife. For our ignorance of those ways—which one portion of mankind calls the ways of Providence, dark and intricate, while another sees in them the action of blind Fatalism, and a third, simple chance, with neither gods nor devils to guide them—would surely disappear, if we would but attribute all these to their correct cause. With right knowledge . . . the two-thirds of the World's evil would vanish into thin air.[77]

It is not the Theosophical movement, however, that is likely to bring this about; for as most observers recognize, it is no longer a force in the world. Perhaps this is because it, like Hinduism, acquired the God idea, and thus ceased to truly represent the Wisdom Tradition.

NOTES

1. *H. P. Blavatsky Collected Writings*, [ed. by Boris de Zirkoff,] vol. 14, Wheaton, Illinois: Theosophical Publishing House, 1985, p. 310; from "The Post-Christian Successors to the Mysteries," section 34 of *The Secret Doctrine*, vol. 3, 1897; or vol. 5 of the 6-volume Adyar ed., 1938.
2. *The Secret Doctrine*, by H. P. Blavatsky, 2 vols., 1st ed., 1888; many reprints since; I use the definitive edition prepared by Boris de Zirkoff (pagination unchanged), Adyar, Madras: Theosophical Publishing House, 1978, vol. 2, p. 584.
3. *Isis Unveiled*, by H. P. Blavatsky, 2 vols., 1st ed., 1877; reprint, [ed. by Boris de Zirkoff] (pagination unchanged), Adyar, Madras: Theosophical Publishing House, 1972, vol. 1, p. 589.
4. *The Mahatma Letters to A. P. Sinnett*, transcribed and compiled by A. T. Barker, 1st ed., 1923; 2nd (corrected) ed., London: Rider & Co., 1926; facsimile reprint, Pasadena: Theosophical University Press, 1975; 3rd rev. ed., Adyar, Madras: Theosophical Publishing House,

1962, letter #10, p. 52; chronological ed., Quezon City, Metro Manila, Philippines: Theosophical Publishing House, 1993, pp. 269-270.

5. *The Mahatma Letters,* letter #54, 3rd ed. p. 300. See also letter #23B, 3rd ed. p. 152: ". . . Mr. Hume's MSS., 'On God'—that he kindly adds to our Philosophy, something the latter had never contemplated before—. . ."

6. Some have regarded this utilization of the term "God" in the Djwhal Khul/Alice Bailey writings as "skillful means"; that is, the use of teachings that are not ultimately true in order to benefit a spiritually immature audience, one that is presently incapable of assimilating the actual truth. To move a largely Christian audience from an anthropomorphic conception of God to a much more abstract conception of God as the Solar Logos, rather than causing them to reject the Ageless Wisdom teachings altogether as being Godless, would be considered in Buddhism as skillful means.

Others have considered the Mahatma letters to be of questionable authenticity, and have therefore doubted whether their denial of God accurately represents the position of the Ageless Wisdom Tradition. This is based on the statement in Alice Bailey's *The Rays and the Initiations,* p. 342: "The Master K.H., in one of the few (the very few) paragraphs in *The Mahatma Letters* which are genuine and not simply the work of H.P.B. . . ." H. P. Blavatsky said the same thing in an 1886 letter, published by C. Jinarajadasa in the Introduction to *The Early Teachings of the Masters*: "It is very rarely that Mahatma K.H. *dictated verbatim*; and when he did there remained the few sublime passages found in Mr. Sinnett's letters from him." Blavatsky points out here that "the Masters would not stoop for one moment to give a thought to *individual,* private matters relating but to one or even ten persons, their welfare, woes and blisses in this world of Maya, to nothing except questions of really universal importance." The Mahatma letters in question, letters #10 and #22, on the topic of God, certainly pertain to questions of really universal importance. A study of the more than 100 Mahatma letters shows that these two are almost certainly among the few that are genuine (along with letter #2, which is apparently the one referred to in the Bailey passage cited above, and two other letters not found in *The Mahatma Letters,* namely, the first letter of K.H. to A. O. Hume, and the Mahā-Chohan's letter, besides parts of others).

There is a passage that deals directly with this question in Alice Bailey's *Esoteric Psychology,* vol. 2, pp. 229-230: "We have spoken here of God in terms of *Person,* and we have used therefore the pronouns, He and His. Must it therefore be inferred that we are dealing with a stupendous Personality which we call God, and do we therefore belong to that school of thought which we call the anthropomorphic? The Buddhist teaching recognises no God or Person. Is it, therefore, wrong from our point of view and approach, or is it right?" The answer is: "Both schools of thought are right and in no way contradict each other." The author says further: "In form and when in manifestation, the only way in which the human mind and brain can express its recognition of the conditioning divine life is to speak in terms of Person, of Individuality. Hence we speak of God as a Person, of His will, His nature and His form." This statement holds true only for the Western Christian audience to whom it was addressed, since Buddhists and Jainas have in fact developed spiritual systems that have functioned effectively for thousands of years without ever speaking in terms of Person. This answer is reminiscent of a famous editorial that appeared in *The New York Sun* at the end of the nineteenth century, which said in answer to the question of 8-year-old Virginia O'Hanlan, "Yes, Virginia, there is a Santa Claus. He exists as certainly as love and generosity and devotion exist." How else could a question like this be answered? Just as a professor of physics will answer the same question one way when speaking to a class of beginning physics students, and another way when speaking to another physics professor, we may assume that the Tibetan, D.K., would have dealt with this question very differently to an audience of Tibetan Buddhists.

7. *The Mahatma Letters*, letter #10, 3rd ed. p. 52.

8. The *Tattvārthādhigama-sūtra*, written by Umāsvāti or Umāsvāmi, has recently been published in the West in English as *That Which Is*, translated by Nathmal Tatia, Harper Collins Publishers, 1994. A previous translation by J. L. Jaini, *Tattvarthadhigama Sutra*, Sacred Books of the Jainas, vol. 2, 1920, was reprinted by AMS Press, New York, in 1974. A translation with the early commentary of Pūjyapāda called *Sarvārtha-siddhi* was published under the title, *Reality*, by S. A. Jain, Calcutta: Vira Sasana Sangha, 1960. A translation with a modern commentary was published as *Pt. Sukhlalji's Commentary on Tattvārtha Sūtra of Vācaka Umāsvāti*, Ahmedabad: L. D. Institute of Indology, 1974.

When the *Tattvārthādhigama-sūtra* was written, approximately two millenniums ago, Jainas made up a significant percentage of India's population. Today, Jainas make up less than one percent of India's population. Jainas today, living in a sea of Hindus who all believe in God, have sometimes adopted the word God for their *paramātman*, or *muktātman*, or *mukta-jīva*, or *siddha-parameṣṭhi*, which all refer to a liberated soul, perfectly pure, and completely freed from karmic bondage; the goal held out for all souls. This, of course, is not God as understood in other religions. Thus, one may occasionally see references to God in modern Jaina writings, but Jainism has in fact never postulated the existence of God. This is because, as put by Subodh Kumar Pal in "A Note on Jaina Atheism": "—it is *karma* alone which fructuates and determines the course of an individual through different births. Because *the Jaina believes in the inexorable moral law of karma which no mercy can bend.*" (*Jain Journal*, vol. 24, no. 2, Oct. 1989, p. 52; italics his.)

9. The *Abhidharma-kośa*, written by Vasubandhu, has now been published in English with its auto-commentary, as *Abhidharmakośabhāṣyam*, first translated into French by Louis de La Vallée Poussin, 1923-1931, then translated from French into English by Leo M. Pruden, 4 vols., Asian Humanities Press: Berkeley, 1988-1990.

10. *The World's Religions: Our Great Wisdom Traditions*, by Huston Smith, HarperSanFrancisco, 1991, p. 115. This is a revised and updated edition of his 1958 book, *The Religions of Man.*

11. *The Perennial Philosophy*, by Aldous Huxley, New York and London: Harper & Brothers Publishers, 3rd ed., 1945 (1st ed., 1944), p. 22. This shows that Huxley did not conceive of Godhead without God, even though he popularized the use of the term Godhead as something that could be distinguished from God (contrary to standard dictionaries, which define Godhead as God). God is, for him, an inherent aspect of Godhead. He writes, for example, on pp. 23-24: "It would be a mistake, of course, to suppose that people who worship one aspect of God to the exclusion of all the rest must inevitably run into the different kinds of trouble described above. If they are not too stubborn in their ready-made beliefs, if they submit with docility to what happens to them in the process of worshipping, the God who is both immanent and transcendent, personal and more than personal, may reveal Himself to them in his fulness."

12. *The Perennial Philosophy*, p. 21. The Hindu "God-without-form," or impersonal Godhead, is *nirguṇa brahman. Brahman* is equated with *ātman*, the self of all, in the Upaniṣads. Buddhism, with its cardinal doctrine of *anātman*, "no-self," denies the *ātman*. There have, however, been several attempts to show that original Buddhism did not deny *ātman* in the sense taught in the old Upaniṣads, where it is identified with the impersonal *brahman*. Only one of these attempts has been regarded seriously, that of Kamaleswar Bhattacharya in his book, *L'Ātman-Brahman dans le Bouddhisme ancien*, Paris: École française d'Extrême-Orient, 1973 (an English translation is forthcoming). This

book came about as a result of Bhattacharya's studies on Cambodia. While working on old Buddhist inscriptions found there, he was struck by one which read, "Let the Buddha give you enlightenment, by whom the doctrine of no-self was well-taught, as the means of attaining the highest self (*paramātman*), though [apparently] in contradiction." He attempts to show in this book, on the basis of the Pāli and Sanskrit Buddhist scriptures, that the Buddha does not deny the *ātman* taught in the Upaniṣads, but on the contrary indirectly affirms it, in denying that which is falsely believed to be the *ātman.*

The Cambodia connection is of particular interest to students of the Wisdom Tradition. H. P. Blavatsky had said about Angkor Wat, "After the Pyramids this is the most occult edifice in the whole world" (see her entry, "Nagkon Wat," the name used for Angkor Wat, in *The Theosophical Glossary,* p. 223). Paul Brunton's posthumously published notebooks provided further information. See chapter 4, section 7, "The Secret Doctrine of the Khmers," in *The Notebooks of Paul Brunton, vol. 10, The Orient: Its Legacy to the West,* Burdett, New York: Larson Publications, 1987, pp. 197-202. Brunton's informant, a Mongolian Lama, said that Dorjeff and Blavatsky were co-disciples of the same guru. On Dorjeff's life, see: *Buddhism in Russia, The Story of Agvan Dorzhiev, Lhasa's Emissary to the Tsar,* by John Snelling, Element, 1993.

Cambodia was described by Brunton's informant as one of three centers of the secret doctrine, along with south India and Tibet. The headquarters of this tradition shift locations every seven hundred years. This tradition was centered in Cambodia from the sixth to the thirteenth centuries C.E. Before that it was centered in south India. After Cambodia it was centered in Tibet, up till 1939. In Cambodia, it thrived during most of the Khmer Empire, which lasted from the ninth to the fifteenth centuries C.E., and which was centered at Angkor. However, little is known about religion in the Khmer Empire, other than that it included both Hinduism and Mahāyāna Buddhism (which latter apparently included the Ādi-Buddha teaching, found in Kālacakra). This is because, as noted in a recent *National Geographic* article, "The Temples of Angkor," by Douglas Preston, Aug. 2000, p. 86: "Its extensive libraries of writings on palm leaves or animal skins vanished without a trace centuries ago, leaving us only a scattering of puzzling stone inscriptions."

13. *The Mahatma Letters,* letter #10, 3rd ed. pp. 53-56.

14. *Buddhism—A Non-Theistic Religion,* by Helmuth von Glasenapp, London: George Allen and Unwin, 1970, p. 107. This is an English translation of the original German book, *Buddhismus und Gottesidee,*

Wiesbaden, 1954. See also p. 119: "Thus Nirvāna cannot be equated with the Christian God for it lacks most of the distinguishing marks of God: it is not a personality; it does not think, feel, or will; it did not create the world, nor does it rule it, etc."

15. The *Brahma-jāla Sutta* is the first Sutta of the Dīgha Nikāya, so can be found in the Pali Text Society's edition and translation of the latter. A recent English translation is *The Long Discourses of the Buddha*, Boston: Wisdom Publications, 1995 (published as *Thus Have I Heard* in 1987). The idea of Brahmā as the creator is refuted in 2.3-6.

16. This treatise, titled *Īśvara-kartṛtva-nirākṛtir Viṣṇor-eka-kartṛtva-nirākaraṇam*, "Refutation of Īśvara as Creator; refutation of Viṣṇu as Sole Creator," is attributed to Nāgārjuna in the Tibetan Tanjur. It was first published, in Sanskrit and Tibetan, by F. W. Thomas in his "Notes from the Tanjur," *Journal of the Royal Asiatic Society*, 1903, pp. 345-349. An English translation of it is included in: "Two Early Buddhist Refutations of the Existence of Īśvara as the Creator of the Universe," by George Chemparathy, *Wiener Zeitschrift für die Kunde Süd- und Ostasiens*, vol. 12-13, 1968/1969, p. 85-100. The other refutation he includes is from the *Yogācāra-bhūmi*, by Asaṅga.

17. *Encyclopaedia of Buddhism*, ed. G. P. Malalasekera, published by the Government of Sri Lanka, vol. 5, fasc. 2, 1991, p. 346; entry "God," by Gunapala Dharmasiri and Jonathan S. Walters.

18. *The Mahatma Letters*, letter #22, 3rd ed. pp. 137-138.

19. *The Mahatma Letters*, letter #22, 3rd ed. p. 139.

20. *The Mahatma Letters*, letter #22, 3rd ed. pp. 139-140.

21. Incomplete manuscripts of a few other commentaries on the Vedas were discovered in the early 1900s, those of Skanda-svāmin, Udgītha, and Veṅkata Mādhava, all pre-Sāyaṇa. Skanda-svāmin's, the oldest, may possibly date to the 7th century C.E. This is still far removed from the time of the Vedas. Their approach does not differ substantially from Sāyaṇa's.

Sāyaṇa employs a ritualistic interpretation of the Vedas, having reference to sacrifice, and this line of interpretation has by default conditioned modern understanding of the Vedas. But from references found in a much older text, the *Nirukta*, we see that this is only one of three lines of Vedic interpretation. While explaining certain Vedic passages, the *Nirukta* occasionally refers to these three kinds of interpretation (see: *Nirukta* 3.12, 10.26, 11.4, 12.37, 12.38): *adhiyajña*, having reference to sacrifice (the one used by Sāyaṇa); *adhidaivata*, having reference to the deity; and *adhyātma*, having reference to the self or spirit, i.e., the inner. This last kind of interpretation had been almost entirely lost, but in the twentieth century attempts were made by writers such as Vasudeva S. Agrawala to revive it.

Vasudeva S. Agrawala (1904-1966) was the main writer in English on the *adhyātma* tradition of Vedic interpretation. His teacher was Pandit Motilal Sastri, a disciple of Madhusudan Ojha, Raja Pandit of Jaipur. These two wrote many books, but not in English. Agrawala first called attention to this line of interpretation in his 1939 article, "The Vedas and Adhyātma Tradition," *Indian Culture*, vol. 5, pp. 285-292. I am aware of only one other publication in English preceding this that advocated the *adhyātma* approach: "Indra—The Ṛg-Vedic Ātman," by O. K. Anantalakshmi, *Journal of Oriental Research*, Madras, vol. 1, 1927, pp. 27-44. Agrawala went on to publish several books utilizing this approach. His magnum opus is *The Thousand-Syllabled Speech, I. Vision in Long Darkness*, Varanasi: Prithivi Prakashan, 1963, an annotated translation of *Ṛg-veda* hymn 1.164.

22. See: *The Secret Doctrine*, vol. 1, pp. xxiii-xxx. For a list of the "real, original" Sanskrit works once found in India, see "The Strange Story of a Hidden Book," in *The Science of the Sacred Word, Being a Summarized Translation of The Pranava-vada of Gargyayana*, by Bhagavan Das, vol. 1, Adyar, Madras: The Theosophist Office, 1910, pp. i-lxxxi, especially pp. xii-xiv, xl-xlvii. This describes "a special literature which existed and was extant and matter of public knowledge and study in India, some thousands of years ago, and which still exists, but now inextant and hidden, and to be rediscovered by single-minded and laborious search only" (p. lx). The *Praṇava-vāda* is one of these works, whose summarized English translation by Bhagavan Das was published in three volumes, 1910-1913. Two volumes of its original Sanskrit were published: *Pranava Vada of Maharshi Gargyayana and Pranava Vadartha Deepika of Swami Yogananda*, ed. by K. T. Sreenivasachariar, vol. I, Madras: The Brahmavadin Press, 1915; vol. II, Madras: The Modern Printing Works, 1919, Suddha Dharma Mandala Series no. 5 (a-1). The Suddha Dharma Mandala also brought out other of these hidden Sanskrit works, most notably what they call the original *Bhagavad-gītā*, having 745 verses rather than 700 as in the now extant version.

23. *Coomaraswamy, 2: Selected Papers, Metaphysics*, edited by Roger Lipsey, Princeton: Princeton University Press, 1977; Bollingen Series, 89; p. 175; from his 1936 article, "Vedic 'Monotheism.'"

24. *The Cultural Heritage of India*, vol. 1, Calcutta: The Ramakrishna Mission Institute of Culture, 2nd ed., 1958, pp. 327-328.

25. Vasudeva S. Agrawala, *The Thousand-Syllabled Speech, I. Vision in Long Darkness*, Varanasi: Prithivi Prakashan, 1963, p. 180.

26. *Nirukta*, 7.14 (Agni as the first deity), 7.17 (Agni as all the deities; this is found in the *Brāhmaṇas*), and 7.18 (quotation of Vedic verse). See: *The Nighaṇṭu and the Nirukta*, ed. and trans. by Lakshman Sarup, 1st ed. 1920-1927; reprint, Delhi: Motilal Banarsidass, 1967.

27. *Nirukta*, 7.4; *Coomaraswamy, 2: Selected Papers, Metaphysics*, p. 166; Sarup, *The Nighaṇṭu and the Nirukta*, English p. 115, Sanskrit p. 134; also cited by Agrawala, "Yāska and Pāṇini," in *The Cultural Heritage of India*, vol. 1, 2nd ed., p. 300.

28. Sarup, *The Nighaṇṭu and the Nirukta*, p. 115, fn. 10.

29. *Sāyaṇa's Preface to the Ṛgvedabhāṣya*, trans. Peter Peterson, Poona: Bhandarkar Oriental Research Institute, 1974, p. 2 (first published in *Handbook to the Study of the Rigveda*, Bombay Sanskrit Series, 41, 1890).

30. *Rig-Veda-Samhitâ . . . with the Commentary of Sâyanâkârya*, vol. I, ed. F. Max Müller, 2nd ed., London: Henry Frowde, 1890, p. 2, lines 27-29; for English, see: Peterson, *Sāyaṇa's Preface*, p. 6.

31. See: George Chemparathy, "Some Observations on Dayānanda Sarasvatī's Conception of the Veda," *Wiener Zeitschrift für die Kunde Südasiens*, vol. 38, 1994, p. 235-236. On p. 236, he writes: "The reason for the strikingly subordinate position accorded to the Upaniṣads may be sought in the very nature of their central teachings, which could not at all be brought into harmony with Dayānanda's own conception of God, man, and the external world. The Upaniṣads view the Ultimate Reality as absolutistic and monistic. . . . By contrast, Dayānanda accepts a single personal supreme God as the creator of the universe. . . . A strict monotheistic belief . . . could not be constructed on the monistic and idealistic underpinnings of the Upaniṣadic thought." Earlier, on p. 232, he wrote: ". . . Dayānanda set about his work of reform by re-interpreting the Vedic texts in such a way as to present Hinduism as a monotheistic religion, purged of all forms of polytheism and idolatry. In order to achieve this end he had to repudiate certain traditional conceptions on the nature of the Veda and to interpret the Vedic texts in such a way as to make them suit his own ideas."

Others agree that a single, all-powerful God cannot be found in the Vedas. Leading Vedic scholar R. N. Dandekar in his article, "God in Hindu Thought," *Annals of the Bhandarkar Oriental Research Institute*, vols. 48 & 49, 1968, p. 440, writes: "In spite of all such indications, it must be clearly stated that monotheism in the sense of a single ethical god who, while being intimately involved in the world-process, is yet transcendental in character had not developed in the Vedic period." Similarly, leading Western Vedic scholar Jan Gonda in his study, "The Concept of a Personal God in Ancient Indian Religious Thought,"

Selected Studies, vol. 4: *History of Ancient Indian Religion,* Leiden: E. J. Brill, 1975, pp. 1-26, was unable to find this kind of God in the Vedas.

32. "A Mental Puzzle," *The Theosophist,* vol. 3, no. 9, June 1882, Supplement, p. 7. "Man. X., R. 129" is Maṇḍala 10, Sūkta 129. The "R" is apparently a misprint for "S." The line quoted from this Sūkta or hymn is the first line of Ṛk 1, or verse 1.

33. See also: *Sāṃkhya-sūtra* 5.2-10, 6.64. I cite this and like titles as *sūtra* rather than *sūtras,* although both are correct, the Sanskrit being either *sūtram* (singular) or *sūtrāṇi* (plural). For an English translation of the *Sāṃkhya-sūtra* along with the commentaries of Aniruddha and Vijñāna Bhikṣu, see: *The Samkhya Philosophy,* trans. Nandalal Sinha, Sacred Books of the Hindus, vol. 11, Allahabad: 1915; reprint, New York: AMS Press, 1974; reprint, New Delhi: Oriental Books Reprint Corporation, 1979. The *Sāṃkhya-sūtra* is supposed to be the textbook of the Sāṃkhya system, but the extant *Sāṃkhya-sūtra* is clearly a later compilation. It does, however, include undeniably ancient Sāṃkhya teachings. The *Sāṃkhya-kārikā* serves in its place as the textbook of the Sāṃkhya system. The *Sāṃkhya-kārikā* does not mention *īśvara.*

34. Besides Vijñāna Bhikṣu's commentary on *Sāṃkhya-sūtra* 1.92, see his introduction to his commentary (in the Sinha translation cited in note 33, pp. 6-8). His view is followed by Jag Mohan Lawl in his translation of the *Sāṃkhya-sūtra,* titled *The Sankhaya Philosophy of Kapila,* Edinburgh: Orpheus Publishing House, 1921. Lawl says in his explanatory notes on verse 1.92, p. 57: "Some translators make a mistake here by thinking that Sankhaya Philosophy is atheistic, but they are mistaken: he simply means that the inability of the worldly mind to prove the existence of God does not prove there is no God, for Yogis with higher consciousness can see and prove for themselves." In a similar vein, K. P. Bahadur in his translation of the *Sāṃkhya-sūtra,* titled *The Wisdom of Saankhya,* New Delhi: Sterling Publishers, 1978, notes on verse 1.92, p. 75: "It should be noted that it is not said that God does not exist, only that the evidence of His existence is not there."

35. See: *The Mahatma Letters,* letter #10, 3rd ed. p. 52: "Nevertheless we deny most emphatically the position of agnosticism . . ."; p. 53: "Pantheistic we may be called—agnostic NEVER."; letter #54, p. 300: "He makes of us *Agnostics*!! . . ."

36. Summarized from *The Mahatma Letters,* letter #22.

37. Buddhist scholars such as Edward Conze have written that Buddhism is agnostic. See his *Buddhism: Its Essence and Development,* 1951, p. 39: ". . . the Buddhists adopt an attitude of agnosticism to the

question of a personal creator. . . ." This is a general assumption based on the Buddhist teaching of the fourteen undefined points (*avyākṛta-vastu*), that the Buddha refused to discuss. However, it does not take account of the fact that the Buddha is shown in the *Brahma-jāla Sutta* specifically denying that the world was created by God, Brahmā, and in the *Aggañña Sutta* stating how it in fact came about. This is hardly an agnostic position.

Some Buddhist scholars have also attributed something akin to monotheism to one phase of Buddhism, the Tantric phase involving the concept of an Ādi-Buddha (e.g., Conze, op. cit., pp. 43, 191). This attribution was made before these teachings became available in their context (which happened after 1959 when Tibetan refugees brought these teachings with them to India), and before many of the original sources had been published, such as the *Kālacakra Tantra* and its *Vimalaprabhā* commentary, or the *Pradīpoddyotana* commentary on the *Guhyasamāja Tantra*. It is now clear that they are non-theistic like the rest of Buddhism.

38. For more on the Sāṃkhya worldview, particularly in its relation to the Wisdom Tradition, see my article, "Sāṃkhya and the Wisdom-Religion," *Fohat*, vol. 4, no. 4, Winter 2000, pp. 84-86, 92-94.

Some have claimed that Sāṃkhya was originally theistic, and later became non-theistic. The main evidence for this is found in the *Mahābhārata*, where God is included in passages that give distinctly Sāṃkhya teachings. But as shown by Pulinbihari Chakravarti in his *Origin and Development of the Sāṃkhya System of Thought*, pp. 54-58, the *Mahābhārata* presupposes the existence of earlier Sāṃkhya writings. Thus it could easily have incorporated these Sāṃkhya ideas into its own theistic setting.

Others have noted references in early writings such as the Jaina *Ṣaḍ-darśana-samuccaya* and the Buddhist *Tattva-saṃgraha* to both a Sāṃkhya without God (*nirīśvara*), and a Sāṃkhya with God (*seśvara*). However, the latter almost certainly refers to the Yoga system, since the Yoga system was not described separately in these writings.

Johannes Bronkhorst, "God in Sāṃkhya," *Wiener Zeitschrift für die Kunde Südasiens*, vol. 27, 1983, pp. 149-164, attempts to show that the earlier commentators on the *Sāṃkhya-kārikā* accepted the existence of God, *īśvara*. These references appear to me to refer to the *īśvara* of the Yoga system rather than *īśvara* as God. See below.

39. *Yoga-sūtra* 1.23, 1.24, 2.1, 2.32, 2.45.

40. Gangānātha Jhā, *The Yoga-Darshana*, 2nd ed., Adyar, Madras: Theosophical Publishing House, 1934, p. xiv. Nagin Shah has tried to

show that *īśvara* in the *Yoga-sūtra* refers to an "extra-ordinary person" who has achieved the goal of yoga, for as long as he remains in the body. See his article, "An Alternative Interpretation of Patañjali's Three Sūtras on Īśvara," *Sambodhi*, vol. 4, no. 1, April 1975, pp. 1-6. He provides a useful analysis of *sūtra* 1.25 on omniscience.

41. M. D. Shastri, "History of the Word 'Īśvara' and Its Idea," *Proceedings and Transactions of the Seventh All-India Oriental Conference, Baroda, December 1933*, Baroda: Oriental Institute, 1935, pp. 487-503; reprinted with a few additions in *The Princess of Wales Sarasvati Bhavana Studies*, vol. 10, ed. M. D. Shastri, Benares: Government Sanskrit Library, 1938, pp. 35-63.

42. T. M. P. Mahadevan, *Outlines of Hinduism*, Bombay: Chetana, (1st ed. 1956, 2nd ed. 1960,) reprint 1966, p. 138. Mahadevan here echoes M. Hiriyanna, *Outlines of Indian Philosophy*, London: George Allen & Unwin, 1932, pp. 323-324: "Whatever stimulus is required for such change to take place comes from the past karma of the selves that are on life's pilgrimage at the time. This means the abolition of the idea of God from the system, which is indeed a strange tenet to be held by a school claiming to be orthodox *par excellence*."

For the views of the early Pūrva Mīmāṃsā authors on God, and their denial of his existence, see: Ganganatha Jha, *Pūrva-Mīmāṃsā in Its Sources*, Benares: Benares Hindu University, 1942, chap. 5, "God," pp. 43-52.

43. Gaṅgānātha Jhā, *The Prābhākara School of Pūrva Mīmāṃsā*, 1st ed., 1911; reprint, Delhi: Motilal Banarsidass, 1978, pp. 249-250. Even outside of the Pūrva Mīmāṃsā system, there is a question of what the Vedic deities really are. The word that is translated as "god" or "deity" is *deva* or *devatā*. As noted by several scholars, the word *deva* does not really mean a "god." Vidhushekhara Bhattacharya writes: "Its literal sense is 'a shining one' and it is used to denote anything that shines in any way, or that which has some sort of glory or power" (*The Āgamaśāstra of Gauḍapāda*, Calcutta: University of Calcutta, 1943; reprint, Delhi: Motilal Banarsidass, 1989, p. 22). He then gives references to the Upaniṣads where the following things are called *devas*: ether, air, fire, earth, speech, mind, eye, ear, breath, etc.

Some scholars have felt that "angel" is a better translation of *deva* than "god" or "deity." See, for example, Ananda K. Coomaraswamy, "Angel and Titan: An Essay in Vedic Ontology," *Journal of the American Oriental Society*, vol. 55, no. 4, Dec. 1935, pp. 373-419.

Sri Aurobindo saw the Vedic "gods" as outer symbols of inner psychological experience. The various gods represent various aspects of the psyche and what pertains to it. Thus, translations of the Vedas produced by his school may use will-force, divine mind, intuition, etc., in place of Agni, Indra, Saramā, etc.

44. *Bṛhad-āraṇyaka Upaniṣad* 1.4.8, 4.4.22, 6.4.14-18. The other nine principal Upaniṣads are *Īśā, Kena, Kaṭha, Praśna, Muṇḍaka, Māṇḍūkya, Taittirīya, Aitareya,* and *Chāndogya.* This is the traditional list, having ten only. Many modern translations include other Upaniṣads, and sometimes also call these other ones principal.

45. Shastri, "History of the Word 'Īśvara' and Its Idea," 1938, p. 47. Shastri does not give the Upaniṣad references, but refers instead to "Concordance to the Principal Upaniṣads," which as all readers know, is by G. A. Jacob. Jacob lists under the entry "*īśvara*" only the *Bṛhad-āraṇyaka Upaniṣad* among the ten principal Upaniṣads, and gives for it only 1.4.8 and 6.4.14-18. These are what Shastri refers to here. His conclusion that *īśvara* is found in only one of the ten older Upaniṣads and only in this sense is incorrect. Two more *īśvara* references in the principal Upaniṣads may be found in Jacob's *Concordance* under the compound form, "*sarveśvara.*" These are to *Bṛhad-āraṇyaka Upaniṣad* 4.4.22, and *Māṇḍūkya Upaniṣad,* paragraph 6.

46. Shastri, "History of the Word 'Īśvara' and Its Idea," 1938, p. 38.

47. Shastri, "History of the Word 'Īśvara' and Its Idea," 1938, p. 47.

48. See: Paul Hacker, "Relations of Early Advaitins to Vaiṣṇavism," *Wiener Zeitschrift für die Kunde Süd- und Ostasiens,* vol. 9, 1965, p. 147; reprinted in *Philology and Confrontation: Paul Hacker on Traditional and Modern Vedānta,* ed. Wilhelm Halbfass, Albany: State University of New York Press, 1995, p. 33.

49. See: Paul Hacker, "Distinctive Features of the Doctrine and Terminology of Śaṅkara: Avidyā, Nāmarūpa, Māyā, Īśvara," in *Philology and Confrontation,* ed. Wilhelm Halbfass, Albany: State University of New York Press, 1995, p. 94. This is an English translation of his "Eigentümlichkeiten der Lehre und Terminologie Śaṅkaras: Avidyā, Nāmarūpa, Māyā, Īśvara," *Zeitschrift der Deutschen Morgenländischen Gesellschaft,* vol. 100, 1950, pp. 246-286.

50. See: David Reigle, "The Original Śaṅkarācārya," *Fohat,* vol. 5, no. 3, Fall 2001, pp. 57-60, 70-71.

51. This letter was first published in "Echoes from the Past," *The Theosophist,* vol. 28, June 1907, quotation from p. 702 (this printing has "impressional" for "impersonal"); reprinted in *Letters from the Masters of the Wisdom,* compiled by C. Jinarajadasa, [First Series,] Adyar, Madras: Theosophical Publishing House, 1919, no. XXX, p. 79; 5th ed., 1964, p. 66. Corrections were made in the third edition, where this letter was

now "transcribed from the original at Adyar." In the 1907 printing it is dated 1881. Jinarajadasa says its date is probably 1882.

52. Śaṅkarācārya, in attempting to show that *brahman* is conscious, takes as his primary opponent the Sāṃkhya teaching of non-conscious primary substance (*pradhāna*). It would seem that some people at that time equated *brahman* with *pradhāna*. Gauḍapāda, in his commentary on *Sāṃkhya-kārikā* 22, gives *brahman* as a synonym of *pradhāna*, also called *prakṛti*. In the list of Sāṃkhya topics from the lost *Ṣaṣṭi-tantra* found in the *Ahirbudhnya-saṃhitā*, *brahman* is given first, where one would expect *pradhāna* or *prakṛti*, and this is followed by *puruṣa*. Several other early sources attribute the teaching of *brahman* to Sāṃkhya, including the recently discovered *Yukti-dīpikā* Sāṃkhya commentary. For a listing of these, with references, see: Pulinbihari Chakravarti, *Origin and Development of the Sāṃkhya System of Thought*, Calcutta: Metropolitan Printing and Publishing House, 1951; reprint, New Delhi: Oriental Books Reprint Corporation, 1975; pp. 26-28.

53. Summarized from: T. M. P. Mahadevan, "The Idea of God in Advaita," *The Vedanta Kesari*, vol. 53, no. 1, May 1966, pp. 35-38.

54. Although Nyāya means logic, it is somewhat misleading to think of the Nyāya system as only concerned with logic. Ingalls opens his article cited in note 57 below as follows: "It has often seemed to me that the teachings of the early Nyāya might better be called a philosophy of man than an exposition of logic. Certainly the greater part of the *Nyāyasūtra* deals with human problems rather than logical ones: with man's senses, mind and soul; with the means of knowledge he may use and how he may best use them. Again, the method of dealing with these subjects, as the Naiyāyikas themselves admit, is prevailingly that of perception and experience (*pratyakṣa*) rather than that of logic (*anumāna*)."

55. Karl H. Potter, *Encyclopedia of Indian Philosophies*, vol. 2, *Indian Metaphysics and Epistemology: The Tradition of Nyāya-Vaiśeṣika up to Gaṅgeśa*, Princeton: Princeton University Press, 1977, p. 7.

56. Ganganath Jha, "The Theism of Gautama, the Founder of 'Nyāya,'" *Proceedings & Transactions of the First Oriental Conference, Poona, Held on the 5th, 6th and 7th of November 1919*, Poona: Bhandarkar Oriental Research Institute, vol. II, 1922, p. 283. Jha in his translation of these three Nyāya texts does not bring out the fact that Gautama's position has here been reversed by the commentators. This translation was published serially in *Indian Thought*, vols. 4-11, 1912-1919, and then reprinted in book form in 3 vols.; this was reprinted in 1984 by Motilal Banarsidass, Delhi, and again in 4 vols. by the same publisher

in 1999, as *The Nyāya-Sūṭras of Gauṭama, with the Bhāṣya of Vātsyāyana and the Vārṭika of Uḍḍyoṭakara.* In a footnote on p. 1456, Jha tells us that: "In regard to this Section there is a difference among Commentators. According to the *Bhāṣya,* the *Vārṭika* and Vishvanātha, it is meant to propound the Naiyāyika *Siḍḍhānta* that the Universe has been created by God. . . . It is this interpretation that we have adopted in the translation." So a reader of Jha's English translation will never know that the commentators have here reversed Gautama's position.

Another translation, that of Mrinalkanti Gangopadhyaya titled *Nyāya: Gautama's Nyāya-sūtra with Vātsyāyana's Commentary,* Calcutta: Indian Studies, 1982, follows the interpretation of Phaṇibhūṣaṇa Tarkavāgīśa, a modern translator of this text into Bengali. He regards these verses as refuting the view that God alone—as independent of the actions of living beings—is the cause of the world. He gives this section a Sanskrit title stating this, *kevala-īśvara-kāraṇatā-nirākaraṇa prakaraṇa,* as if this is part of Vātsyāyana's text, but it is not. Vātsyāyana titles this section, *īśvara-upādānatā-prakaraṇa,* which Jha fills out as "Examination of the Theory that God is the Cause of the Universe." It appears that Phaṇibhūṣaṇa here offers yet another interpretation of these verses, unlike those of the classical commentators. Unlike Vātsyāyana and Uddyotakara, but like Vācaspati Miśra and Udayana, he regards verse 4.1.19 as the view of another that is to be refuted. But unlike Vācaspati Miśra and Udayana, he does this by saying that God alone as the cause (independent of human effort) is to be refuted, rather than that God as material cause is to be refuted while God as efficient cause is to be accepted. So a reader of Gangopadhyaya's translation, who assumes that this is Vātsyāyana's interpretation, is in fact getting Phaṇibhūṣaṇa's interpretation. This is to say nothing of the original position of the author, Gautama.

57. Daniel H. H. Ingalls, "Human Effort Versus God's Effort in the Early Nyāya (*NS.* 4. 1. 19-21)," *Felicitation Volume Presented to Professor Sripad Krishna Belvalkar,* ed. S. Radhakrishnan, et al., Banaras: Motilal Banarasi Dass, 1957, p. 229.

58. See, for example, the clarification of meaning of *Nyāya-sūtra* 4.1.21 in Chandra Sodha, "A Fresh Approach to Īśvaropādānatā in Nyāya Sūtra," *Glory of Knowledge (Professor Ram Murti Sharma Felicitation Volume),* ed. S. G. Kantawala, et al., Delhi: Eastern Book Linkers, 1990, pp. 211-216. Ingalls had noted that this verse is extremely ambiguous because one must fill in an understood subject and pronoun. Ingalls understood it as saying that God is caused to act by human effort, thus reflecting the Nyāya primacy of human effort, but still not denying the

existence of God. Sodha provides a more natural understanding of it, as saying that the fruit is caused by the actions of man; it does not refer to God (p. 216). This is stated more clearly by Francis X. Clooney, S.J., in "The Existence of God, Reason, and Revelation in Two Classical Hindu Theologies," *Faith and Philosophy, Journal of the Society of Christian Philosophers*, vol. 16, no. 4, Oct. 1999, pp. 523-543. He translates:
"4.1.19. The Lord is the cause, since we see that human action is fruitless.
"4.1.20. This is not so since, as a matter of fact, no fruit is accomplished without human action.
"4.1.21. Since that [action] is efficacious [only due to human effort], the reason [put forth in 4.1.19, regarding the need to posit a Lord] lacks force" (p. 527; bracketed material is his).

C. Bulcke, S.J., says in his 1947 monograph, *The Theism of Nyaya-Vaisesika: Its Origin and Early Development* (Delhi: Motilal Banarsidass, 1968), p. 26: ". . . we intend to show, that whatever may have been the position of Gautama, theism was not an original tenet of Nyāya. The doctrine of karma as exposed in the *Nyāya-Sūtras* leaves little room for Īśvara and all Naiyāyikas will be faced with the problem of a Supreme Lord and a mechanical and inevitable law of retribution."

Gopikamohan Bhattacharyya in his 1961 book, *Studies in Nyāya-Vaiśeṣika Theism* (Calcutta: Sanskrit College), focuses on Udayana's *Nyāya-kusumāñjali*, expounding the proofs for the existence of God. Bhattacharyya therefore does not really deal with early Nyāya. He opens his book with, "The Nyāya-Vaiśeṣika philosopher is an uncompromising theist. . . ." He concludes his book with, "Monotheism is the cream of Indian thought." For a criticism of Bhattacharyya's book, see George Chemparathy, "Theism and Early Vaiśeṣika System," *Kavirāj Abhinandana Grantha*, 1967, pp. 120-121, note 16.

John Vattanky, S.J., in his 1993 book, *Development of Nyāya Theism* (New Delhi: Intercultural Publications), deals somewhat with early Nyāya, but surprisingly, he seems to be unaware of the researches of his predecessors in this area. Ingalls, for example, is neither referred to nor cited in the bibliography. Vattanky can therefore naively say on pp. 22-23: "The intuition of Gautama that God is to be considered the cause of the world has remained the cornerstone of Nyāya theism and for this reason alone Gautama deserves to be called the father of Nyāya theism."

59. Vātsyāyana twice acknowledges that Gautama's verse on *īśvara* is the view of another. First, he introduces this section at 4.1.14 with the words, *ataḥ paraṃ prāvādukānāṃ dṛṣṭayaḥ pradarśyante*, which Jha

translates as, "We now proceed to show up the doctrines of philosophers (of several schools)—" (p. 1449). Second, he introduces verse 4.1.19, Gautama's verse on *īśvara*, with the words, *athāpara āha*, which Jha translates as, "Another philosopher says—" (p. 1457). Yet in his commentary Vātsyāyana treats this as Gautama's own view.

60. See: S. Kuppuswami Sastri, "Rāvaṇa-Bhāṣya," *Journal of Oriental Research*, Madras, vol. 3, 1929, p. 5: "Such considerations may lend support to the conjecture that the earlier Rāvaṇa-Bhāṣya was perhaps dominated by atheistic and pro-Buddhist proclivities, such as might have been quite in keeping with the text of the Vaiśeṣika sūtras, and with the spirit of the tradition characterising the Vaiśeṣikas as *ardha-vaināśikas*, while the work of Praśastapāda gave the Vaiśeṣika system a theistic turn and presented its doctrines in an anti-Buddhist Āstika setting."

61. See: Johannes Bronkhorst, "God's Arrival in the Vaiśeṣika System," *Journal of Indian Philosophy*, vol. 24, 1996, p. 283: "We can conclude that the Kaṭandī [the commentary by Rāvaṇa] did not yet refer to God in its account of the destruction and creation of the world." See also p. 285.

The title of the present article is adapted from the title of this one by Johannes Bronkhorst, which I acknowledge with appreciation.

62. See: Śaṅkarācārya, *Brahma-sūtra-bhāṣya*, 2.2.11-12. The relevant passages were translated and discussed by George Chemparathy in his, "Theism and Early Vaiśeṣika System," *Kavirāj Abhinandana Grantha*, Lucknow: Akhila Bhāratīya Saṃskṛta Pariṣad, 1967, on pp. 113-114. Johannes Bronkhorst provides evidence that Śaṅkarācārya's summary was probably based on the commentary by Rāvaṇa, in his article, "God's Arrival in the Vaiśeṣika System," pp. 282-284.

63. The *Daśa-padārtha-śāstra* is one of two Hindu texts, the other being the *Sāṃkhya-kārikā*, found in the Chinese Buddhist canon. Its Sanskrit original is lost. An English translation was made from the Chinese by H. Ui, and published in *The Vaiśeṣika Philosophy, according to the Daśapadārtha-śāstra*, London: Royal Asiatic Society, 1917; reprint, Varanasi: Chowkhamba Sanskrit Series Office, 1962. Another English translation was made by Keiichi Miyamoto, along with a re-translation from Chinese back into Sanskrit, and a critical edition of the Chinese text. This was published in *The Metaphysics and Epistemology of the Early Vaiśeṣikas*, Pune: Bhandarkar Oriental Research Institute, 1996. Two other re-translations of this book into Sanskrit have been published: *Dasa-Padarthi*, trans. Uma Ramana Jha, Jammu: Shri Ranbir Kendriya Sanskrit Vidyapeetha, 1977; and "Daśapadārthaśāstra," by Karunesha

Shukla, in *Journal of the Ganganatha Jha Research Institute*, vol. 19, 1962-1963, pp. 147-158; vol. 20-21, 1963-1965, pp. 111-130. These were both made from H. Ui's English translation, not from the Chinese text.

64. *Padārthadharmasaṅgraha of Praśastapāda, with the Nyāyakandalī of Śrīdhara*, trans. Gaṅgānātha Jhā, originally published in *The Pandit*, vols. 25-37, 1903-1915; reprint, Benares: E. J. Lazarus and Co., 1916; reprint, Varanasi: Chaukhambha Orientalia, 1982. On this see also George Chemparathy's article, "The Īśvara Doctrine of Praśastapāda," *Vishveshvaranand Indological Journal*, vol. 6, 1968, pp. 65-87. This should be supplemented by George Chemparathy's study of two fragments from a lost text or texts of Praśastapāda and/or his followers that were quoted in Kamalaśīla's *Tattva-saṃgraha-pañjikā*, "Two Little-Known Fragments from Early Vaiśeṣika Literature on the Omniscience of Īśvara," *Adyar Library Bulletin*, vol. 33, 1969, pp. 117-134.

65. *Vaiśeṣikasūtra of Kaṇāda, with the Commentary of Candrānanda*, ed. Muni Śrī Jambuvijayaji, Baroda: Oriental Institute, 1961, Gaekwad's Oriental Series, 136, p. 2. On this recently discovered commentary and its views on God, see also George Chemparathy's article, "The Īśvara Doctrine of the Vaiśeṣika Commentator Candrānanda," *Ṛtam, Journal of the Akhila Bharatiya Sanskrit Parishad*, vol. 1, no. 2, Jan. 1970, pp. 47-52.

66. *The Vaiśeshika Darśana, with the Commentaries of Śankara Miśra and Jayanáráyana Tarka Panchánana*, ed. Jayanáráyana Tarka Panchánana, Calcutta: Baptist Mission Press, 1861, Bibliotheca Indica 34, p. 8; *The Vaiśesika Sûtras of Kanâda, with the Commentary of Śaṅkara Miśra*, trans. Nandalal Sinha, Allahabad: Pâṇini Office, 1911, Sacred Books of the Hindus, 6; reprint, New York: AMS Press, 1974; reprint, Delhi: S. N. Publications, 1986; p. 7; 2nd ed., revised and enlarged, Allahabad: Pâṇini Office, 1923, p. 7.

67. *Vaiśeṣikadarśana of Kaṇāda, with an Anonymous Commentary*, ed. Anantalal Thakur, Darbhanga: Mithila Institute of Post-Graduate Studies and Research in Sanskrit Learning, 1957, p. 2. Although this commentary was published as being anonymous, Anantalal Thakur later identified the author of it as Bhaṭṭa Vādīndra. See his article, "Bhaṭṭavādīndra—The Vaiśeṣika," *Journal of the Oriental Institute*, Baroda, vol. 10, no. 1, Sep. 1960, pp. 22-31.

68. George Chemparathy, "The Testimony of the Yuktidīpikā Concerning the Īśvara Doctrine of the Pāśupatas and Vaiśeṣikas," *Wiener Zeitschrift für die Kunde Süd- und Ostasiens*, vol. 9, 1965, p. 146.

69. *Letters from the Masters of the Wisdom*, [First Series,] letter #1, 1st ed. p. 9; 5th ed. p. 7; *Combined Chronology*, by Margaret Conger,

Pasadena: Theosophical University Press, 1973, p. 46; *The Mahatma Letters*, chron. ed. p. 479.

70. *The Mahatma Letters*, letter #10, 3rd ed. p. 52.

71. *The Mahatma Letters*, letter #10, 3rd ed. pp. 57-58; this letter then continues: "If it is objected that we too have temples, we too have priests and that our lamas also live on charity . . . let them know that the objects above named have in common with their Western equivalents, but the name. Thus in our temples there is neither a god nor gods worshipped, only the thrice sacred memory of the greatest as the holiest man that ever lived. If our lamas to honour the fraternity of the *Bhikkhus* established by our blessed master himself, go out to be fed by the laity, the latter often to the number of 5 to 25,000 is fed and taken care of by the *Sangha* (the fraternity of lamaic monks), the lamassery providing for the wants of the poor, the sick, the afflicted. Our lamas accept food, never money, and it is in those temples that the origin of evil is preached and impressed upon the people. There they are taught the four noble truths—*ariya sacca*, and the chain of causation, (the 12 *nidānas*) gives them a solution of the problem of the origin and destruction of suffering."

72. *The Mahatma Letters*, letter #10, 3rd ed. p. 53.

73. *The Secret Doctrine*, vol. 2, pp. 273-274. For the problem that this hitherto unknown fact regarding belief in God makes for students of the Wisdom Tradition, see: *The Mahatma Letters*, letter #134, 3rd ed. pp. 454-456.

74. *The Secret Doctrine*, vol. 2, p. 200; see also vol. 2, p. 139 fn. The other two monotheistic faiths now make up the bulk of the sons of Abraham. In reference to these, an article titled, "The Akhund of Swat," *H. P. Blavatsky Collected Writings*, vol. 1, 1966, pp. 369-375, is of considerable interest. It gives an account of a Sikh adept who in 1858 foretold the death of the Akhund twenty years later, saying further (p. 374): "Then, the first hour will strike of the downfall of those twin foes of truth—Christianity and Islam. The first, as the more powerful, will survive the second, but both will soon crumble into fragmentary sects, which will mutually exterminate each other's faith."

75. *Letters from the Masters of the Wisdom*, [First Series,] letter #1, 1st ed. p. 11; 5th ed. p. 9; *Combined Chronology*, p. 47; *The Mahatma Letters*, chron. ed. p. 480.

76. *The Secret Doctrine*, vol. 1, p. 653.

77. *The Secret Doctrine*, vol. 1, p. 643.

SELECTED BIBLIOGRAPHY

General Indian

Gonda, Jan. "The Concept of a Personal God in Ancient Indian Religious Thought." In his *Selected Studies*, vol. 4: *History of Ancient Indian Religion*, pp. 1-26. Leiden: E. J. Brill, 1975 (first published in *Studia Missionalia*, Roma, vol. 17, 1968, pp. 111-136).

Kaviraj, Gopinath. "Theism in Ancient India." In his *Aspects of Indian Thought*, pp. 45-71. Burdwan: The University of Burdwan, [1966] (first published in *The Princess of Wales Sarasvati Bhavana Studies*, Benares, vol. 2, 1923, pp. 93-111, and vol. 3, 1924, pp. 67-77).

Shastri, M. D. "History of the Word 'Īśvara' and Its Idea." *Proceedings and Transactions of the Seventh All-India Oriental Conference, Baroda, December 1933*, pp. 487-503. Baroda: Oriental Institute, 1935; reprinted with a few additions in *The Princess of Wales Sarasvati Bhavana Studies*, vol. 10, ed. M. D. Shastri, pp. 35-63. Benares: Government Sanskrit Library, 1938.

General Hinduism

Dandekar, R. N. "God in Hindu Thought." *Annals of the Bhandarkar Oriental Research Institute*, vols. 48 & 49, 1968, pp. 433-465.

Radhakrishnan, S. "The Hindu Idea of God." *The Spectator*, May 30, 1931; reprinted in *The Heart of Hinduism*. Madras: G. A. Natesan & Co., 1936; reprinted in *The Voice of Śaṅkara*, vol. 28, no. 2, 2003, pp. 32-37.

Veda

Coomaraswamy, Ananda K. "Vedic Exemplarism." *Harvard Journal of Asiatic Studies*, vol. 1, 1936, pp. 44-64; addenda and corrigenda, p. 281; reprinted in *Coomaraswamy, 2: Selected Papers, Metaphysics*, edited by Roger Lipsey, pp. 177-197. Bollingen Series, 89. Princeton: Princeton University Press, 1977.

_____. "Vedic 'Monotheism.'" First published in *Dr. S. Krishnaswami Aiyangar Commemoration Volume*, pp. 18-25. Madras, 1936; revised reprint in *Journal of Indian History*, vol. 15, 1936, pp. 84-92; reprinted with the author's further revisions in *Coomaraswamy, 2: Selected Papers, Metaphysics*, edited by Roger Lipsey, pp. 166-176. Bollingen Series, 89. Princeton: Princeton University Press, 1977.

Shende, N. J. "The Devas in the Later Vedic Literature." *Journal of the University of Bombay*, Arts Number 36, vol. 30 n.s., part 2, Sep. 1961, pp. 1-10.

Nyāya

Bulcke, C., S.J. *The Theism of Nyaya-Vaisesika: Its Origin and Early Development.* 1st ed., Calcutta, 1947; reprint, Delhi: Motilal Banarsidass, 1968.

Clooney, Francis X., S.J. "The Existence of God, Reason, and Revelation in Two Classical Hindu Theologies." *Faith and Philosophy, Journal of the Society of Christian Philosophers*, vol. 16, no. 4, Oct. 1999, pp. 523-543.

Ingalls, Daniel H. H. "Human Effort Versus God's Effort in the Early Nyāya (*NS.* 4. 1. 19-21)." In *Felicitation Volume Presented to Professor Sripad Krishna Belvalkar*, pp. 228-235. Banaras: Motilal Banarasi Dass, 1957.

Jha, Ganganath. "The Theism of Gautama, the Founder of 'Nyāya.'" *Proceedings & Transactions of the First Oriental Conference, Poona, Held on the 5th, 6th and 7th of November 1919*, vol. 2, pp. 281-285. Poona: Bhandarkar Oriental Research Institute, 1922.

Sodha, Chandra. "A Fresh Approach to Īśvaropādānatā in Nyāya Sūtra." In *Glory of Knowledge [Professor Ram Murti Sharma Felicitation Volume]*, ed. S. G. Kantawala and Priti Sharma, pp. 211-216. Delhi: Eastern Book Linkers, 1990.

Vaiśeṣika

Bhattachary[y]a, Gopikamohan. "Is Kaṇāda an Atheist?" *Indian Historical Quarterly*, vol. 31, no. 1, Mar. 1955, pp. 85-89; also published in his *Studies in Nyāya-Vaiśeṣika Theism*, Appendix A, pp. 160-163. Calcutta: Sanskrit College, 1961.

Bronkhorst, Johannes. "God's Arrival in the Vaiśeṣika System." *Journal of Indian Philosophy*, vol. 24, 1996, pp. 281-294.

Chemparathy, George. "The Testimony of the Yuktidīpikā Concerning the Īśvara Doctrine of the Pāśupatas and Vaiśeṣikas." *Wiener Zeitschrift für die Kunde Süd- und Ostasiens*, vol. 9, 1965, pp. 119-146.

_____. "Theism and Early Vaiśeṣika System." In *Kavirāj Abhinandana Grantha*, pp. 109-125. Lucknow: Akhila Bhāratīya Saṃskṛta Pariṣad, 1967.

_____. "The Doctrine of Īśvara as Exposed in the Nyāyakandalī." *Journal of the Ganganatha Jha Research Institute*, vol. 24, parts 1-4, Jan.-Oct. 1968, pp. 25-38.

_____. "The Īśvara Doctrine of Praśastapāda." *Vishveshvaranand Indological Journal*, vol. 6, 1968, pp. 65-87.

_____. "Two Little-Known Fragments from Early Vaiśeṣika Literature on the Omniscience of Īśvara." *Adyar Library Bulletin*, vol. 33, 1969, pp. 117-134.

_____. "Praśastapāda and His Other Names." *Indo-Iranian Journal*, vol. 12, 1969-1970, pp. 241-254.

_____. "The Īśvara Doctrine of the Vaiśeṣika Commentator Candrānanda." *Ṛtam, Journal of the Akhila Bharatiya Sanskrit Parishad*, vol. 1, no. 2, Jan. 1970, pp. 47-52.

_____. "The Number of Qualities (*Guṇa*) in Īśvara according to Śrīdhara: A Reconsideration." *Journal of the Ganganatha Jha Kendriya Sanskrit Vidyapeetha*, vol. 27, parts 1-2, Jan.-Apr. 1971, pp. 11-16.

_____. *An Indian Rational Theology: Introduction to Udayana's Nyāyakusumāñjali*. Publications of the De Nobili Research Library, vol. 1. Vienna: 1972.

_____. "A Discussion of the Early Nyāya-Vaiśeṣikas on the Nature of Īśvara." *Bhāratīya Vidyā*, vol. 39, no. 1, 1979, pp. 31-38.

Muir, J. "Does the Vaiśeshika Philosophy Acknowledge a Deity, or Not?" *Journal of the Royal Asiatic Society of Great Britain & Ireland*, vol. 20, part 1, 1862, pp. 22-30.

Sāṃkhya

Bhattacharya, Tarapada. "The Sāṃkhya and God." *Calcutta Review*, third series, vol. 169, no. 2, Nov. 1963, pp. 227-232.

Bronkhorst, Johannes. "God in Sāṃkhya." *Wiener Zeitschrift für die Kunde Südasiens und Archiv für indische Philosophie*, vol. 27, 1983, pp. 149-164.

Hattori, Masaaki. "On Seśvara-Sāṃkhya." *Asiatische Studien*, vol. 53, no. 3, 1999, pp. 609-618.

Mishra, Surendramohan. "On the Problem of God in the Sāṃkhya." *Vishveshvaranand Indological Journal*, vol. 22, 1984, pp. 178-183.

Pal, Subodh Kumar. "A Note on Sāṃkhya Denial of a Creator God." *Visva-Bharati Journal of Philosophy*, vol. 31, no. 2, 1995, pp. 37-44.

Wezler, Albrecht. "Der Gott des Sāṃkhya: zu *Nyāyakusumāñjali* 1.3." *Indo-Iranian Journal*, vol. 12, 1969-1970, pp. 255-262.

Yoga

Bronkhorst, Johannes. "Yoga and Seśvara Sāṃkhya." *Journal of Indian Philosophy*, vol. 9, 1981, pp. 309-320.

Feuerstein, Georg. "The Concept of God (Īśvara) in Classical Yoga." *Journal of Indian Philosophy*, vol. 15, 1987, pp. 385-397.

Pflueger, Lloyd W. "Person, Purity, and Power in the *Yogasūtra*." In *Theory and Practice of Yoga: Essays in Honour of Gerald James Larson*, ed. Knut A. Jacobsen, pp. 29-59. Leiden: Brill, 2005.

Shah, Nagin. "An Alternative Interpretation of Patañjali's Three Sūtras on Īśvara." *Sambodhi*, vol. 4, no. 1, April 1975, pp. 1-6.

Pūrva-Mīmāṃsā

Chatterjee, K. N. "Deities in Mīmāṃsā—Verbal or Physical?" *Bhāratīya Vidyā*, vol. 39, no. 3, 1979, pp. 26-30.

Clooney, Francis X. "What's a God? The Quest for the Right Understanding of *devatā* in Brāhmaṇical Ritual Theory (*mīmāṃsā*)." *International Journal of Hindu Studies*, vol. 1, no. 2, 1997, pp. 337-385.

Jha, Ganganatha. *Pūrva-Mīmāṃsā in Its Sources*, chap. 5, "God," pp. 43-52. Benares: Benares Hindu University, 1942.

Vedānta

Mahadevan, T. M. P. "The Idea of God in Advaita." *Vedanta Kesari*, vol. 53, no. 1, May 1966, pp. 35-38.

Sankaranarayana, S. "The Technique of Taking Refuge in God and Śāṅkara Vedānta." In *Kalyāṇa-mitta: Professor Hajime Nakamura Felicitation Volume*, ed. V. N. Jha, pp. 123-126. Delhi: Sri Satguru Publications, 1991.

Sharma, Arvind. "The Advaitic Conception of God." In his *The Philosophy of Religion and Advaita Vedānta: A Comparative Study in Religion and Reason*, pp. 1-14. University Park, Pennsylvania: Pennsylvania State University Press, 1995.

Sharma, Arvind. "The Vedantic Concept of God." In *Perspectives on Vedānta: Essays in Honor of Professor P. T. Raju*, ed. S. S. Rama Rao Pappu, pp. 114-131. Leiden: E. J. Brill, 1988.

Tapasyananda, Swami. "Hindu (Vedantic) Idea of God." *Vedanta Kesari*, vol. 53, no. 5, Sep. 1966, pp. 227-232.

Warrier, A. G. Krishna. *God in Advaita*. Simla: Indian Institute of Advanced Study, 1977.

Jainism

Pal, Subodh Kumar. "A Note on Jaina Atheism." *Jain Journal,* vol. 24, no. 2, Oct. 1989, pp. 48-53.
Pandey, Brij Kishore. "Is Jain Philosophy an Antitheistic Philosophy?" *Jaina Antiquary,* vol. 25, no. 2, Dec. 1973, pp. 7-12.
Shastri, Damodar. "Jain Concept of God." *Vaishali Institute Research Bulletin,* no. 3, 1982, pp. 108-116.
Singh, S. P. "Concept of God and Jain Philosophy." *Jaina Antiquary,* vol. 24, no. 2, Dec. 1968, pp. 1-9.
Upadhye, A. N. "The Jaina Conception of Divinity." *Wiener Zeitschrift für die Kunde Süd- und Ostasiens,"* vol. 12-13, 1968/1969, pp. 389-393.
Van den Bossche, Frank. "Jain Arguments Against Nyāya Theism: A Translation of the Īśvarotthāpaka Section of Guṇaratna's Tarka-Rahasya-Dīpikā." *Journal of Indian Philosophy,* vol. 26, 1998, pp. 1-26.

Buddhism

Chemparathy, George. "Two Early Buddhist Refutations of the Existence of Īśvara as the Creator of the Universe." *Wiener Zeitschrift für die Kunde Süd- und Ostasiens,* vol. 12-13, 1968/1969, pp. 85-100.
Cheng, Hsueh-Li. "Nāgārjuna's Approach to the Problem of the Existence of God." *Religious Studies,* vol. 12, 1976, pp. 207-216.
Dharmasiri, Gunapala. *A Buddhist Critique of the Christian Concept of God.* Colombo: Lake House Investments Ltd, 1974; [2nd rev. ed.,] Antioch, California: Golden Leaves Publishing Company, 1988.
_____, and Jonathan S. Walters. "God." In *Encyclopaedia of Buddhism,* ed. G. P. Malalasekera, vol. 5, fasc. 2, 1991, pp. 345-347. Published by the Government of Sri Lanka.
Glasenapp, Helmuth von. *Buddhism—A Non-Theistic Religion.* London: George Allen and Unwin, 1970; translated by Irmgard Schloegl from the original German *Buddhismus und Gottesidee.* Wiesbaden, 1954.
Hayes, Richard P. "Principled Atheism in the Buddhist Scholastic Tradition." *Journal of Indian Philosophy,* vol. 16, 1988, pp. 5-28.
Jackson, Roger. "Dharmakīrti's Refutation of Theism." *Philosopy East and West,* vol. 36, no. 4, Oct. 1986, pp. 315-348.
_____. "Atheology and Buddhology in Dharmakīrti's *Pramāṇavārttika.*" *Faith and Philosophy, Journal of the Society of Christian Philosophers,* vol. 16, no. 4, Oct. 1999, pp. 472-505.

Shukla, Karunesha. "Dharmakīrti and Īśvarasiddhi: A Review." *Ṛtam, Journal of Akhila Bharatiya Sanskrit Parishad*, vols. 2-6, 1970-1975, pp. 165-173.

Thera, Nyanaponika. *Buddhism and the God-Idea: Selected Texts.* Kandy: Buddhist Publication Society, 1962; 2nd ed. 1970; The Wheel Publication no. 47 (included in *The Wheel*, vol. 3).

Thomas, F. W. "Notes from the Tanjur, Part 1: *Īśvarakartṛtvanirākṛtir Viṣṇorekakartṛtvanirākaraṇam.*" *Journal of the Royal Asiatic Society of Great Britain and Ireland*, 1903, pp. 345-349.

[The foregoing article was written by David Reigle, and published in *Fohat*, A Quarterly Publication of Edmonton Theosophical Society, vol. 7, no. 1, Spring 2003, pp. 6-11, and no. 2, Summer 2003, pp. 35-39, 46-47, without the notes.]

Tsongkhapa and the Teachings of the Wisdom Tradition

Tsongkhapa (1357-1419) was the founder of the Gelugpa or "Yellow Hat" order of Tibetan Buddhism. This soon became the dominant order in Tibet, making Tsongkhapa Tibet's most influential teacher. Not only was this great reformer the leading teacher of the known or exoteric teachings, but according to Theosophical sources, he was also the leading teacher of the secret or esoteric teachings, the Wisdom Tradition. Some of these hitherto secret teachings were brought out in the late 1800s under the name Theosophy. We would therefore expect that, allowing for the differences necessitated by a different audience, and for what in his time had to remain secret, the basic or core teachings of Theosophy would be the same as the basic or core teachings of Tsongkhapa. But they are not. No, Tsongkhapa specifically and pointedly denied the first and third of what were brought out in 1888 by H. P. Blavatsky as the three fundamental propositions of the Secret Doctrine.

Tsongkhapa is described in Theosophical sources as "the reformer of esoteric as well as of vulgar Lamaism":

> When our great Buddha—the patron of all the adepts, the reformer and the codifier of the occult system, reached first *Nirvana* on earth, he became a Planetary Spirit; *i.e.*—his spirit could at one and the same time rove the interstellar spaces *in full consciousness,* and continue at will on Earth in his original and individual body. For the divine Self had so completely dis-franchised itself from matter that it could create at will an inner substitute for itself, and leaving it in the human form for days, weeks, sometimes years, affect in no wise by the change either

> the vital principle or the physical mind of its body. By the way, that is the highest form of adeptship man can hope for on our planet. But it is as rare as the Buddhas themselves, the last Khobilgan who reached it being Tsong-ka-pa of Kokonor (XIV Century), the reformer of esoteric as well as of vulgar Lamaism.[1]

Tsongkhapa is also described in Theosophical sources as "the founder of the *Gelukpa* ("yellow-cap") Sect, and of the mystic Brotherhood connected with its chiefs,"[2] and again as "the founder of the secret School near Shigatse, attached to the private retreat of the Teshu-Lama":

> As a supplement to the *Commentaries* there are many secret folios on the lives of the Buddhas and Bodhisattvas, and among these there is one on Prince Gautama and another on His reincarnation in Tsong-Kha-pa. This great Tibetan Reformer of the fourteenth century, said to be a direct incarnation of Amita-Buddha, is the founder of the secret School near Shigatse, attached to the private retreat of the Teshu-Lama. It is with Him that began the regular system of Lamaic incarnations of Buddhas (Sang-gyas), or of Śākya-Thub-pa (Śākyamuni).[3]

The Teshu-Lama, or Tashi-Lama, more properly known as the Paṇchen Lama, is the head of Tashi-lhunpo monastery located near Shigatse. This is where the secret Brotherhood alleged to have been the source of the Theosophical teachings was said to be centered. Tsongkhapa is therefore seen in Theosophical writings as being not only the reformer of exoteric Buddhism and the founder of the Gelugpa order, but also as the reformer of the esoteric teachings that we may call the Wisdom Tradition, and the founder, or at least re-organizer, of the secret school or Brotherhood in Tibet that the Mahatma/Bodhisattva[4] teachers behind the Theosophical movement belonged to.

Further, Tsongkhapa's reforms are seen in Theosophical writings as necessary correctives that he undertook, as a Buddha incarnation, in order to put the Buddha's teachings back in line with the Buddha's secret doctrines:

> The records preserved in the Gon-pa, the chief Lamasery of Tashi-lhumpo, show that Sang-gyas left the regions of the "Western Paradise" to incarnate Himself in Tsong-kha-pa, in consequence of the great degradation into which His secret doctrines had fallen. . . . Until the Tsong-kha-pa period there had been no Sang-gyas (Buddha) incarnations in Tibet.[5]

We may then expect his exoteric reforms to be directly related to the esoteric teachings.

It is clear that the Mahatma/Bodhisattva teachers behind the Theosophical movement regarded themselves as followers of Tsongkhapa and his Gelugpas.[6] The teacher referred to as the Maha-Chohan, the chief of the secret Brotherhood, is recorded as saying, after specifically referring to Tsongkhapa, "we, the humble disciples of these perfect lamas":

> Among the few glimpses obtained by Europeans of Tibet and its mystical hierarchy of "perfect lamas," there is one which was correctly understood and described. "The incarnations of the Bodhisattva Padmapani or Avalokitesvara and of Tsong-kha-pa, that of Amitabha, relinquish at their death the attainment of Buddhahood—*i.e.* the summum bonum of bliss, and of individual *personal* felicity—that they might be born again and again for the benefit of mankind."* In other words, that they might be again and again subjected to misery, imprisonment in flesh and all the sorrows of life, provided that by such a self sacrifice repeated throughout long and dreary centuries they might become the means of securing salvation and bliss in the hereafter for a handful of men chosen among but one of the many races of mankind. And it is we, the humble disciples of these perfect lamas, who are expected to allow the T.S. [Theosophical Society] to drop its noblest title, that of the Brotherhood of Humanity to become a simple school of psychology? No, no, good brothers, you have been labouring under the mistake too long already.[7]

What teachings did these Mahatmas/Bodhisattvas of the secret Brotherhood give out as their basic or core teachings?

The brotherhood of humanity formed the first object of the Theosophical Society, closely related to compassion, which forms the cornerstone of Tibetan Buddhism. Besides this, their basic or core doctrinal teachings were formulated as the three fundamental propositions of the Secret Doctrine. These are given in the Proem to H. P. Blavatsky's book, *The Secret Doctrine*, the major sourcebook of the Theosophical teachings:[8]

> Before the reader proceeds to the consideration of the Stanzas from the Book of Dzyan which form the basis of the present work, it is absolutely necessary that he should be made acquainted with the few fundamental conceptions which underlie and pervade the entire system of thought to which his attention is invited. [p. 13]
>
> The Secret Doctrine establishes three fundamental propositions:
>
> (*a*) An Omnipresent, Eternal, Boundless, and Immutable PRINCIPLE on which all speculation is impossible, since it transcends the power of human conception and could only be dwarfed by any human expression or similitude. It is beyond the range and reach of thought—in the words of *Māṇḍūkya Upanishad*, "unthinkable and unspeakable." To render these ideas clearer to the general reader, let him set out with the postulate that there is one absolute Reality which antecedes all manifested, conditioned, being. [p. 14]
>
> Further, the Secret Doctrine affirms:
>
> (*b*) The Eternity of the Universe *in toto* as a boundless plane; periodically "the playground of numberless Universes incessantly manifesting and disappearing," called "the manifesting stars," and the "sparks of Eternity." . . . This second assertion of the Secret Doctrine is the absolute universality of that law of periodicity, of flux and reflux, ebb and flow, which physical science has observed and recorded in all departments of nature. [pp. 16-17]

Moreover, the Secret Doctrine teaches:

> (*c*) The fundamental identity of all Souls with the Universal Over-Soul, the latter being itself an aspect of the Unknown Root; and the obligatory pilgrimage for every Soul—a spark of the former—through the Cycle of Incarnation (or "Necessity") in accordance with Cyclic and Karmic law, during the whole term. [p. 17]

What, then, does Tsongkhapa have to say on these three ideas, the fundamental propositions of the Secret Doctrine? Even though Tsongkhapa's major works are now available in English translation, I will purposely avoid quoting them here, reserving this for an appendix. I will instead quote statements of his views made by modern Gelugpas, to avoid any possibility of taking his words out of context, as someone not trained in his tradition could easily do. It is obvious to all that the present Dalai Lama, being the direct heir to the unbroken Gelugpa tradition of Tsongkhapa, represents his views authoritatively.

Ultimate reality in the Gelugpa tradition is "emptiness"; that is, the fact that everything lacks, or is empty of, any real or independent existence of its own. Things do exist, but only in dependence on other things. They exist depending on causes and conditions. Things arise due to causes, and disappear due to causes. Nothing remains unchanged. Therefore, everything lacks an unchanging inherent nature, or *svabhāva*, that would allow it to exist always staying the same. Everything is empty of such an inherent existence, or *svabhāva*. This is the doctrine of emptiness, *śūnyatā*. While some have attempted to find in this emptiness an "absolute Reality which antecedes all manifested, conditioned, being," as is postulated in the first fundamental proposition of the Secret Doctrine, for Gelugpas emptiness is not this. As the Dalai Lama explains:

> It's important for us to avoid the misapprehension that emptiness is an absolute reality or an independent truth. [pp. 114-115] It is important to clarify that we are not speaking of emptiness as some kind of absolute strata of reality, akin to, say, the

> ancient Indian concept of *Brahman,* which is conceived to be an underlying absolute reality from which the illusory world of multiplicity emerges. Emptiness is not a core reality, lying somehow at the heart of the universe, from which the diversity of phenomena arise. [pp. 117-118][9]

The Dalai Lama's longtime translator is Thupten Jinpa, who completed the traditional Gelugpa monastic curriculum, receiving the highest degree, Geshe Lharam. He made a special study of the writings of Tsongkhapa. He then went on to take a Ph.D. at Cambridge University. His thesis has been revised and published in 2002 as *Self, Reality and Reason in Tibetan Philosophy: Tsongkhapa's Quest for the Middle Way.* In this book we have the most comprehensive and authoritative statement in English of Tsongkhapa's philosophical thought, that of the Middle Way or Madhyamaka. The following quote from this book summarizes from Tsongkhapa what the Dalai Lama said in the above quote.

> What is being denied by all these terms of exclusion is the notion that something positive, perhaps a deeper reality, is being affirmed in the aftermath of negation. This is in direct contrast to those who think that the ultimate nature of reality according to Madhyamaka thought is some kind of an absolute—something along the lines of Leibnizian plenitude or Vedānta's Brahman—that serves in some way as the fundamental substratum of reality. According to Tsongkhapa, anyone who characterizes the ultimate nature of reality in positive terms ultimately falls victim to the deeply ingrained human tendency towards reification [i.e., attributing reality to something that is not real]. No matter what terms you may use to describe it, be it Brahman, plenitude, buddha-nature, the absolute, and so on, such a reified entity still remains an essentialist, metaphysical concept. Only a thoroughgoing negation can lead to full liberation from our tendency for grasping.[10]

Jinpa's term "essentialist" comes from *svabhāva,* "essence," or "inherent nature," understood to mean "inherent existence," or "intrinsic being." *Svabhāva* is a key term in the Theosophical teachings. It occurs seven times in the Stanzas of Dzyan given in *The Secret Doctrine*, and is used in the Mahatma letters to describe a basic reality:

> We will perhaps be near correct to call it *infinite life* and the source of all life visible and invisible, an essence inexhaustible, ever present, in short Swabhavat [*svabhāva*].[11]

It is this, above all, that Tsongkhapa's Gelugpa Madhyamaka doctrine repudiates. The ultimate truth of emptiness is, more fully, the emptiness of inherent existence. This is literally the emptiness of, or lack of, *svabhāva*. As explained by Jinpa, Tsongkhapa's repudiation of *svabhāva* is total and unequivocal.

> First and foremost, he [Tsongkhapa] wants to make it clear that the Mādhyamika's rejection of *svabhāva* ontology must be unqualified and absolute. . . . The negation of *svabhāva*, i.e. intrinsic being, must be absolute and universal, yet it should not destroy the reality of the everyday world of experience. . . . [p. 297] [T]he Mādhyamika's emptiness is the absolute negation of intrinsic being—i.e. it is a mere absence of intrinsic being with no positive content. [p. 299][12]

That is, Tsongkhapa's denial of *svabhāva* is absolute, with no implication of affirming *svabhāva* in some deeper reality. It is not like saying John Doe does not see with his left eye, thereby implying that he sees with his right eye. Tsongkhapa's denial of *svabhāva* is a non-implicative, absolute negation. Moreover, this absence of *svabhāva* is itself the ultimate nature of reality.

> In that Tsongkhapa saw the Madhyamaka's *śūnyatā* (emptiness) to be a non-implicative, absolute negation is beyond question. It is, however, not a mere negation *per se*; it is an absolute negation of *svabhāva* (intrinsic being). By maintaining this, Tsongkhapa is suggesting that the absence of intrinsic being is the ultimate nature of reality![13]

Tsongkhapa, then, denies *svabhāva* altogether, saying that the very absence of *svabhāva* is the ultimate nature of reality. So the ultimate nature of reality is the fact of emptiness, the fact that everything lacks an absolute essence. Emptiness here is a description of the way things are, not a description of what is. Theosophy, too, describes its ultimate reality, which it calls "space," as emptiness, adopting an early translation of *śūnyatā*.[14] But in Theosophy it is a description of what is, not a description of the way things are. In *The Secret Doctrine* we read:

> "What is that which was, is, and will be, whether there is a Universe or not; whether there be gods or none?" asks the esoteric Senzar Catechism. And the answer made is—SPACE.[15]

As Blavatsky had explained earlier in another place:

> Hence, the Arahat secret doctrine on cosmogony admits but of one absolute, indestructible, eternal, and uncreated UNCONSCIOUSNESS (so to translate), of an element (the word being used for want of a better term) absolutely independent of everything else in the universe; a something ever present or ubiquitous, a Presence which ever was, is, and will be, whether there is a God, gods or none; whether there is a universe or no universe; existing during the eternal cycles of Maha Yugas, during the *Pralayas* as during the periods of *Manvantara*: and this is SPACE, ... Space, then, or *Fan, Bar-nang* (*Mahā-Śūnyatā*) or, as it is called by Lao-tze, the "Emptiness" is the nature of the Buddhist Absolute.[16]

Space or emptiness (*śūnyatā*) as taught in Theosophy is a description of what ultimately is, a name of the omnipresent, eternal, boundless, and immutable principle taught as the first fundamental proposition of the Secret Doctrine. It is not, as in Tsongkhapa's teachings, a description of the way things are, the fact of their emptiness, or lack of *svabhāva*. It is not the total negation of *svabhāva*, absolute essence, but on the contrary is even equated with it. Blavatsky explains further:

> *Prakriti, Svabhavat* or *Ākāśa* is—SPACE as the Tibetans have it; Space filled with whatsoever substance or no substance at all; *i.e.*, with substance so imponderable as to be only metaphysically conceivable. . . . "That which we call form (*rūpa*) is not different from that which we call space (*Śūnyatā*) . . . Space is not different from Form. . . ." (Book of *Sin-king* or the *Heart Sutra*. . . .)[17]

This is not at all how Tsongkhapa teaches emptiness. For him, following the *Heart Sūtra* just cited, form is indeed not different from emptiness. But this emptiness is not space as described above. Rather, it is the ultimate nature of things. It is a nature (*svabhāva*) that is no nature (*niḥsvabhāva*). Everything is empty, without *svabhāva*. There is no underlying metaphysical essence, no "one absolute Reality." Jinpa explains further:

> Since Tsongkhapa's ontology contains no notion of an underlying unitary substratum, it cannot be defined by any criterion as monistic. Although Tsongkhapa undeniably accepts that emptiness is the sole ultimate (*paramārtha*), there is no suggestion that it (emptiness) is some kind of underlying hidden absolute with unique ineffable metaphysical properties. For emptiness too is 'relative' in that its identity and existence are contingent upon the things on which it is defined. For Tsongkhapa, apart from the emptinesses of individual things and persons, there is no 'universal,' all-encompassing emptiness that can be characterized as some kind of great 'mother-emptiness.'[18]

But the Wisdom Tradition teaches exactly a universal emptiness or space that can be characterized as a great mother-emptiness.

> Space is called in the esoteric symbolism "the Seven-Skinned Eternal Mother-Father." It is composed from its undifferentiated to its differentiated surface of seven layers.[19]

Moreover, the Stanzas of Dzyan refer to this Mother-Father as *svabhāva*. Describing the period of rest before the manifestation of a new universe, they say:

> Darkness alone filled the boundless all, for father, mother and son were once more one, . . . [1.5]
> . . . Darkness alone was father-mother, Svabhavat, and Svabhavat was in darkness. [2.5][20]

From this father-mother, space or emptiness, having an essence or *svabhāva,* and being a substance so imponderable as to be only metaphysically conceivable, springs the universe at the time of re-awakening. According to a secret commentary:

> "The Initial Existence in the first twilight of the Mahā-Manvantara [after the MAHĀ-PRALAYA that follows every age of Brahmā] is a CONSCIOUS SPIRITUAL QUALITY. . . .
> "It is substance to OUR spiritual sight. It cannot be called so by men in their WAKING STATE; therefore they have named it in their ignorance 'God-Spirit.'
> ". . . As its substance is of a different kind from that known on earth, the inhabitants of the latter, seeing THROUGH IT, believe in their illusion and ignorance that it is empty space. There is not one finger's breadth [ANGULA] of void Space in the whole Boundless [Universe]. . . ."[21]

"All is empty" teaches Mahāyāna Buddhism. Tsongkhapa explains that all is empty of any inherent existence or *svabhāva,* and that this fact of their emptiness is the sole ultimate reality. Theosophy explains "all is empty" as meaning that all consists of the imponderable something called space, an emptiness that is the sole ultimate reality. While everything in the phenomenal universe lacks any *svabhāva* or inherent existence of its own, it all consists of space, the one and only thing that does have an inherent nature or *svabhāva.* So Tsongkhapa and Theosophy fundamentally disagree on the most basic teachings of *svabhāva,* or an ultimate nature, and emptiness, or the ultimate reality.

As a last resort, can we possibly find something akin to the first fundamental proposition of the Secret Doctrine in the idea of the buddha-nature (*tathāgata-garbha*) that is held to be found within all? No, insists Tsongkhapa! As put by Jinpa:

> Tsongkhapa is extremely sensitive to any temptation to perceive buddha-nature (*tathāgatagarbha*) as some kind of absolute, primordial entity similar to an eternal soul. He vehemently argues that to subscribe to any notion of a substantial entity called an essence is equal to adhering to the non-Buddhist concept of *ātman*. For Tsongkhapa, to adhere to such concepts is, as it were, to bring back the ghost of an eternal self through the back door![22]

We are therefore unable to find any point of agreement, as we would expect to find, between the teachings of Tsongkhapa and the first fundamental proposition of the Secret Doctrine, an omnipresent, eternal, boundless, and immutable principle. On the contrary, Tsongkhapa pointedly refutes any such thing, and makes this denial the basic platform of his teachings. It is one thing to not speak about an esoteric teaching, leaving the possibility that one actually accepts it but cannot speak about it; it is another to pointedly refute it, and to make this the central platform of one's teachings. It could even be said that the first fundamental proposition of Tsongkhapa's Gelugpa order is the denial of an omnipresent, eternal, boundless, and immutable principle. This is a very real problem for Theosophists, who hold Tsongkhapa to be the reformer of the secret Brotherhood to which their Mahatma/Bodhisattva teachers belonged.

The third fundamental proposition of the Secret Doctrine fares no better with Tsongkhapa. It is the fundamental identity of all souls with the universal oversoul, itself an aspect of the unknown root. In East Asian Buddhism, the *tathāgata-garbha* (the buddha-nature) is equated with the "one mind" (*eka-citta*) or universal mind. It is also equated with the *ālaya-vijñāna*, "storehouse consciousness," or "foundational consciousness." This is likened to the ocean and its waves. A wave rises and falls, like the individual consciousness that comprises an individual person, yet does not differ from the ocean, like the storehouse consciousness is the same as the one mind. But as just seen, Tsongkhapa rejects any understanding of the *tathāgata-garbha* as a universal mind in the sense of something that all minds or consciousnesses or souls could be one with. For him, any such statement found in the Buddhist sūtras requires interpretation. Thus, the *tathāgata-garbha* is understood by Tsongkhapa as the emptiness of the mind. The *ālaya-vijñāna* as equated with the *tathāgata-garbha* is understood as emptiness. The *ālaya-vijñāna* as an individual consciousness, the highest part of the aggregate of consciousness (*vijñāna-skandha*) of a person, was specifically denied to exist by Tsongkhapa, even conventionally.[23] Like the *tathāgata-garbha*, the mind of clear light (*prabhāsvara-citta*) was understood as an individual potential. Any idea of a universal oversoul was pointedly rejected by Tsongkhapa. There is no universal oversoul that all souls could be one with, nor is there an unknown root that it could be an aspect of.

What, then, are students of the Wisdom Tradition to do, when Tsongkhapa, who their Mahatma/Bodhisattva teachers claim to follow, specifically and pointedly refutes the first and third fundamental propositions of the Secret Doctrine? I have attempted to show elsewhere that the doctrinal position of the Wisdom Tradition is Great Madhyamaka, and that this agrees with the fundamental propositions of the Secret Doctrine.[24] It is well known that when the Great Madhyamaka teachings were brought out in Tibet by Dolpopa and his Jonangpa order, they were forcefully refuted by Tsongkhapa and his Gelugpa order. It is also well known that one of Theosophy's main purposes, in harmony with its brotherhood ideal, is to attempt to reconcile all the religions and philosophies of the world. Less known in the West is that in the latter part of the 19th century, the same time that the Theosophical teachings were being brought out, another movement with similar aims was launched in Tibet. This is the Ri-mé, or non-sectarian movement. One of its main teachers was Ju Mipham. Mipham attempted a reconciliation of the long opposed Jonangpa and Gelugpa doctrinal positions. As described in a recent article by Dorji Wangchuk:

> [Mi-pham] attempted to reconcile these seemingly irreconcilable positions. According to him, it is only in their approaches, and not in their intended goal that the Jo-naṅ-pas and the dGe-lugs-pas differ. Mi-pham viewed the difference between the

Jo-naṅ emphasis on the positive aspect and the dGe-lugs stress on the negative aspect as a difference in the strategies (*thabs*: *upāya*) employed to argumentatively establish (*sgrub*) *nirvāṇa* and eliminate (*'joms*) *saṃsāra*, respectively.[25]

Mipham is saying that the approach of the Jonangpa position is to emphasize the positive aspect by the strategy of establishing *nirvāṇa*, the intended goal, while the approach of the Gelugpa position is to emphasize the negative aspect by the strategy of eliminating *saṃsāra*, our worldly existence, in order to reach the same intended goal of *nirvāṇa*, the state of enlightenment. The one approach is to establish what is; the other approach is to eliminate what is not. Thus the first uses positive descriptions of what is; the other uses negative descriptions or negations of what is not. To say, then, that buddha-nature truly exists, as say Jonangpas, or that there is an omnipresent, eternal, boundless, and immutable principle, as say Theosophists, does not have to contradict that everything is empty of inherent existence, as say Gelugpas. But for six hundred years these two approaches have been seen as irreconcilably contradictory, and it will take more than a simple statement like this to reconcile them. So Mipham explains, using the needed technical terms, specifically how the two could agree. As summarized in the same article:

Although often ignored by both the parties, Mi-pham indeed saw a common element upon which they could agree. According to him, Dol-po-pa had accepted the idea that reality as experienced in meditative equipoise is free from manifoldness. Hence, if what one experiences in meditative equipoise is indeed ultimate reality, then even for Dol-po-pa, the highest reality is "freedom from manifoldness." . . . Similarly, according to Tsoṅ-kha-pa, so long as one holds the "appearances [of phenomena characterised by] dependent origination" (*snaṅ ba rten 'byuṅ*) and their emptiness (*stoṅ pa*) apart, one has not yet perfected one's view. One's view becomes only then perfect when the "appearances" [of phenomena] and their "emptiness" are perceived simultaneously. . . . This "union of appearance and

> emptiness" is, for Mi-pham, identical with "freedom from manifoldness." Thus, according to him, both Dol-po-pa and Tsoṅ-kha-pa, like many other Indian and Tibetan scholars and sages, were referring to one and the same absolute truth upon which, ironically, both vehement disputes and reconciliation hinged.[26]

If this is true, that both were referring to one and the same absolute truth, it would be a matter of each approach using the strategy or means it regarded as necessary to reach the goal. The ultimate test of whether or not any given doctrinal position is an appropriate means, according to both Mahāyāna Buddhist values and Wisdom Tradition values, is that it must result in the furthering of compassion in the individual, and of brotherhood in the world. It is certainly the case that Tsongkhapa's teaching of the ultimate reality of emptiness, as the fact that everything lacks any inherent existence, has passed this test, despite the seeming lack of any self who could feel compassion. Jinpa says:

> Perhaps the most important test of valid insight into emptiness for Tsongkhapa is how one's understanding manifests in action. If, as a result of prolonged contemplation on emptiness, the individual becomes more and more desensitized to the sufferings of the world, there is a serious flaw in one's understanding of the teachings on no-self. According to Tsongkhapa, a deepening of one's understanding of emptiness must naturally lead to a deepening of one's belief in the principles of causality and karma. In other words, profound awareness of the truly empty nature of things and events must manifest in compassionate ethical behaviour. . . . One could say that compassionate action is the *authentic* way of being in no-self. . . . One could say that in the ethical sense, this refers to living a totally altruistic way of life, for all actions that pertain to others now stem from a perspective that is no longer rooted in the notion of a 'truly' important, egoistic self. From the philosophical point of view, such a way of life represents a mode of being that is free from grasping at supposedly 'real' entities.[27]

The basic ethical teachings of Tsongkhapa have been seen to agree with those of the Wisdom Tradition, while the basic doctrinal teachings have been seen to disagree. Students of the Wisdom Tradition, those who look upon Tsongkhapa as a main teacher in their lineage, will not say of the doctrinal teachings that one is right and one is wrong. So they are obliged to try and reconcile them. While the reconciliation proposed by Mipham has not yet found acceptance among Tsongkhapa's Gelugpas, nor is it likely to any time soon, it may well fare better among students of the Wisdom Tradition.[28]

NOTES

1. *The Mahatma Letters to A. P. Sinnett from the Mahatmas M. & K. H.*, transcribed and compiled by A. T. Barker, first edition, London: 1923; second edition, corrected, London: 1926; third and revised edition, edited by Christmas Humphreys and Elsie Benjamin, Adyar, Madras: Theosophical Publishing House, 1962, pp. 43-44; . . . in chronological sequence, arranged and edited by Vicente Hao Chin, Jr., Quezon City, Philippines: Theosophical Publishing House, 1993, p. 62.

2. *The Theosophical Glossary*, by H. P. Blavatsky, 1892; photographic reprint, Los Angeles: The Theosophy Company, 1971, p. 305.

3. *H. P. Blavatsky Collected Writings*, [compiled by Boris de Zirkoff,] vol. 14, Wheaton, Ill.: Theosophical Publishing House, 1985, p. 425, from her "Amita Buddha, Kwan-shai-yin, and Kwan-yin—What the 'Book of Dzyan' and the Lamaseries of Tsong-kha-pa Say."

4. The teachers behind the Theosophical movement were not known as Mahatmas in Tibet, but rather as Byang chubs, pronounced Chang chub, the Tibetan translation of the Sanskrit word Bodhisattva. See on this: *The Mahatma Letters to A. P. Sinnett*, letter no. 49, 1st and 2nd eds., p. 285; 3rd ed., p. 281; chronological ed., letter no. 20, p. 75 (Byang-tzyoobs, Tchang-chubs); and *H. P. Blavatsky Collected Writings*, vol. 4, p. 16 (Byang-tsiub); vol. 6, pp. 97, 101, 109, 273 (Byang-tsiubs). Mahatma is only an Indian name for them adopted by Theosophical writers then living in India, because it was better known among the people there. See: *Esoteric Buddhism*, by A. P. Sinnett, fifth ed., 1885,

pp. 7-8. Nonetheless, the term Mahātma can be found in old Buddhist texts such as the *Yukti-ṣaṣṭikā* by Nāgārjuna, verses 4, 50, 54, 58. For an English translation of this text, see: *Nagarjuniana: Studies in the Writings and Philosophy of Nāgārjuna*, by Chr. Lindtner, 1982, pp. 100-119. This text has also been translated as "The *Yuktiṣaṣṭikākārikā* of Nāgārjuna," by Fernando Tola and Carmen Dragonetti, *Journal of the International Association of Buddhist Studies*, vol. 6, no. 2, 1983, pp. 94-123; reprinted in their 1995 book, *On Voidness: A Study on Buddhist Nihilism*, pp. 19-51. A new translation is *Nāgārjuna's Reason Sixty with Chandrakīrti's Reason Sixty Commentary*, by Joseph John Loizzo and the AIBS Translation Team, 2007.

5. *H. P. Blavatsky Collected Writings*, vol. 14, p. 427. See also vol. 4, p. 11, which appears to be the original source of this statement.

6. Among the many Theosophical references indicating this are, for example: *H. P. Blavatsky Collected Writings*, vol. 6, p. 198: "In Sikkim and Tibet they are called Dug-pas (red-caps), in contra-distinction to the Geluk-pas (yellow-caps), to which latter most of the adepts belong." Ibid., p. 272: "Even Csoma de Körös knew very little of the *real gelukpas* and Esoteric Lamaism." Vol. 4, p. 18: "a lamasery, with a school attached where the orphans of Red Caps, and the converted Shammars should be instructed in the 'Good Doctrine' of the Gelukpas." Vol. 14, p. 433: "None of these has ever received his information from a genuine Gelugpa source: all have judged Buddhism from the bits of knowledge picked up at Tibetan frontier lamaseries, in countries thickly populated by Bhutanese and Lepchas, Böns, and red-capped Dugpas, along the line of the Himālayas. . . . None of these have anything to do with the real philosophical Buddhism of the Gelugpas, or even of the most educated among the Sakyapa and Kadampa sects."

7. "View of the Chohan on the T.S.," more commonly known as the Maha-Chohan's letter, published in a number of places, including *The Mahatma Letters to A. P. Sinnett*, chronological ed., p. 480, and also is available online here at: www.easterntradition.org. The asterisked quote within this quote is given in the original as from "Rhys Davids," but appears instead to be a paraphrase from *Narratives of the Mission of George Bogle to Tibet and of the Journey of Thomas Manning to Lhasa*, edited by Clements R. Markham, London: Trübner and Co., 1876, p. xlvii.

8. *The Secret Doctrine,* by H. P. Blavatsky, 2 vols., first edition, 1888; many reprints; I use the definitive edition prepared by Boris de Zirkoff (pagination unchanged), Adyar, Madras: Theosophical Publishing House, 1978, vol. 1, pp. 13-17. The fundamental propositions of the Secret Doctrine are also found re-stated and expanded in *A Treatise on Cosmic Fire,* by Alice Bailey, New York: 1925, pp. 3-7.

9. *Essence of the Heart Sutra: The Dalai Lama's Heart of Wisdom Teachings,* Boston: Wisdom Publications, 2002.

10. Thupten Jinpa, *Self, Reality and Reason in Tibetan Philosophy: Tsongkhapa's Quest for the Middle Way,* London: RoutledgeCurzon, 2002, p. 60.

11. *The Mahatma Letters to A. P. Sinnett,* letter no. 15, 3rd ed. p. 89. See also letter no. 11, 3rd ed. p. 60: "To comprehend my answers you will have first of all to view the eternal *Essence,* the Swabhavat not as a compound element you call spirit-matter, but as the one element for which the English has no name." In addition, see letter no. 22, 3rd ed. p. 136: "Study the laws and doctrines of the Nepaulese Swabhavikas, the principal Buddhist philosophical school in India, and you will find them the most learned as the most scientifically logical wranglers in the world. Their plastic, invisible, eternal, omnipresent and unconscious Swabhavat is Force or *Motion* ever generating its electricity which is life."

12. Thupten Jinpa, "Delineating Reason's Scope for Negation: Tsongkhapa's Contribution to Madhyamaka's Dialectical Method," *Journal of Indian Philosophy,* vol. 26, no. 4, Aug. 1998, pp. 297, 299. This is restated in his book, *Self, Reality and Reason in Tibetan Philosophy,* on pp. 62-63. I have quoted this from his journal article rather than from his book, because when he slightly rephrased this in his book, he took out the word "*svabhāva*" and used instead the words "essentialist" and "intrinsic existence," respectively, in the two occurrences.

13. Thupten Jinpa, ibid., p. 295. This is paraphrased in his book on p. 61. Note that the word "suggesting" used in Jinpa's sentence, "Tsongkhapa is suggesting that the absence of intrinsic being is the ultimate nature of reality," is only a concession to modern scholarly norms of usage. It has become customary in scholarly circles to only "suggest" things, not to declare them. But in fact, Tsongkhapa is here doing more than just suggesting; this is his firmly held position.

14. "Space" as the translation of *śūnyatā* was adopted from the early translation of the *Heart Sūtra* by Samuel Beal, found in his book, *A Catena of Buddhist Scriptures from the Chinese*, London: Trübner & Co., 1871, pp. 282-284. This translation was quoted by Blavatsky in her notes to T. Subba Row's article, "The Aryan-Arhat Esoteric Tenets on the Sevenfold Principle in Man," published in *The Theosophist*, vol. 3, no. 4, January, 1882, pp. 93-99. This article along with her notes was reprinted in *H. P. Blavatsky Collected Writings*, vol. 3, where the "space (sûnyatâ)" quote occurs on pp. 405-406.

Then in the Proem to *The Secret Doctrine*, vol. 1, pp. 14 ff., where the three fundamental propositions are given, absolute abstract space is one of the two aspects under which the first proposition, namely, an omnipresent, eternal, boundless, and immutable principle, is said to be symbolized. The second of the two aspects under which it is said to be symbolized is absolute abstract motion. However, when speaking of this boundless, immutable principle, it is often simply called "space," as in the esoteric Senzar Catechism quoted immediately below.

The reason that space must be primary, when the omnipresent, eternal, boundless, and immutable principle in symbolized under two aspects, is that for motion to exist, there must be something to move (see Mahatma letter no. 22, 3rd ed. p. 139). Hence, space is in some sense substantial, however imponderable, and cannot here be a mere absence. [Later research indicates that "space" is here the translation not of *śūnyatā* but of *dhātu*, meaning both "basic space" (Tib. *dbyings*) and "element" (Tib. *khams*), as in the one element.]

15. *The Secret Doctrine*, vol. 1, p. 9.

16. Blavatsky's notes on "The Aryan-Arhat Esoteric Tenets on the Sevenfold Principle in Man," in *H. P. Blavatsky Collected Writings*, vol. 3, p. 423.

17. Blavatsky's notes, ibid., pp. 405-406 fn.

18. Thupten Jinpa, *Self, Reality and Reason*, pp. 174-175.

19. *The Secret Doctrine*, vol. 1, p. 9.

20. *The Secret Doctrine*, vol. 1, pp. 27, 28.

21. *The Secret Doctrine*, vol. 1, p. 289. These are "Extracts from a private commentary, hitherto secret."

22. Thupten Jinpa, *Self, Reality and Reason*, p. 139. On the *ātman* question, see "Ātman/Anātman in Buddhism and Its Implication for

the Wisdom Tradition," by Nancy Reigle, published as chapter 8 of this book.

23. This denial of even the conventional existence of the *ālaya-vijñāna* is found in Tsongkhapa's *Notes on the Eight Great Difficult Points of the Mūla-madhyamaka-kārikā* (*rTsa ba shes rab kyi dka' gnad chen po brgyad kyi brjed byang*), written down from his lectures by his disciple rGyal-tshab-rje. It was made known in Lobsang Dargyay's article, "Tsong-Kha-pa's Understanding of Prāsaṅgika Thought," *Journal of the International Association of Buddhist Studies*, vol. 10, no. 1, 1987, pp. 55-65. He summarizes this point on p. 60 as follows:

> (1) Negation of *ālayavijñāna*: Tsong-kha-pa claims that the Prāsaṅgika system denies the existence of *ālayavijñāna* even on the conventional (*saṃvṛti*) level, not to mention on the ultimate (*paramārtha*) level.

These eight difficult points, or unique tenets, formed the subject of a Ph.D. thesis by Daniel Cozort that was later revised and published as *Unique Tenets of the Middle Way Consequence School*, Ithaca, N.Y.: Snow Lion Publications, 1998. This book includes translations of three commentaries on them. The text itself of the eight difficult or crucial points was translated by David Seyfort Ruegg in *Two Prolegomena to Madhyamaka Philosophy: Candrakīrti's Prasannapadā Madhyamaka-vṛttiḥ on Madhyamakakārikā I.1, and Tsoṅ kha pa Blo bzaṅ grags pa/rGyal tshab Dar ma rin chen's dKa' gnad/gnas brgyad kyi zin bris, Annotated Translations. Studies in Indian and Tibetan Madhyamaka Thought, Part 2.* Wiener Studien zur Tibetologie und Buddhismuskunde, vol. 34. Wien: Arbeitskreis für Tibetische und Buddhistische Studien, Universität Wien, 2002. The denial of the *ālaya-vijñāna* is the first of these eight difficult or crucial points, or unique tenets.

24. See "The Doctrinal Position of the Wisdom Tradition: Great Madhyamaka," the next chapter of this book.

25. From Dorji Wangchuk, "The rÑiṅ-ma Interpretations of the Tathāgatagarbha Theory," *Wiener Zeitschrift für die Kunde Südasiens*, vol. 48, 2004, p. 199.

26. Ibid., pp. 200-201. For a source statement by Mipham on this, see *Speech of Delight: Mipham's Commentary on Śāntarakṣita's Ornament of the Middle Way*, translated by Thomas Doctor, Ithaca, N.Y.: Snow Lion

Publications, 2004, pp. 130-133; the same statement in *The Adornment of the Middle Way: Shantarakshita's Madhyamakalankara with Commentary by Jamgön Mipham*, translated by the Padmakara Translation Group, Boston: Shambhala Publications, 2005, pp. 139-140.

The technical term, "freedom from manifoldness" (*niṣprapañca, spros dang bral ba*), is not at all easy to render into meaningful English. Thomas Doctor uses "freedom from constructs" here (p. 133), while the Padmakara Translation Group here uses "absence of conceptual extremes" (p. 139).

27. Thupten Jinpa, *Self, Reality and Reason*, p. 183.

28. In a recent account of Mipham's position on emptiness and his qualms about the Gelugpa understanding of it, Mipham is shown as holding that Tsongkhapa's final understanding of emptiness is the same as his, but that Tsongkhapa taught a provisional understanding of emptiness that his Gelugpas mistook for definitive and final. See *Mipham's Dialectics and the Debates on Emptiness*, by Karma Phuntsho, London and New York: RoutledgeCurzon, 2005:

> Mipham's reconciliatory tone is heard best in his repeated approbation of Tsongkhapa and his final understanding of Emptiness. [p. 211]

> . . . despite the fact that most of [Mipham's] polemical writings are critiques of Tsongkhapa's interpretation and the Gelukpa understanding of Emptiness, he even went as far as to eulogize Tsongkhapa and identify his final understanding of Emptiness with the Primordial Purity (*ka dag*) of Dzogchen thought. He repeatedly argued that Tsongkhapa and other eminent Gelukpa masters like Changkya Rolpai Dorje (1717-86) held views consonant with the Nyingmapa and other Ngarabpa viewpoints, although they taught a provisional understanding of Emptiness that their followers, the Gelukpas, mistook for definitive and final. [p. 16]

Naturally, the Gelugpas, who received Tsongkhapa's teachings in a direct lineage of transmission, find this hard to accept. Nonetheless, if something like this is not the case, there is no real way to achieve the reconciliation that Mipham attempted.

Appendix 1:
Tsongkhapa on No Ultimately Existing Principle

1. From his very early work, *Golden Garland of Eloquence: Legs bshad gser phreng*, translated by Gareth Sparham, vol. 1: First Abhisamaya, Fremont, Calif.: Jain Publishing Company, 2008, pp. 457-459 [single brackets are Sparham's] [[double brackets are my additions]]:

> The assertion, then, [of Dolpopa Shayrap Gyeltsen] that the later works of Maitreya, and the scriptures of the two brothers [Asaṅga and Vasubandhu] are getting at an unconditioned, ultimately established, final outcome [[*pariniṣpanna*]] empty of all conditioned phenomena is simply the fabricated nonsense of coarse minds. . . .
>
> And in the section of the emptiness of ultimate reality it [[*Defense of the Three Sūtras*]] says,
>
>> "Even nirvāṇa is empty of nirvāṇa." The ultimate reality—nirvāṇa—is empty of imaginary nirvāṇa. But does [the Lord] not say that nirvāṇa is "unmoved [[*kuṭastha*]]?" Though that is the philosophy of some thinkers in the Listener vehicle, ultimately there is no dharma called "nirvāṇa" at all.
>
> Thus here and elsewhere, in many sections, it says again and again that there is an agreement between both [the Lord's] statements that the ultimate, and emptiness are empty of their own-being [[*svabhāva*]], and [the Lord's] assertion that the ultimate and emptiness are unmoving and permanent as the fundamental state that is not empty of being actual emptiness. This [*Defense*] says, "the true nature of dharmas does not exist in its imaginary aspect, and does *not* not exist in the state of

non-duality" intending the way dharmas actually exist, worried that negating the own-being free from all extremes in a demonstration of what is finally there when the two things that have to be negated have been negated will lead to establishing [that final reality] as an actual extreme [of total annihilation]. It does not say so within asserting that that [true nature of dharmas] is established as permanent and unmoving in fact, because in the emptiness of the unconditioned section it says, "If even in the Listener system they do not ultimately exist, what need to mention that this is also the case in the Emptiness system." It thus says that the unconditioned is not established as fact.

2. From his middle period work, *Ocean of Reasoning; A Great Commentary on Nāgārjuna's Mūlamadhyamakakārikā*, translated by Geshe Ngawang Samten and Jay L. Garfield, New York and Oxford: Oxford University Press, 2006, p. 217, commenting on chapter 7, verse 33cd:

> Since, as explained earlier, produced things do not exist inherently in any way, how could these four unproduced phenomena—cessation occasioned by analysis, cessation not occasioned by analysis, space, and reality—exist inherently? They cannot! This is explained clearly.
>
> It follows from the extensive refutation of the true existence of produced things that there is no way that unproduced phenomena can truly exist. The point of asserting this in this text is that even those who maintain that the unproduced truly exists must maintain that it is an object of authoritative cognition. In that case, this argument refutes them: "The object to be measured is not measured." Even if they maintain them to be objects to be achieved, "Whatever is to be achieved is not achieved" refutes them. Even if they maintain that it abides on a certain ground, "Whatever endures does not endure" refutes them. Even if they posit them as the cause of achievement, they are refuted as it is explained in the "Examination of the Aggregates." Those who posit them in terms of characteristics and characterized should be refuted as it is explained in the "Examination

of the Elements." Following these examples, the arguments explained in the other previous chapters could be reformulated as refutations.

If these arguments could not refute the true existence of the unproduced as objects to be achieved, etc., it would be impossible to refute the true existence of produced things. These cases are completely similar. Thus, if one develops a good understanding of the arguments advanced by the master, in each chapter all such misunderstandings will be eliminated. Therefore, to say that although the produced are not truly existent, the unproduced are truly existent is the statement of a philosophical neophyte.

3. From one of his last works, the *Medium-Length Exposition of the Stages of the Path to Enlightenment,* the section on "special insight," translated by Jeffrey Hopkins in *Tsong-kha-pa's Final Exposition of Wisdom,* Ithaca, N.Y.: Snow Lion Publications, 2008, p. 101, referring to Nāgārjuna's *Praise of the Element of Attributes*:

> He says that the absence of an inherently established nature in these phenomena is the element of attributes [[*dharmadhātu*]] that is the object of meditation, and he says that just meditation on it is the supreme purifier of the mind. Therefore, how could it be suitable to cite this [*Praise of the Element of Attributes*] for the position that the emptiness that is the absence of the inherent establishment of phenomena appearing in this way is an annihilatory emptiness and that, therefore, a truly existent emptiness separate from it is to be posited as the emptiness that is the object of meditation!
>
> This is like propounding that in order to remove the suffering of fright upon apprehending a snake in the east despite there being no snake there, the demonstration that there is no snake in the east will not serve as an antidote to it, but rather one should indicate, "There is a tree in the west." For, one is propounding that in order to remove the suffering upon adhering to the true existence of what appears in this way to sentient beings, realization that those bases [that is, objects]—which are

> apprehended to truly exist—do not truly exist will not serve as an antidote, but that rather one must indicate that some other senseless base truly exists.

The same section of this same Lam-rim work of Tsong-kha-pa's has also been translated by Robert Thurman. Since these works are often not easy to understand, it is always helpful to compare another translation when available. Here is this same passage from *The Life and Teachings of Tsong Khapa*, Dharamsala: Library of Tibetan Works and Archives, 1982, pp. 150-151:

> Therefore, Nāgārjuna, from the very same *Praise*, says, . . . , i.e., that the Ultimate Realm [[*dharma-dhātu*]] to be contemplated is the very intrinsic nonreality of all things, and that such contemplation is the supreme cultivator of the mind.
>
> Thus, how can it be proper to quote this (in support of) the position that, since the emptiness which is intrinsic realitylessness of things is a nihilistic emptiness, one must employ some different, truly established emptiness as the emptiness to be contemplated? This would be like saying that, to dispel the pain of terror from mistakenly thinking there is a snake to the east, "Showing there is no snake there would not serve as remedy, so one must show that there is a tree to the west!" For, what one is saying here is that the realization of the truthlessness of the objects of truth-habits is no remedy to cure beings' suffering from truth-notions about such apparent things, and that rather one must show that some other irrelevant object truly exists.

4. From his most definitive work, the *Essence of Eloquence*, translated by Robert A. F. Thurman as *Tsong Khapa's Speech of Gold in the Essence of True Eloquence: Reason and Enlightenment in the Central Philosophy of Tibet*, Princeton: Princeton University Press, 1984, pp. 193-194:

> Therefore, anyone who maintains that the statements of the intrinsic unreality of all things in scriptures such as the *Transcendent Wisdom* intend all superficial things and do not intend the

> absolute, contradicts the *Elucidation* and the treatises of Aryasanga and Vasubandhu, and also departs from the system of the Holy Father and Son [Nāgārjuna and Āryadeva].
>
> The inquiry into the intention of the statement of intrinsic unreality asks both the intention in declaring unreality and the actual mode of unreality, and the answer deals with both in order. To explain the first, (the Buddha) collected all the statements of unreality or identitylessness with regard to all different categories of things, from form to omniscience, into three unrealities, intending that the explanation of their mode of unreality be easy to understand, since all superficial and ultimate things are contained within these three. However, though (the Buddha) needed to use such a technique, who is there in his right mind who would say that the ultimate was not included among the things declared to be unreal, when the *Mother Scripture*, etc., declared that all things, such as the five aggregates, the twelve media, and the eighteen elements, are non-existent, identityless, unreal; and particularly mentions the intrinsic unreality of all the synonyms of the absolute, such as "emptiness," the "ultimate element," and "reality," etc.?

The same passage has also been translated by Jeffrey Hopkins in his book, *Emptiness in the Mind-Only School of Buddhism; Dynamic Responses to Dzong-ka-ba's The Essence of Eloquence: I.* Berkeley and Los Angeles: University of California Press, 1999, pp. 83-85:

> Hence [it is contradictory for some, namely, Dol-bo-ba and others] to explain that the statements in the Perfection of Wisdom Sūtras, and so forth, that all phenomena are natureless are in consideration [only] of all conventional phenomena [which, according to them, are self-empty in the sense of being empty of their own true establishment] but do not refer to the ultimate [which, they say, is itself truly established and empty of being any conventional phenomenon]. They thereby contradict the *Sūtra Unraveling the Thought* as well as the texts of Asaṅga and his brother [Vasubandhu] and are also outside the system of the Superior father [Nāgārjuna], his spiritual sons, and so forth.

It is thus: [When Paramārthasamudgata] asks about that in consideration of which [Buddha] spoke of non-nature, he is asking (1) about what [Buddha] was thinking when he taught non-nature and (2) about the modes of non-nature. Also, the answer indicates those two respectively. From between those two, let us explain the first [that is, what Buddha had as the basis in his thought when in the Perfection of Wisdom Sūtras he taught that all phenomena are natureless. There, Buddha] said that the limitless divisions of instances of phenomena ranging from forms through to exalted knowers-of-all-aspects have no nature or inherent nature. These phenomena are included in the three non-natures [that is, three natures—imputational, other-powered, and thoroughly established natures]. Thinking that when it is explained how those are natureless, it is easy to understand [the individual modes of thought that were behind his statement in the Perfection of Wisdom Sūtras], he included [all phenomena] into the three non-natures [that is, three natures. For] all ultimate and conventional phenomena are included within those three. Also, with respect to the need for [Buddha's] doing thus, in the Mother Sūtras [that is, the Perfection of Wisdom Sūtras] and so forth, all phenomena—the five aggregates, the eighteen constituents, and the twelve sense-spheres—are described as without thingness, without an inherent nature, and natureless. In particular, mentioning all the terminological variants of the ultimate—emptiness, the element of [a Superior's] qualities, thusness, and so forth—he said that these are natureless. Therefore, who with a mind would propound that the ultimate is not among the phenomena about which it is said that phenomena are natureless!

NOTE TO APPENDIX 1

One may ask, if there is no ultimately existing principle such as the omnipresent, eternal, boundless, and immutable principle taught as the first fundamental proposition of the Secret Doctrine, what, then, does exist? As summed up by Thupten Jinpa, for Tsongkhapa there is only conventional existence, only the lived-in world of our everyday experience. Jinpa sums this up in his 2002 book, *Self, Reality and Reason in Tibetan Philosophy: Tsongkhapa's Quest for the Middle Way*:

> . . . for Tsongkhapa, to exist is to exist on the conventional level. On the ultimate level, however, no entity's existence remains tenable. [pp. 211-212]
>
> Existence consists of both conventional and ultimate realities. Emptiness, the mode of being of all things and events, is the ultimate, while all other phenomena, both transitory and non-transitory, are conventional realities. However, emptiness cannot be said to exist in-and-of-itself, for this would mean that it is an absolute. So, although emptiness is not a conventional reality, it nevertheless exists on the conventional level. This is because nothing exists as an absolute. Seen in this way, conventional existence equals existence. Thus, one can say that for Tsongkhapa, to exist is to exist in the conventional sense. [pp. 152-153]
>
> Therefore, according to Tsongkhapa, metaphysical postulates such as *ātman*, *brahman*, eternal *dharmas*, indivisible atoms, *ālaya* consciousness, *svasaṃvedanā* (self-cognizing awareness), and so on are all unnecessary phantom additions to the repertoire of existing things and events. Because of their essentialist metaphysical nature, according to Tsongkhapa, if these entities were to exist, they would possess a categorically distinct ontological status. This is because if they existed, they would have to do so as absolutes. But as we have seen, any notion of absolute is untenable from Tsongkhapa's point of view. . . . By including this third criterion, Tsongkhapa wishes to demonstrate that metaphysical postulates such as *ātman*, *ālaya*, eternal *dharmas*, and so on cannot be accepted as conventionally existent, for these metaphysical categories are incapable of withstanding ultimate analysis. . . . For Tsongkhapa, as shown earlier, the conventional (*saṃvṛti*) and the ultimate (*paramārtha*) are not two distinct entities with a categorically different ontological status. Rather, they are two aspects of one and the same world. There is only one world, the lived-in world of our everyday experience. [pp. 155, 157, 158]

Appendix 2:
On Errors in H. P. Blavatsky's Writings

It is important to recognize that many of H. P. Blavatsky's statements are not her own. That is, they are not her own in the sense of coming from her adept teachers, but rather they come from the published books available at the time she wrote. This means that, since the information found in these early books is very often faulty, so Blavatsky's statements are very often faulty. In the case at hand, that of Tsongkhapa, Blavatsky wrote:

> In an article, "Reincarnations in Tibet," everything that could be said about Tsong-kha-pa was published.[1]

All of the information found in this article, published in 1882, has been regarded by Theosophists as coming from Blavatsky's adept teachers, when in fact some of it came from books that were then available. About Tsongkhapa, Blavatsky wrote in this article:

> It was because, among many other reforms, Tsong-Kha-pa forbade necromancy (which is practiced to this day with the most disgusting rites, by the Böns—the aborigines of Tibet—with whom the Red Caps, or Shammars, had always fraternized), that the latter resisted his authority. This act was followed by a split between the two sects. Separating entirely from the Gelukpas, the Dugpas (Red Caps)—from the first in a great minority—settled in various parts of Tibet, chiefly its borderlands, and principally in Nepal and Bhutan. But, while they retained a sort of independence at the monastery of Sakya-Jong, the Tibetan residence of their spiritual(?) chief Gong-sso Rinpoche, the Bhutanese have been from their beginning the tributaries and vassals of the Taley-Lamas.[2]

Compare this with what is found in an 1876 book by Clements R. Markham, *Narratives of the Mission of George Bogle to Tibet, and of the Journey of Thomas Manning to Lhasa,* a book that is directly referred to by Blavatsky in her article. From p. xlvi:

> In the middle of the fourteenth century a great reforming Lama arose in Tibet, named Tsong-khapa, who proved to be an incarnation of one of the Dhyani Buddhas, named Amitabha. . . . He forbade clerical marriages, prohibited necromancy, and introduced the custom of frequent conferences among the Lamas. His reforms led to a schism in the Tibetan church. The old sect, which resisted all change, adhered to their dress, and are called Shammars, or Dukpas, and Red Caps. Their chief monastery is at Sakia-jong, and they retain supremacy in Nepal and Bhutan.

Then on p. lii, after repeating that "the adherents of the older, but now heretical Red sect, still have a large monastery at Sakia-jong, and have retained supremacy among the Buddhists in Nepal and Bhutan," Markham adds in a footnote:

> The Abbot of the Red Cap monastery at Sakia, in Tibet, has the title of Gongso Rimboché. (Turner, p. 315.)

From this comparison, it is clear that Markham is the source of Blavatsky's above-quoted statements. But this was not known to Theosophists; and A. P. Sinnett in his influential Theosophical classic, *Esoteric Buddhism,* quoted this very same passage from Blavatsky's article, saying about it:

> . . . for the complete trustworthiness of which in all its mystic bearings I have the highest assurance . . .[3]

Blavatsky, too, repeated this information again in her article, "Tsong-kha-pa—Lohans in China":

> Tsong-kha-pa gave the signs whereby the presence of one of the twenty-five Bodhisattvas or of the Celestial Buddhas (Dhyāni-

> Chohans) in a human body might be recognized, and He strictly forbade necromancy. This led to a split amongst the Lamas, and the malcontents allied themselves with the aboriginal Böns against the reformed Lamaism. Even now they form a powerful sect, practising the most disgusting rites all over Sikkim, Bhutan, Nepal, and even on the borderlands of Tibet.[4]

Diehard Theosophists might here say that this information is in fact vouched for by Blavatsky's adept teachers, and that it happens to correspond to what Markham wrote, so Blavatsky was free to use his statements as a source. However, a few lines later in Blavatsky's above-quoted article, she wrote:

> The Tashi-Lamas were always more powerful and more highly considered than the Taley-Lamas. The latter are the creation of the Tashi-Lama, Nabang-Lob-Sang, the sixth incarnation of Tsong-Kha-pa—himself an incarnation of Amitabha, or Buddha.[5]

Similarly, a few lines later in Markham's above-quoted book, we find the source of this erroneous statement that the Dalai Lamas are the creation of the Tashi-Lama:

> Thus arose the two powerful Abbots of Galdan and Teshu Lumbo, both of the Gelupka or Yellow sect; but the former were soon eclipsed by the superior piety and learning of the incarnations of Teshu Lumbo; and the sixth in succession of those incarnations made himself master of all Tibet, and founded the successions of the Dalai and Teshu Lamas as they now exist. This was Navang Lobsang. He rebuilt the palace or monastery of Potala, at Lhasa, in 1643, and in 1650 he visited the Emperor of China, and accepted the designation of Dalai (or ocean) Lama. After a long reign he went away to reappear as two infants, if not three; for, although he was the fifth Teshu Lama, he was the first Dalai; and since his time there have been two great incarnations of equal rank: the Dalai Lama at Potala, who is an incarnation of the Buddhisatwa Avalokiteswara (or Padma Pani); and the Teshu Lama at Teshu Lumbo, the incarnation of the Dhyani

> Buddha Amitabha, and also of Tsong-khapa, who was himself the incarnation of Amitabha.[6]

Again, Blavatsky later repeated her erroneous statement in a footnote in her article, "Tsong-kha-pa—Lohans in China":

> It is curious to note the great importance given by European Orientalists to the Dalai Lamas of Lhasa, and their utter ignorance as to the Tda-shu (or Teshu) Lamas, while it is the latter who began the hierarchical series of Buddha-incarnations, and are *de facto* the "popes" in Tibet: the Dalai Lamas are the creations of Nabang-lob-Sang, the Tda-shu Lama, who was Himself the sixth incarnation of Amita, through Tsong-kha-pa, though very few seem to be aware of that fact.[7]

In the latter half of the twentieth century, full and reliable historical information about Tibet has become available. It is now well known that Nawang Lobsang was the fifth Dalai Lama, and he created the Tashi Lamas, or Panchen Lamas, not the other way around, as is stated and repeated by Blavatsky. The source of this confusion is obviously Markham's book. Nawang Lobsang was not the first Dalai Lama and fifth Teshu Lama, the sixth incarnation of Tsongkhapa, as Markham says. Markham was led to make this error by information he gives in an intervening paragraph, one that Blavatsky also quotes from him:

> Gedun-tubpa, another great reformer, is said to have received the spirit of Tsong-khapa in 1419, and to have died in 1474. He built the monastery at Teshu Lumbo in 1445, and it was in the person of this perfect Lama, as he was called, that the system of perpetual incarnation commenced. He was himself the incarnation of the Buddhisatwa Padma Pani, and on his death he relinquished the attainment of Buddha-hood that he might be born again and again for the benefit of mankind.[8]

This information is correct enough, but Gedun-tubpa (dGe 'dun grub pa) was retroactively made the first Dalai Lama, not the first Tashi Lama, even though he in fact founded the monastery of Teshu Lumbo, or Tashi-lhunpo. The incorrect assumption made by Markham that Gedun-tubpa was the first Tashi Lama, or Panchen Lama, caused his error, an error then copied by Blavatsky. This is a straightforward error of historical facts, one that could hardly have been made by an adept living in Tibet. In brief, Markham got it wrong, and Blavatsky copied this error and put it forth as fact. Many Theosophists think it is gospel truth coming from her adept teachers, when in fact it is nothing more than an old error repeated. I do not think that, when Theosophists know this, they would be willing to attribute such an error to Blavatsky's adept teachers.

So with the other errors copied from Markham. Sakya-Jong is the chief monastery of the Sakya order, only one of three main "red hat" orders. Markham's statement that it is the head-quarters of the Red Cap sect is therefore incorrect.

> . . . the great monastery of Sakia-jong, the head-quarters of the Red Cap sect of Buddhists.[9]

It is the headquarters of only the Sakya order, not the Nyingma and Kagyu orders, which are also "red hat" orders. Moreover, to call the "red hats" all Dugpas is also incorrect. It is a different "red hat" order, the Kagyu, or more precisely, the Dugpa Kagyu sub-order, which actually has the name Dugpa (*'brug pa*), also phoneticized as Dukpa or Drukpa. This is the state religion of Bhutan. Blavatsky wrote in this same article, about the other "red hat" order, the Nyingma:

> The "Dug-pa or Red Caps" belong to the old Nyingmapa sect, who resisted the religious reform introduced by Tsong-Kha-pa between the latter part of the fourteenth and the beginning of the fifteenth centuries.[10]

Thus, Blavatsky, like other writers of the time, referred to all three of the "red hat" orders as Dugpas. So with further errors. There is no evidence that Tsongkhapa "forbade necromancy," as stated by Markham and repeated by Blavatsky, or even that necromancy was then practiced in Tibet, with or without "the most disgusting rites." On the contrary, another major article written by Blavatsky, or in this case translated by her on behalf of her Tibetan informants, specifically counters the idea that Buddhists were Spiritualists, i.e., necromancers, as was claimed by Arthur Lillie in his book, *Buddha and Early Buddhism.* The whole point of this article, titled "Tibetan Teachings," is that Buddhists, like Hindus, avoid contact with the dead, so would hardly be involved in invoking the spirits of the departed, like Spiritualists were then doing in Western countries. This article, too, like "Reincarnations in Tibet," although having much new information, is not free from erroneous information copied from then existing books. It certainly includes important and hitherto unknown information about Tsongkhapa, including the following:

> Our world-honoured Tsong-kha-pa closing his fifth Dam-ngag reminds us that "every sacred truth, which the ignorant are unable to comprehend under its true light, ought to be hidden within a triple casket concealing itself as the tortoise conceals his head within his shell; ought to show her face but to those who are desirous of obtaining the condition of Anuttara Samyak Sambodhi"—the most merciful and enlightened heart.[11]

And this:

> A prophecy of Tsong-kha-pa is current in Tibet to the effect that the true doctrine will be maintained in its purity only so long as Tibet is kept free from the incursions of western nations, whose crude ideas of fundamental truth would inevitably confuse and obscure the followers of the Good Law. But, when the western world is more ripe in the direction of philosophy, the incarnation of Pan-chhen-rin-po-chhe—the Great Jewel of Wisdom—one of the Teshu Lamas, will take place, and the splendour of truth will then illuminate the whole world. We have here the true key to Tibetan exclusiveness.[12]

But it also includes some unfortunate errors, that can only have been copied from then existing books, such as the following statement:

> In the book known as the *Avatamsaka Sūtra,* in the section on "the Supreme Ātman—Self—as manifested in the character of the Arhats and Pratyeka Buddhas," it is stated that "Because from the beginning, all sentient creatures have confused the truth, and embraced the false; therefore has there come into existence a hidden knowledge called Alaya Vijñāna."[13]

This statement was repeated by Blavatsky in her article, "The Secret Books of 'Lam-rim' and Dzyan."[14] Compare Samuel Beal's 1871 book, *A Catena of Buddhist Scriptures from the Chinese,* pp. 124-125, where Beal is translating a work by Jin Cha'u that has been quoting the *Avataṃsaka Sūtra*:

> But now it may be asked "From what cause then did these worlds innumerable spring?" We reply, "They come from the heart (âtman) alone; they are made by that alone." But because from the very first, all sentient creatures have confused the truth, and embraced the false; therefore has there come into being a hidden knowledge called, "Alaya vijnyâna," and because of this, all the various transformations in the world without and the senses within, have been produced. Hence the Scriptures say, "Because of the primeval fallacy (fallacious cause), the whole phenomenal world has been originated, and from this cause too has sprung not only the various modes of birth, but the idea of Nirvâna itself."

Beal added a footnote just before this paragraph began, which is the source of Blavatsky's statement, "the Supreme Ātman—Self—as manifested in the character of the Arhats and Pratyeka Buddhas":

> The whole of this section is expressed in technical language, which it is difficult to put in an English form. The Supreme Self

> (âtman) or Heart, is supposed not only to manifest itself under three forms or persons, but to occupy four "lands," or discharge four supreme functions. 1. In its supreme condition, perfectly at rest, and yet ever glorious; 2. As manifested in the character of all the Bôdhisatwas; 3. As manifested in the character of the Rahats and Pratyêka Buddhas; 4. As manifested in the condition of Holy men (Buddhists) and worldly philosophers (heretics).

In 1871, when this was published, little was known of the doctrines of the Yogācāra school of Mahāyāna Buddhism. So it is not surprising that Beal mistranslated their technical term *ālaya-vijñāna* as "hidden knowledge." But as has long since been known, the correct meaning is "storehouse consciousness," or "foundational consciousness," or "substratum consciousness," or "mind basis-of-all." It has nothing to do with any hidden knowledge. This is clear even in Beal's translated paragraph cited above. The whole phenomenal world has originated from the *ālaya-vijñāna*, and this itself has come into being from the primeval fallacy of people confusing the truth and embracing the false. This is basic Yogācāra doctrine, and has been known at least since the time of D. T. Suzuki's 1904 article, "Philosophy of the Yogācāra":

> The Ālīya is a magazine, the efficiency of which depends on the habit-energy (*hsi ch'i* in Chinese) of all defiled dharmas, and in which all the seeds are systematically stowed away. In one respect this vijñāna of all seeds is the actual reason whereby the birth of all defiled dharmas becomes possible, but in another respect its own efficiency depends on the habit-energy which is discharged by multitudinous defiled dharmas since beginningless time. In other words, the Ālīya is at once the cause and the effect of all possible phenomena in the universe.[15]

These few examples are sufficient, I believe, to show that along with whatever new things Blavatsky brought out are a number of erroneous statements that were copied from the published books available at the time. The explanation for this is, I think, not far to seek. Blavatsky, like the secretary of any busy executive today, was given certain basic materials and then left on her own to make a coherent presentation of them. This meant supplementing them with whatever sources were then available. She herself would not necessarily have known that the publicly available sources were faulty, any more than anyone else at that time would have. Her adept teachers were busy men, and simply did not have time to check everything she wrote. This is only common sense, and would have been taken for granted in any other situation. Blavatsky repeatedly disclaimed infallibility for her writings. It is quite unreasonable to assume that everything she wrote is free from errors, as some of her followers assumed. Because much of her material came from her adept teachers, they thought that all of it did. In her article, "My Books," Blavatsky wrote that these "friends, as unwise as they were kind," spread this idea, "and this was seized upon by the enemy and exaggerated out of all limits of truth." She there continues:

> It was said that the whole of *Isis [Unveiled]* had been dictated to me *from cover to cover* and *verbatim* by these invisible Adepts. And, as the imperfections of my work were only too glaring, the consequence of all this idle and malicious talk was, that my enemies and critics inferred—as they well might—that either these invisible inspirers had no existence, and were part of my "fraud," or that they lacked the cleverness of even an average good writer.[16]

So even though Blavatsky's writings contain much hitherto unavailable information found nowhere else, they must be read critically like anything else.

NOTES TO APPENDIX 2

1. *H. P. Blavatsky Collected Writings*, vol. 14, p. 427.
2. *H. P. Blavatsky Collected Writings*, vol. 4, p. 12.
3. *Esoteric Buddhism*, by A. P. Sinnett, 5th ed., 1885, p. 182.

4. *H. P. Blavatsky Collected Writings*, vol. 14, p. 427.
5. *H. P. Blavatsky Collected Writings*, vol. 4, p. 12.
6. Clements R. Markham, ed., *Narratives of the Mission of George Bogle to Tibet, and of the Journey of Thomas Manning to Lhasa*, London: Trübner and Co., 1876, p. xlvii.
7. *H. P. Blavatsky Collected Writings*, vol. 14, pp. 427-428.
8. Markham, op. cit., p. xlvii. This is quoted by Blavatsky in *H. P. Blavatsky Collected Writings*, vol. 4, p. 13 fn.
9. Markham, op. cit., p. xxviii; see also pp. lii, 179-180.
10. *H. P. Blavatsky Collected Writings*, vol. 4, pp. 10-11.
11. *H. P. Blavatsky Collected Writings*, vol. 6, pp. 99-100.
12. *H. P. Blavatsky Collected Writings*, vol. 6, p. 105.
13. *H. P. Blavatsky Collected Writings*, vol. 6, pp. 100-101.
14. *H. P. Blavatsky Collected Writings*, vol. 14, p. 423.
15. *Le Muséon*, n.s., vol. 5, 1904, p. 377.
16. *H. P. Blavatsky Collected Writings*, vol. 13, pp. 195-196.

[The foregoing article was written by David Reigle, and presented as part of the program, "Theosophy's Tibetan Connection," at the Annual Meeting of the Texas Federation of the Theosophical Society in America, San Antonio, April 18-20, 2008.]

The Doctrinal Position of the Wisdom Tradition: Great Madhyamaka

It has now become possible to identify the specific school or tradition of Buddhism in Tibet that represents the doctrinal position of the Wisdom Tradition known today as Theosophy. It is the "Great Madhyamaka" or "Great Middle Way" (in Tibetan, *dbu ma chen po*)[1] school or tradition. This tradition, preserved for the last millennium in Tibet, has only become known to us in recent years.

Theosophy is said to represent a secret Wisdom Tradition that was once universal. But knowledge of its very existence long ago disappeared from public consciousness. It became hidden, or more colloquially, went "underground." In recent centuries, it is supposed to have been preserved by a secret brotherhood located in Tibet. From two members of this brotherhood, H. P. Blavatsky learned of the existence of this Wisdom Tradition. Under their instruction, she made its existence known to the world, and brought out some of its teachings. She called these teachings Theosophy. They were greeted with much skepticism when they came out in the late 1800s, as would be expected of any allegedly secret teachings. Theosophy never claimed to be Tibetan Buddhism; but many, among its critics and supporters alike, thought that its teachings should be found therein.

The teachings found in Tibet are those of Mahāyāna or Northern Buddhism. They are usually thought of in terms of wisdom and compassion. Wisdom is the teaching of emptiness (*śūnyatā*), coming in the lineage of the bodhisattva Mañjuśrī through the teacher Nāgārjuna in the school or tradition called Madhyamaka, the "Middle Way." The teaching of compassion (*karuṇā*), comes in the lineage of the bodhisattva Maitreya through the teacher Asaṅga in the school or tradition called Yogācāra, "Practice of Yoga," where yoga means meditation.

As the teachings of Tibet became accessible in the last few decades of the twentieth century, it could be seen that these agreed with those of Theosophy on the fundamental teaching of compassion, but they did not agree on the basic doctrinal teaching of emptiness. This basic Madhyamaka teaching was accepted by all schools of Tibetan Buddhism as their doctrinal position. Thus, even though all schools accepted the Yogācāra teachings on compassion, they did not accept as ultimately true the Yogācāra doctrinal position. This position was characterized as Citta-mātra, "Mind-Only," meaning that there is nothing but mind. Rather, following the basic Madhyamaka teaching of emptiness, Tibetan Buddhists held that the mind is empty of any inherent or ultimate existence. Holding the Madhyamaka doctrinal position, however, did not stop them in the least from adopting and applying the Yogācāra teachings on compassion. Indeed, nowhere else on earth has compassion been developed and cultivated to the extent it was in Tibet; so much so, that it is seen as Tibetan Buddhism's most characteristic feature.

Similarly, Theosophy's basic platform is "brotherhood," the brotherhood of all humanity, a quite radical idea in the late 1800s when it was brought out. That this was based on the Mahāyāna Buddhist idea of compassion, the bodhisattva ideal, can be seen throughout the Theosophical writings, above all in *The Voice of the Silence*.[2] This small treatise is said to have been translated by Blavatsky from *The Book of the Golden Precepts*. These precepts, she says, "are written variously, sometimes in Tibetan but mostly in ideographs."[3] The language of these ideographs she calls "Senzar," describing it as a secret sacerdotal language. From this language she also translated the "Stanzas of Dzyan," on the origin of the cosmos and of humanity, published in her greatest work, *The Secret Doctrine*. She tells us that both of her sources, *The Book of Dzyan* and *The Book of the Golden Precepts*, form part of the same series.[4] In her translation of parts of the latter as *The Voice of the Silence*, we find the key term "Ālaya" used eight times.[5] In her translation of the "Stanzas of Dzyan" in *The Secret Doctrine*, "Ālaya" is featured in the last verse of the first stanza.[6] This is a distinctive Yogācāra doctrinal term.

The term *ālaya*, usually understood to stand for the fuller *ālaya-vijñāna*,[7] is the single most characteristic Yogācāra term. *Ālaya-vijñāna* has been translated as "storehouse consciousness," "substratum consciousness," "foundational consciousness," or "mind basis-of-all." It is defined by Asaṅga as *citta*, "mind,"[8] as in Cittamātra, "Mind-Only," the distinctive doctrinal position that is usually held to characterize the Yogācāra school or tradition. We find further that the distinctive Yogācāra doctrinal term *pariniṣpanna* is also used in the "Stanzas of Dzyan," twice.[9] This is one of three terms that together give the Yogācāra description of everything that is. Things partake of three characteristics (*lakṣaṇa*), or natures (*svabhāva*): the "imagined" (*parikalpita*), which is unreal, the "dependent" (*paratantra*), which is partially real, and the "perfected" (*pariniṣpanna*), which is real. Since *pariniṣpanna*, like *ālaya*, is not used elsewhere, these provide us with good evidence for tracing Theosophy's doctrinal affiliation to the Yogācāra school or tradition of Buddhism.

However, Theosophy does not teach the doctrine of "Mind-Only" (*citta-mātra*), or its other name, "Consciousness-Only" (*vijñapti-mātra*). No, Theosophy clearly does not accept an ultimate consciousness.[10] So what Theosophy teaches cannot be described as *vijñāna-vāda*, the "doctrine of consciousness" [as ultimate reality]. These three terms are used to characterize the Yogācāra doctrinal position. Despite using Yogācāra terms, this is not the doctrinal position of Theosophy. No more than the Mādhyamikas of Tibet does Theosophy accept the Yogācāra doctrinal position as ultimate. But neither can Theosophy be identified with the widely known Madhyamaka or "Middle Way" doctrinal positions, teaching emptiness (*śūnyatā*).

In recent years there has come to be known in the West a school or tradition that calls itself "Great Madhyamaka." It is different from the two well-known forms of Madhyamaka, the Svātantrika Madhyamaka and Prāsaṅgika Madhyamaka. When the Madhyamaka teaching, the teaching of emptiness, first reached Tibet from India, it was in the form of what later came to be called Svātantrika Madhyamaka, the Madhyamaka that uses autonomous or independent inferences in its reasoning to prove emptiness. This form of Madhyamaka comes down from the teacher Nāgārjuna through the commentator Bhavya (or Bhā[va]viveka). Then at the beginning of the twelfth century C.E., through the work of the translator Pa-tsap Nyima Drak, Prāsaṅgika Madhyamaka came into Tibet.[11] This became the dominant form of Madhyamaka there. It comes down from Nāgārjuna through the commentators Buddhapālita and later Candrakīrti. In its reasonings to prove emptiness it employs a type of statement that shows the unwanted consequences of whatever may be postulated by others. So both of these forms of Madhyamaka prove emptiness, but by using different methods. Such are the two kinds of Madhyamaka that are described in the standard textbooks on tenets since the fifteenth century.[12] There is no mention of a third kind, Great Madhyamaka.

Great Madhyamaka is described in the section on tenets of *The Treasury of Knowledge*, written by the co-founder of the Ri-mé or nonsectarian movement, Jamgon Kongtrul, in the latter part of the nineteenth century. It draws on earlier works by the Jonang teacher Tāranātha and by the Sakya teacher Shakya Chokden. An English translation of this section was published in 2007.[13] The work by Tāranātha that it draws on, *The Essence of Other-Emptiness*, was also published in English in 2007.[14] Jamgon Kongtrul first distinguishes the kinds of Madhyamaka, placing the two well-known kinds, Svātantrika and Prāsaṅgika, together as Rangtong Madhyamaka, and calling the third kind Shentong Madhyamaka. Great Madhyamaka is the original name for this used by the Jonang teacher Dolpopa, who first prolumgated it in Tibet in the fourteenth century. The Tibetan term Rangtong (*rang stong*) means "self-empty"; Shentong (*gzhan stong*) means "other-empty." They are descriptive terms used to distinguish the respective doctrines of emptiness.

Rangtong Madhyamaka, both Svātantrika and Prāsaṅgika, teaches the emptiness of "self-nature" (*svabhāva*), meaning real existence, of all *dharmas*, the elements of existence that make up the world, often translated as "phenomena." They are "self-empty"; they do not ultimately exist. Shentong Madhyamaka also accepts this emptiness, but says that this is not the whole picture. It adds that in ultimate truth there is something that is not empty of real or inherent existence, but that really exists. It is empty of everything other than itself; it is "other-empty." Jamgon Kongtrul explains the differences between the two in the *Treasury of Knowledge*, here quoted from Ringu Tulku's 2006 book, *The Ri-me Philosophy of Jamgön Kongtrul the Great.*

> For both Rangtong and Shentong Madhyamaka, all phenomena included in the relative truth are emptiness, and there is the cessation of all fabricated extremes in meditation. Their views do not differ on these points. However, in relation to post-meditation, to clearly distinguish the tenet systems, merely in terms of the way they use terminology, Shentong says that the dharmata, or true nature, is there, and Rangtong says the dharmata is not there. In the ultimate analysis, using the reasoning that examines the ultimate, Shentong says nondual primordial wisdom is truly established, and Rangtong says primordial wisdom is not truly established. These two statements delineate their main differences.[15]

He is saying that for both of them, all conventional phenomena, our whole world, is empty, i.e., "self-empty," and therefore does not exist in the ultimate sense. For Shentong Madhyamaka, however, the *dharmatā*, which is the inscrutable true nature of all things or all phenomena (*dharmas*), and primordial wisdom (*jñāna*), do exist in the ultimate sense. They are "other-empty," i.e., empty of everything other than themselves. But these, for Rangtong Madhyamaka, are "self-empty" like everything else; hence they do not exist in the ultimate sense. As may be seen, the doctrinal difference between the two is significant. In the spirit of Ri-mé nonsectarianism, Ringu Tulku comments here:

> So, their difference lies in the words they use to describe the dharmata and primordial wisdom. Shentong describes the dharmata, the true nature, as ultimately real, while Rangtong philosophers fear that if it is described in that way, people might understand it as the concept of a soul or atma. The Shentong

> philosophers think there is a greater chance of misunderstanding if the enlightened state is described as unreal and void. Their debates rest on how to phrase the teachings to have the least danger of misinterpretation. Kongtrul finds the Rangtong presentation best for dissolving concepts, and the Shentong presentation best for describing the actual experience.[16]

It must be noted that the Shentong doctrinal position accepts the Rangtong doctrinal position, but the Rangtong doctrinal position does not accept the Shentong doctrinal position. The debates on this in Tibet, therefore, were historically not very conciliatory. For the numerically dominant proponents of the Rangtong position, the Shentong position was akin to the non-Buddhist *ātman* or soul doctrine of the Hindus, and thus was heretical. For them, i.e., for most Tibetan Buddhists, the same would be true of the doctrinal position of Theosophy.

The Shentong or Great Madhyamaka doctrinal position, like that of Rangtong Madhyamaka, and in agreement with that of Theosophy, says the entire phenomenal universe is empty of any inherent nature that would make it ultimately real, or exist in the ultimate sense. But for Shentong the real ultimates for which we have no adequate words do exist in the ultimate sense, being empty of everything other than themselves. This teaching is very much in agreement with what is taught in Theosophy. In its most basic statement, "The Secret Doctrine establishes three fundamental propositions," the first of which is:

> An Omnipresent, Eternal, Boundless, and Immutable PRINCIPLE on which all speculation is impossible, since it transcends the power of human conception and could only be dwarfed by any human expression or similitude. It is beyond the range and reach of thought—in the words of *Māṇḍūkya Upanishad,* "unthinkable and unspeakable."[17]

Thus, both Great Madhyamaka and Theosophy are willing to postulate something that is ultimately real beyond the dualities of thought, beyond concepts.

Great Madhyamaka does not trace its origin to the teacher Nāgārjuna, and hence to the bodhisattva Mañjuśrī, as do both Svātantrika and Prāsaṅgika Madhyamaka, but rather traces it to the teacher Asaṅga, and hence to the bodhisattva Maitreya.[18] This is of much significance to the present inquiry. It means that Great Madhyamaka finds its origin in the five treatises of Maitreya, and in the exegetical works thereon by Asaṅga and his brother Vasubandhu. These, of course, are Yogācāra treatises. But here they are understood as teaching Great Madhyamaka rather than Cittamātra, "Mind-Only." Their Yogācāra terms are here used to teach Shentong, "other-empty." We now see how the "Stanzas of Dzyan" may use the distinctive Yogācāra terms *ālaya* and *pariniṣpanna*, and yet not teach "Consciousness-Only," but rather a boundless and immutable principle beyond the range and reach of thought. Indeed, like Great Madhyamaka, the origin of these stanzas, too, is traced to Maitreya.

The "Book of Dzyan," from which stanzas are given in *The Secret Doctrine*, is said by Blavatsky to be "utterly unknown to our philologists, or at any rate was never heard of by them under its present name."[19] This is because it is only a generic name, in which "Dzyan" is a Tibetan phonetic rendering of the Sanskrit term *jñāna*, meaning "primordial wisdom."[20] As seen above, this is distinguished as ultimately real in Great Madhyamaka. While she gave us no clue of its actual name there in *The Secret Doctrine*, she did write in an earlier private letter to A. P. Sinnett:

> I have finished an enormous Introductory Chapter, or *Preamble*, Prologue, call it what you will; just to show the reader that the text as it goes, every Section beginning with a page of translation from the Book of *Dzyan* and the Secret Book of "Maytreya Buddha" *Champai chhos Nga* (in prose, not the five books in verse known, which are a blind) are no fiction.[21]

The wording here could indicate either that the Book of Dzyan and the Secret Book of Maitreya Buddha are the same book or two different books, but the translation we have of the stanzas does not show two different portions. She may be referring to the combined ancient Senzar stanzas with later Sanskrit glosses that she says she blended together in her translation.[22] In any case, she here identifies the Book of Dzyan with the Secret Book of Maitreya, and distinguishes it from the known five books of Maitreya in verse. With this we no longer have to merely infer from the presence of distinctive Yogācāra terms that the source of her "Stanzas of Dzyan" is Maitreya. It is stated for us.

In conclusion, we now know that there exists a school or tradition of Buddhism in Tibet known as Great Madhyamaka, tracing its origin to Maitreya and using Yogācāra terms to teach an ultimate that is not consciousness, but is beyond it. It teaches the ultimate existence of something that is Shentong, or "empty of other," and an ultimately existing primordial wisdom (*jñāna* or *dzyan*). We may reasonably identify this Great Madhyamaka as the doctrinal position of the Wisdom Tradition known today as Theosophy. We may say, in brief, that the doctrinal position of Theosophy is Great Madhyamaka.

Confirmation from a Mongolian Lama

Confirmation of this has come from a quite unexpected and independent source. Paul Brunton when visiting Angkor in Cambodia in the 1930s met there a Mongolian lama who was also visiting at that time. This Mongolian teacher told him of a secret tradition that is the same as the Wisdom Tradition known today as Theosophy. The information he gave came out in 1987 in Brunton's posthumously published notebooks.

> There is first a secret tradition which has combined and united Hinduism, the religion of many Gods, and Buddhism, the religion without a God. There is next an unbroken line of sages who held and taught this doctrine as being the real and final truth about life. . . . The tradition itself was limited by the mental incapacity of the masses to the circle of a few sages and their immediate disciples. Vedanta and Mahayana are corruptions of this pure doctrine, but of all known systems they come closest to it.[23]

Regarding this unbroken line of sages, Brunton asked him "if they are the same adepts as those spoken of by H. P. Blavatsky."[24] The Mongolian lama then gave an account of how Blavatsky came to study with them, and of her younger co-disciple, Lama Dorzhiev, who we can infer was this Mongolian lama's teacher. About the adepts of Tibet, he said, "Their location was always a secret; even most of the High Lamas never knew it."[25] What he told Brunton about their doctrine, through a translator, was to change his life. Brunton then gave out some of this to the world in modern English as "mentalism."

> Through the services of an educated Chinese disciple who was with him, we were able to converse about Buddhism and other matters. He gave out a teaching which formed the basis of mentalism and which was occasionally so subtle that it went above my head, but which I understood sufficiently to revolutionize my outlook. Some of its tenets were incorporated in the mentalism explained in my books *The Hidden Teaching Beyond Yoga* [1941], and *The Wisdom of the Overself* [1943].[26]

Brunton carefully avoided using any Sanskrit terms when formulating this teaching, since he believed that it had to be given in modern terms.[27] Nonetheless, through stray comments he made, we are able to verify that the "mentalism" he derived from this lama's teachings is in fact Yogācāra, or Cittamātra, "Mind-Only," or Vijñaptimātra, "Consciousness-Only."[28] He did not, however, regard mentalism as the ultimate truth, as he makes clear in a few places.[29] But when he wrote, in the 1940s, nothing was known of any teaching like Great Madhyamaka that used Yogācāra terminology to teach something beyond "Mind-Only," or mentalism. He therefore took Yogācāra as "Mind-Only" and constructed his mentalism accordingly. It is clear that the teaching he got from this Mongolian lama was Yogācāra based. This provides independent confirmation that the doctrinal basis of the Wisdom Tradition known today as Theosophy is a Yogācāra teaching, a teaching that is ultimately understood as Great Madhyamaka.[30]

Supplement: The Background of Great Madhyamaka

The Madhyamaka Background

The fact that Great Madhyamaka traces its lineage back to Maitreya does not mean that it does not go back to Nāgārjuna. Nāgārjuna is regarded by all as the founder of Madhyamaka, in the sense of being the one who first formulated the Buddha's teachings given in the Perfection of Wisdom (*prajñā-pāramitā*) *sūtras* into a philosophical school or tradition, the Madhyamaka or "Middle Way." Emptiness (*śūnyatā*) is the primary teaching of this tradition, whether Svātantrika Madhyamaka, Prāsaṅgika Madhyamaka, or Great Madhyamaka. For its understanding of emptiness as Shentong, or "other-empty," Great Madhyamaka utilizes the hymns of Nāgārjuna.[31] It is in these hymns, they say, that Nāgārjuna reveals the highest understanding of emptiness.

Nāgārjuna's greatest work is the *Mūla-madhyamaka-kārikā*. This is normally understood, even by Great Mādhyamikas, to teach emptiness as Rangtong, or "self-empty." This teaching, that all things (*dharma*) are empty of any self-nature (*svabhāva*) that would allow them to exist on their own, is considered in Svātantrika Madhyamaka and Prāsaṅgika Madhyamaka to be the highest understanding of emptiness. This teaching is also accepted in Great Madhyamaka, but as the next to highest. The question of exactly what understanding of emptiness Nāgārjuna ultimately intended is an open one. There is a brief text among "The Hundred and Eight Guidebooks of the Jo nang pas" that says Great Madhyamaka is the ancient tradition of Madhyamaka following the original texts of Nāgārjuna and his spiritual son Āryadeva, not yet divided into Svātantrika and Prāsaṅgika.

> Concerning the *dBu ma chen po'i khrid* ["The Guidance on the Great Middle Way"]: it was received by the bodhisattva Zla ba rgyal mtshan from the Newar Pe nya pa, one who belonged to the lineage of Nāgārjuna, father and son [i.e., Nāgārjuna and Āryadeva]. He taught it to rDzi lung pa 'Od zer grags pa, and he to Gro ston, who propounded it widely. There are some

> who hold that this was the lineage of the *dBu ma lta khrid* ["The Guidance on the View of the Middle Way"] that came to the venerable Red mda' ba from mNga' ris, in West Tibet, but that is uncertain. This is [also] called the *gZhung phyi mo'i dbu ma* ["The Middle Way according to the Original Texts," i.e., of Nāgārjuna and Āryadeva], and so is the ancient tradition, not yet divided into Prāsaṅgika and Svātantrika. That which is distinguished as the special doctrine of Red mda' ba, however, is the unblemished adherence to the Prāsaṅgika tradition, that follows the texts of the glorious Candrakīrti.[32]

While Prāsaṅgika Madhyamaka was dominant in Tibet since the fifteenth century, preceded by centuries when Svātantrika held the field there, these divisions did not exist previously in India. There was simply Madhyamaka, with different teachers giving different emphases. Only later and retrospectively were their teachings classified as Svātantrika and Prāsaṅgika. Moreover, in the earlier centuries of the first millennium C.E., even Yogācāra and Madhyamaka were not yet separate schools of Buddhism.[33] Indeed, we have Yogācāra writers producing commentaries on Nāgārjuna's great work, the *Mūla-madhyamaka-kārikā*, including even Asaṅga. None of these were translated into Tibetan, but a couple were translated into Chinese. Prof. Seyfort Ruegg writes:

> It is to be noted that among the earlier commentaries on Nāgārjuna's writings there are some by important masters of the Yogācārin/Vijñānavādin school. . . . The existence of such commentaries on the MMK [*Mūla-madhyamaka-kārikā*] by leading authorities of the Vijñānavāda clearly indicates that Nāgārjuna's work was not considered to be the exclusive property of the Mādhyamikas in the narrow sense of a particular school, and that it was regarded as fundamental by Mahāyānist thinkers of more than one tendency.[34]

So it is entirely possible that Great Madhyamaka was an early tradition of Madhyamaka using the Yogācāra terminology employed by Maitreya and Asaṅga to explain the original texts of Nagārjuna and Āryadeva, before the time of Buddhapālita and Bhā[va]viveka, who were later considered the founders of the Prāsaṅgika and Svātantrika divisions, respectively.

As for the question of what understanding of emptiness Nāgārjuna ultimately intended, this will have to remain open. Despite the repeated assertions of many Tibetan lamas today that it is definitely the Prāsaṅgika understanding, and the fact that this dominated in Tibet for the last six centuries, this was not the dominant understanding in India. In Madhyamaka's original homeland the Svātantrika understanding was equally widespread, if not more so. Not only was Prāsaṅgika not the dominant understanding of Madhyamaka in India, but even Madhyamaka itself was not the dominant understanding of Buddhism there, as it was in Tibet. In India, the Yogācāra form of Buddhism was equally widespread, if not more so. We learn in standard histories of Buddhism that the pivotal Prāsaṅgika teacher Candrakīrti was continually defeated in debate by the Yogācāra teacher Candragomin over several years at Nālandā monastic university.[35] We may recall here that the Yogācāra commentaries on Nāgārjuna's *Mūla-madhyamaka-kārikā* never reached Tibet. All this serves to show that, historically speaking, no one understanding of emptiness is clearly demonstrable as being what Nāgārjuna ultimately intended. For this we will have to await the discovery of Nāgārjuna's own commentary.

It is a strange and inexplicable fact that Nāgārjuna's own commentary on his greatest work, the *Mūla-madhyamaka-kārikā*, is apparently lost. The one attributed to him now found in the Tibetan canon, titled *Akutobhaya*, is not authentic according to Tsongkhapa and others.[36] It is a brief commentary, consisting of only 70 folios in its Tibetan translation as found in the Derge edition of the Tengyur. Had this brief commentary actually been by Nāgārjuna, they say, it would have been cited by all later commentators. Yet it is not cited by any of them, even though much of it is incorporated into Buddhapālita's commentary.[37] But the early biography of Nāgārjuna translated into Chinese by Kumārajīva in 405 C.E. describes the *Akutobhaya* commentary, the original one, as very extensive, of 100,000 verses measure.

> He [Nāgārjuna] explains the *Mahāyāna* in detail and composes the *Upadeśa* of 100,000 *Gāthās*. Besides, he writes *the Splendid Way of the Buddha of 5000 Gāthās, the great Śāstra* (textbook) *on the art of compassion of 5,000 Gāthās, the Madhyamaka-śāstra of 500 Gāthās.* He causes the spreading of the *Mahāyāna* doctrine far into India. He also composes the *Akutobhaya-śāstra with 100,000 Gāthās; the Madhyamaka-śāstra* is contained therein.[38]

It would be easy for us to dismiss such seemingly extravagant numbers as fantasy, except that Kumārajīva actually translated the *Upadeśa* of 100,000 verses measure into Chinese, and this is extant today.[39] We therefore have reason to trust his very early account that Nāgārjuna's own original *Akutobhaya* commentary on the *Mūla-madhyamaka-kārikā*, which Kumārajīva refers to as the *Madhyamaka-śāstra of 500 Gāthās*, consisted of the measure of 100,000 verses. But inexplicably, it is lost.

What we can deduce from the earliest available sources is that the basic understanding of the *Mūla-madhyamaka-kārikā* was probably what later came to be called Prāsaṅgika, but that this approach using negative dialectic was not seen as contradictory to an approach using more positive language. That is, it was not exclusively Prāsaṅgika, as it became in Tibet for the Gelugpas. This may be deduced from the fact that the earliest available commentary, the brief *Chung lun* translated by Kumārajīva into Chinese along with the the *Mūla-madhyamaka-kārikā* in 402 C.E., takes a basically Prāsaṅgika approach.[40] The *Chung lun* is closely similar to the brief *Akutobhaya* commentary that was translated into Tibetan five centuries later,[41] although in China it was not attributed to Nāgārjuna as it was in Tibet. It is now known that fully a third of the *Akutobhaya* is incorporated verbatim into the commentary by Buddhapālita.[42] It is this commentary that came to be seen as the source of the Prāsaṅgika understanding of Madhyamaka, when Candrakīrti in his commentary defended it against the method used by Bhā[va]viveka in his commentary, later to become known as Svātantrika. The Prāsaṅgika method found in Buddhapālita's commentary, then, can be traced back to the *Chung lun* translated by Kumārajīva, our earliest extant source. Kumārajīva obviously accepted it as correctly giving the basic import of the *Mūla-madhyamaka-kārikā*. At the same time, he also obviously accepted the lengthy *Upadeśa* translated by him as correctly giving Nāgārjuna's import, a text known for its more positive approach to reality. Prof. Seyfort Ruegg writes:

> Especially noteworthy are the references found in the *Upadeśa to a positive theory of reality (*dharmatā, tathatā, dharmadhātu, bhūtakoṭi*).[43]

It is this positive theory of reality that Great Madhyamaka finds in Nāgārjuna's hymns, especially the *Dharmadhātu-stava*.[44] It may be that Nāgārjuna's original *Akutobhaya* commentary of 100,000 verses measure, like his *Upadeśa* of 100,000 verses measure, also includes positive descriptions of reality. We know at least that Kumārajīva apparently saw no conflict between the *Upadeśa* with its positive characterization of reality and the *Chung lun* with its use of the Prāsaṅgika dialectic of negations. This was before Madhyamaka was divided into Svātantrika and Prāsaṅgika, and may reflect the ancient tradition of "The Middle Way according to the Original Texts," as Great Madhyamaka called itself. For Great Madhyamaka, too, there is no conflict in using Prāsaṅgika dialectic to negate the ultimate reality of all phenomenal existence, and using positive terms for an ultimate reality beyond conception, as is done in some of the hymns of Nāgārjuna.[45]

If Great Madhyamaka is in fact the ancient tradition of "The Middle Way according to the Original Texts," it would have drawn upon Nāgārjuna's now lost *Akutobhaya* commentary of 100,000 verses measure for its understanding of emptiness. The custodians of the Wisdom Tradition claim to have access to all such works as this one even now. Works of this importance were not lost, they say, but were withdrawn.[46] The fact that there is full doctrinal agreement between the Wisdom Tradition and Great Madhyamaka would point to this understanding being the original one intended by Nāgārjuna. The time may soon come when we once again have access to Nāgārjuna's own *Akutobhaya* commentary. Only then can we know for sure.

The Yogācāra Background

Great Madhyamaka traces its lineage back to Asaṅga and Maitreya, as we learn from only recently available materials. In a 2007 Ph.D. thesis, Michael Sheehy provides a quotation from Ngag dbang Blo gros Grags pa's *Lamp of the Moon: A History of the Jonang Tradition* on the origin of Great Madhyamaka.

> With the arrival of the venerable Ārya Asaṅga (ca. 4th-5th cent.), the chariot tradition of the Great Madhyamaka of definitive meaning was elegantly distinguished and established within the three planes of existence. This was the founding of the definitive secret of the consummate intent of the victorious ones and has been praised as the supreme distinction between the provisional and definitive sections of the Mahāyāna sūtras.[47]

Then, addressing a praise to Ārya Asaṅga for doing this, Ngag dbang Blo gros Grags pa continues:

> In particular, you transcribed the principal intended meaning of the final turning from the Regent Maitreya, the tradition of commentaries on the general intent of the sūtra sections of the Mahāyāna. These include the *Uttaratantra,* the two differentiations, and the two ornaments which together compose the *Five Treasures of Maitreya.* When you studied with these masters, you acquired each of the individual entrances of meditative concentration through merely studying the specific points of meaning. Since these teachings of Maitreya are the intent of the victorious one, they are the consummate definitive meaning composed according to irreversible advice. Exactly as is, this is the vast illumination of the view and meditation of the Gzhan stong Great Madhyamaka.[48]

The writings received by Asaṅga from Maitreya, then, form the basis of the Great Madhyamaka school or tradition. As is well known, these writings have always been described as Yogācāra, and have usually been thought to teach Mind-Only (*citta-mātra*).

If these texts really teach Great Madhyamaka, why are they so widely believed to teach Mind-Only? According to sources now available, the Mind-Only or Cittamātra understanding of Yogācāra arose with 500 earlier teachers including Avitarka. As explained in *The Treasury of Knowledge* by Jamgon Kongtrul:

> The great exalted one of Jonang [Dolpopa] and his followers maintain that Asaṅga and his brother [Vasubandhu] were Madhyamaka masters and that their system of philosophical tenets is the Great Madhyamaka (*dBu ma chen po*).
>
> You may wonder, in that case, who were the founding masters of the Chittamātra system? [The founders and promulgators of the Chittamātra system] were five hundred Mahāyāna masters, great exalted ones of earlier times, such as Avitarka, and others. "Others" means some of their followers and some later Proponents of Mere Cognition (Vijñaptimātra).[49]

Jamgon Kongtrul's source for this is a text by Tāranātha, who there explains further:

> It was well known that there were five hundred Yogāchāra masters, such as the great venerable Avitarka, Jñānatala, and others. Their treatises were not translated into Tibetan, in the same way that the treatises of the eighteen orders [were not translated into Tibetan].[50]

Tāranātha makes clear in his *History of Buddhism in India* that these 500 teachers were the first Mahāyāna teachers, and hence preceded Maitreya and Asaṅga by centuries. He reports that they were all followers of the path of Yogācāra Cittamātra.[51] Thus, Mind-Only or Cittamātra is not the teaching of Maitreya and Asaṅga, but arose earlier. Ngag dbang Blo gros Grags pa writes:

> Accordingly, after these three councils on the Hīnayāna discourses had convened, it is said that five hundred teachers of

the dharma including the great honorable Avitarka and others came about as adherents of the Mahāyāna. These scriptural collections of the Mahāyāna including the *Laṅkāvatāra-sūtra*, the *Gaṇḍavyūha-sūtra* and many of the Mahāyāna sūtras were then discovered in various regions, and these teachings were then kept and diffused. From these, the Mahāyāna tradition of the Cittamātra system that asserts actual existence (*dngos smra ba'i sems tsam lugs*) arose.[52]

This last statement refers to the tenet of the Mind-Only or Cittamātra system that consciousness (*vijñāna*) is truly existent. This is the source of the confusion. Great Madhyamaka does not accept this tenet. Jamgon Kongtrul opens his chapter on Cittamātra tenets with this statement:

Chittamātras state that consciousness is truly existent.[53]

The translator of Jamgon Kongtrul's text points out that according to him, this is the difference between Mind-Only or Cittamātra and Great Madhyamaka or Shentong Madhyamaka:

The opening verse is a concise statement of one of the Chittamātras' main tenets: they assert consciousness to be truly existent. According to Jamgon Kongtrul, this assertion distinguishes this tenet system from Shentong-Madhyamaka.[54]

Great Madhyamaka holds not that consciousness (*vijñāna*) is truly existent, but rather that primordial wisdom (*jñāna*) is truly existent. These two have often been confused, and thus the Yogācāra teachings of Maitreya, Asaṅga, and Vasubandhu have often been taken as teaching Mind-Only or Cittamātra. But, says Jamgon Kongtrul, this is a mistake.

This is simply the mistake of those who speak deviously by not distinguishing between Vasubandhu's assertion that primordial wisdom is truly existent and the Chittamātra system's statement that consciousness is truly existent.[55]

So the Great Madhyamaka tradition takes as its sources the Yogācāra works of Maitreya, Asaṅga, and Vasubandhu, but it does not understand them as teaching Mind-Only or Cittamātra like they are usually understood elsewhere.

The main point, then, is that Great Madhyamaka understands the Yogācāra texts differently than Mind-Only. This is true whether the Mind-Only understanding was taught by 500 early teachers including Avitarka or by some other teachers, and whether these teachers preceded or came after Maitreya and Asaṅga. Granting this, it will still be worthwhile to see how far the account of 500 early teachers including Avitarka from Tāranātha's *History of Buddhism in India* can be verified.

The origin of Yogācāra is normally thought to lie with Maitreya and Asaṅga. They lived, agreeably to both traditional accounts and modern research, at least a couple centuries after Nāgārjuna. Thus, when references to Yogācāra ideas are found in a work by Nāgārjuna, the authenticity of this work is called into question. This work is the *Bodhicitta-vivaraṇa,* which gives a sustained critique of Mind-Only ideas in its verses 22-56.[56] But the researches of Christian Lindtner, showing that this text is quoted as a work of Nāgārjuna's by many early Madhyamaka writers, have provided convincing evidence that it is in fact an authentic Nāgārjuna work.[57] Now the question is where did the Yogācāra Mind-Only ideas critiqued in it come from.

Yogācāra Mind-Only ideas are found in Mahāyāna *sūtras* such as the *Laṅkāvatāra-sūtra.* Tāranātha's account names this and several other *sūtras* as being brought out at the time of the 500 early teachers including Avitarka.[58] Lindtner's research agrees that the *Laṅkāvatāra-sūtra* was sufficiently early to be Nāgārjuna's source for the Yogācāra Mind-Only ideas that he critiques, and in fact was.[59] This answers the question of where these ideas could have come from. But there is an important weakness in this picture. It is unlikely that any Buddhist writer would directly critique a *sūtra,* supposed to contain the words of the Buddha. They would only critique later Buddhist writers' interpretations of a *sūtra.* We are therefore practically obliged to assume that some teachers were then teaching Mind-Only based on these *sūtras*. Thus some early teachers such as the 500 including Avitarka become not only plausible, but necessary. Their works have been lost, just like the works of the eighteen early Hīnayāna orders that, as said by Tāranātha above, were not translated into Tibetan.[60]

Tāranātha tells us that Avitarka was the teacher of Rahulabhadra, who was the teacher of Nāgārjuna.[61] So the Mind-Only ideas promulgated by these early teachers reached Nāgārjuna directly. Nāgārjuna, after obtaining the Perfection of Wisdom or *Prajñā-pāramitā sūtras* from the Nāgas, and seeing the central role of the teachings on emptiness in these *sūtras*, was then in a position to say that emptiness was the highest teaching of the Buddha. So emptiness must also be what the Buddha primarily intended in the *Laṅkāvatāra* and other Mahāyāna *sūtras* that had come out earlier, even if Yogācāra Mind-Only teachings are also found in them. Thus, the earlier teachers were wrong in taking Mind-Only as what these *sūtras* ultimately teach, and this needed to be countered. This Nāgārjuna did in his *Bodhicitta-vivaraṇa*. He did this a couple centuries before Asaṅga arrived on the scene. The Madhyamaka teaching, taking emptiness as the primary teaching of all the Mahāyāna *sūtras*, was thus in place when Asaṅga arrived.

Great Madhyamaka fully agrees with Nāgārjuna's rejection of Mind-Only, and his making emptiness the primary teaching of the Mahāyāna. Nāgārjuna's Madhyamaka was only furthered by Asaṅga and Maitreya, not opposed by them. Asaṅga spent twelve years in meditation trying to understand the import of the Perfection of Wisdom *sūtras* that Nāgārjuna brought out.[62] Maitreya then showed Asaṅga how the path to enlightenment was hidden away in these Perfection of Wisdom *sūtras*, teaching him the *Abhisamayālaṃkāra*, a book destined to become the main textbook on the path used in all the Tibetan monasteries. Maitreya also taught Yogācāra treatises to Asaṅga. Mahāyāna at that time still remained a single tradition. It was not until later that Madhyamaka and Yogācāra were seen as separate branches of Mahāyāna. Bhā[va]viveka was the first writer known to have distinguished Madhyamaka and Yogācāra as different schools, specifically naming Asaṅga and Vasubandhu with Yogācāra, and opposing it.[63] Candrakīrti followed him in this, continuing to distinguish the two, and continuing to oppose Yogācāra.[64] Thus the distinction of Yogācāra and Madhyamaka coincided with what was later viewed as the separation of the Svātantrika and Prāsaṅgika schools of Madhyamaka, of Bhā[va]viveka and Candrakīrti respectively. Great Madhyamaka traces its lineage back to before that separation, when the Yogācāra treatises of Maitreya were not regarded as conflicting with Madhyamaka, but only as further explaining it.

Just as Nāgārjuna had furthered the Mahāyāna teachings by showing that emptiness is their primary intent, rather than Mind-Only, so Maitreya and Asaṅga and Vasubandhu furthered the Madhyamaka teachings by showing that other-emptiness or Shentong is their ultimate intent, rather than self-emptiness or Rangtong. Such is the Great Madhyamaka position. According to this tradition, Vasubandhu wrote a great commentary on the Perfection of Wisdom *sūtras* that explained them by way of the distinctive Yogācāra teaching of the three natures (*svabhāva*):[65] the "imagined" (*parikalpita*), the "dependent" (*paratantra*), and the "perfected" (*pariniṣpanna*). These three natures were given in slightly different terms in the "Questions of Maitreya" section of the Perfection of Wisdom *sūtras* in 18,000 lines and in 25,000 lines.[66] This section was regarded by Dolpopa as the Buddha's own commentary, by which the *sūtras* should be interpreted.[67] Vasubandhu did so in his commentary. In this commentary it is possible to distinguish emptiness in two different senses, said Dolpopa.[68] It is these that he widely promoted as self-emptiness or Rangtong and other-emptiness or Shentong.

Great Madhyamaka was known as the meditative tradition (*sgom lugs*) of the works of Maitreya, in contradistinction to the analytical tradition (*thos bsam gyi lugs*).[69] It was primarily an oral tradition that was transmitted privately, and thus long remained little known. This explains the lack of historical references to it until its revival in India by Maitrīpa in the eleventh century, and its subsequent transmission to Tibet, where Dolpopa spread it widely in the fourteenth century.[70]

NOTES

1. On Great Madhyamaka, see Stearns, *The Buddha from Dolpo*, pp. 7, 49, 88, etc.; Tāranātha, *The Essence of Other-Emptiness*, pp. 62 ff.; and Dolpopa, *Mountain Doctrine*, pp. 6, 56, etc.

2. To give just one example from *The Voice of the Silence*, see p. 71:

> Now bend thy head and listen well, O Bodhisattva—Compassion speaks and saith: "Can there be bliss when all that lives must suffer? Shalt thou be saved and hear the whole world cry?"

3. *The Voice of the Silence*, Preface, p. vii.

4. Ibid., p. vi.

5. Of these eight occurrences of "Ālaya" in *The Voice of the Silence*, the first three are on p. 24:

> Alas, alas, that all men should possess Alaya, be one with the great Soul, and that possessing it, Alaya should so little avail them!
> Behold how like the moon, reflected in the tranquil waves, Alaya is reflected by the small and by the great, is mirrored in the tiniest atoms, yet fails to reach the heart of all. Alas, that so few men should profit by the gift, the priceless boon of learning truth, the right perception of existing things, the Knowledge of the non-existent!

The fourth is on pp. 49-50:

> Of teachers there are many; the MASTER-SOUL is one, Alaya, the Universal Soul. Live in that MASTER as ITS ray in thee. Live in thy fellows as they live in IT.

The next two are on p. 57:

> Thou hast to saturate thyself with pure Alaya, become as one with Nature's Soul-Thought. At one with it thou art invincible; in separation, thou becomest the playground of Samvriti, origin of all the world's delusions.

> All is impermanent in man except the pure bright essence of Alaya. Man is its crystal ray; a beam of light immaculate within, a form of clay material upon the lower surface. That beam is thy life-guide and thy true Self, the Watcher and the silent Thinker, the victim of thy lower Self.

The seventh is on p. 67:

> Know that the stream of superhuman knowledge and the Deva-Wisdom thou hast won, must, from thyself, the channel of Alaya, be poured forth into another bed.

The last is on pp. 69-70:

> Yet, one word. Canst thou destroy divine COMPASSION? Compassion is no attribute. It is the LAW of LAWS—eternal Harmony, Alaya's SELF; a shoreless universal essence, the light of everlasting Right, and fitness of all things, the law of love eternal.

In addition to these, Blavatsky uses it in her note on p. 88:

> The "MASTER-SOUL" is *Alaya,* the Universal Soul or Atman, each man having a ray of it in him and being supposed to be able to identify himself with and to merge himself into it.

6. This verse of *The Secret Doctrine,* Stanza 1, verse 9, is:

> But where was the Dangma when the Alaya of the universe was in Paramartha and the great wheel was Anupadaka?

The *ālaya* is defined by Blavatsky here as "Soul as the basis of all, Anima Mundi" (p. 47), explaining that "Alaya is literally the 'Soul of the World' or Anima Mundi, the 'Over-Soul' of Emerson" (p. 48). So the *ālaya* is "Cosmic Ideation, Mahat or Intelligence, the Universal World-Soul" of her chart summary following the first fundamental proposition of the Secret Doctrine (p. 16). It is the "Universal Over-Soul" in the third fundamental proposition of the Secret Doctrine, teaching "The fundamental identity of all Souls with the Universal Over-Soul" (p. 17).

7. Great Madhyamaka makes a point to distinguish the *ālaya* from the *ālaya-vijñāna,* equating the former with the eternal *jñāna,* or primordial wisdom, and describing the latter as consciousness, or

vijñāna, which is ephemeral and is existent only conventionally, but not ultimately. Certainly, the sixth occurrence of *ālaya* in *The Voice of the Silence* shows this distinction where it says, "All is impermanent in man except the pure bright essence of Alaya." Similarly, Blavatsky says in *The Secret Doctrine*, vol. 1, p. 48, "Alaya, though eternal and changeless in its inner essence on the planes which are unreachable by either men or Cosmic Gods (Dhyani Buddhas), alters during the active life-period with respect to the lower planes, ours included."

8. *Abhidharmasamuccaya: The Compendium of the Higher Teaching (Philosophy)*, by Asaṅga, translated into French by Walpola Rahula, English version by Sara Boin-Webb, Fremont, Calif.: Asian Humanities Press, 2001, p. 21.

9. The first occurrence of *pariniṣpanna* is Stanza 1, verse 6:

> The seven sublime lords and the seven truths had ceased to be, and the Universe, the son of Necessity, was immersed in Paranishpanna, to be outbreathed by that which is and yet is not. Naught was.

The other occurrence of *pariniṣpanna* is Stanza 2, verse 1:

> Where were the builders, the luminous sons of Manvantaric dawn? In the unknown darkness in their Ah-hi Paranishpanna. The Producers of form from no-form—the root of the world—the Devamatri and Svâbhâvat, rested in the bliss of non-being.

On the term *pariniṣpanna*, usually incorrectly spelled as *paranishpanna* in *The Secret Doctrine*, but once correctly as *parinishpanna* (vol. 1, p. 23), see also, "Book of Dzyan Research Report: Technical Terms in Stanza I," by David Reigle, found in *Blavatsky's Secret Books*, pp. 73-81, or online at www.easterntradition.org.

10. On this point, that Theosophy does not accept an ultimate consciousness, see, for example, *The Secret Doctrine*, Stanza 1, verse 8:

> Alone the one form of existence stretched boundless, infinite, causeless, in dreamless sleep; and life pulsated unconscious in universal space, throughout that all-presence which is sensed by the opened eye of the Dangma.

The Mahatma Letters, letter #10, 3rd ed., p. 53:

> If people are willing to accept and to regard as God our ONE LIFE immutable and unconscious in its eternity they may do so and thus keep to one more gigantic misnomer. . . .

"The Aryan-Arhat Esoteric Tenets on the Sevenfold Principle in Man," *H. P. Blavatsky Collected Writings*, vol. 3, p. 423:

> Hence, the Arahat secret doctrine on cosmogony admits but of one absolute, indestructible, eternal, and uncreated UNCONSCIOUSNESS (so to translate), of an element (the word being used for want of a better term) absolutely independent of everything else in the universe; . . .

11. The fullest account of this and the role of Pa-tsap Nyima Drak (sPa-tshab Nyi-ma-grags) in it is found in "Spa-tshab Nyi-ma-grags and the Introduction of Prāsaṅgika Madhyamaka into Tibet," by Karen Christina Lang, in *Reflections on Tibetan Culture: Essays in Memory of Turrell V. Wylie*, edited by Lawrence Epstein & Richard F. Sherburne, Lewiston, N.Y.: Edwin Mellen Press, 1990, pp. 127-141.

12. For an overview of textbooks on tenets, see "The Tibetan Genre of Doxography: Structuring a Worldview," by Jeffrey Hopkins, in *Tibetan Literature: Studies in Genre, Essays in Honor of Geshe Lhundup Sopa*, edited by José Ignacio Cabezón and Roger R. Jackson, Ithaca, N.Y.: Snow Lion Publications, 1996, pp. 170-186. To Jeffrey Hopkins we are also indebted for a complete translation of the largest such textbook, *Maps of the Profound: Jam-yang-shay-ba's Great Exposition of Buddhist and Non-Buddhist Views on the Nature of Reality*, Ithaca, N.Y.: Snow Lion Publications, 2003. With Geshe Lhundup Sopa, Hopkins translated a brief such textbook, dKon mchog 'jigs med dbang po's *Precious Garland of Tenets*, published in *Practice and Theory of Tibetan Buddhism*, New York: Grove Press, 1976. This book was revised and reissued as *Cutting Through Appearances: Practice and Theory of Tibetan Buddhism*, Ithaca, N.Y.: Snow Lion Publications, 1989.

13. Elizabeth M. Callahan, trans., *The Treasury of Knowledge, Book Six, Part Three: Frameworks of Buddhist Philosophy*.

14. Jeffrey Hopkins, trans., *The Essence of Other-Emptiness*.

15. Ringu Tulku, *The Ri-me Philosophy of Jamgön Kongtrul the Great*, pp. 9-10. I quote this from Ringu Tulku's book rather than Elizabeth Callahan's translation (see note 13 above) because I follow by quoting

Ringu Tulku's comment on this passage. Callahan's translation of it is, pp. 258-259:

> The Rangtong and Shentong [systems] do not differ over the way that conventional [phenomena] are empty, nor do they disagree that the extremes of conceptual elaborations cease during meditative equipoise. They differ over whether, as a convention, dharmatā exists during subsequent attainment or not, and over whether primordial wisdom is truly established at the end of analysis or not. [The Shentong system] asserts that [if] ultimate reality were simply a nonimplicative negation, whereby its nature is not established, it would be an inanimate emptiness. [Shentong Proponents] present [ultimate reality] as being primordial wisdom empty of dualism, as being reflexive awareness. This is asserted to be the profound view linking the Sūtra and Mantra [systems].

16. Ringu Tulku, op. cit., p. 10.

17. H. P. Blavatsky, *The Secret Doctrine*, vol. 1, p. 14.

18. See the opening few verses of Tāranātha's *Supplication to the Profound Zhentong Madhyamaka Lineage*, at www.jonangfoundation.org. See also on this: Tāranātha, *The Essence of Other-Emptiness*, p. 62; Jamgon Kongtrul, *The Treasury of Knowledge, Book Six, Part Three: Frameworks of Buddhist Philosophy*, p. 249; Ringu Tulku, *The Ri-me Philosophy of Jamgön Kongtrul the Great*, p. 214.

19. H. P. Blavatsky, *The Secret Doctrine*, vol. 1, p. xxii.

20. See on this, *The Books of Kiu-te, or the Tibetan Buddhist Tantras: A Preliminary Analysis*, by David Reigle, San Diego: Wizards Bookshelf, 1983, pp. 46-47.

21. *The Letters of H. P. Blavatsky to A. P. Sinnett*, 1925; reprint, Pasadena: Theosophical University Press, 1973, p. 195.

22. H. P. Blavatsky, *The Secret Doctrine*, vol. 1, p. 23.

23. *The Notebooks of Paul Brunton*, vol. 10, *The Orient: Its Legacy to the West*, Burdett, N.Y.: Larson Publications, 1987, chap. 4, section 7, "The Secret Doctrine of the Khmers," p. 199.

24. Ibid., p. 201.

25. Ibid., p. 201.

26. Ibid., p. 202.

27. Paul Brunton, *The Hidden Teaching Beyond Yoga*, new revised edition, New York: E. P. Dutton & Co., 1942, pp. 99-100:

> Although our unconventional presentation of this knowledge is a modern and Western one, its original source is an ancient and Indian one. Both silent texts and living voices which have informed our writing are mostly Indian, supplemented by some Tibetan documents and a personal Mongolian esoteric instruction. A million men may gainsay the tenability of the tenets unfolded here but none can gainsay the fact that they are Indian tenets, albeit little-known, without twisting the most authoritative ancient documents to suit their mediocre minds. If we do not quote those texts here it is because our readers are primarily Western and we do not wish to burden them with the troublesome necessity of exploring exhaustive glossaries for unfamiliar Sanskrit names.

Paul Brunton, *The Hidden Teaching Beyond Yoga*, pp. 409-410:

> This quality of the timelessness of truth thrust itself powerfully into the present writer's meditations one evening in a land of steaming jungles and dense forests, where forgotten Indian sages had carried their culture long ago. He sat amid the vast deserted ruins of ancient Angkor, in Cambodian Indo-China, . . . Was it not wonderful that the immemorial wisdom of these men, who flourished and taught when Europe lay benighted in the dark ages, could be known and studied today and would be known and studied yet again when another two millenniums had once more passed over this planet? Out of the burial-urn of the Past this same wisdom has been extricated. But because it has here been moulded in an ultra-modern form to suit both our time and need, its authenticity or truth may not be plainly recognizable to its present-day Indian inheritors. Yet there is not a single important tenet here which cannot be found phrased in the old Sanskrit writings. We are only the inheritors and not the discoverers of this ever-ancient but ever-new lore.

Paul Brunton, *The Wisdom of the Overself*, New York: E. P. Dutton & Co., 1943, pp. 13-14:

> Hundreds of texts were examined in the effort to trace and collate basic ideas. . . . The Ariadne's thread which finally led me through this metaphysical maze was indeed placed in my hands whilst visiting Cambodian China where I encountered amid the deserted shrines of majestic Angkor another visitor in the person of an Asiatic philosopher. From him I received an unforgettable personal esoteric instruction . . . . All this is but a preamble to the statement that with these volumes a doctrine is presented which in all essential principles is not a local Indian tradition but an all-Asiatic one. . . . It would have been much easier to emulate a portentous academic parrot and merely write down what other men had written or said as it would have been more self-flattering to parade the breadth of my learning by peppering both volumes with a thousand Sanskrit, Tibetan and Chinese quotations, names or words. But life to-day points a challenging sword at us. I was too sensitive to the iconoclastic spirit of our age, too enamoured of the austere figure of truth rather than of her discarded robes, too troubled by what I had physically seen and personally experienced in this world-shaking epoch to be satisfied with anything less than a fresh living reconstruction.

28. Paul Brunton, *The Wisdom of the Overself*, p. 26:

> Mentalism derives its name from its fundamental principle that Mind is the only reality, the only substance, the only existence; things being our ideas and ideas finding their support in our mind. Mentalism in short is the doctrine that in the last analysis there is nothing but Mind.

This is obviously a straightforward statement of Yogācāra understood as Cittamātra, or "Mind-Only." While he carefully avoided using these Sanskrit terms, we can derive them directly from his comment on the mentalist schools of China and Japan. In *The Notebooks of Paul Brunton*, vol. 13, part 3, p. 96, para. 214, he writes:

> The mentalist schools of Chinese Buddhism existed only from 600 A.D. to 1100 A.D. They were named the Fa-hsiang and the Wei-shih. The mentalist school of Japanese Buddhism was the Hosso.

Fa-hsiang is the name of the Yogācāra school in China. This school is also known as Wei-shih, meaning *vijñapti-mātra*, "consciousness only." Hosso is the name of the same school in Japan. Moreover, we can find this in Angkor as well. In *The Notebooks of Paul Brunton*, vol. 13, part 3, p. 2, he writes:

> One thousand years ago the doctrine of mentalism was taught at Angkor, according to an inscription of that time which I saw there, the inscription of Srey Santhor. It likened the appearance of the doctrine in the world of faith and culture to the sun bringing back the light.

See the inscription from Vat Sithor from about 968 C.E., concerning a Buddhist prelate named Kīrtipaṇḍita, given in David Snellgrove's 2004 book, *Angkor—Before and After: A Cultural History of the Khmers*, Trumbull, Conn.: Weatherhill, and Bangkok: Orchid Press, p. 82:

> "In him the sun of the doctrines of 'Non-Self' (*nairātyma*), 'Mind Only' (*cittamātra*) and the like, which have been eclipsed in the night of false teachings, shone once again in full daylight."

Snellgrove adds in a note on this (n. 17, p. 226):

> The preferred school of Buddhist philosophy is thus that of Yogacāra or 'Mind Only' (*Cittamātra*), representing the latest and 'Third Turning' of the Wheel of the Doctrine, as promulgated by the Bodhisattva Maitreya and the Sage Asanga . . . .

29. See on this, Paul Brunton, *The Hidden Teaching Beyond Yoga*, pp. 362-363:

> And we may now see the deep and practical wisdom of the early Indian teachers who prescribed yoga to those whose intellectual power was not strong enough to grasp the truth of mentalism through reasoned insight, for thus these men were enabled to arrive at the same goal through feeling, not through knowledge. . . . Yet we must never forget that mentalism is only a step leading to ultimate truth. . . . It is also a temporary ground which the questing mind must occupy whilst consolidating its first victory, the victory over matter. Once the consolidation is fully effected it must begin to move onwards again; it must leave mentalism! The

ultimate reality cannot consist of thoughts because these are fated to appear and vanish; it must have a more enduring basis than such transiency. Nevertheless we may see in thoughts, to which we have reduced everything, intimations of the presence of this reality and apart from which they are as illusory as matter. The further and final battle must lead to victory over the idea itself. Both materialism and mentalism are tentative viewpoints which must be taken up and then deserted when the ultimate viewpoint is reached. Then alone may we say: "*This is real.*" . . . Meanwhile it is essential to study well this basis of mentalism because upon it shall later be reared a superstructure of stupendous but reasoned revelation.

30. Further confirmation of this is found in "a work written in Chinese by a Tibetan, and published in the monastery of Tientai," quoted by Blavatsky in, "The 'Doctrine of the Eye' & the 'Doctrine of the Heart,' or the 'Heart's Seal,'" in *H. P. Blavatsky Collected Writings*, vol. 14, pp. 450-451:

> No profane ears having heard the mighty Chau-yan [secret and enlightening *precepts*] of Wu-Wei-chen-jen [Buddha *within* Buddha], of our beloved Lord and Bodhisattva, how can one tell what his thoughts really were? The holy Sang-gyas-Panchen never offered an insight into the *One Reality* to the unreformed [uninitiated] Bhikkhus. Few are those even among the Tu-fon [Tibetans] who knew it; as for the Tsung-men Schools, they are going with every day more down hill . . . . Not even the Fa-hsiang-Tsung can give one the wisdom taught in real Naljor-chod-pa [Sanskrit: Yogacharyā]: . . . it is all "Eye" Doctrine, and no more. The loss of a restraining guidance is felt; since the Tch'-an-si [teachers] of inward meditation [self-contemplation or Tchung-kwan] have become rare, and the Good Law is replaced by idol-worship [Siang-kyan]. It is of this [idol- or image-worship] that the Barbarians [Western people] have heard, and know nothing of Bas-pa-Dharma [the secret Dharma or doctrine]. Why has truth to hide like a tortoise within its shell? Because it is now found to have become like the Lama's tonsure knife, a weapon too dangerous to use even for the Lanoo. Therefore no one can

> be entrusted with the knowledge [Secret Science] before his time. The Chagpa-Thog-med have become rare, and the best have retired to Tushita the Blessed.

Two sentences confirm this: "Not even the Fa-hsiang-Tsung can give one the wisdom taught in real Naljor-chod-pa [Sanskrit: Yogacharyā]: . . . it is all 'Eye' Doctrine, and no more." "The Chagpa-Thog-med have become rare, and the best have retired to Tushita the Blessed." The term Fa-hsiang-Tsung is the name of the Yogācāra school in China. The term Naljor-chod-pa is, as shown, the Tibetan translation of the Sanskrit term Yogācāra, or Yogacharyā. The term Chagpa-Thog-med is the Tibetan translation of Ārya Asaṅga, the founder of the Yogācāra school. Its meaning in this sentence is apparently followers of Asaṅga, i.e., of the "real" Yogācāra school. This would be, as we have seen, the Great Madhyamaka school or tradition.

Great Madhyamaka teaches Shentong, or "other-emptiness." The Tibetan writer quoted here goes on to say, p. 452, that one should ultimately be enabled to see, "the faithful reflection of Self . . . . First, this; then Tong-pa-nyi, lastly; Sammā Sambuddha." He here brings in the Madhyamaka term Tong-pa-nyi, which is the Tibetan translation of the Sanskrit term *śūnyatā*, "emptiness."

31. See, for example, Dudjom Rinpoche, Jikdrel Yeshe Dorje, *The Nyingma School of Tibetan Buddhism: Its Fundamentals and History*, Boston: Wisdom Publications, 1991, vol. 1, book 1, part 3, chapter 7, "The Two Truths According to Great Madhyamaka," p. 216, where Nāgārjuna's hymns are called eulogies:

> One should know that the entire intention of the sūtras and the tantras, which are the scriptures of the Tathāgata, is subsumed in a single nucleus, just as butter is condensed from milk, and cream from butter, so that the climax of the philosophical systems, according to the causal vehicle of dialectics, is this Great Madhyamaka, supreme among vehicles. Its meaning is revealed in the texts of Maitreya, such as the *Supreme Continuum of the Greater Vehicle*, and in the sublime Nāgārjuna's *Collection of Eulogies*, which subsume the essence of the definitive meaning of both the intermediate and final promulgations of the transmitted precepts."

32. From "gDams ngag: Tibetan Technologies of the Self," by Matthew Kapstein, in *Tibetan Literature: Studies in Genre, Essays in Honor of Geshe Lhundup Sopa,* edited by José Ignacio Cabezón and Roger R. Jackson, Ithaca, N.Y.: Snow Lion Publications, 1996, p. 282. Bracketed material is Kapstein's.

33. On this, see Won ch'uk's comments from his commentary on the *Saṃdhi-nirmocana-sūtra,* quoted by Tsong kha pa in his *Ocean of Eloquence,* translated by Gareth Sparham, Albany: State University of New York Press, 1993, p. 49:

> Since at that time [the time of Asaṅga] the doctrine was of one taste, there was no controversy between those asserting emptiness and those asserting existence (*bhava*). This is the reason why Ācārya Nye ba'i 'od (=Bandhu-prabhā/ Prabhā-mitra) said: "A thousand years ago the taste of Buddha's teaching was one. Thereafter, mindfulness (*smṛti*) and wisdom (*prajñā*) gradually deteriorated and those asserting emptiness and those asserting existence (*bhava*) spread widely in the world."

"Those asserting emptiness" are those who follow Madhyamaka, and "those asserting existence" are those who follow Yogācāra. For a good example of a text written before the separation of these two schools took place, and so reflecting their harmony, see Kambala's *Ālokamālā,* translated by Chr. Lindtner, in *Miscellanea Buddhica,* Indiske Studier 5, Copenhagen: Akademisk Forlag, 1985; reprinted as *A Garland of Light: Kambala's Ālokamālā,* Fremont, Calif.: Asian Humanities Press, 2003.

Notice also that the full title of the famous Madhyamaka work by Nāgārjuna's spiritual son Āryadeva, the *Catuḥ-śataka,* "Four Hundred [Verses]," is *Bodhisattva-Yogācāra-Catuḥ-śataka,* where Yogācāra clearly refers to the "yoga practice" (*yogācāra*) of a Bodhisattva, its original meaning, and not to the later separated school of that name.

34. David Seyfort Ruegg, *The Literature of the Madhyamaka School of Philosophy in India,* A History of Indian Literature, vol. 7, fasc. 1, p. 49, Wiesbaden: Otto Harrassowitz, 1981. The part omitted by me in the ellipsis is:

> A portion of a commentary ascribed to Asaṅga on the beginning of the MMK is preserved in Chinese (Taishō 1565, translated in 543); it refers to Rāhulabhadra and comments also on the

> preliminary stanzas to the MMK concerned with the eight negative epithets applied to *pratītyasamutpāda.* A commentary by Sthiramati is also preserved in Chinese (Taishō 1567, translated about 1000); it evidently knows Bhāvaviveka's commentary on the MMK. In addition, a commentary by Sthiramati's master Guṇamati which is no longer extant is known to tradition; it seems to have been known to Bhāvaviveka.

Tradition also knows a commentary on the *Mūla-madhyamaka-kārikā* by the Yogācāra master Dharmapāla that is no longer extant. See: Leonard W. J. van der Kuijp, *Contributions to the Development of Tibetan Buddhist Epistemology,* Alt- und Neu-Indische Studien 26, Wiesbaden: Franz Steiner Verlag, 1983, p. 281, n. 146. Dharmapāla's commentary on Āryadeva's *Catuḥśataka,* however, is extant, although in Chinese. See John P. Keenan's translation of its tenth chapter, *Dharmapāla's Yogācāra Critique of Bhāvaviveka's Mādhyamika Explanation of Emptiness: The Tenth Chapter of Ta-Ch'eng Kuang Pai-Lun Shih Commenting on Āryadeva's Catuḥśataka Chapter Sixteen,* Lewiston, N.Y.: Edwin Mellen Press, 1997.

35. See, for example, *Indian Buddhist Pandits, from "The Jewel Garland of Buddhist History,"* translated by Losang Norbu Tsonawa, [Dharamsala]: Library of Tibetan Works & Archives, 1985, p. 24:

> Chandragomī held the Cittamatrin view of Asanga and Chandrakīrti held Nāgārjuna's Prāsangika Mādhyamika viewpoint as explained by Buddhapalita. It is said that they debated for seven years. The people witnessed the debate over the years and those who understood some of the arguments and viewpoints they expounded made up a song:
>
> Ah! Nāgārjuna's texts,
> For some people are medicine
> But are poison for others.
> But Maitreya and Asanga's texts
> Are medicine for everyone.

36. See *Tsong Khapa's Speech of Gold in the Essence of True Eloquence; Reason and Enlightenment in the Central Philosophy of Tibet,* translated by Robert A. F. Thurman, Princeton: Princeton University Press, 1984, pp. 265-266, regarding the *Akutobhaya,* "No Fear from Anywhere":

> As for the *No Fear from Anywhere*, in comment on the twenty-seventh chapter, it cites evidence from the *Four Hundred*: "As the revered Aryadeva declares: Very rarely does it happen that there are teacher, listener, and that worth hearing. Hence, in short, cyclic life is neither limited nor limitless!" This means that the *No Fear from Anywhere* is not an autocommentary, as is also recognized from the fact that not even the smallest fragment of its commentary is cited in the commentaries of Buddhapalita, Bhavaviveka, or Chandrakirti.

See also *Mkhas grub rje's Fundamentals of the Buddhist Tantras*, translated by Ferdinand D. Lessing and Alex Wayman, The Hague: Mouton, 1968, reprinted under the changed title, *Introduction to the Buddhist Tantric Systems*, Delhi: Motilal Banarsidass, 1978, p. 89:

> This *Akutobhaya* is maintained by the older catalogs, and by many persons following them, to have been composed by Nāgārjuna; but that is certainly not so, because there is not a single instance of its being quoted in the works of his disciples, and while commenting on the twenty-seventh chapter [of the *Prajñā-mūla*] it says, quoting the *Catuḥśataka* (Toh. 3846), "Āryadeva also says."

For a fuller statement of mKhas grub rje's views on this, see *A Dose of Emptiness: An Annotated Translation of the sTong thun chen mo of mKhas grub dGe legs dpal bzang*, translated by José Ignacio Cabezón, Albany: State University of New York Press, 1992, pp. 82-84.

37. See the study of the *Akutobhaya* by C. W. Huntington, Jr., "A Lost Text of Early Madhyamaka," *Asiatische Studien/Études Asiatiques*, vol. 49, 1995, pp. 693-767. He there writes on p. 708:

> BP [Buddhapālita's commentary] has clearly incorporated lines, phrases, lengthy passages and almost entire chapters from the earlier commentary. We know that BP borrowed from ABh [*Akutobhayā*], and not the reverse, because of the relative chronology of the two texts. When two translated texts are identical, as are these two in so many places, then we must assume that the original texts were also identical in these same places. In this case, out of a total of 4,399 lines found in the present edition of ABh, fully 1,437 were lifted verbatim and incorporated into the

body of BP. This means that almost exactly one third of ABh has been reproduced verbatim in BP.

38. *The Life of Nāgārjuna from Tibetan and Chinese Sources,* by M. Walleser, Delhi: Nag Publishers, 1979, p. 29. This book is a reprint of the article published in *Asia Major,* Hirth Anniversary Volume, 1923, pp. 421-455, where this quote occurs on p. 447. This passage was again translated by Richard H. Robinson in *Early Mādhyamika in India and China,* Madison: [University of Wisconsin Press], 1967, p. 26:

> Explaining the Mahāyāna at great length, he wrote the *Upadeśa* in 100,000 ślokas. He also wrote the *Buddha-mārga-alaṃkāra-śāstra* (?) in 5,000 ślokas, the *Mahāmaitri-upāya-śāstra* (?) in 5,000 ślokas, and the *Madhyamaka-śāstra* in 500 ślokas, and caused the Mahāyāna doctrine to have a great vogue throughout India. He also wrote the *Akutobhayā-śāstra* (?) in 100,000 ślokas, out of which the *Madhyamaka-śāstra* comes.

39. The first part of the *Upadeśa,* or *Mahāprajñāpāramitāśāstra,* was translated from Chinese into French by Étienne Lamotte in five heavily annotated volumes totaling 2451 pages, as *Le Traité de la Grande Vertu de Sagesse de Nāgārjuna (Mahāprajñāpāramitāśāstra),* Louvain, 1944-1980. For an English study of it, see *Nāgārjuna's Philosophy as Presented in the Mahā-Prajñāpāramitā-Śāstra,* by K. Venkata Ramanan, Tokyo, 1966. The latter part of the *Upadeśa* was not translated into Chinese completely, but only summarized by Kumārajīva. Although Lamotte later came to doubt that the *Upadeśa* was written by the same Nāgārjuna who wrote the *Mūla-madhyamaka-kārikā,* his reasons for this were not convincing to other scholars, such as J. W. de Jong (see his review of Lamotte's vol. 3, in *Asia Major,* vol. 17, 1971, pp. 105-112). Venkata Ramanan in his book listed above was not convinced either. Since Kumārajīva probably lived only a century after Nāgārjuna, the traditions of authorship in his time would carry much weight.

40. The *Chung lun* was translated into English by Brian Bocking, *Nāgārjuna in China: A Translation of the Middle Treatise,* Lewiston, N.Y.: Edwin Mellen Press, 1995.

41. Huntington, pp. 705-706: "Close comparison of the texts of Abh and CL confirms that both commentaries stem from one original Indic source."

42. See note 37 above.

43. Seyfort Ruegg, p. 33. He here refers the reader to K. Venkata Ramanan's book (see note 39 above), pp. 16, 44-45, 251 sq.

44. English translations of Nāgārjuna's *Dharmadhātu-stava* have recently become available. Donald S. Lopez, Jr., translated it under the title, "In Praise of Reality," in the book, *Buddhist Scriptures*, edited by him, London: Penguin Books, 2004, pp. 464-477. Karl Brunnhölzl has given us a whole book on this hymn of 101 verses, under the title, *In Praise of Dharmadhātu*, Ithaca, N.Y.: Snow Lion Publications, 2007. It includes the commentary by the 3rd Karmapa. Here are verses 20-22 as translated by Lopez:

> When a fireproof garment, stained by various stains, is placed in a fire, the stains are burned but the garment is not. (20)
> In the same way, the mind of clear light is stained by desire. The stains are burned by the fire of wisdom; just that clear light is not. (21)
> All the *sūtras* setting forth emptiness spoken by the teacher turn back the afflictions; they do not impair the element. (22)

45. Besides the *Dharmadhātu-stava* (see the previous note), in which this is frequent, see, for example, Nāgārjuna's *Acintya-stava*, "Hymn to the Inconceivable [Buddha]," verses 37-39. As edited and translated by Chr. Lindtner in his *Nagarjuniana: Studies in the Writings and Philosophy of Nāgārjuna*, Copenhagen: Akademisk Forlag, 1982; reprint, Delhi: Motilal Banarsidass, 1987, pp. 152-153:

> bhāvābhāvadvayātītam anatītaṃ ca kutra cit |
> na ca jñānaṃ na ca jñeyaṃ na cāsti na ca nāsti yat ||
> yan na caikaṃ na cānekaṃ nobhayaṃ na ca nobhayam |
> anālayam athāvyaktam acintyam anidarśanam ||
> yan nodeti na ca vyeti nocchedi na ca śāśvatam |
> tad ākāśapratīkāśaṃ nākṣarajñānagocaram ||
> [That which] has transcended the duality of being and non-being without, however, having transcended anything at all; that which is not knowledge or knowable, not existent nor non-existent, not one nor many, not both nor neither; [that which is] without foundation, unmanifest, inconceivable, incomparable; that which arises not, disappears not, is not to be annihilated

> and is not permanent, *that* is [Reality] which is like space [and] not within the range of words [or] knowledge (*akṣarajñāna*).

Nāgārjuna then goes on in verse 45 to describe this ultimate reality as *svabhāva*, "inherent nature," or "inherent existence," *prakṛti*, "essential nature," or "(primary) substance," *tattva*, "reality," *dravya*, "substance," *vastu*, "a real thing," and *sat*, "true being," terms that are thoroughly negated by him as applied to everything else. This is especially true of the first one, *svabhāva*; the whole theme of Madhyamaka being that everything is empty of *svabhāva* (*svabhāva-śūnya*), inherent nature or inherent existence.

This hymn, along with three others forming the *Catuḥstava* of Nāgārjuna, has also been published in Sanskrit and English in the book by Fernando Tola and Carmen Dragonetti, *On Voidness: A Study on Buddhist Nihilism*, Delhi: Motilal Banarsidass, 1995.

46. See *The Secret Doctrine*, vol. I, p. xxiii:

> The members of several esoteric schools—the seat of which is beyond the Himālayas, and whose ramifications may be found in China, Japan, India, Tibet, and even in Syria, besides South America—claim to have in their possession the *sum total* of sacred and philosophical works in MSS. and type: all the works, in fact, that have ever been written, in whatever language or characters, since the art of writing began; from the ideographic hieroglyphs down to the alphabet of Cadmus and the Devanāgarī.
>
> It has been claimed in all ages that ever since the destruction of the Alexandrian Library, every work of a character that might have led the profane to the ultimate discovery and comprehension of some of the mysteries of the Secret Science, was, owing to the combined efforts of the members of the Brotherhoods, diligently searched for. It is added, moreover, by those who know, that once found, save three copies left and stored safely away, such works were all destroyed.

47. Michael Sheehy, *The Gzhan stong Chen mo*, p. 66.

48. Michael Sheehy, *The Gzhan stong Chen mo*, p. 67.

49. Jamgon Kongtrul, *The Treasury of Knowledge*, p. 192. See also: Tāranātha's *The Essence of Other-Emptiness*, p. 72.

50. Jamgon Kongtrul, *The Treasury of Knowledge*, p. 364, n. 593.

51. *Tāranātha's History of Buddhism in India*, trans. Lama Chimpa, Alaka Chattopadhyaya, ed. Debiprasad Chattopadhyaya, Simla: Indian Institute of Advanced Study, 1970, pp. 98-100. The translators give the Tibetan term in footnote 25, p. 100: *rnal-'byor-spyod-pa-sems-tsam-pa.*

52. Michael Sheehy, *The Gzhan stong Chen mo*, pp. 66, 111-112.

53. Jamgon Kongtrul, *The Treasury of Knowledge*, p. 176.

54. Elizabeth M. Callahan, Introduction, in Jamgon Kongtrul, *The Treasury of Knowledge*, p. 37.

55. Jamgon Kongtrul, *The Treasury of Knowledge*, pp. 39, 191.

56. The *Bodhicitta-vivaraṇa* has been published in Tibetan and translated into English by Chr. Lindtner in his *Nagarjuniana: Studies in the Writings and Philosophy of Nāgārjuna*, pp. 180-217; verses 22-56 are on pp. 192-201.

57. Chr. Lindtner, *Nagarjuniana*, p. 180.

58. *Tāranātha's History of Buddhism in India*, p. 98.

59. Christian Lindtner, "The Laṅkāvatārasūtra in Early Indian Madhyamaka Literature," *Asiatische Studien/Études Asiatiques*, vol. 46, 1992, pp. 244-279. The *Bodhicitta-vivaraṇa* is discussed on pp. 260-264.

60. The works of the eighteen early Hīnayāna orders apparently were lost long ago, as they were not translated into Chinese, either. On these eighteen early orders, see Vasumitra's *Samaya-bhedoparacana-cakra*, translated by Jiryo Masuda as, "Origin and Doctrines of Early Indian Buddhist Schools: A Translation of the Hsüan-chwang Version of Vasumitra's Treatise," *Asia Major*, vol. 2, 1925, pp. 1-78.

61. *Tāranātha's History of Buddhism in India*, p. 102.

62. According to the traditional histories of Buddhism compiled in Tibet, Asaṅga was unable to understand the Perfection of Wisdom *sūtras* due to their great length and diffusiveness. After twelve years of meditation, Maitreya appeared to him and taught him how the path to enlightenment is found in them. This was then written in his book, the *Abhisamayālaṃkāra*. For a convenient account of this, summarized from the histories by Bu-ston and Tāranātha, see Geshe Wangyal's book, *The Door of Liberation*, 1973 ed., pp. 52-54; 1995 ed., pp. 31-33.

63. Bhā[va]viveka's full critique of Yogācāra is found in the fifth chapter of his *Madhyamaka-hṛdaya* and his *Tarka-jvālā* commentary thereon. At the beginning of the latter he specifically names Asaṅga

and Vasubandhu. A more brief critique is found in his *Prajñā-pradīpa* commentary on Nāgārjuna's *Mūla-madhyamaka-kārikā*, as an appendix to chapter 25. He also critiques Yogācāra in the fourth chapter of his *Madhyamaka-ratna-pradīpa*. Here is a bibliographic listing, by date of publication, of these sources:

Lindtner, Christian. "Bhavya's Controversy with Yogācāra in the Appendix to *Prajñāpradīpa*, Chapter XXV." In *Tibetan and Buddhist Studies Commemorating the 200th Anniversary of the Birth of Alexander Csoma de Körös*, edited by Louis Ligeti, vol. 2, pp. 77-97. Bibliotheca Orientalis Hungarica, vol. 29. Budapest: Akadémiai Kiadó, 1984 (gives critical edition of the Tibetan text).

Eckel, M. David. "Bhāvaviveka's Critique of Yogācāra Philosophy in Chapter XXV of the *Prajñāpradīpa*." In *Miscellanea Buddhica*, edited by Chr. Lindtner, pp. 25-75. Indiske Studier 5. Copenhagen: Akademisk Forlag, 1985 (gives English translation).

Lindtner, Christian. "Bhavya's Critique of Yogācāra in the *Madhyamakaratnapradīpa*, Chapter IV." In *Buddhist Logic and Epistemology: Studies in the Buddhist Analysis of Inference and Language*, edited by Bimal Krishna Matilal and Robert D. Evans, pp. 239-263. Studies of Classical India, vol. 7. Dordrecht: D. Reidel Publishing Company, 1986 (gives English translation).

Lindtner, Christian. "Materials for the Study of Bhavya." In *Kalyāṇa-mitrārāgaṇam: Essays in Honour of Nils Simonsson*, edited by Eivind Kahrs, pp. 179-202. Oslo: Norwegian University Press, 1986 (includes critical edition of the Tibetan text of *Madhyamaka-ratna-pradīpa*, chap. 4).

Lindtner, Chr. "Bhavya's Madhyamakahṛdaya (Pariccheda Five) Yogācāratattvaviniścayāvatāra." *Adyar Library Bulletin*, vol. 59, 1995, pp. 37-65. Reprint, Adyar Library Pamphlet Series, no. 48, 1995. Also found in his edition of the whole text: *Madhyamakahṛdayam of Bhavya*. Chennai: Adyar Library and Research Centre, 2001, pp. 58-71 (in Sanskrit).

64. Candrakīrti's critique of Yogācāra is found in chapter 6 of his *Madhyamakāvatāra*, verses 45-97, and his own commentary thereon. This text is not yet available in Sanskrit, although a manuscript of it is reported to exist in Lhasa. Its Tibetan translation, with commentary,

was published in the Bibliotheca Buddhica series, vol. 9, 1907-1912. Both the root text and commentary of this critique are available in a French translation, and the root text in several English translations. There are also two articles summarizing the critique. Here follows a bibliographic listing, by date of publication, of these sources:

La Vallée Poussin, Louis de. "Madhyamakāvatāra: Introduction au Traité du Milieu, de l'Ācārya Candrakīrti, avec le commentaire de l'auteur, traduit d'après la version tibétaine." *Le Muséon*, n.s., vol. 8, 1907, pp. 249-317 (chaps. 1-5); vol. 11, 1910, pp. 271-358 (chap. 6, verses 1-80); vol. 12, 1911, pp. 235-328 (chap. 6, verses 81-165); unfinished (the Yogācāra critique is found in the second installment, pp. 324-358, and the third installment, pp. 236-255).

Olson, Robert F. "Candrakīrti's Critique of Vijñānavāda." *Philosophy East and West*, vol. 24, 1974, pp. 405-411.

Fenner, Peter G. "Candrakīrti's Refutation of Buddhist Idealism," *Philosophy East and West*, vol. 33, 1983, pp. 251-261 (includes English translation of *Madhyamakāvatāra*, chap. 6, verses 45-77).

Batchelor, Stephen. In *Echoes of Voidness*, by Geshe Rabten. London: Wisdom Publications, 1983, pp. 47-91 (gives English translation of *Madhyamakāvatāra*, chap. 6).

Huntington, C. W., Jr., with Geshé Namgyal Wangchen. In *The Emptiness of Emptiness: An Introduction to Early Indian Mādhyamika.* Honolulu: University of Hawaii Press, 1989, pp. 143-196; notes to this, pp. 218-267 (gives English translation of the whole *Madhyamakāvatāra*).

Fenner, Peter. In *The Ontology of the Middle Way.* Studies of Classical India, vol. 11. Dordrecht: Kluwer Academic Publishers, 1990, pp. 209-302 (gives English translation of the whole *Madhyamakāvatāra*, and includes Tibetan text).

Stöter-Tillmann, Jürgen, and Tashi Tsering. In Rendawa Shönnu Lodrö's *Commentary on the 'Entry into the Middle,' Lamp which Elucidates Reality.* The Dalai Lama Tibeto-Indological Series, vol. 23. Sarnath, Varanasi: Central Institute of Higher Tibetan Studies, 1997 (includes English translation of the whole *Madhyamakāvatāra*).

Padmakara Translation Group. *Introduction to the Middle Way: Chandrakirti's Madhyamakavatara with Commentary by Jamgön*

Mipham. Boston: Shambhala Publications, 2002.

Goldfield, Ari, et al. *The Moon of Wisdom: Chapter Six of Chandrakirti's Entering the Middle Way, with Commentary from the Eighth Karmapa, Mikyö Dorje's Chariot of the Dakpo Kagyü Siddhas*. Ithaca, N.Y.: Snow Lion Publications, 2005 (includes Tibetan text).

65. Vasubandhu's commentary is a combined commentary on the 100,000 line, 25,000 line, and 18,000 line Perfection of Wisdom *sūtras*, called the *Śata-sāhasrikā-pañcaviṃśati-sāhasrikāṣṭādaśa-sāhasrikā-prajñā-pāramitā-bṛhaṭ-ṭīkā*. Tsongkhapa did not accept Vasubandhu's authorship of it, but said it was written by the much later Daṃṣṭrāsena instead (see *Tsong Khapa's Speech of Gold in the Essence of True Eloquence: Reason and Enlightenment in the Central Philosophy of Tibet*, trans. Robert A. F. Thurman, Princeton: Princeton University Press, 1984, pp. 247-248). However, Daṃṣṭrāsena may only have revised Vasubandhu's work. There had to have been in existence an early interpretation of the Perfection of Wisdom *sūtras* by way of the three natures, since this is exactly what Bhā[va]viveka refutes in his *Madhyamaka-hṛdaya*, where his major refutation of Yogācāra occurs. Here in chapter 5, verses 1-7, the Yogācāra position is stated, that he will go on to refute in verses 8 onward. In verses 5-6 the three natures are stated, and verse 7 says that this is how the Perfection of Wisdom is understood in Yogācāra. The rest of the chapter is his refutation of the three natures.

Moreover, Vasubandhu's disciple Diṅnāga states clearly in his *Prajñāpāramitā-piṇḍārtha-saṃgraha* (*Collection of the Essential Meaning of the Perfection of Wisdom*) that the three natures are the basis for understanding the Perfection of Wisdom, and that in fact, there is no other teaching than this in these sacred texts:

prajñāpāramitāyāṃ hi trīn samāśritya deśanā |
kalpitaṃ paratantraṃ ca pariniṣpannam eva ca || 27 ||
nāstīty-ādi-padaiḥ sarvaṃ kalpitaṃ vinivāryate |
māyopamādi-dṛṣṭāntaiḥ paratantrasya deśanā || 28 ||
caturdhā-vyavadānena pariniṣpanna-kīrtanam |
prajñāpāramitāyāṃ hi nānyā buddhasya deśanā || 29 ||

27. In the Perfection of Wisdom, the teaching is based on the three [natures]: the imagined, the dependent, and the perfected.

28. By the words, "it does not exist," etc., all the imagined is refuted. By the examples of [being] like an illusion, etc., [is given] the teaching of the dependent.
29. By the fourfold purification [is made] the proclamation of the perfected. In the Perfection of Wisdom there is no other teaching of the Buddha.

The Sanskrit text quoted above may be found in the following editions, both of which agree completely for these three verses. The Tucci edition also includes Tibetan and English translations. I have given a more literal translation rather than Tucci's looser translation, which was made before *prajñā-pāramitā* became standardly translated as Perfection of Wisdom, due to the work of Edward Conze. Tucci here translated it as the "gnosis."

Tucci, Giuseppe. "Minor Sanskrit Texts on the Prajñā-pāramitā: 1. The Prajñā-pāramitā-piṇḍārtha of Diṅnāga." *Journal of the Royal Asiatic Society*, 1947, pp. 53-75.

Frauwallner, Erich. In "Dignāga, sein Werk und seine Entwicklung." *Wiener Zeitschrift für die Kunde Süd- und Ostasiens, und Archiv für Indische Philosophie*, vol. 3, 1959, pp. 83-164; *Prajñā-pāramitā-piṇḍārtha-saṃgraha* on pp. 140-144.

66. The original Sanskrit text of this section was published in "'Maitreya's Questions' in the Prajñāpāramitā," by Edward Conze and Iida Shotaro, *Mélanges D'Indianisme a la Mémoire de Louis Renou*, Paris: Éditions E. de Boccard, 1968, pp. 229-242. An English translation may be found in *The Large Sutra on Perfect Wisdom*, translated by Edward Conze, Berkeley and Los Angeles: University of California Press, 1975, pp. 644-652. The terms for the three natures used there, p. 238, are *parikalpita, vikalpita,* and *dharmatā,* translated by Conze, p. 648, as "imagined," "discerned," and "dharmic nature." The second one can also be translated as "conceptualized" or "constructed by thought," and the third as "true nature."

67. See Dolpopa's *Bka' bsdu bzhi pa'i rang 'grel*, folio 615, in *The Collected Works (Gsuṅ 'Bum) of Kun-mkhyen Dol-po-pa Śes-rab-rgyal-mtshan (1292-1361): Reproduced from eye copies of prints from the Rgyal-rtse Rdzoṅ blocks preserved at the Kyichu Monastery in the Paro Valley, Bhutan,* vol. 1, Paro, Bhutan/Delhi: Lama Ngodrup and Sherab Drimay, 1984. This

same text is also found in *The 'Dzam-thang Edition of the Collected Works (Gsung-'bum) of Kun-mkhyen Dol-po-pa Shes-rab Rgyal-mtshan*, vol. 5 (yā), collected and presented by Matthew Kapstein. Delhi: Shedrup Books, 1992, folios 269-329.

68. See the section, "Delineating well all emptinesses as the two, self-emptiness and other-emptiness," in Dolpopa's *Mountain Doctrine*, pp. 324-334, where Vasubandhu's Perfection of Wisdom commentary is quoted on p. 330. It may be helpful to note that the term translated here by Jeffrey Hopkins as "non-entities," is translated by others as "non-existence."

69. On these two traditions of the works of Maitreya, see *The Blue Annals*, translated by George N. Roerich, 1949; reprint, Delhi: Motilal Banarsidass, 1976, etc., pp. 347-350, for the account by 'Gos Lo-tsā-ba Gzhon-nu-dpal (1392-1481); Leonard W.J. van der Kuijp, *Contributions to the Development of Tibetan Buddhist Epistemology, From the eleventh to the thirteenth century*, Alt- und Neu-Indische Studien 26, Wiesbaden: Franz Steiner Verlag, 1983, pp. 42-44, including the account by Gser-mdog Paṇ-chen Śākya-mchog-ldan (1428-1509); S. K. Hookham, *The Buddha Within: Tathagatagarbha Doctrine According to the Shentong Interpretation of the Ratnagotravibhaga*, Albany: State University of New York Press, 1991, pp. 269-271, for the account by 'Jam-mgon Kong-sprul Blo-gros-mtha'-yas (1813-1899); Karl Brunnhölzl, *The Center of the Sunlit Sky: Madhyamaka in the Kagyü Tradition*, Ithaca, N.Y.: Snow Lion Publications, 2004, pp. 461-462, for a summary of the meditative tradition lineage up to the present; and Cyrus Stearns, "Dol-po-pa Shes-rab rgyal-mtshan and the Genesis of the *Gzhan-stong* Position in Tibet," *Asiatische Studien/Études Asiatiques*, vol. 49, no. 4, 1995, p. 840, for a note by Jo-nang Kun-dga' grol-mchog (1507-1566) from a notebook by Bstan kha-bo-che (b. 1021) quoting his teacher Sajjana, the source of the two lines of transmission into Tibet.

70. Dolpopa believed that he was restoring the true teachings from the bygone "Age of Perfection" (*kṛta-yuga*), or "Age of Truth" (*satya-yuga*), called by other traditions the "Golden Age." These had been lost through the faulty interpretations of later commentators who no longer had the true understanding of the Buddha's teachings. Corroboration of Dolpopa's claims comes from a most unexpected source, although one that may be doubted because of dating, namely,

from the Hindu sage Gauḍapāda. Gauḍapāda was the teacher of the teacher of Śaṅkarācārya, and hence his date depends on the date of Śaṅkarācārya. Śaṅkarācārya is generally placed around the seventh or eighth century of the Common Era, and no doubt most of the now extant writings attributed to him are from that time. However, there is considerable evidence that the original Śaṅkarācārya was born in the year 509 B.C.E. (this evidence is gathered and presented in my paper, "The Original Śaṅkarācārya"). This would make his teacher's teacher Gauḍapāda a contemporary of the Buddha, following the traditional dating of the Buddha's death as 543 B.C.E.

It is now well known, thanks to the research of Vidhushekhara Bhattacharya, that Gauḍapāda's greatest work, the *Māṇḍūkya-kārika,* uses Buddhist terminology and ideas liberally (see *The Āgamaśāstra of Gauḍapāda,* University of Calcutta Press, 1943). These are found in the fourth and last section of that book, which has every appearance of being written at a later time than the first three sections. It has, for example, an opening salutation like would normally be found at the beginning of a work. This salutation, moreover, is addressed to the "best of men," a standard epithet of the Buddha. With all the other evidence that Bhattacharya provided, we may infer that Gauḍapāda wrote this after coming into contact with Buddhist ideas, or perhaps, after coming into contact with the Buddha himself.

In the "Replies to Inquiries Suggested by 'Esoteric Buddhism,'" published in *The Theosophist,* vol. 5, 1883, is the section, "Sakya Muni's Place in History" (pp. 38-43), which draws on unpublished esoteric records to give facts about the Buddha's life and date. This section was presumably written by Blavatsky's teacher, Morya, and was reprinted in the book, *Five Years of Theosophy,* and also in *H. P. Blavatsky Collected Writings,* vol. 5, 1950, pp. 241-259. It is said therein (p. 256) that the Hindu Brahmans expected the coming of the Buddha, and at that time met him as an Avatar:

> It is no better than loose conjecture to argue that it would have entered as little into the thoughts of the Brahmans of noting the day of Buddha's birth "as the Romans, or even the Jews, [would have] thought of preserving the date of the birth of Jesus before he had become the founder of a religion." (M. Müller's *History of Ancient Sanskrit Literature,* p. 263.) For, while the Jews had been

from the first rejecting the claim of Messiahship set up by the Chelas of the Jewish prophet, and were not expecting their Messiah at that time, the Brahmans (the initiates, at any rate) knew of the coming of him whom they regarded as an incarnation of divine wisdom and therefore were well aware of the astrological date of his birth. If, in after times in their impotent rage, they destroyed every accessible vestige of the birth, life and death of Him, who in his boundless mercy to all creatures had revealed their carefully concealed mysteries and doctrines in order to check the ecclesiastical torrent of ever-growing superstitions, there had been a time when he was met by them as an Avatar.

Meeting him as an avatar, it would have only been natural for the great Brahman sage, Gauḍapāda, to have sought out the Buddha and received teachings from him. It may thus be that in Gauḍapāda's text we have the earliest direct record of the Buddha's teachings to have come down to us. Ironically, this text has come down to us within the Hindu tradition. In the Buddhist tradition, what we have is the orally passed down discourses of the so-called Hīnayāna tradition, only later written down. The discourses or *sūtras* of the Mahāyāna tradition are said by tradition to have disappeared forty years after the Buddha's passing, and then to have reappeared in later centuries. Proceeding on the assumption that the Buddha in fact taught Mahāyāna ideas during his lifetime, and that Gauḍapāda was there to hear and record them, some interesting facts emerge.

Dolpopa goes against the standard received Yogācāra teachings, insisting that the second of the three natures is illusory just like the first of them. It is not the case, says he, that the third or perfected nature (*pariniṣpanna*) is the second or dependent nature (*paratantra*) when freed of the first or imagined nature (*parikalpita*), as Yogācāra is normally thought to teach. Only the third or perfected nature is truly existent. Neither the first nor the second are truly existent. This, claims Dolpopa, is the true original understanding of the Buddha's teachings on this. Gauḍapāda says the very same thing.

Gauḍapāda's *Māṇḍūkya-kārikā,* also known as the *Āgama-śāstra,* section 4, verse 73, reads:

yo 'sti kalpita-saṃvṛtyā paramārthena nâsty asau |
paratantrâbhisaṃvṛtyā syān nâsti paramārthataḥ || 73 ||

> That which exists conventionally as the imagined does not exist ultimately. [That which] may exist conventionally as the dependent [also] does not exist ultimately.

So Gauḍapāda, too, rejects the ultimate existence of the second or dependent nature, just like Dolpopa does, and in opposition to the standard Yogācāra or Cittamātra teachings as normally understood. Dolpopa, utilizing the Great Madhyamaka understanding of Yogācāra to do this, believed that he was restoring the original teachings of the Buddha. The evidence provided by Gauḍapāda may well corroborate this claim of Dolpopa's. Moreover, a verse quoted in *The Secret Doctrine*, vol. 1, p. 48, also agrees with this.

> "No Arhat, oh mendicants, can reach absolute knowledge before he becomes one with Paranirvana. *Parikalpita* and *Paratantra* are his two great enemies" (Aphorisms of the Bodhisattvas).

It seems that all three, Dolpopa, Gauḍapāda, and *The Secret Doctrine*, agree in this distinctive doctrine of rejecting the ultimate existence of the second or dependent nature (*paratantra*), thus setting them apart from standard Yogācāra or Cittamātra. We may assume, then, that this Great Madhyamaka doctrine is a doctrine of the Wisdom Tradition.

Selected Bibliography on Great Madhyamaka

Dolpopa, translated by Jeffrey Hopkins. *Mountain Doctrine; Tibet's Fundamental Treatise on Other-Emptiness and the Buddha-Matrix*, by Dol-bo-ba Shay-rap-gyel-tsen. Ithaca, N.Y.: Snow Lion Publications, 2006. (This is a complete translation of Dolpopa's greatest work, the *Ri chos nges don rgya mtsho.*)

Hopkins, Jeffrey. *Tsong-kha-pa's Final Exposition of Wisdom.* Ithaca, N.Y.: Snow Lion Publications, 2008. (Part Two is "Comparing Dol-po-pa's and Tsong-kha-pa's Views")

Hookham, S. K. *The Buddha Within: Tathagatagarbha Doctrine According to the Shentong Interpretation of the Ratnagotravibhaga.* Albany: State University of New York Press, 1991.

Kongtrul, Jamgon, Lodro Taye, translated by Elizabeth M. Callahan. *The Treasury of Knowledge, Book Six, Part Three: Frameworks of Buddhist Philosophy, A Systematic Presentation of the Cause-Based Philosophical Vehicles.* Ithaca, N.Y.: Snow Lion Publications, 2007. (This is the only available text on tenet systems that includes Shentong Madhyamaka.)

Ringu Tulku. *The Ri-me Philosophy of Jamgön Kongtrul the Great: A Study of the Buddhist Lineages of Tibet.* Boston: Shambhala Publications, 2006.

Sheehy, Michael R. *The Gzhan stong Chen mo: A Study of Emptiness according to the Modern Tibetan Buddhist Jo nang Scholar 'Dzam thang mKhan po Ngag dbang Blo gros Grags pa (1920-75).* Ph.D. thesis, California Institute of Integral Studies, 2007.

Stearns, Cyrus. *The Buddha from Dolpo: A Study of the Life and Thought of the Tibetan Master Dolpopa Sherab Gyaltsen.* Albany: State University of New York Press, 1999; revised and enlarged edition, 2010. (This includes complete translations of Dolpopa's *A General Commentary on the Doctrine,* and his last major work, *The Great Calculation of the Doctrine Which Has the Significance of a Fourth Council.*)

Tāranātha, translated by Jeffrey Hopkins. *The Essence of Other-Emptiness*, by Tāranātha. Ithaca, N.Y.: Snow Lion Publications, 2007. (This is a concise work on Shentong by the second most famous Jonangpa writer, Tāranātha.)

[The foregoing article was written by David Reigle, and presented as part of the program, "Theosophy's Tibetan Connection," at the Annual Meeting of the Texas Federation of the Theosophical Society in America, San Antonio, April 18-20, 2008.]

Ātman/Anātman in Buddhism and Its Implication for the Wisdom Tradition

Does Christianity believe in reincarnation? Of course it does not. Yet, students of the Wisdom Tradition may seek to find evidence that early Christians did accept reincarnation. Similarly in Buddhism. Does Buddhism believe in the *ātman*, the permanent self? Certainly the Buddhist religion does not. Yet, there is evidence that the Buddha when teaching his basic doctrine of *anātman*, no-self, only denied the abiding reality of the personal or empirical *ātman*, but not the universal or authentic *ātman*.

The Wisdom Tradition known as Theosophy teaches the existence of "An Omnipresent, Eternal, Boundless, and Immutable PRINCIPLE,"[1] often compared to the Hindu *ātman*, the universal "self," while Buddhism with its doctrine of *anātman*, "no-self," is normally understood to deny any such universal principle. In regard to Buddhism, however, there have been several attempts to show that the Buddha did not deny the existence of the authentic *ātman*, the self.[2] Only one of these attempts seems to have been taken seriously by scholars[3]; namely, the work of Kamaleswar Bhattacharya. His book on this subject, written in French, *L'Ātman-Brahman dans le Bouddhisme ancien*, was published in Paris in 1973; and an English translation of this work, *The Ātman-Brahman in Ancient Buddhism*, was published in 2015.[4] It is here that he set forth his arguments for the existence of the Upaniṣadic *ātman* in early Buddhism. This is the work that we will discuss.

How must we understand the Sanskrit term *ātman*, or in Pāli, *attā*? The word *ātman* has been translated into English a number of different ways by writers; sometimes as soul, or self, or ego.[5] The consensus among scholars for some time now has been to translate *ātman* as "self," which we will do here.[6] And likewise, we will translate Sanskrit *anātman*, or Pāli *anattā*, as "no-self." Translating *ātman* as "self" also avoids confusion between "soul" and "self" when it distinguishes *ātman*, the eternal and unchanging self, from the reincarnating and evolving soul.

One of the basic teachings of Buddhism is that all existence has three defining characteristics (*tri-lakṣaṇa*): suffering (*duḥkha*), impermanence (*anitya*), and no-self (*anātman*).[7] If these are the Buddha's basic teachings, then why question his teaching of *anātman* (no-self)?

In the case of Kamaleswar Bhattacharya, while he was doing research in the Sanskrit inscriptions of ancient Cambodia, he came across an inscription that caused him to question the teaching of *anātman*.[8] The inscription that caught his attention began with the following stanza. Note that *nairātmya* (non-self, absence of self) is a synonym of *anātman* (no-self). It reads:

> *Buddho bodhiṃ vidadhyād vo yena nairātmyadarśanam* |
> *viruddhasyāpi sādhūktaṃ sādhanaṃ paramātmanaḥ* ||[9]

> The concept of *paramātman* [the highest self] is in contradiction (*viruddha*) with the doctrine of *nairātmya* [non-self]; nevertheless, the Buddha taught that same doctrine [of non-self] as a means (*sādhana*) of attaining to *paramātman* [the highest self]![10]

This may be restated as:

The Buddha taught that through the cultivation of non-self (*nairātmya*), one reaches the highest self (*paramātman*). The idea here is that by emptying yourself of your personality, your lower self, you are able to reach or ascend to your highest self, your spiritual essence.

Interestingly enough, Paul Brunton talks about this same inscription in one of his notebooks. He renders it as:

> Let the Buddha give you the Bodhi, by Whom has been taught well the philosophy denying the existence of the individual soul

and teaching the cult of the universal soul though [the two teachings seem to be] contradictory.[11]

When George Cœdès, who was later to became Bhattacharya's mentor, first saw this inscription in 1908, he thought that it had been contaminated by Hindu influence.[12] But after Sylvain Lévi published his edition and translation of the *Mahāyāna-Sūtrālaṃkāra* in 1907 and 1911, it became apparent that no contamination had taken place.[13]

This important Buddhist text supported the idea that *paramātma* (the highest self) and *nairātmya* (non-self), found together in the inscription, were not contradictory:

> In utterly pure Emptiness, the Buddhas have attained to the summit of the *ātman*, which consists in Impersonality [*nairātmya*, non-self]. Since they have found, thus, the pure *ātman*, they have reached the heights of *ātman*.
>
> And, in this Plan Without-Outflowing, is indicated the *paramātman* of the Buddhas—How so?—Because their *ātman* consists in the essential Impersonality [*nairātmya*, non-self].—*Mahāyāna-Sūtrālaṃkāra*, 9.23, with beginning of commentary.[14]

Note that Lévi has translated *nairātmya* as "Impersonality," instead of "non-self," which has been used here.

Bhattacharya then quoted another Mahāyāna text, the *Ratnagotravibhāga* commentary, to support this idea further:

> The Tathāgata [Buddha], on the other hand, by virtue of his absolute knowledge (*yathābhūtajñānena*), has gained perfect intuition of the Impersonality [*nairātmya*] of all separate elements. This Impersonality [*nairātmya*] accords, from every point of view (*yathā-darśanam*), with the characteristics of the *ātman*. It is thus always regarded as *ātman*, because it is Impersonality [*nairātmya*] which is *ātman* (*nairātmyam evātmeti kṛtvā*).[15]

From this we can see that the two seemingly contradictory ideas of *paramātman* (the highest self) and *nairātmya* (non-self) found in the Cambodian inscription are *not* incompatible with Buddhist scriptures. Bhattacharya concludes:

> The idea of *paramātman* is thus not contrary to the doctrine of *nairātmya*; the two terms rather designate the same thing from two different points of view.[16]

Another scholar, R. Grousset, commenting on the passage quoted above from the *Mahāyāna-Sūtrālaṃkāra*, says that the *nairātyma* idea is also found in the Upaniṣads, known for their teaching of *ātman*. He writes:

> . . . such a conception recalls, curiously enough, material from some of the Upaniṣads; the *ātman* consisting essentially in *nairātmya*, or, if preferred, the person being resolved in its very depths in impersonality, we there approach the impersonal *ātman* of the *Bṛhadāraṇyaka* [*Upaniṣad*].[17]

It is Bhattacharya's belief that the Buddha did not deny this impersonal, eternal *ātman* of the Upaniṣads.

Bhattacharya distinguishes two types of *ātman*:

1) the authentic *ātman*, and 2) the empirical *ātman*.[18]

The authentic *ātman* is the true spiritual *ātman* of the Upaniṣads, eternal and unchanging. The empirical *ātman* is the psycho-physical individuality,[19] the person, which is ephemeral and changing. This psycho-physical individuality is made up of five components, which are called *skandha*s, or aggregates. These five *skandha*s are:

1. form, or body (*rūpa*),
2. feeling (*vedanā*),
3. perception and conception (*saṃjñā*),
4. karma formations, or karmic seeds (*saṃskāra*),
5. consciousness (*vijñāna*).

In other words, the five *skandha*s, or aggregates, make up what we would call the everyday person. As we saw earlier, just like everything else in existence, the *skandhas*, too, are characterized by suffering (*duḥkha*), impermanence (*anitya*), and no-self (*anātman*).

Throughout the Buddhist scriptures of the Pāli canon, we find the Buddha repeatedly denying the existence of the *ātman* in the five *skandhas*. The following dialogue is one example, where the Buddha says:

> "Now what think you, Soṇa? Is body permanent or impermanent?"
>
> "Impermanent, lord."
>
> "And what is impermanent, is that woe or weal?"
>
> "Woe, lord."
>
> "And is it fitting to hold such views as 'this is mine,' 'this am I,' or 'this is the self of me,' about that which is impermanent and unstable?"
>
> "Surely not, lord."
>
> "Is feeling . . . perception . . . the activities [karma formations] . . . is consciousness permanent or impermanent? (as before). . . ."
>
> "Surely not, lord."
>
> "Wherefore, Soṇa, whatsoever body there be, whether past, future or present, inward or outward, gross or subtle, low or lofty, far or near . . . every body should thus be regarded as it really is by right insight. Thus 'this is not mine,' 'this am not I,' 'this of me is not the self.'"
>
> And so also with regard to feeling, perception, the activities [karma formations] and consciousness (so should they be regarded). —*Saṃyutta-Nikāya*, 22.49.[20]

This type of negation is meant to dispel the idea of a permanent, truly existing personality, the *satkāya-dṛṣṭi*.[21] It is clear that the *skandhas*, the ephemeral person, cannot be the eternal, unchanging *ātman*.

While the Buddha clearly and repeatedly said that there was no *ātman* in the *skandhas*, he did not directly or specifically deny the existence of the eternal *ātman* of the Upaniṣads. As Bhattacharya says:

The Buddha did not say, "There is no *ātman*." He simply said, in speaking of the *skandhas/khandhas*, ephemeral and painful, which constitute the psycho-physical being of a man: *n' etaṃ mama, n' eso 'ham asmi, na m' eso attā*, "This is not mine, I am not this, this is not my *ātman*."[22]

Ananda Coomaraswamy, in his book, *Hinduism and Buddhism*, agrees: "the repeated expression 'That is not my Self' has so often been misinterpreted to mean 'There is no Self.'"[23]

Bhattacharya cites another passage from the Pāli canon to illustrate that the Buddha did not deny the existence of the authentic *ātman*. This passage speaks of an "unborn," "unproduced," "uncreated." This is reminiscent of the immutable principle spoken of in *The Secret Doctrine*.[24] The Buddha says in this passage:

> There is, monks, an unborn, unproduced, uncreated, unformed. If there were not, monks, an unborn, unproduced, uncreated, unformed, there would be no issue [escape] for the born, the produced, the created, the formed. (*Udāna*, 8.3)[25]

Bhattacharya elaborates on this passage from the *Udāna*, with scriptural support from the *Saṃyutta Nikāya*:

> Note that the "unborn, unproduced, uncreated, unformed" (*ajāta, abhūta, akata, asaṃkhata*), in a word, the Unconditioned, is not another world, situated beyond the "born, produced, created, formed" (*jāta, bhūta, kata, saṃkhata*). It is in us, is our very selves: it is our essential nature. It must, then, be discovered in the depths of our being, by transcending our phenomenal existence.[26]

Kamaleswar Bhattacharya's thesis is that when the Buddha denied the *ātman* in the *skandhas*, he was *indirectly affirming* the existence of the authentic, Upaniṣadic *ātman*.[27]

To support his position, Bhattacharya cites the Indian logician Uddyotakara of the Hindu Nyāya school, who said that this type of negation, "This is not mine, I am not this, this is not my *ātman*," doesn't make sense logically unless one accepts that the *ātman* exists. This is called a *specific negation*. Uddyotakara says:

> This negation is a specific negation (*viśeṣapratiṣedha*), not a universal negation (*sāmānyapratiṣedha*). One who does not accept the *ātman* must employ a universal negation: 'I am not,' 'You are not.' A specific negation always implies a corresponding affirmation: when, for example, I say, 'I do not see with my left eye,' it is understood that I do see with my right eye. . . ."[28]

In this case, the specific negation of *ātman* in the *skandhas* would have for its corresponding affirmation the existence of the authentic, Upaniṣadic *ātman*.

The eminent Buddhist scholar, La Vallée Poussin, commenting on a passage from the *Majjhima-Nikāya*,[29] corroborates Bhattacharya's thesis when he says:

> In the light of this text, which really is quite straightforward, we may understand several sermons, and notably the sermon of Benares, not as the negation of the *ātman* as do the Buddhists—but as the affirmation of an *ātman* distinct from the *skandhas*.[30]

This brings us back to the teaching of the stanza in the inscription that we began with:

> The Buddha taught the doctrine of *nairātmya* [non-self] as the means (*sādhana*) of attaining to *paramātman* [the highest self].[31]

Here, the stanza teaches us to cultivate the specific negation of *nairātmya* [non-self], in order to attain to its corresponding affirmation of *paramātman* [the highest self]. The two Mahāyāna texts we cited earlier to support these ideas (the *Mahāyāna-Sūtrālaṃkāra* and the commentary to the *Ratnagotravibhāga*) treated *nairātmya* and *paramātman* as synonyms.[32] In other words, once understood, they become two different sides of the same coin. *Nairātmya*, the negation of the empirical self, reveals *paramātman,* the highest authentic self, which is inexpressible.

This type of logic can be fruitfully employed when referring to truth or the absolute, such as *ātman* or *paramātman.*[33] Since truth is beyond discursive thought, it can be referred to in negative terms only, such as the *neti neti* "not this, not that" of the Upaniṣads. As Bhattacharya says:

> All truths as can be formulated are, in fact, but approximations of Truth, which is inexpressible; none of them can be identified with Truth itself. They aid us in reaching it, they guide our progress towards it; but they must be transcended if it is to be reached.[34]

It is perhaps for this reason that when the itinerant monk Vatsagotra (Pāli: Vacchagotta) came to the Buddha and asked him if there is an *ātman* or not, the Buddha remained silent. Also, it is there explained that had the Buddha answered either way, Vatsagotra would have misunderstood him due to his preconceptions. To have given any answer would have been misleading.[35]

What are some reasons for possible confusion concerning the *ātman* in Buddhism?

1. The Buddha's silence on pertinent questions, such as whether the *ātman* exists, as we have just seen in the Vatsagotra story, has been a long-standing source of confusion for readers of the Buddhist scriptures. While the Buddha taught that the *skandhas* are *anātman,* he did not say that "There is no *ātman.*"[36] If he had wanted to dispel the *ātman* itself, he could have done so directly, to avoid confusion.[37]

2. Despite the fact that the Buddha repeatedly taught the doctrine of *anātman* relative to the *skandhas*, there are, nevertheless, numerous occurrences of the word *ātman* throughout the Buddhist scriptures that may not be used only as a pronoun.

Citing the Pāli canon alone, Pérez-Remón says:

> In fact the references to *attā* [*ātman*] in the five Nikāyas are as overwhelming, as regards their numbers, as the references to *anattā* [*anātman*], and plenty of those references are extremely significant.[38]

With all the emphasis the Buddha placed on the teaching of *anātman*, the many references to *ātman* can be confusing.

3. Although both positive and negative formulations of *ātman* are found in the Buddhist scriptures, it is the negative formulations that predominate. Bhattacharya says:

> There certainly are positive expressions, relative to the *ātman*, in the Pāli Canon. . . . But these positive expressions—often moreover wrongly interpreted—are almost drowned in the mass of negative expressions. . . . It is this predilection for negative expression which would seem to have been responsible for the pernicious theory of the "negation of the *ātman*."[39]

4. Another source of confusion in the Buddhist scriptures is the fact that the word *ātman* can be used in more than one sense. Not only can *ātman* have the meaning of the authentic, Upaniṣadic *ātman*, but it can and often is used simply as a reflexive personal pronoun. As Steven Collins says:

> *Attā* [*Ātman*] is the regular reflexive pronoun in Pali, used in the masculine singular for all numbers and genders.[40]

Thus, as a reflexive pronoun, the word *attā* [*ātman*] can be used for "myself," "yourself," "himself," "herself," "ourselves," etc.

As we have seen, the word *ātman* can be used to indicate either the empirical self designated by the personal pronoun, or the authentic, Upaniṣadic self. Hence the possible confusion that can arise in translation in certain contexts. Bhattacharya cites a verse from the *Dhammapada* illustrating the different usages of the word *ātman* within a single verse (emphasis added):

> *attā hi attano nātho ko hi nātho paro siyā* |
> *attanā hi sudantena nāthaṃ labhati dullabhaṃ* ||

> The *ātman* is the refuge of the self.
> What other refuge can there be?
> When the (phenomenal) *ātman* is properly subdued,
> a refuge, difficult to find, is obtained.
> (*Dhammapada*, 160)[41]

Walpola Rahula, the distinguished Sinhalese monk and Buddhist scholar, interprets this verse differently. Here is his translation (emphasis added):

> Oneself is one's own protector (refuge);
> what other protector (refuge) can there be?
> With oneself fully controlled,
> one obtains a protection (refuge) which is hard to gain.
> (*Dhammapada*, 160)[42]

Note that Rahula translates each occurrence of "*ātman*" as the reflexive pronoun ("oneself"), while Bhattacharya translates the first occurrence of "*ātman*" as the authentic *ātman*, followed by the empirical *ātman*.

Bhattacharya also cited some verses from the *Bhagavadgītā* (6.5-7) to show a precedent for this alternating translation of "*ātman*" as the empirical and the authentic *ātman*. Here is verse 6.5 (emphasis added):

> *uddhared ātmanātmānaṃ nātmānam avasādayet* |
> *ātmaiva hy ātmano bandhur ātmaiva ripur ātmanaḥ* ||

May one be saved by himself,
may one not let himself perish.
The (phenomenal) *ātman* is the friend of the (true) *ātman*,
and it is also its enemy.
(*Bhagavadgītā*, 6.5)[43]

This example from the *Bhagavadgītā* clearly shows the juxtaposition of *ātman* in its two meanings within a single verse. Some of the confusion in interpreting the *ātman* in Buddhism could be avoided by distinguishing between the two. As Bhattacharya says:

> The Buddha certainly denied the *ātman*. That *ātman*, however, is not the Upaniṣadic *ātman*.[44]

And elsewhere:

> Before stating that Buddhism has denied the *ātman*, modern authors should, therefore, have been precise as to which *ātman* is meant.[45]

Bhattacharya cites a statement from the great Buddhist master Vasubandhu, "which perfectly elucidates the so-called 'negation of *ātman*' in Buddhism":[46]

> It is by virtue of that nature of things, consisting in subject and object, which the ignorant imagine, that the things are devoid of self, not by virtue of that ineffable Self which is the domain of the Enlightened Ones. (*Viṃśatikā-vṛtti*, verse 10)

Kamaleswar Bhattacharya has a panoramic view of Buddhism within the larger Indian context. He believes that it didn't come out of a vacuum, but that in fact the Buddha "was continuing the Upaniṣadic tradition."[47] Comparing the teachings of the Pāli canon with those of the Upaniṣads, Bhattacharya writes:

> The existence of similarities between two traditions does not imply total identity. But the difference between the teachings of the Pali Canon and those of the Upaniṣad[s] has too often been exaggerated. The Buddha's Absolute appears to be the same as that of the Upaniṣads.[48]

And in another place he repeats this same statement, concluding in an even stronger manner:

> . . . The Buddha's Absolute is the same as that of [the] Upaniṣads; the gulf was created later, by the scholastic interpretations.[49]

Bhattacharya sees the difference between the Upaniṣads and Buddhism as "simply a difference in emphasis."[50] He says that "Buddhism is, first and foremost, a doctrine of salvation."[51] Whereas the authors of the Upaniṣads were more philosophers than saviors, the Buddha was more a savior than a philosopher. While the Upaniṣadic authors spoke "much more of the Infinite than of the finite, much more of the Goal than of the Way," the Buddha spoke "more of the finite than of the Infinite, more of the Way than of the Goal." But he says that the goal of the philosopher and the savior are the same, and that goal is "Knowledge which is Deliverance."[52]

Bhattacharya has said that deliverance, or liberation, is "rediscovering our true being by transcending our phenomenal existence."[53] But he notes that deliverance isn't complete for a Bodhisattva until the entire world is delivered, "since he and the world are identical."[54] The Buddha shows "the way which leads from the ephemeral to the Eternal, from the mortal to the Immortal, from the sorrow of the finite to the Bliss of the Infinite."[55]

Transcending our phenomenal existence to realize the authentic *ātman* leads us from the ephemeral to the eternal. Realizing the *anātman* (or *nairātmya*), the no-self of the person, leads us to the realization of the *ātman* (or *paramātman*), the true spiritual self. When understood correctly, we can see that there is no contradiction between them. As Bhattacharya says:

There is no contradiction between *ātman* and *anātman*. The *ātman*, which is denied, and that which is affirmed, through that negation itself, pertains to two different levels. It is only when we have not succeeded in distinguishing between them, that the terms *ātman* and *anātman* seem to us to be opposed.[56]

When Kamaleswar Bhattacharya found the Cambodian inscription that spoke of *nairātmya* and *paramātman*, it led him to make a thorough investigation of the question of *ātman* in Buddhism. He concluded:

Does not Buddhism deny the *ātman*? . . . I have but one answer which I have tried to formulate in various ways in this book, on the basis, invariably, of a study of the Pāli canon and of the Nikāyas in particular,[57] that is: the Buddha does not deny the Upaniṣadic *ātman*; on the contrary, he indirectly affirms it, *in denying that which is falsely believed to be the ātman.*[58]

The implication of this for the Wisdom Tradition is clear. Bhattacharya in his book has provided substantial evidence, from exoteric Buddhist sources, that the Buddha did not deny the Upaniṣadic *ātman* or self, a universal principle comparable to that taught in the Wisdom Tradition. Blavatsky has provided us with an esoteric Buddhist source that states this outright. She calls this "An Unpublished Discourse of Buddha." It says:

Said the All-Merciful: Blessed are ye, O Bhikshus, happy are ye who have understood the mystery of Being and *Non-Being* explained in Bas-pa [(secret)[59] Dharma, Doctrine], and have given preference to the latter, for ye are verily my Arhats. . . . The elephant, who sees his form mirrored in the lake, looks at it, and then goes away, taking it for the real body of another elephant, is wiser than the man who beholds his face in the stream, and looking at it, says, "Here am I . . . I am I"—for the "I," his Self, is not in the world of the twelve Nidānas and mutability, but in that of Non-Being, the only world beyond the snares of Māyā. . . .

> That alone, which has neither cause nor author, which is self-existing, eternal, far beyond the reach of mutability, is the true "I" [Ego], the Self of the Universe. . . . He who listens to my secret law, preached to my select Arhats, will arrive with its help at the knowledge of Self, and thence at perfection.[60]

Thus, esoteric Buddhism does accept the true spiritual self or *ātman*, as shown in this unpublished discourse of the Buddha. This is the position of the Wisdom Tradition. In a similar way, Bhattacharya describes the Upaniṣadic *ātman* (the self) that is not denied by the Buddha, even using the same terms, being and non-being:

> It is the Being in itself, one, all-encompassing, absolute. From the objective standpoint, as we have seen, it is a non-being. But it is this non-being which is the authentic Being, the ground of all beings.[61]

The great value of Bhattacharya's work for students of the Wisdom Tradition is that it shows the acceptance of the true spiritual self or *ātman* from extant exoteric Buddhist sources. The Buddha's fundamental doctrine of *anātman* or no-self is a denial of only the personal self, thereby leading one to the realization of the universal self. This universal *ātman* is a principle that is in full agreement with the omnipresent, eternal, boundless, and immutable principle of *The Secret Doctrine*, described in the words of the *Māṇḍūkya Upaniṣad* as inconceivable and inexpressible.[62] It is no wonder that the Buddha couldn't speak about the true, spiritual *ātman*.

NOTES

1. "An Omnipresent, Eternal, Boundless, and Immutable PRINCIPLE on which all speculation is impossible, since it transcends the power of human conception and could only be dwarfed by any human expression or similitude. It is beyond the range and reach of thought—in the words of *Māṇḍūkya Upanishad*, 'unthinkable and unspeakable.'" In H. P. Blavatsky, *The Secret Doctrine*, ed. Boris de Zirkoff (pagination unchanged), 1st ed., 1888 (Adyar, Madras: Theosophical Publishing House, 1978), vol. 1, p. 14.

2. There are quite a number of scholars over the years who have been more or less sympathetic to this idea, including: A. Coomaraswamy, Erich Frauwallner, Sue Hamilton, I. B. Horner, Christmas Humphries, Joaquín Pérez-Remón, S. Radhakrishnan, and Carolyn Rhys Davids.

3. See for example: J. W. de Jong, "Lamotte and the Doctrine of Non-Self," p. 152; and *A Brief History of Buddhist Studies in Europe and America* (Tokyo: Kôsei Publishing Co., 1997), p. 98.

David Seyfort Ruegg, *Buddha-nature, Mind and the Problem of Gradualism in a Comparative Perspective: On the Transmission and Reception of Buddhism in India and Tibet*, Jordan Lectures in Comparative Religion, 13 (London: School of Oriental and African Studies, University of London, 1989), p. 54.

4. Kamaleswar Bhattacharya, *L'Ātman-Brahman dans le Bouddhisme ancien*, Publications de l'École française d'Extrême-Orient, vol. 90 (Paris: École française d'Extrême-Orient, 1973); *The Ātman-Brahman in Ancient Buddhism* (Cotopaxi, Colo.: Canon Publications, 2015).

5. Walpola Rahula, *What the Buddha Taught*, Second and Enlarged Edition (New York: Grove Press, 1974), p. 51.

6. "There seems to be no other way of translating *parato* than 'as other', and we must therefore translate *attato* as 'as self', since English recognises the opposition between 'self' and 'other', but not between 'soul' and 'other'. If we have to translate *attā* as 'self' in these contexts, then for the sake of consistency we must do the same elsewhere." (K. R. Norman, "A Note on Attā in the Alagaddūpama-sutta," pp. 27-28.)

7. Pāli: *ti-lakkhaṇa*. Here is the *ti-lakkhaṇa* formula as found in the *Dhammapada* of the Pāli canon, verses 277-279:

"sabbe saṃkhārā aniccā" . . .

"sabbe saṃkhārā dukkhā" . . .

"sabbe dhammā anattā" . . .

—*Dhammapada,* ed. O. von Hinüber and K. R. Norman (Oxford: Pali Text Society, 1995), p. 78.

"All conditioned things are impermanent." . . .

"All conditioned things are suffering." . . .

"All phenomena are non-self." . . .

—*The Word of the Doctrine (Dhammapada),* trans. by K. R. Norman (Oxford: Pali Text Society, 1997), p. 41.

8. Professor Kamaleswar Bhattacharya, who retired from the Centre National de la Recherche Scientifique in Paris as Director of Research in 1996, was one of the leading experts in the field of the Khmer civilization of ancient Cambodia, specializing in Sanskrit epigraphy.

9. Inscription B from Bàt Cŭṃ during the reign of Rājendravarman, 944-968 A.D. In K. Bhattacharya, *Ātman-Brahman,* p. 1.

10. K. Bhattacharya, *Ātman-Brahman,* p. 1 (brackets mine).

11. Paul Brunton, *The Notebooks of Paul Brunton,* vol. 10, The Orient: Its Legacy to the West (Burdett, NY: Larson Publications, 1987), p. 206.

12. K. Bhattacharya, *Ātman-Brahman,* p. 1.

13. Ibid. *Mahāyāna-Sūtrālaṃkāra,* 2 vols., Sylvain Lévi, ed. and trans., Bibliothèque de l'École des Hautes Études, Sciences historiques et philologiques (Paris: Librairie Honoré Champion, 1907 and 1911), fascs. 159 and 190.

14. S. Lévi's translation, slightly modified by K. Bhattacharya in *Ātman-Brahman,* p. 2. The text has been quoted on p. 1:

śūnyatāyāṃ viśuddhāyāṃ nairātmyātmāgralābhataḥ |

buddhāḥ suddhātmalābhitvād gatā ātmamahātmatām ||

tatra cānāsrave dhātau buddhānāṃ paramātmā nirdiśyate.—kiṃ kāraṇam?—agranairātmyātmakatvāt.—Mahāyāna-Sūtrālaṃkāra, 9.23, with beginning of *vyākhyā.*

15. K. Bhattacharya, *Ātman-Brahman,* pp. 4-5. *The Ratnagotravibhāga Mahāyānottaratantraśāstra,* E. H. Johnston, ed. (Patna: Bihar Research Society, 1950), p. 31:

Tathāgataḥ punar yathābhūtajñānena sarvadharmanairātmyaparapārami-

prāptaḥ. tac cāsya nairātmyam anātmalakṣaṇena yathā-darśanam avisaṃvāditatvāt sarvakālam ātmābhipretaḥ, nairātmyam evātmeti kṛtvā. (1.36) Bhattacharya notes corrections to the text on p. 40, nn. 8, 9, and 10.

16. K. Bhattacharya, *Ātman-Brahman*, p. 5.

17. René Grousset, *Les philosophies indiennes*, vol. 2 (Paris: Desclée de Brouwer, 1931), p. 28. Cited in K. Bhattacharya, *Ātman-Brahman*, p. 5.

18. K. Bhattacharya, *Ātman-Brahman*, p. 207.

19. Ibid., p. 6.

20. *The Book of the Kindred Sayings* (*Saṃyutta-Nikāya*) *or Grouped Suttas*, Part 3, trans. F. L. Woodward (London: Pali Text Society, 1925), p. 43.

21. K. Bhattacharya, *Ātman-Brahman*, p. 31.

22. Ibid., p. 6. This teaching occurs many times in the Pāli scriptures. See, for example, *The Book of the Kindred Sayings* (*Saṃyutta-Nikāya*) *or Grouped Suttas*, Part 3, trans. F. L. Woodward, 22.76 (pp. 68-69):

" . . . What is impermanent, that is suffering. What is suffering, that is not the Self.

"What is not the Self, 'that is not mine, that am not I, that is not the Self of me.' This is the way one should regard things as they really are, by right insight."

(*Saṃyutta-Nikāya*, Pali Text Society edition, vol. 3, p. 76):
yad aniccaṃ taṃ dukkhaṃ; yaṃ dukkhaṃ tad anattā; yad anattā taṃ n' etaṃ mama, n' eso 'ham asmi, na m' eso attā ti evam etaṃ yathābhūtaṃ sammappaññāya daṭṭhabbaṃ.

23. Ananda K. Coomaraswamy, *Hinduism and Buddhism* (New York: Philosophical Library, [n.d.]), p. 72.

24. *The Secret Doctrine*, vol. 1, p. 14: "An Omnipresent, Eternal, Boundless, and Immutable PRINCIPLE on which all speculation is impossible, since it transcends the power of human conception."

25. K. Bhattacharya, *Ātman-Brahman*, p. 33. I have modified the translation slightly: "non-born" has been changed to "unborn," "non-produced" has been changed to "unproduced," etc.

The full quotation from the Pāli reads:

atthi, bhikkhave, ajātaṃ abhūtaṃ akataṃ asaṅkhataṃ | no cetaṃ, bhikkhave, abhavissa ajātaṃ abhūtaṃ akataṃ asaṅkhataṃ, nayidha jātassa bhūtassa katassa saṅkhatassa nissaraṇaṃ paññāyetha | yasmā ca kho, bhikkhave, atthi ajātaṃ abhūtaṃ akataṃ asaṅkhataṃ, tasmā jātassa bhūtassa katassa saṅkhatassa nissaraṇaṃ paññāyati.—Udāna, 8.3.

Cited from: *The Khuddakapāṭha-Dhammapada-Udāna-Itivuttaka-Suttanipāta* (*Khuddakanikāya*, vol. 1), ed. Bhikkhu J. Kashyap, Nālandā-Devanāgarī-Pāli-Series ([N.p.]: Pāli Publication Board, 1959), p. 163.

26. K. Bhattacharya, *Ātman-Brahman*, pp. 47-48, n. 38. See *The Book of the Kindred Sayings* (*Saṃyutta-Nikāya*) *or Grouped Suttas*, Part 1, trans. Mrs. Rhys Davids (London: Pali Text Society, 1917), 2.3.6 (p. 86):

". . . It is in this fathom-long carcase, friend, with its impressions and its ideas that, I declare, lies the world, and the cause of the world, and the cessation of the world, and the course of action that leads to the cessation of the world."

(Saṃyutta-Nikāya, Pali Text Society editions, 1884: vol. i, p. 62; 1998: vol. 1, pp. 144-145): *api ca khvāhaṃ āvuso imasmiññ eva vyāmamatte kaḷevare [sa]saññimhi samanake lokañ ca paññāpemi lokasamudayañ ca lokanirodhañ ca lokanirodhagāminiñ ca paṭipadaṃ.*

27. K. Bhattacharya, *Ātman-Brahman*, p. ix.

28. Ibid., p. 32. Uddyotakara is cited from the *Tattva-saṃgraha-pañjikā* of Kamalaśīla (Embar Krishnamacharya ed., 1926), pp. 130-131 (cf. *Nyāyavārttika*, 3.1.1). Bhattacharya adds that although he agrees with Uddyotakara's logic "to prove that the Buddha did not deny all *ātman*," he disagrees with Uddyotakara's view when he sees in the words of the Buddha "an affirmation of the *ātman* as conceived by the Naiyāyikas, that is: as the individual ego, distinct from the aggregates (pp. 32-33)."

29. "Monks, if someone came into this copse of Jeta where we are, and took for burning, the grass, wood, branches, leaves, could you say that he took you and burned you?—No, Lord, for all that is not us, none of that belongs to us.—In the same way, monks, reject what is not of yourselves. . . ." (*Majjhima-Nikāya*, 1, p. 141, cited in K. Bhattacharya, *Ātman-Brahman*, p. 34.)

30. K. Bhattacharya, *Ātman-Brahman*, p. 109, n. 243, from: Louis de La Vallée Poussin, *Le Dogme et la Philosophie du Bouddhisme*, 2nd ed. (Paris, 1930), p. 101. For a similar statement, see Louis de La Vallée Poussin, "The *Ātman* in the Pāli Canon," p. 823: "Body and mind are not the *ātman*, not because the *ātman* does not exist (as the later doctors maintain), but because body and mind being transitory and painful, cannot be, cannot have any intimate connection with, the *ātman*: for the *ātman* is by definition eternal and happy. Our text

perhaps postulates a transcendent *ātman*, an individual one. Such an *ātman* is well known in the old Indian speculation: the Puruṣa of the Sāṃkhya school who remains untouched by the biological and psychological activities, who neither acts nor feels."

31. K. Bhattacharya, *Ātman-Brahman*, p. 207 (brackets mine); see also p. 1.

32. Ibid., p. 34.

33. It should be here noted, however, that the Gelugpa school of Tibetan Buddhism, following Tsong-khapa, uses a different type of logic regarding the ultimate. While they teach that everything in the universe is empty (*śūnya*), that is, empty of inherent existence (*svabhāva*), this does not imply the existence of some transcendent absolute. They call this a non-affirming negation.

In India, the well-known example of the affirming negation is that of Devadatta: The fat Devadatta doesn't eat in the day. This implies that he eats during the night. It is therefore an affirming negation.

So what we have here with the Gelugpas regarding the teaching of emptiness (*śūnyatā*) is a non-affirming negation: in denying one thing it does not affirm another.

34. K. Bhattacharya, *Ātman-Brahman*, p. 9.

35. Ibid., p. 25, cited from *Abhidharmakośa*, Chapter 9. See Vasubandhu's *Abhidharmakośabhāṣyam*, vol. 4, translated into English by Leo M. Pruden from the French of Louis de La Vallée Poussin (Berkeley, Calif.: Asian Humanities Press, 1990), pp. 1333-34.

36. K. Bhattacharya, *Ātman-Brahman*, p. 6. Other scholars, too, have noted that the Buddha did not specifically deny the existence of *attā/ātman* in the Pāli canon. Karel Werner says: "But there is no statement in the Sutta Piṭaka about the ultimate existence or non-existence of *atta*." (Karel Werner, "Indian Concepts of Human Personality in Relation to the Doctrine of the Soul," pp. 94-95.)

K. R. Norman: "It may be true to say that the Buddha does not specifically deny the existence of the *attā* anywhere in the Pāli canon, in the sense that he does not state explicitly 'The *attā* does not exist'." (K. R. Norman, "A Note on Attā in the Alagaddūpama-sutta," p. 28.)

This, of course, does not mean that these scholars necessarily hold that the Pāli canon accepts the existence of the *attā/ātman*.

37. Sue Hamilton has remarked: "I have argued elsewhere that

interpreting the Buddha's doctrine of *anattā* as simply stating 'there is no self,' misses the point. I will not rehearse my arguments here (though it is tempting to ask rhetorically why, if this were his meaning, he did not just say so in reply to all the questions he did not answer about the nature of the soul) . . ." In: Sue Hamilton, "The Dependent Nature of the Phenomenal World," p. 282.

38. Joaquín Pérez-Remón, *Self and Non-Self in Early Buddhism*, Religion and Reason, 22 (The Hague: Mouton Publishers, 1980), p. 4.

39. K. Bhattacharya, *Ātman-Brahman*, p. 38.

40. Steven Collins, *Selfless persons: Imagery and thought in* Theravāda *Buddhism* (Cambridge: Cambridge University Press, 1982), p. 71.

41. K. Bhattacharya, *Ātman-Brahman*, p. 31. *Dhammapada*, 160 (or *Dhamma-pada*, 12.4).

42. Walpola Rahula, *What the Buddha Taught*, p. 130.

43. K. Bhattacharya, *Ātman-Brahman*, p. 30.

44. Ibid., p. 207.

45. Ibid., p. 34.

46. Kamaleswar Bhattacharya, "The Anātman Concept in Buddhism," p. 224:

yo bālair dharmāṇāṃ svabhāvo grāhyagrāhakādiḥ parikalpitas tena kalpitenātmanā teṣāṃ nairātmyaṃ na tv anabhilāpyenātmanā yo buddhānāṃ viṣayaḥ (Vasubandhu's auto-commentary on *Viṃśatikā*, verse 10). This statement of Vasubandhu is cited in K. Bhattacharya, *Ātman-Brahman*, p. 33, but in the somewhat different translation by Sylvain Lévi.

47. K. Bhattacharya, *Ātman-Brahman*, p. 190.

48. Kamaleswar Bhattacharya, "Some Thoughts on Ātman-Brahman in Early Buddhism," p. 72.

49. Kamaleswar Bhattacharya, "Brahman in the Pali Canon and in the Pali Commentaries," p. 23.

50. K. Bhattacharya, *Ātman-Brahman*, p. 209.

51. Ibid., p. 37.

52. Ibid., pp. 209-210.

53. Ibid., p. 145.

54. Ibid., p. 16.

55. Ibid., p. 6. Here Bhattacharya has used descriptions from the Upaniṣads to describe the state of deliverance.

56. Ibid., p. 207.

57. Bhattacharya here follows what has been acknowledged by Buddhist scholars to be the correct methodology since 1911, namely to rely on the old Pāli Nikāyas, i.e., the Sutta Piṭaka texts, rather than on the later Theravāda interpretations. As Karel Werner writes while commenting on Steven Collins's book (*Selfless persons*):

"In the context of the Sutta Piṭaka texts by themselves, whose analysis Collins neglects, constantly projecting into them later Theravāda interpretations, . . . Collins's interpretations do, of course, reflect quite correctly the Theravāda position from whose point of view he wrote his thesis as expressed by its subtitle. Where he is wrong is when he reads the Sutta Piṭaka in the light of Theravāda orthodoxy as interpreted in the Abhidhamma and commentaries, regarding even the late Buddhaghosa's *Visuddhimagga,* the main compendium of Theravāda orthodoxy, as spelling out explicitly what is contained implicitly in the original Sutta Piṭaka (p. 22), a stance fully embraced in Theravāda circles of learned monks, but untenable on the level of academic scholarship, at least since Karl Seidenstücker published his *Pali-Buddhismus in Übersetzungen* (Breslau 1911) in which he 'allowed the texts of the Canon themselves to speak without the rather dubious help of later commentaries' and maintained that 'we have to tackle the oldest sources' with our own understanding as best we can, thus 'avoiding the risk of adopting the position of a particular school by trusting later exegetical interpretations' (p. X). Which does not, of course, rule out careful consideration and evaluation of later views. Seidenstücker's stance has since been adopted by most scholars of Buddhism as well as Buddhist thinkers." (Karel Werner, "Indian Concepts of Human Personality in Relation to the Doctrine of the Soul," p. 90, n. 9.)

This methodology, Werner notes, was followed by Joaquín Pérez-Remón (*Self and Non-Self in Early Buddhism*): ". . . the whole platform from which he undertook his investigations, namely the Sutta Piṭaka with only a limited use of the Vinaya Piṭaka and almost complete rejection of Theravāda interpretations." (Karel Werner, "Indian Concepts of Human Personality in Relation to the Doctrine of the Soul," p. 94, n. 14.)

58. K. Bhattacharya, *Ātman-Brahman*, p. ix.

59. The word "secret" is not found in the original quote. It has been added to define "Bas-pa" (Tibetan: *sbas-pa*).

60. "An Unpublished Discourse of Buddha," *H. P. Blavatsky Collected Writings*, vol. 14 (Wheaton, Ill.: Theosophical Publishing House, 1985), pp. 408-409.

61. Kamaleswar Bhattacharya, "The Anātman Concept in Buddhism," p. 223.

62. *The Secret Doctrine*, vol. 1, p. 14; *Māṇḍūkya Upaniṣad*, v. 7.

SELECTED BIBLIOGRAPHY

Albahari, Miri. "Against No-*Ātman* Theories of *Anattā*." *Asian Philosophy*, vol. 12, no. 1, 2002, pp. 5-20.

Anacker, Stefan. "No Self, 'Self', and Neither-Self-Nor-Non-Self in Mahāyāna Writings of Vasubandhu." *Communication & Cognition* (Special issue: The Notion of 'Self' in Buddhism), vol. 32, no. 1/2, 1999, pp. 85-95.

Bhattacharya, Kamaleswar. "The Anātman Concept in Buddhism." *Navonmeṣa: Mahamahopadhyaya Gopinath Kaviraj Commemoration Volume*, vol. 4: English. Varanasi: M. M. Gopinath Kaviraj Centenary Celebration Committee, 1987, pp. 213-224. [This article is a concise statement of many of the key points found in his *L'Ātman-Brahman dans le Bouddhisme ancien.*]

———. *L'Ātman-Brahman dans le Bouddhisme ancien.* Publications de l'École française d'Extrême-Orient, vol. 90. Paris: École française d'Extrême-Orient, 1973.

Review by André Bareau. *Revue de l'histoire des religions*, vol. 187, no. 1, 1975, pp. 99-100 (in French).

Review by Richard Gombrich. *Archives Internationales d'Histoire des Sciences*, vol. 28, 1978, pp. 128-129.

Review by Friedhelm Hardy. *Journal of the Royal Asiatic Society of Great Britain & Ireland*, 1975, no. 1, pp. 78-79.

Review by Mario Piantelli. *East and West*, n.s., vol. 25, nos. 1-2, 1975, pp. 239-240.

———. *The Ātman-Brahman in Ancient Buddhism*. Cotopaxi, Colo.: Canon Publications, 2015. [English translation of the above.]

———. "The *Ātman* in Two Prajñāpāramitā-Sūtra-s." *Our Heritage*, Special Number: 150th Anniversary Volume, 1824-1974. Calcutta: Sanskrit College, 1979, pp. 39-45.

———. "Brahman in the Pali Canon and in the Pali Commentaries." *Amalā Prajñā: Aspects of Buddhist Studies, Professor P. V. Bapat Felicitation Volume*, ed. N. H. Samtani. Bibliotheca Indo-Buddhica, no. 63. Delhi: Sri Satguru Publications, 1989, pp. 15-31. Previously printed: *Studies in Orientology: Essays in Memory of Prof. A. L. Basham*, ed. S. K. Maity, et al. Agra: Y. K. Publishers, 1988, pp. 95-112.

———. "Diṭṭhaṃ, Sutaṃ, Mutaṃ, Vinnātaṃ" [*sic* for Viññātaṃ]. In *Buddhist Studies in Honour of Walpola Rahula*, ed. Somaratna Balasooriya, et al. London: Gordon Fraser, 1980, pp. 10-15. [On a passage from the *Alagaddūpama-sutta*.]

———. "A Note on Anātman in the Work of E. Lamotte." *Premier Colloque Étienne Lamotte (Bruxelles et Liège 24-27 septembre 1989)*. Publications de L'Institut Orientaliste de Louvain, 42. Louvain-la-Neuve: Institut Orientaliste, Université Catholique de Louvain, 1993, pp. 25-26.

———. "A Note on the Anatta Passage of the *Mahānidāna-sutta*." *Recent Researches in Buddhist Studies: Essays in Honour of Professor Y. Karunadasa*, ed. Kuala Lumpur Dhammajoti, et al. Colombo: Y. Karunadasa Felicitation Committee, 1997, pp. 47-50.

———. "On the Brahman in Buddhist Literature." *Sri Venkateswara University Oriental Journal*, vol. 18, pts. 1 and 2, Jan.-Dec. 1975, pp. 1-8.

———. "Once More on a Passage of the *Alagaddūpama-sutta*." In *Bauddhavidyāsudhākaraḥ: Studies in Honour of Heinz Bechert on the Occasion of His 65th Birthday*, ed. Petra Kieffer-Pülz and Jens-Uwe Hartmann. Indica et Tibetica, vol. 30. Swisttal-Odendorf: Indica et Tibetica Verlag, 1997, pp. 25-28.

———. "Once More on Two Passages of the Pāli Canon." *Indologica Taurinensia*, vol. 17-18, 1991-1992 (published 2000), pp. 63-67.

———. "Some Thoughts on Ātman-Brahman in Early Buddhism." *Dr. B. M. Barua Birth Centenary Commemoration Volume, 1989*. Calcutta: Bauddha Dharmankur Sabha, 1989, pp. 63-83. [This article, after the first four pages, reproduces the basic part of his "Brahman in the Pali Canon and in the Pali Commentaries."]

———. *Some Thoughts on Early Buddhism, with Special Reference to Its Relation to the Upaniṣads.* Pune: Bhandarkar Oriental Research Institute, 1998. Acharya Dharmananda Kosambi Memorial Lectures (third series). [A 31-page booklet.]

———. "Unity in Diversity: Anattā Revisited." *Sanskrit Studies Centre Journal* (Silpakorn University, Bangkok, Thailand), vol. 2, 2006, pp. 1-7.

———. REVIEW of Claus Oetke, *"Ich" und das Ich. Analytische Untersuchungen zur buddhistisch-brahmanischen Ātmankontroverse.* Stuttgart, 1988. In *Bulletin d'Etudes Indiennes,* vol. 9, 1991, pp. 279-281.

———. REVIEW of Cristina Anna Scherrer-Schaub, *Yuktiṣaṣṭikāvṛtti, Commentaire à la soixantaine sur le raisonnement ou Du vrai enseignement de la causalité par le Maître indien Candrakīrti.* Bruxelles, 1991. In *Journal of Indian Philosophy,* vol. 22, 1994, pp. 391-393. [Says two kinds of *viññāṇa* must be distinguished in the *Kevaddha-sutta.*]

Bhattacharya, Vidhushekhara. "Ātmavāda as in the Yogācārabhūmi of Ācārya Asaṅga." In *Dr. C. Kunhan Raja Presentation Volume: A Volume of Indological Studies.* Madras: The Adyar Library, 1946, pp. 27-37. [The main content of this article is in Sanskrit.]

———. "The Doctrine of Ātman and Anātman." *Proceedings and Transactions of the Fifth Indian Oriental Conference, November 19, 20, 21 and 22, 1928,* vol. 2. Lahore: University of the Panjab, 1930, pp. 995-1008.

Chakravarti, Arindam. "The Nyāya Proofs for the Existence of the Soul." *Journal of Indian Philosophy,* vol. 10, no. 3, Sept. 1982, pp. 211-238.

Chatterji, Jagadish Chandra. "The Buddha and the Ātman." *Prabuddha Bharata,* vol. 68, March 1963, pp. 91-98.

Chowdhury, R. P. "Interpretation of the 'Anatta' Doctrine of Buddhism: A New Approach." *Indian Historical Quarterly,* vol. 31, no. 1, March 1955, pp. 52-67.

Collins, Steven. *Selfless persons: Imagery and thought in* Theravāda *Buddhism.* Cambridge: Cambridge University Press, 1982.

REVIEW by George D. Bond. In *History of Religions,* vol. 23, no. 2, November 1983, pp. 186-189.

REVIEW by Paul Griffiths. In *Philosophy East and West,* vol. 33, no. 3, July 1983, pp. 303-305.

REVIEW by Matthew Kapstein, "Collins, Parfit, and the problem of personal identity in two philosophical traditions—A review of Selfless Persons . . . and Reasons and Persons." In *Philosophy East and West*, vol. 36, no. 3, July 1986, pp. 289-298.

REVIEW by Joy Manné Lewis. In *Bulletin of the School of Oriental and African Studies*, vol. 46, no. 2, 1983, pp. 363-364.

REVIEW by Vijitha Rajapakse. In *Journal of the International Association of Buddhist Studies*, vol. 8, no. 1, 1985, pp. 117-122.

REVIEW by Prabal Sen. In *Journal of Indian Philosophy*, vol. 14, 1986, pp. 99-106.

———. "What Are Buddhists *Doing* When They Deny the Self?" *Religion and Practical Reason: New Essays in the Comparative Philosophy of Religions*, ed. Frank E. Reynolds and David Tracy. Albany: State University of New York Press, 1994, pp. 59-86.

Dessein, Bart. "Self, Dependent Origination and Action in Bactrian and Gandhāran Sarvāstivāda Abhidharma Texts." *Communication & Cognition* (Special issue: The Notion of 'Self' in Buddhism), vol. 32, no. 1/2, 1999, pp. 53-83.

Fuji, Kyoko. "On the Ātman Theory in the Mahāparinirvāṇasūtra." *Premier Colloque Étienne Lamotte (Bruxelles et Liège 24-27 septembre 1989)*. Publications de L'Institut Orientaliste de Louvain, 42. Louvain-la-Neuve: Institut Orientaliste, Université Catholique de Louvain, 1993, pp. 27-31.

Gombrich, Richard. "Another Buddhist Criticism of Yājñavalkya." *Buddhist and Indian Studies in Honour of Professor Sodo Mori.* Hamamatsu: Kokusai Bukkyoto Kyokai, 2002, pp. 21-23.

Gómez, Luis O. "The Elusive Buddhist Self: Preliminary Reflections on its Denial." *Communication & Cognition* (Special issue: The Notion of 'Self' in Buddhism), vol. 32, no. 1/2, 1999, pp. 21-51.

Hamilton, Sue. "Anattā: A Different Approach." *The Middle Way*, vol. 70, no. 1, May 1995, pp. 47-60.

———. "The Dependent Nature of the Phenomenal World." *Recent Researches in Buddhist Studies: Essays in Honour of Professor Y. Karunadasa*, ed. Kuala Lumpur Dhammajoti, et al. Colombo: Y. Karunadasa Felicitation Committee, 1997, pp. 276-291.

———. *Early Buddhism: A New Approach, The I of the Beholder.* Richmond, Surrey: Curzon Press, 2000.

Harvey, Peter. *The Selfless Mind: Personality, Consciousness and Nirvāṇa in Early Buddhism.* Richmond, Surrey: Curzon Press, 1995.

Jong, J. W. de. "Lamotte and the Doctrine of Non-Self." *Cahiers d'Extrême-Asie*, vol. 3, 1987, pp. 151-153.

Karunadasa, Y. "The Buddhist Doctrine of Non-Self and the Problem of the Over-Self." *The Middle Way*, vol. 69, no. 2, August 1994, pp. 107-118.

Kritzer, Robert. "An *ātman* by Any Other Name: Two Non-Buddhist Parallels to *antarābhava*." *Journal of Indian and Buddhist Studies*, vol. 47, no. 1, Dec. 1998, pp. 506-500.

Kuan, Tse-Fu. "Rethinking Non-Self: A New Perspective from the *Ekottarika-āgama*." *Buddhist Studies Review*, vol. 26, no. 2, 2009, pp. 155-175.

La Vallée Poussin, Louis de. "The *Ātman* in the Pāli Canon." *Indian Culture*, vol. 2, 1935-1936, pp. 821-824.

Lindtner, Christian. "Magnanimity of Madhyamaka." *Communication & Cognition* (Special issue: The Notion of 'Self' in Buddhism), vol. 32, no. 1/2, 1999, pp. 127-148.

Matilal, Bimal Krishna. "Nyāya Critique of the Buddhist Doctrine of Non-Soul." *Journal of Indian Philosophy*, vol. 17, no. 1, March 1989, pp. 61-79.

Mejor, Marek. "'There Is No Self' (Nātmāsti)—Some Observations from Vasubandhu's Abhidharmakośa and the Yuktidīpikā." *Communication & Cognition* (Special issue: The Notion of 'Self' in Buddhism), vol. 32, no. 1/2, 1999, pp. 97-126.

Nakamura, Hajime. "The Problem of Self in Buddhist Philosophy." In *Revelation in Indian Thought: A Festschrift in Honour of Professor T. R. V. Murti.*, ed. Harold Coward and Krishna Sivaraman. Emeryville, Calif.: Dharma Publishing, 1977.

Norman, K. R. "A Note on Attā in the Alagaddūpama-sutta." In *Studies in Indian Philosophy: A Memorial Volume in Honour of Pandit Sukhlalji Sanghvi*, ed. Dalsukh Malvania and Nagin J. Shah. L. D. Series, 84. Ahmedabad: L. D. Institute of Indology, 1981, pp. 19-29. Reprint in his *Collected Papers*, vol. 2, London: Pali Text Society, 1991.

Oetke, Claus. "About the Assessment of Views on a Self in the Indian Philosophical Tradition." In *Pramāṇakīrtiḥ: Papers Dedicated to Ernst Steinkellner on the Occasion of His 70th Birthday*, ed. by Birgit

Kellner, et al., Part 2, pp. 567-585. Wiener Studien zur Tibetologie und Buddhismuskunde, no. 70.2. Wien: Arbeitskreis für Tibetische und Buddhistische Studien, Universität Wien, 2007.

———. *"Ich" und das Ich. Analytische Untersuchungen zur buddhistisch-brahmanischen Ātmankontroverse.* Alt- und Neu-Indische Studien, vol. 33. Stuttgart: Franz Steiner Verlag Wiesbaden, 1988.

REVIEW by Kamaleswar Bhattacharya. In *Bulletin d'Etudes Indiennes*, vol. 9, 1991, pp. 279-281.

REVIEW by J. Bronkhorst. In *Wiener Zeitschrift für die Kunde Südasiens*, vol. 33, 1989, pp. 223-225.

REVIEW by E. Franco and K. Preisendanz. In *Journal of the American Oriental Society*, vol. 111, 1991, pp. 840-842.

REVIEW by J. W. de Jong. In *Indo-Iranian Journal*, vol. 34, 1991, pp. 144-147.

REVIEW by Karel Werner. In *Journal of the Royal Asiatic Society*, 1989, no. 1, pp. 171-172.

Pérez-Remón, Joaquín. *Self and Non-Self in Early Buddhism.* Religion and Reason, 22. The Hague: Mouton Publishers, 1980.

REVIEW by André Bareau. *Revue de l'histoire des religions*, vol. 199, no. 3, 1982, pp. 335-336 (in French).

REVIEW by George D. Bond. In *History of Religions*, vol. 23, no. 2, November 1983, pp. 186-189.

REVIEW ARTICLE by Steven Collins. In *Numen*, vol. 29, fasc. 2, December 1982, pp. 250-271.

REVIEW by Vijitha Rajapakse. In *Journal of the International Association of Buddhist Studies*, vol. 8, no. 1, 1985, pp. 122-126.

REVIEW by Tilmann Vetter. In *Wiener Zeitschrift für die Kunde Südasiens*, vol. 27, 1983, pp. 211-215 (in German).

Renou, Louis. "On the Word Ātmán." *Vāk*, no. 2, December 1952, pp. 151-157. [Discusses *ātman* in the Vedic literature.]

Rhys Davids, C. A. F. "The Self: An Overlooked Buddhist Simile." *Journal of the Royal Asiatic Society of Great Britain & Ireland*, 1937, pp. 259-264.

Sanderson, Alexis. "The Sarvāstivāda and its Critics: Anātmavāda and the Theory of Karma." *Buddhism into the Year 2000: International Conference Proceedings.* Bangkok and Los Angeles: Dhammakaya Foundation, 1994, pp. 33-48.

Sen, Sushanta. "The Buddhist Doctrine of No-Soul (Nairātma Vāda)." *Visva-Bharati Journal of Philosophy*, vol. 10, no. 1, August 1973, pp. 62-77.

Shukla, Karunesha. "Ātman in Buddhist Philosophy," Chapter II: "The Upaniṣadic Ātman and the Conception of Attā in the Teachings of the Buddha." *Poona Orientalist*, vol. 27, nos. 3-4, 1962, pp. 114-132.

———. "*Ātman* in Buddhist Philosophy: View-point of the Buddha." *Proceedings of the Twenty-Sixth International Congress of Orientalists, New Delhi, January 4-10, 1964*, vol. 3, part 1. Poona: Bhandarkar Oriental Research Institute, 1969, p. 521 (summary).

———. "Buddhist Ātmavāda and Asaṅga." *Journal of the Ganganatha Jha Research Institute*, vol. 23, pts. 1-4, Jan. 1967-Dec. 1967, pp. 29-49.

Venkataramanan, K. "Did the Buddha Deny the Self?" *Philosophical Quarterly*, Amalner, vol. 28, no. 4, Jan. 1956, pp. 273-280.

———. "Sāmmitīyanikāya Śāstra." *Visva-Bharati Annals*, vol. 5, 1953, pp. 153-243.

Werner, Karel. "Indian Conceptions of Human Personality." *Asian Philosophy*, vol. 6, no. 2, 1996, pp. 93-107.

———. "Indian Concepts of Human Personality in Relation to the Doctrine of the Soul." *Journal of the Royal Asiatic Society of Great Britain & Ireland*, 1988, pp. 73-97.

Wijebandara, Chandima. "Ananda Coomaraswamy and the Buddha's Refutation of Ātmavāda." *Ānanda: Papers on Buddhism and Indology, A Felicitation Volume Presented to Ananda Weihena Palliya Guruge on his sixtieth birthday*, ed. Y. Karunadasa. Colombo: Felicitation Volume Editorial Committee, 1990, pp. 317-322.

Winternitz, M. "Self and Non-Self in Early Buddhism." *Jhā Commemoration Volume: Essays on Oriental Subjects.* Poona Oriental Series, no. 39. Poona: Oriental Book Agency, 1937, pp. 457-468.

[The foregoing article was written by Nancy Reigle, and presented as part of the program, "Theosophy's Tibetan Connection," at the Annual Meeting of the Texas Federation of the Theosophical Society in America, San Antonio, April 18-20, 2008.]

A Compilation on the First Fundamental Proposition of the Secret Doctrine: The One Reality (from early Theosophical writings)

prepared by David Reigle

Outline

1. The first fundamental proposition of the Secret Doctrine: the one reality
2. The radical unity, or non-duality, of the one reality
3. The two aspects of the one reality
4. The one reality described as space
   a. space as both a limitless void and a conditioned fullness
   b. space as a limitless void (i.e., as emptiness)
   c. space as a conditioned fullness (i.e., not just empty space)
5. The one reality described as substance (or matter)
6. The one reality described as darkness
7. The one reality described as the one element
8. The aspect of the one reality described as motion, the great breath, the one life, unconditioned consciousness (or spirit), *svabhāva* ("inherent nature"), or force

1. The first fundamental proposition of the Secret Doctrine: the one reality

An Omnipresent, Eternal, Boundless, and Immutable PRINCIPLE on which all speculation is impossible, since it transcends the power of human conception and could only be dwarfed by any human expression or similitude. It is beyond the range and reach of thought—in the words of *Māṇḍūkya Upanishad,* "unthinkable and unspeakable."
—*The Secret Doctrine,* vol. 1, p. 14

To render these ideas clearer to the general reader, let him set out with the postulate that there is one absolute Reality which antecedes all manifested, conditioned, being. This Infinite and Eternal Cause—dimly formulated in the "Unconscious" and "Unknowable" of current European philosophy—is the rootless root of "all that was, is, or ever shall be." It is of course devoid of all attributes and is essentially without any relation to manifested, finite Being. It is "Be-ness" rather than Being (in Sanskrit, *Sat*), and is beyond all thought or speculation.
—*The Secret Doctrine,* vol. 1, p. 14

The fundamental Law in that system, the central point from which all emerged, around and toward which all gravitates, and upon which is hung the philosophy of the rest, is the One homogeneous divine SUBSTANCE-PRINCIPLE, the one radical cause.
—*The Secret Doctrine,* vol. 1, p. 273 (from the recapitulation in "Summing Up")

2. The radical unity, or non-duality, of the one reality:

The radical unity of the ultimate essence of each constituent part of compounds in Nature—from Star to mineral Atom, from the highest Dhyāni-Chohan to the smallest infusoria, in the fullest acceptation of the term, and whether applied to the spiritual, intellectual, or physical worlds—this is the one fundamental law in Occult Science.
—*The Secret Doctrine,* vol. 1, p. 120

No matter what one may study in the S.D. let the mind hold fast, as the basis of its ideation, to the following ideas:

The FUNDAMENTAL UNITY OF ALL EXISTENCE. This unity is a thing altogether different from the common notion of unity—as when we say that a nation or an army is united; or that this planet is united to that by lines of magnetic force or the like. The teaching is not that. It is that existence is ONE THING, not any collection of things linked together. Fundamentally there is ONE BEING. This BEING has two aspects, positive and negative. The positive is Spirit, or CONSCIOUSNESS. The negative is SUBSTANCE, the subject of consciousness. This Being is the Absolute in its primary manifestation. Being absolute there is nothing outside it. It is ALL-BEING. It is indivisible, else it would not be absolute. If a portion could be separated, that remaining could not be absolute, because there would at once arise the question of COMPARISON between it and the separated part. Comparison is incompatible with any idea of absoluteness. Therefore it is clear that this fundamental ONE EXISTENCE, or Absolute Being must be the REALITY in every form there is.

. . . .

The Atom, the Man, the God (she says) are each separately, as well as all collectively, Absolute Being in their last analysis, that is their REAL INDIVIDUALITY. It is this idea which must be held always in the background of the mind to form the basis for every conception that arises from study of the S.D. The moment one lets it go (and it is most easy to do so when engaged in any of the many intricate aspects of the Esoteric Philosophy) the idea of SEPARATION supervenes, and the study loses its value.

—"The 'Secret Doctrine' and Its Study" (notes of personal teachings given by H. P. Blavatsky to Robert Bowen), cited from *An Invitation to The Secret Doctrine*, pp. 3-4

3. The two aspects of the one reality:

This "Be-ness" is symbolized in the Secret Doctrine under two aspects. On the one hand, absolute abstract Space, representing bare subjectivity, the one thing which no human mind can

either exclude from any conception, or conceive of by itself. On the other, absolute abstract Motion representing Unconditioned Consciousness. Even our Western thinkers have shown that Consciousness is inconceivable to us apart from change, and motion best symbolizes change, its essential characteristic. This latter aspect of the one Reality, is also symbolized by the term "The Great Breath," a symbol sufficiently graphic to need no further elucidation. Thus, then, the first fundamental axiom of the Secret Doctrine is this metaphysical ONE ABSOLUTE—BE-NESS—symbolized by finite intelligence as the theological Trinity.
—*The Secret Doctrine,* vol. 1, p. 14

Considering this metaphysical triad as the Root from which proceeds all manifestation, the Great Breath assumes the character of pre-cosmic Ideation. It is the *fons et origo* [source and origin] of force and of all individual consciousness, and supplies the guiding intelligence in the vast scheme of cosmic Evolution. On the other hand, pre-cosmic root-substance (*Mūlaprakṛiti*) is that aspect of the Absolute which underlies all the objective planes of Nature.

Just as pre-cosmic Ideation is the root of all individual consciousness, so pre-cosmic Substance is the substratum of matter in the various grades of its differentiation.
—*The Secret Doctrine,* vol. 1, p. 15

The ONE REALITY; its *dual* aspects in the conditioned Universe.
—*The Secret Doctrine,* vol. 1, p. 16

4. The one reality described as space:

"What is that which was, is, and will be, whether there is a Universe or not; whether there be gods or none?" asks the esoteric Senzar Catechism. And the answer made is—SPACE.
—*The Secret Doctrine,* vol. 1, p. 9

The Occult Catechism contains the following questions and answers:

"What is it that ever is?" "Space, the eternal Anupadaka [*upapāduka*]." "What is it that ever was?" "The Germ in the Root." "What is it that is ever coming and going?" "The Great Breath." "Then, there are three Eternals?" "No, the three are one. That which ever is, is one, that which ever was, is one, that which is ever being and becoming, is also one: and this is Space."
—*The Secret Doctrine,* vol. 1, p. 11

What is the one eternal thing in the universe independent of every other thing?

Space.
—"Cosmological Notes," *The Letters of H. P. Blavatsky to A. P. Sinnett,* Appendix II, p. 376 (by Mahatma Morya)

Hence, the Arahat secret doctrine on cosmogony admits but of one absolute, indestructible, eternal, and uncreated UNCONSCIOUSNESS (so to translate), of an element (the word being used for want of a better term) absolutely independent of everything else in the universe; a something ever present or ubiquitous, a Presence which ever was, is, and will be, whether there is a God, gods or none; whether there is a universe or no universe; existing during the eternal cycles of Maha Yugas, during the *Pralayas* as during the periods of *Manvantara*: and this is SPACE, the field for the operation of the eternal Forces and natural Law, the *basis* (as our correspondent rightly calls it) upon which take place the eternal intercorrelations of Ākāśa-Prakriti, guided by the unconscious regular pulsations of *Śakti*—the breath or power of a conscious deity, the theists would say—the eternal energy of an eternal, unconscious Law, say the Buddhists. Space, then, or *Fan, Bar-nang* (*Mahā-Śūnyatā*) or, as it is called by Lao-tze, the "Emptiness" is the nature of the Buddhist Absolute.
—"The Aryan-Arhat Esoteric Tenets on the Sevenfold Principle in Man," *H. P. Blavatsky Collected Writings,* vol. 3, p. 423

Prakriti, Svabhavat or *Ākāśa* is—SPACE as the Tibetans have it; Space filled with whatsoever substance or no substance at all; *i.e.*, with substance so imponderable as to be only metaphysically conceivable. . . . "That which we call form (*rūpa*) is not different from that which we call space (*Śūnyatā*) . . . Space is not different from Form. . . ." (Book of *Sin-king* or the *Heart Sutra*. . . .)
—"The Aryan-Arhat Esoteric Tenets on the Sevenfold Principle in Man," *H. P. Blavatsky Collected Writings*, vol. 3, pp. 405-406 fn.

4a. space as both a limitless void and a conditioned fullness:

Space is neither a "limitless void," nor a "conditioned fullness," but both: being, on the plane of absolute abstraction, the ever-incognizable Deity, which is void only to finite minds, and on that of *māyāvic* perception, the Plenum, the absolute Container of all that is, whether manifested or unmanifested: it is, therefore, that ABSOLUTE ALL.
—*The Secret Doctrine*, vol. 1, p. 8

Space is the *one eternal thing* . . . . It is, as taught in the esoteric catechism, neither limitless void, nor conditioned fullness, but both. It was and ever will be.
—*The Secret Doctrine*, vol. 1, p. 35

4b. space as a limitless void (i.e., as emptiness):

This "Be-ness" is symbolized in the Secret Doctrine under two aspects. On the one hand, absolute abstract Space, representing bare subjectivity, the one thing which no human mind can either exclude from any conception, or conceive of by itself. . . .
—*The Secret Doctrine*, vol. 1, p. 14

Space is the *one eternal thing* that we can most easily imagine, immovable in its abstraction and uninfluenced by either the presence or absence in it of an objective Universe. It is without dimension, in every sense, and self-existent.
—*The Secret Doctrine*, vol. 1, p. 35

. . . the One All is, like Space—which is its only mental and physical representation on this Earth, or our plane of existence—neither an object of, nor a subject to, perception.
—*The Secret Doctrine,* vol. 1, p. 8

4c. space as a conditioned fullness (i.e., not just empty space):

"As its substance is of a different kind from that known on earth, the inhabitants of the latter, seeing THROUGH IT, believe in their illusion and ignorance that it is empty space. There is not one finger's breadth [ANGULA] of void Space in the whole Boundless [Universe]."
—*The Secret Doctrine,* vol. 1, p. 289, "Extracts from a private commentary, hitherto secret"

"Creation"—out of pre-existent eternal substance, or matter, of course, which substance, according to our teachings, is boundless, ever-existing space.
—*The Secret Doctrine,* vol. 2, p. 239 fn.

Space, however, viewed as a "Substantial Unity"—the "living Source of Life"—as the "Unknown Causeless Cause," is the oldest dogma in Occultism, millenniums earlier than the *Pater-Aether* of the Greeks and Latins.
—*The Secret Doctrine,* vol. 1, pp. 9-10 fn.

. . . "Space, the all containing uncontained, is the primary embodiment of simply unity . . . boundless extension." . . . [Space is] "The *unknown container of all, the Unknown FIRST CAUSE.*" This is a most correct definition and answer, most esoteric and true, from every aspect of occult teaching. *SPACE,* which, in their ignorance and iconoclastic tendency to destroy every philosophic idea of old, the modern wiseacres have proclaimed "an abstract idea" and a *void,* is, in reality, the container and *the body of the Universe* with its seven principles.
—*The Secret Doctrine,* vol. 1, p. 342

Space is called in the esoteric symbolism "the Seven-Skinned Eternal Mother-Father." It is composed from its undifferentiated to its differentiated surface of seven layers.
—*The Secret Doctrine,* vol. 1, p. 9

The Second idea to hold fast to is that THERE IS NO DEAD MATTER. Every last atom is alive. It cannot be otherwise since every atom is itself fundamentally Absolute Being. Therefore there is no such thing as "spaces" of Ether, or Akasha, or call it what you like, in which angels and elementals disport themselves like trout in water. That's the common idea. The true idea shows every atom of substance no matter of what plane to be in itself a LIFE.
—"The 'Secret Doctrine' and Its Study" (notes of personal teachings given by H. P. Blavatsky to Robert Bowen), cited from *An Invitation to The Secret Doctrine,* p. 4

5. The one reality described as substance (or matter):

"The Initial Existence in the first twilight of the Mahā-Manvantara [after the MAHĀ-PRALAYA that follows every age of Brahmā] is a CONSCIOUS SPIRITUAL QUALITY. . . .

"It is substance to OUR spiritual sight. It cannot be called so by men in their WAKING STATE; therefore they have named it in their ignorance 'God-Spirit.'

". . . As its substance is of a different kind from that known on earth, the inhabitants of the latter, seeing THROUGH IT, believe in their illusion and ignorance that it is empty space. There is not one finger's breadth [ANGULA] of void Space in the whole Boundless [Universe]. . . ."
—*The Secret Doctrine,* vol. 1, p. 289, "Extracts from a private commentary, hitherto secret"

The first primordial matter, eternal and coeval with Space, "which has neither a beginning nor an end," is "neither hot nor cold, but is of its own special nature," says the Commentary (Book II).
—*The Secret Doctrine,* vol. 1, p. 82

The expansion "from within without" of the Mother, called elsewhere the "Waters of Space," "Universal Matrix," etc., does not allude to an expansion from a small centre or focus, but, without reference to size or limitation or area, means the development of limitless subjectivity into as limitless objectivity. "The ever (to us) invisible and immaterial Substance present in eternity, threw its periodical shadow from its own plane into the lap of Māyā."
—*The Secret Doctrine*, vol. 1, pp. 62-63

If people are willing to accept and to regard as God our ONE LIFE immutable and unconscious in its eternity they may do so and thus keep to one more gigantic misnomer. . . .

When we speak of our One Life we also say that it penetrates, nay is the essence of every atom of matter; and that therefore it not only has correspondence with matter but has all its properties likewise, etc.—hence *is* material, is *matter itself*. . . .

Matter we know to be eternal, *i.e.*, having had no beginning (*a*) because matter is Nature herself (*b*) because that which cannot annihilate itself and is indestructible exists necessarily—and therefore it could not begin to be, nor can it cease to be (*c*) because the accumulated experience of countless ages, and that of exact science show to us matter (or nature) acting by her own peculiar energy, of which not an atom is ever in an absolute state of rest, and therefore it must have always existed, *i.e.*, its materials ever changing form, combinations and properties, but its principles or elements being absolutely indestructible. . . .

In other words we believe in MATTER alone, in matter as visible nature and matter in its invisibility as the invisible omnipresent omnipotent Proteus with its unceasing motion which is its life, and which nature draws from herself since she is the great whole outside of which nothing can exist. . . .

The existence of matter then is a fact; the existence of motion is another fact, their self existence and eternity or indestructibility is a third fact. And the idea of pure spirit as a Being or an Existence—give it whatever name you will—is a chimera, a gigantic absurdity.
—*The Mahatma Letters*, letter #10, 3rd ed., pp. 53-56

The conception of matter and spirit as entirely distinct, and both eternal could certainly never have entered my head, however little I may know of them, for it is one of the elementary and fundamental doctrines of Occultism that the two are one, and are distinct but in their respective manifestations, and only in the limited perceptions of the world of senses. . . . matter *per se* is indestructible, and as I maintain coeval with spirit—that spirit which we know and can conceive of. . . . Motion is eternal because spirit is eternal. But no modes of motion can ever be conceived unless they be in connection with matter.
—*The Mahatma Letters*, letter #22, 3rd ed., pp. 138-139

Purusha and Prakriti are in short the two poles of the one eternal element, and are synonymous and convertible terms. . . . Therefore, whether it is called Force or Matter, it will ever remain the Omnipresent Proteus of the Universe, the one element—LIFE—Spirit or Force at its *negative*, Matter at its *positive* pole; the former the MATERIO-SPIRITUAL, the latter, the MATERIO-PHYSICAL Universe—Nature, Svabhavat or INDESTRUCTIBLE MATTER.
—"What is Matter and What is Force?" *H. P. Blavatsky Collected Writings*, vol. 4, pp. 225-226 (Blavatsky says that this article is by Mahatma K.H.)

[The Almora Swami asks:] Will the Editor satisfy us by proving the assertion that "matter is as eternal and indestructible as spirit"? . . .

[T. Subba Row replies:] To our utter amazement, we are called upon to prove that matter is indestructible; at any rate, that "matter is as eternal and indestructible as spirit"! . . .

Our "assertion" then means the following: Undifferentiated cosmic matter or *Mūlaprakṛiti*, as it is called in Hindu books, is *uncreated* and eternal. . . . In every objective phenomenon perceived, either in the present plane of consciousness or in any other plane requiring the exercise of spiritual faculties, there is but change of cosmic matter from one form to another. There is not a single instance, or the remotest suspicion of the annihilation of an atom of matter ever brought to light either by Eastern Adepts or Western scientists. When the common experience of generations of Adepts in their own spiritual or psychic field of observation, and of the ordinary people in theirs—(*i.e.*, in the domain of physical science) points to the conclusion that there never has been the utter annihilation of a single material particle, we are justified, we believe, in saying that matter is indestructible, though it may change its forms and properties and appear in various degrees of differentiation. Hindu and Buddhist philosophers have ages ago recognized the fact that *Purusha* and *Prakṛiti* are eternal, co-existent, not only correlative and interdependent, but positively one and the same thing for him who can read between the lines. Every system of evolution commences with postulating the existence of *Mūlaprakṛiti* or *Tamas* (primeval darkness). . . .

[Subba Row then gives two quotations in Sanskrit to show this, one using *tamas*, "darkness," and one using *asat*, "non-being": *tama eva purastāt abhavat viśvarūpam*, literally, "darkness alone was the form of the all in the beginning" (compare "Book of Dzyan," stanza I, verse 5: "Darkness alone filled the boundless all"); and *asad vā idam agra āsīt*, "this (universe) was verily non-being in the beginning."]

. . . And primeval cosmic matter, whether called *Asat* or *Tamas*, or *Prakṛiti* or *Śakti*, is ever the same, and held to be eternal by both Hindu and Arhat philosophers, while *Purusha* is inconceivable, hence non-existent, save when manifesting through *Prakṛiti*. In its undifferentiated condition, some Advaitis refuse to recognize it as matter, properly so called. Nevertheless this entity is their PARABRAHMAN, with its dual aspect of *Purusha* and *Prakṛiti*. In their opinion it can be called neither; hence in some passages of the Upanishads we find the expression, "PRAKṚITI-*layam*" mentioned; but in all such passages the word "Prakṛiti" means, as we can prove—*matter in a state of differentiation*, while *undifferentiated* cosmic matter in conjunction with, or rather in its aspect of, *latent* spirit is always referred to as "MAHĀ-ĪŚVARA," "Purusha" and "Paramapada."

—"In Re Advaita Philosophy," *A Collection of Esoteric Writings of T. Subba Row*, 1895, pp. 109-113; *Esoteric Writings*, 1980, pp. 480-486; *T. Subba Row Collected Writings*, 2001, vol. 1, pp. 134-141

Your all-pervading supreme power exists, but it is exactly matter, whose life is motion, will, and nerve power, electricity. Purusha can think but through Prakriti.
—"Cosmological Notes," *The Letters of H. P. Blavatsky to A. P. Sinnett,* Appendix II, p. 381 (by Mahatma Morya)

. . . matter *in abscondito* [hidden, invisible], as it is called by the Alchemists, is eternal, indestructible, without beginning or end. It is regarded by Eastern Occultists as the eternal Root of all, . . . the Divine Essence, in short, or Substance; the radiations from This are periodically aggregated into graduated forms, from pure Spirit to gross Matter; the Root, or Space, is in its abstract presence the Deity Itself, the Ineffable and Unknown One Cause.
—*The Secret Doctrine,* 3rd ed., vol. 3, p. 223; "Eastern and Western Occultism," *H. P. Blavatsky Collected Writings,* vol. 14, pp. 233-234

The reader must bear in mind that, according to our teaching, which regards this phenomenal Universe as a great *Illusion,* the nearer a body is to the UNKNOWN SUBSTANCE, the more it approaches *reality,* as being removed the farther from this world of *Maya.*
—*The Secret Doctrine,* vol. 1, pp. 145-146

The One reality is *Mulaprakriti* (undifferentiated Substance)—the "Rootless root," the . . . But we have to stop, lest there should remain but little to tell for your own intuitions.
—*The Mahatma Letters,* letter #59, 3rd ed., p. 341

6. The one reality described as darkness:

Every system of evolution commences with postulating the existence of *Mūlaprakṛiti* or *Tamas* (primeval darkness).
—"In Re Advaita Philosophy," *A Collection of Esoteric Writings of T. Subba Row,* 1895, p. 113; *Esoteric Writings,* 1980, p. 485; *T. Subba Row Collected Writings,* 2001, vol. 1, p. 140

DARKNESS ALONE FILLED THE BOUNDLESS ALL, FOR FATHER, MOTHER AND SON WERE ONCE MORE ONE, AND THE SON HAD NOT AWAKENED YET FOR THE NEW WHEEL, AND HIS PILGRIMAGE THEREON.

—*The Secret Doctrine*, vol. 1, p. 27 (Stanza I, verse 5, of the "Book of Dzyan")

"Darkness" . . . is that of which no attributes can be postulated: it is the Unknown Principle filling Cosmic Space. . . . it is not Darkness as absence of Light . . . .

—"Transactions of the Blavatsky Lodge of the Theosophical Society," *H. P. Blavatsky Collected Writings*, vol. 10, p. 331

Let us turn to Stanza I of the *Book of Dzyan* for an example.

The *Zohar* premises, as does the Secret Doctrine, a universal, eternal Essence, passive—because absolute—in all that men call attributes. . . .

This, then, is the meaning:

"Darkness alone filled the Boundless All, for Father, Mother and Son were once more One."

Space was, and is ever, as it is between the Manvantaras. The Universe in its pre-kosmic state was once more homogeneous and one—outside its aspects. . . .

Says the Secret Doctrine:

It is called to life. The mystic Cube in which rests the Creative Idea, the manifesting Mantra [or articulate speech—Vāch] *and the holy Purusha* [both radiations of *prima materia*] *exist in the Eternity in the Divine Substance in their latent state*

—during Pralaya.

—*The Secret Doctrine*, 3rd ed., vol. 3, pp. 180-181; "The Eastern Gupta Vidyā and the Kabalah," *H. P. Blavatsky Collected Writings*, vol. 14, pp. 185-187; apparently quoting a secret commentary

SPACE filled with darkness, which is primordial matter in its *pre-cosmic* state. . . . and Space is *the* ever Unseen and Unknowable Deity in our philosophy.

—*The Secret Doctrine*, vol. 1, p. 336 fn.

7. The one reality described as the one element:

> However, you will have to bear in mind (*a*) that we recognize but *one* element in Nature (whether spiritual or physical) outside which there can be no Nature since it is *Nature* itself, and which as the *Akasa* pervades our solar system, every atom being part of itself, pervades throughout *space* and *is* space in fact, . . . (*b*) that consequently spirit and matter are *one*, being but a differentiation of states not *essences*, . . . (*c*) that our notions of "cosmic matter" are diametrically opposed to those of western science. Perchance if you remember all this we will succeed in imparting to you at least the elementary axioms of our esoteric philosophy more correctly than heretofore.
> —*The Mahatma Letters,* letter #11, 3rd ed., p. 63

> Yes, as described in my letter—there is but one element and it is impossible to comprehend our system before a correct conception of it is firmly fixed in one's mind. You must therefore pardon me if I dwell on the subject longer than really seems necessary. But unless this great primary fact is firmly grasped the rest will appear unintelligible. This element then is the—to speak metaphysically—one sub-stratum or permanent cause of all manifestations in the phenomenal universe.
> —*The Mahatma Letters,* letter #15, 3rd ed., p. 89

> If the student bears in mind that there is but One Universal Element, which is infinite, unborn, and undying, and that all the rest—as in the world of phenomena—are but so many various differentiated aspects and transformations (correlations, they are now called) of that One, from Cosmical down to microcosmical effects, from super-human down to human and subhuman beings, the totality, in short, of objective existence—then the first and chief difficulty will disappear and Occult Cosmology may be mastered.
> —*The Secret Doctrine,* vol. I, p. 75

. . . the Eastern Occultists hold that there is but one element in the universe—infinite, uncreated and indestructible—MATTER; which element manifests itself in seven states. . . . *Spirit* is the highest state of that matter, they say, since that which is neither matter nor any of its attributes is—NOTHING.
—"From Theosophy to Shakespeare," *H. P. Blavatsky Collected Writings,* vol. 4, p. 602

Light, then, like heat—of which it is the crown—is simply the ghost, the shadow of matter in motion, the boundless, eternal, infinite SPACE, MOTION and DURATION, the trinitarian essence of that which the Deists call God, and we—the One Element; Spirit-matter, or Matter-spirit, whose septenary properties we circumscribe under its triple abstract form in the equilateral triangle.
—"What is Matter and What is Force?" *H. P. Blavatsky Collected Writings,* vol. 4, p. 220 (Blavatsky says that this article is by Mahatma K.H.)

8. The aspect of the one reality described as motion, the great breath, the one life, unconditioned consciousness (or spirit), *svabhāva* ("inherent nature"), or force:

It is a fundamental law in Occultism, that there is no rest or cessation of motion in Nature.
—*The Secret Doctrine,* vol. 1, p. 97

We will say that it is, and will remain for ever demonstrated that since motion is all-pervading and absolute rest inconceivable, that under whatever form or *mask* motion may appear, whether as light, heat, magnetism, chemical affinity or electricity—all these must be but phases of One and the same universal omnipotent Force, a Proteus they bow to as the Great "Unknown" (See Herbert Spencer) and we, simply call the "One Life," the "One Law" and the "One Element."
—*The Mahatma Letters,* letter #23b, 3rd ed., pp. 155-56

However, you will have to bear in mind (*a*) that we recognize but *one* element in Nature (whether spiritual or physical) outside which there can be no Nature since it is *Nature* itself, and which as the *Akasa* pervades our solar system, every atom being part of itself, pervades throughout *space* and *is* space in fact, which pulsates as in profound sleep during the pralayas, . . .
—*The Mahatma Letters,* letter #11, 3rd ed., p. 63

ALONE THE ONE FORM OF EXISTENCE STRETCHED BOUNDLESS, INFINITE, CAUSELESS, IN DREAMLESS SLEEP; AND LIFE PULSATED UNCONSCIOUS IN UNIVERSAL SPACE, THROUGHOUT THAT ALL-PRESENCE WHICH IS SENSED BY THE OPENED EYE OF THE DANGMA.
—*The Secret Doctrine,* vol. 1, p. 27 (Stanza I, verse 8, of the "Book of Dzyan")

Then what do we believe in? Well, we believe in the much laughed at *phlogiston* (see article "What is force and what is matter?" *Theosophist,* September), and in what some natural philosophers would call *nisus,* the incessant though perfectly imperceptible (to the ordinary senses) motion or efforts one body is making on another—the pulsations of inert matter—its life.
—*The Mahatma Letters,* letter #10, 3rd ed., p. 56

We say and affirm that that motion—the universal perpetual motion which never ceases, never slackens nor increases its speed, not even during the interludes between the pralayas, or "nights of Brahma," but goes on like a mill set in motion whether it has anything to grind or not (for the pralaya means the temporary loss of every form, but by no means the destruction of cosmic matter which is eternal)—we say this perpetual motion is the only eternal and uncreated Deity we are able to recognise.
—*The Mahatma Letters,* letter #22, 3rd ed., p. 135

. . . the ceaseless and eternal Cosmic Motion; or rather the Force that moves it, which Force is tacitly accepted as the Deity but never named. It is the eternal *Kāraṇa,* the ever-acting Cause.
—*The Secret Doctrine,* vol. 1, p. 93, fn.

What things are co-existent with space?

(i) Duration.

(ii) Matter.

(iii) Motion, for this is the imperishable life (conscious or unconscious as the case may be) of matter, even during the pralaya, or night of mind.

When Chyang or omniscience, and Chyang-mi-shi-khon—ignorance, both sleep, this latent unconscious life still maintains the matter it animates in sleepless unceasing motion.
—"Cosmological Notes," *The Letters of H. P. Blavatsky to A. P. Sinnett*, Appendix II, p. 377 (by Mahatma Morya)

. . . the world of non-being, where exists the eternal mechanical motion, the uncreated cause from whence proceeds in a kind of incessant downward and upward rotation, the founts of being from non-being, the latter, the reality, the former maya, the temporary from the everlasting, the effect from its cause, the effect becoming in its turn cause *ad infinitum*. During the pralaya, that upward and downward motion ceases, inherent unconscious life alone remaining—all creative forces paralysed, and everything resting in the night of mind.
—"Cosmological Notes," *The Letters of H. P. Blavatsky to A. P. Sinnett*, Appendix II, p. 379 (by Mahatma Morya)

"The Mother sleeps, yet is ever breathing."
—*The Secret Doctrine*, vol. 1, p. 143, apparently quoting a secret commentary

The "Breath" of the One Existence is used in its application only to the spiritual aspect of Cosmogony by Archaic esotericism; otherwise it is replaced by its equivalent in the material plane —Motion. The One Eternal Element, or element-containing Vehicle, is *Space*, dimensionless in every sense; coexistent with which are—endless *duration*, primordial (hence indestructible) *matter*, and *motion*—absolute "perpetual motion" which is the "breath" of the "One" Element. This breath, as seen, can never cease, not even during the Pralayic eternities.
—*The Secret Doctrine*, vol. 1, p. 55

. . . WHERE WAS SILENCE? WHERE THE EARS TO SENSE IT? NO, THERE WAS NEITHER SILENCE NOR SOUND; NAUGHT SAVE CEASELESS, ETERNAL BREATH, WHICH KNOWS ITSELF NOT.
—*The Secret Doctrine*, vol. 1, p. 28 (Stanza II, verse 2, of the "Book of Dzyan")

This "Be-ness" is symbolized in the Secret Doctrine under two aspects. On the one hand, absolute abstract Space, . . . On the other, absolute abstract Motion representing Unconditioned Consciousness. . . . This latter aspect of the one Reality, is also symbolized by the term "The Great Breath," a symbol sufficiently graphic to need no further elucidation.
—*The Secret Doctrine*, vol. 1, p. 14

Its one absolute attribute, which is ITSELF, eternal, ceaseless Motion, is called in esoteric parlance the "Great Breath," which is the perpetual motion of the universe, in the sense of limitless, ever-present SPACE. . . . Occultism sums up the "One Existence" thus: "Deity is an arcane, living (or moving) FIRE, and the eternal witnesses to this unseen Presence are Light, Heat, Moisture"—this trinity including, and being the cause of, every phenomenon in Nature. Intra-Cosmic motion is eternal and ceaseless; cosmic motion (the visible, or that which is subject to perception) is finite and periodical.
—*The Secret Doctrine*, vol. 1, pp. 2-3

"Whatsoever quits the Laya State, becomes active life; it is drawn into the vortex of MOTION [the alchemical solvent of Life]; Spirit and Matter are the two States of the ONE, which is neither Spirit nor Matter, both being the absolute life, latent." (Book of Dzyan, Comm. III, par. 18) . . . . "Spirit is the first differentiation of (and in) SPACE; and Matter the first differentiation of Spirit. That, which is neither Spirit nor matter—that is IT—the Causeless CAUSE of Spirit and Matter, which are the Cause of Kosmos. And THAT we call the ONE LIFE or the Intra-Cosmic Breath."
—*The Secret Doctrine*, vol. 1, p. 258, quoting a secret commentary

There is a moment in the existence of every molecule and atom of matter when, for one cause or another, the last spark of spirit or motion or life (call it by whatever name) is withdrawn, and in the same instant with the swiftness which surpasses that of the lightning glance of thought the atom or molecule or an aggregation of molecules is annihilated to return to its pristine purity of intra-cosmic matter.
—*The Mahatma Letters,* letter #22, 3rd ed., p. 139

Throughout the first two Parts [of vol. I of *The Secret Doctrine*], it was shown that, at the first flutter of renascent life, Svabhavat [*svabhāva*], "the mutable radiance of the Immutable Darkness unconscious in Eternity," passes, at every new rebirth of Kosmos, from an inactive state into one of intense activity; that it differentiates, and then begins its work through that differentiation.
—*The Secret Doctrine,* vol. 1, pp. 634-635

To comprehend my answers you will have first of all to view the eternal *Essence,* the Swabhāvat [*svabhāva*] not as a compound element you call spirit-matter, but as the one element for which the English has no name."
—*The Mahatma Letters,* letter #11, 3rd ed., p. 60

Their [the Svābhāvikas'] plastic, invisible, eternal, omnipresent and unconscious Swabhavat [*svabhāva*] is Force or *Motion* ever generating its electricity which is life.
—*The Mahatma Letters,* letter #22, 3rd ed., p. 136

The world of force is the world of Occultism and the only one whither the highest initiate goes to probe the secrets of being.
—*The Mahatma Letters,* letter #22, 3rd ed., p. 140

. . . did you ever suspect that Universal, like finite, human mind might have two attributes, . . . the "infinite mind," which we name so but for agreement sake, for we call it the infinite FORCE . . ."
—*The Mahatma Letters,* letter #22, 3rd ed., pp. 133-134

Yes; there is a force as limitless as thought, as potent as boundless will, as subtle as the essence of life, so inconceivably awful in its rending force as to convulse the universe to its centre were it but used as a lever, but this Force is not *God*, since there are men who have learned the secret of subjecting it to their will when necessary. Look around you and see the myriad manifestations of life, so infinitely multiform; of life, of motion, of change. What caused these? From what inexhaustible source came they, by what agency? Out of the invisible and subjective they have entered our little area of the visible and objective. Children of Akasa, concrete evolutions from the ether, it was Force which brought them into perceptibility and Force will in time remove them from the sight of man.
—*The Mahatma Letters,* letter #22, 3rd ed., pp. 136-137

The Occultists are taken to task for calling the *Cause* of light, heat, sound, cohesion, magnetism, etc., etc., a *substance.* (The "substance" of the Occultist, however, is to the most refined *substance* of the physicist, what *radiant matter* is to the leather of the Chemist's boots.) . . . In no way—as stated more than once before now—do the Occultists dispute the explanations of Science, as affording a solution of the *immediate* objective agencies at work. Science only errs in believing that, because it has detected in vibratory waves the *proximate* cause of these phenomena, it has, therefore, revealed ALL that lies beyond the threshold of sense. It merely traces the sequence of phenomena on a plane of effects, illusory projections from the region that Occultism has long since penetrated. And the latter maintains that those etheric tremors are not, as asserted by Science, set up by the vibrations of the molecules of *known* bodies—the matter of our terrestrial objective consciousness—but that we must seek for the ultimate causes of light, heat, etc., etc., in MATTER existing in *super-sensuous* states—states, however, as fully objective to the spiritual eye of man, as a horse or a tree is to the ordinary mortal. Light and heat are the ghost or shadow of matter in motion.
—*The Secret Doctrine,* vol. 1, pp. 514-515

Printed in Great Britain
by Amazon

78542637R00169